Hiking New Jersey

A Guide to 50 of the Garden State's
Greatest Hiking Adventures

Paul E. DeCoste
Ronald J. Dupont Jr.

FALCON GUIDES ®

GUILFORD, CONNECTICUT
HELENA, MONTANA
AN IMPRINT OF THE GLOBE PEQUOT PRESS

FALCONGUIDES®

Copyright © 2009 by Morris Book Publishing, LLC

Interior photos by Paul DeCoste unless otherwise
credited
Project manager: Julie Marsh
Interior design: Nancy Freeborn
Layout artist: Maggie Peterson
Maps: DesignMaps Inc. © Morris Book Publishing LLC

Library of Congress Cataloging-in-Publication Data
DeCoste, Paul E.
Hiking New Jersey : a guide to 50 great hiking adven-
tures / Paul E. DeCoste, Ronald J. Dupont, Jr.
p. cm. – (Falconguides)
ISBN 978-0-7627-1119-2
1. Hiking–New Jersey–Guidebooks. 2. Backpacking–
New Jersey–Guidebooks. I. Dupont, Ronald J. II. Title.
GV199.42.N5D43 2009
917.49–dc22
                                        2009003163
Printed in the United States of America
10 9 8 7 6 5 4 3

To the volunteers:
the builders, maintainers, and managers of our trails,
past, present, and future. They make it possible to walk the walk.
And to our friends and families, who fill those walks with love.

Steve Klein, 1930–2001, trail volunteer extraordinaire. COURTESY OF TRUDY ATKINSON

HELP US KEEP THIS GUIDE UP TO DATE

Every effort has been made by the authors and editors to make this guide as accurate and useful as possible. However, many things can change after a guide is published—trails are rerouted, regulations change, techniques evolve, facilities come under new management, and so on.

We would appreciate your comments concerning your experiences with this guide and how you feel it could be improved and kept up to date. While we may not be able to respond to all comments and suggestions, we'll take them to heart, and we'll also make certain to share them with the authors. Please send your comments and suggestions to the following address:

GPP
Reader Response/Editorial Department
P.O. Box 480
Guilford, CT 06437

Or you may e-mail us at: editorial@globepequot.com

Thanks for your input, and happy trails!

Contents

Acknowledgments viii
Introduction 1
Trail Finder Chart 18
Map Legend 22

The Hikes
The Kittatinny Ridge and Valley 23
1   Steenykill Lake and High Point............................... 25
2   Lake Rutherfurd and the Appalachian Trail............. 32
3   The Paulinskill Valley Trail...................................... 37
4   Mount Tammany and Sunfish Pond 46
5   Culvers Gap and Stony Lake 53
6   The Wallkill River Valley 58
7   The Pahaquarry Copper Mines................................ 62
8   Millbrook Village and Van Campens Glen............... 69
9   Buttermilk Falls and Rattlesnake Mountain............ 75

The Highlands Province 80
10 Pochuck Valley to Wawayanda Mountain 82
11 Pyramid Mountain and Tripod Rock 87
12 Bearfort Mountain and Surprise Lake 92
13 The Tourne 96
14 The Pequannock Highlands 100
15 Saffin Pond and Headley Overlook 105
16 Schooley's Mountain...109
17 Terrace Pond 114
18 Wyanokie High Point..118
19 The Black River 124
20 Ken Lockwood Gorge 129
21 Wawayanda Lake...134

The Jersey Piedmont 140
22 The Great Falls of the Passaic.................................142
23 The Hudson Palisades..148
24 The Princeton Woods..153
25 Jockey Hollow 158
26 Watchung Reservation..165
27 The Delaware and Raritan Canal—Millstone Valley 171
28 The Great Swamp..176
29 The Delaware River Valley—Stockton to Bull's Island 182

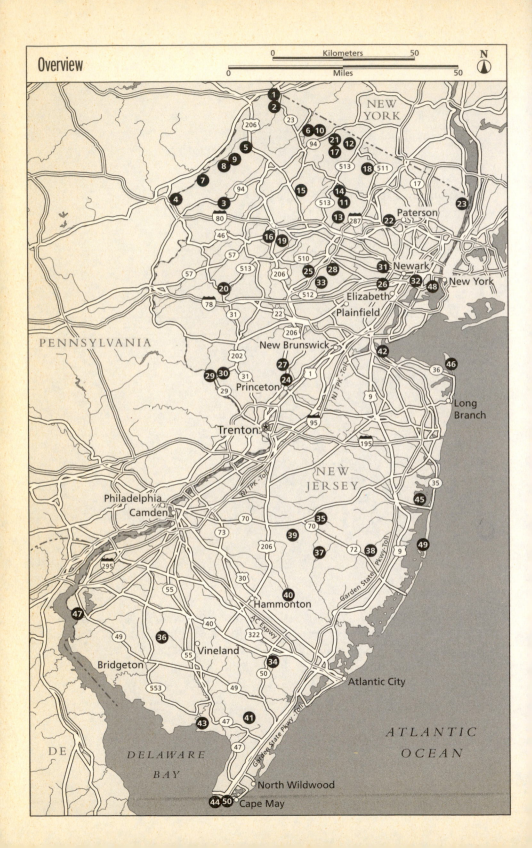

30 The Delaware River Valley—Stockton to Lambertville 187
31 South Mountain and the Rahway River 193
32 The Hackensack Meadowlands 198
33 Lord Stirling Park 202

The Coastal Plain and Pine Barrens 208
34 Belcoville and the South River 210
35 Pakim Pond and Mount Misery 216
36 Parvin Lake 222
37 Bear Swamp Hill and the Pine Plains 226
38 Wells Mills 230
39. Apple Pie Hill 237
40. Batsto Lake 242
41 Lake Nummy and East Creek Pond 248
42. Cheesequake 252

The Jersey Shore and Bays 257
43 The Maurice River Estuary 260
44 Higbee Beach 265
45 Cattus Island 270
46 Sandy Hook 274
47 Finn's Point 281
48 Liberty State Park 285
49 Island Beach 290
50 Cape May Point 297

Honorable Mentions 301
New Jersey Backpacks 302
High Point to Cape May Point 303
Clubs & Trail Groups 305
Further Reading 306
Hike Index 308
About the Authors 309

Acknowledgments

A book like this doesn't get written without the help of many people, and we wish to thank those who helped us. We couldn't have done it without you.

Our fellow author Glenn Scherer helped flesh out the hikes, read portions of the draft, and provided useful comments and criticism. Emilie Dupont read drafts of the sidebars and provided useful suggestions. Pat DeCoste was our sounding board for the hike descriptions. Archaeologist Edward J. Lenik gave generously of his time and knowledge. Ray Whritenour provided assistance with Lenape place names. Matt Tomaso, senior archaeologist, Cultural Resources Consulting Group, provided us with information on the history of the Watchung Reservation. Len Peck assisted with history of the Delaware Water Gap National Rereation Area. Invaluable technical support came from James Walsh, Ron Ceder, and Ian Blundell.

We appreciate the information we received from the following folks: Kevin Holcomb, Fran Stephenson, Helen Hesselgrave, Ann DeGraaf, Dana Loschiavo, Margaret Miller, Lon Everett Sr., Stephanie Fox, Catherine Shrine, Eric Olsen, Sally Vandewater, Michele Stelle, Kathleen Meye, Linda Kay, Madeleine Eno, Marjorie La Pan, Rich Benning, Owen Hyland, Larry Wheelock, Jane Wiltshire, Steven Kahl, Connie Witherby, and Mary Pat Pheil.

For advice, we thank Bob Jonas, John Grob, Jay Schweitzer, Robert Busha, Robert Brill, Rob Jennings, and Mark Texel.

We are in debt to those who generously shared their knowledge: Peter Osborne, Robert DeCoste, Robert Brill, John Galluzzo, James Faczak, Michelle Steele, Dan Barmer, and William Koch.

We are grateful for the exceptionally courteous cooperation we received from the staffs at all the state and county parks and forests in which we hiked and researched, including High Point State Park, Stokes State Forest, Wawayanda State Park, Cheesequake State Park, Island Beach State Park, Parvin State Park, Belleplain State Forest, Brendan T. Byrne State Forest, Cape May State Park, Batsto Village historic site, Essex, Corson, and Wells Mills, Estell Manor County Park, the Morris County Park system, the Ocean County Park system, and the New Jersey Nature Conservancy.

Special thanks are due those who went out of their way to help us: the staff at the Dorothy E. Henry Library and the Sussex County library, Dorothy Decker, Ann M. Bateman, and Sue Kuchinski.

We enjoyed camaraderie along the trails from Jenna Gersie, Walt Palmer, Chris Mazza, Kristine Nelson, Ben Dupont, Jon DeCoste, James DeCoste, Carol DeCoste, and Pat DeCoste.

A tip of the hat to guiding souls who were with us in spirit: John Garcia, Peter Gersie, Steve Klein, and Pete Morrissey.

All-purpose thanks go out to John Keator, William Foley, Al Gomolka, Chris Clause, and Nancy Anderson.

Many thanks to the staff at the Wolverton Inn.

The staff at FalconGuides has been exceptional: Bill Schneider, Russ Schneider, Julie Marsh, Jennifer Blackwell-Yale, and Roberta Monaco.

Our wives and families put up with us during the long gestation of this project and, most important, let us go hiking. We owe them all a debt of gratitude. If we have forgotten anyone, you can (and probably will) take it out of our skin the next time we meet on the trail. Our thanks and apologies.

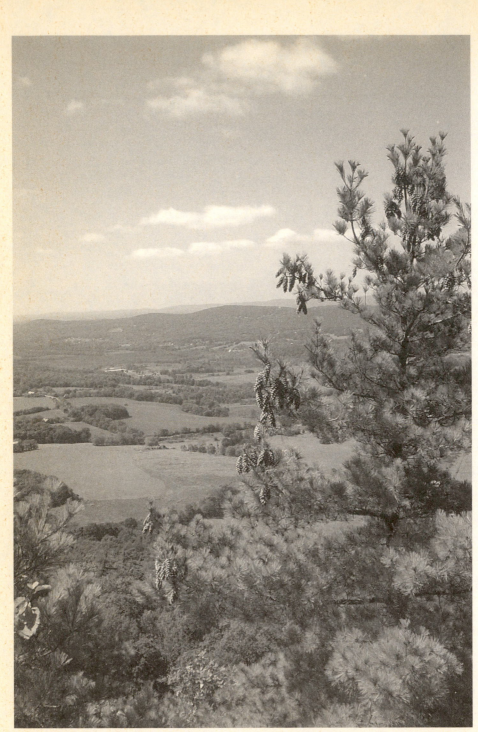

Vernon Valley view from Pinwheel Vistas

Introduction

Do I contradict myself?
Very well then I contradict myself,
(I am large, I contain multitudes.)
—Walt Whitman, *Leaves of Grass,* "Song of Myself," 1855

Few states are as contradictory as New Jersey. It would be hard to find another where gritty urban reality and wild, natural beauty reside in such cheek-by-jowl proximity. Walt Whitman surely appreciated it; he spent the last two decades of his life here.

New Jersey is essentially a sort of peninsula, bounded on the east by the Hudson River, New York Bay, and the Atlantic, and on the south and west by the Delaware Bay and river. Only the New York border on the north is an artificial line. In the northwest, ridges and mountains comprise the Highlands and the Kittatinnies—not big as mountains go, but scenic and surprisingly wild, ruggedly sculpted by the last ice age.

These give way in the center of the state to the rolling hills of the Piedmont, literally foothills, a densely populated corridor running between New York City and Philadelphia. The Piedmont in turn gives way farther south to the broad Coastal

A historic farmstead is found along the Paulinskill Valley Trail among the undulating farmlands.

Plain, a mixture of pine forests, undulating farmland, wetlands, rivers, and coastline. From Sandy Hook, guarding New York harbor, south to Cape May, one of America's first seaside resorts, beaches, and barrier islands greet the Atlantic Ocean.

It is a varied and lovely topography, but too little known by outsiders. Citizens of surrounding states, seeing only the industrial highway corridor between the Big Apple and the City of Brotherly Love, often miss these delights and mislabel New Jersey a wasteland of factories, marshlands, diesel-fumed truck stops, and, perhaps, the remains of Jimmy Hoffa. No place of significance itself, but merely a route between other places. Many have swallowed, sight-unseen, the vision of *Sopranos* New Jersey, of nightclub-joke New Jersey, of "you live in Jersey? Which exit?" Such is the popular stereotype going back even to Colonial times, when Ben Franklin (apocryphally) said that New Jersey was a barrel tapped at both ends.

This grimy industrial stereotype has some truth in it. Since the 1700s, New Jersey has been at the forefront of American industry, technology, and commerce. Our iron mines, forges, and furnaces made armaments for the American Revolution; our mills spun cotton and silk for export and made sails for clipper ships. We made locomotives, guns, and mortars for the Civil War. The first U.S. oil refinery and port were built here, and we still have the largest petroleum storage facilities outside the Middle East. We wove the steel cables for the Brooklyn Bridge, and later, for the Golden Gate Bridge. New Jersey and its citizens gave birth to the lightbulb, the phonograph, the motion picture, the modern submarine, the transistor radio, and the electric guitar (and Bruce Springsteen to play it).

During World War II, we produced a quarter of all U.S. battleships, along with aircraft and rocket engines (one, in a plane flown by Chuck Yeager, broke the sound barrier). We supplied vast quantities of munitions and explosives for both world wars, and we remain America's largest producer of chemicals and pharmaceuticals. When traffic got bad, we invented the cloverleaf intersection.

So yeah, things got a bit messy here and there because of all that. OK, we also have the most toxic waste sites in the nation (about 108, if you must know).

But we can laugh at the stereotype of New Jersey because we've seen the *other* New Jersey, too . . . and so will you. This is the New Jersey of preserved forests and farmland, of streams and waterfalls, of clean beaches and vast wetlands, of endless green mountains. Get this: In the percentage of our land remaining as natural open space, New Jersey outranks *twenty-five* other U.S. states, including Colorado, Arizona, Wisconsin, Hawaii, and Texas.

Equally astonishing: By area, New Jersey has a higher percentage of parks, forests, and preserved farmland than most other states in America; that the Pinelands are the most profoundly and densely wild expanse of land in such proximity to an urban area in the United States; that our wildlife includes not merely white-tailed deer and black bear but also bobcats, bald eagles, and coyotes. In the heart of the Highlands, you could easily imagine yourself in the Adirondacks, while the scrub pine coastal plains are as wild (or wilder) than those found down through the coastal Carolinas and Georgia. We also have the second-largest waterfall east of the Mississippi: the Great Falls of the Passaic.

It's supremely satisfying for us, both Jersey-born and longtime Appalachian Trail (AT) volunteers, to see the reaction of AT thru-hikers entering New Jersey (yes, it goes through New Jersey). Some hikers half expect the AT here to be little more than a footpath between housing developments and shopping malls, more *ba-da-bing* than bucolic.

They are thus astonished at the wonders of the Delaware Water Gap, the grand views from Kittatinny Ridge, and the varied farmlands of the Wallkill Valley. Also by the fact that in the most densely populated state in the nation, they routinely see black bear, sometimes seeing none in their treks through the deepest forests of the southern Appalachians and New England.

New Jersey has more forest today that it did in 1855. The gradual abandonment of old mountain farmsteads, and the creation of state parks and forests, led to the re-growth of thousands of acres from the late 1800s to the mid-1900s. Mixed hardwoods predominate in the north while in the south are the famous Pine Barrens (which do, however, include oak and other hardwoods).

This steady increase in forested land after 1900 prompted a return of animal spe-cies as well. Farmers in 1910 rarely saw a whitetail deer, and hunters seeking them went to the Alleghenies or the Adirondacks. Today they are common to the point of

New Jersey's wildlife includes not only whitetail deer and black bear, but also bobcats, bald eagles, and coyotes.

being a hazard and a nuisance. Beaver, raccoon, skunk, and fox are all common both in rural, suburban, and urban environments. The bald eagle is now present in most rural areas of New Jersey.

Large predators like mountain lion, wolf, and black bear were rendered extinct in New Jersey in the 1800s (wolf scalps brought a bounty). The bear has returned aplenty and is a common sight in the north. Wolves are still long-gone, but an increasing body of anecdote suggests that the mountain lion is beginning to find its way back to its ancestral prowls, fed in no small part by the abundant deer population.

And there are animal newcomers: possum and coyote, neither original to the state, are both residents now. The yowl-yip-howling of a pack of coyotes in deep woods near sunset will, very definitely, send a chill down your spine and put a spring in your step.

Our weather is as diverse as our landscape. Winters, especially in the North, are akin to those in New England, with deep snows and subzero temperatures not uncommon. Winter hiking requires suitable clothing and gear. Elevation change can make a huge difference. A light February rain in the Piedmont can be a blizzard in the Kittatinnies; a pleasant spring day in the Palisades can be bleak winter at High Point.

New Jersey summers can likewise be Southern-style hot, humid, and hazy, with temperatures peaking over 100 degrees at times (don't forget—Cape May *does* fall south of the Mason–Dixon Line). Sunscreen and water are essentials. Many times of year are bug-free in New Jersey, but not all. If one Jersey joke has merit, it's the one about the state bird being the mosquito. The tick, once relatively uncommon, can now be a serious pest. The moral: Wear bug repellent. All times of year have their glories for the hiker—if you are prepared.

Every level of government in New Jersey has acquired public lands and open space. The federal government owns historic sites (including Morristown National Historical Park), recreational areas (including Delaware Water Gap), seashores (including Sandy Hook), and wildlife refuges (Great Swamp, Edwin B. Forsythe, Wallkill River, among others).

The State of New Jersey was among the first in the nation to create a state park and forest system. It is an extensive network of facilities, some of them established over a century ago. These vary from pocket-size parks with densely developed recreational facilities, like Parvin State Park, to vast tracts of wilderness, like Wharton State Forest, over 100,000 acres in area.

The New York–New Jersey region gave birth to a variety of hiking and outing clubs between 1900 and 1920. These groups were mainly composed of folks who wanted to get out of the city and hike in the fresh country air on weekends. They became a force for good, both lobbying for the acquisition and preservation of public lands, and volunteering their time to build trails, shelters, and other facilities. In 1920 most of these groups gathered under the aegis of the New York–New Jersey Trail Conference, which since that time has been an important force in promoting conservation and trail building in the region. The Trail Conference's maps and guidebooks are indispensable for hiking in New Jersey.

The state lands system was given a super-charge in 1961 when the voters approved the first Green Acres bond act to acquire open space. Since then over 1.2 million acres have been preserved in New Jersey. This is good, because the last two decades have seen a neck-and-neck race between land preservation and land development; the race is far from over. Still, our state enjoys a superb state park system—if only its funding were equally superb (it generally isn't).

Most county governments also have park and preserve systems, often very fine ones, as do some local governments. Essex County was the first in the nation to establish a county park system, beginning with Newark's Branch Brook Park (which has more cherry trees than Washington, D.C.) in 1895. Some large municipalities, like Newark, own vast tracts of forest as a watershed for their drinking-water reservoirs, and these also provide recreational opportunities. Morris County alone has a park and historic site system that rivals the state's in quality.

Fortunately, New Jerseyans have long been strong supporters for open space preservation at the ballot box. Almost every year sees the creation of a new recreational opportunity someplace in the state. Needless to say, each type of park has different rules and regulations, and you need to be aware of each.

One advantage of hiking in New Jersey is choosing your "people quotient." On popular trails in peak season, you can be part of the happy throng, if that's your desire. Similarly, you can choose a remote trail in midweek or off-season and not see another soul for a day—maybe a week.

Bloodroot blooms in rich woodlands along trails from March to May.

Preparing this book was both a challenge and a treat. A challenge because limitations of time and space forced the omission of some wonderful hikes (see Honorable Mentions at the end of the book). But also a treat: It led us to explore some places and hikes long on our "to do" list, which we'd never gotten to (and maybe never would). With a mixed sense of awe and embarrassment we encountered oft-ignored riches so close to home. Like the New Yorker who has never been to the top of the Empire State Building, many is the native Jerseyan (not to mention visiting tourist) who has never heard the roar of the Great Falls, been made dizzy by the Palisades, enjoyed the expansive vistas from High Point, been awed by the Water Gap, soaked in the silence of the Pine Barrens, trekked the beaches of Cape May, or savored a dozen other magical places.

Whether native or visitor, heed well: Don't let this happen to you. Strap on your boots and see the *real* New Jersey.

Hiking in New Jersey

As we venture into the outdoors, we have a responsibility to protect our wild places. So please, do what you can. The following section will help you understand better what it means to "do what you can" while still making the most of your hiking experience. Anyone can take a hike, but hiking safely and well is an art requiring preparation and proper equipment.

Trail Etiquette

Zero impact. Always leave an area just like you found it—if not better than you found it. Pack up all of your trash and extra food. Bury human waste at least 100 feet from water sources under 6 to 8 inches of topsoil. Don't bathe with soap in a lake or stream—use prepackaged moistened towels to wipe off sweat and dirt, or bathe in the water without soap.

Stay on the trail. Paths serve an important purpose; they limit impact on natural areas. Straying from a designated trail may seem innocent but it can cause damage to sensitive areas—damage that may take years to recover, if it can recover at all. Even simple shortcuts can be destructive. So, please, stay on the trail.

Leave no weeds. Noxious weeds tend to overtake other plants, which in turn affects animals and birds that depend on them for food. To minimize the spread of noxious weeds, hikers should regularly clean their boots, tents, packs, and hiking poles of mud and seeds. Also brush your dog to remove any weed seeds before heading off into a new area.

Keep your dog under control. Always obey leash laws and be sure to bury your dog's waste or pack it in resealable plastic bags.

Respect other trail users. Often you're not the only one on the trail. With the rise in popularity of multiuse trails, you'll have to learn a new kind of respect, beyond the nod and "hello" approach you may be used to. First investigate whether you're on a multiuse trail, and assume the appropriate precautions. Note that you're not likely to hear a mountain biker coming, so be prepared and know ahead of time whether you share the trail with them. Cyclists should always yield to hikers, but that's little comfort to the hiker. Be aware. When you approach horses on the trail, always step quietly off the trail, preferably on the downhill side, and let them pass. If you're wearing a large backpack, it's often a good idea to sit down. To some animals, a hiker wearing a large backpack might appear threatening. Make sure your dog doesn't harass these animals.

Safety

When you enter the wild, you assume the risk and the responsibility for your own safety. You know yourself and your limitations better than anyone. Although this book attempts to alert you to potential dangers, nature is uncertain and trail maintenance can change over time. For safe, responsible travel, you should listen to your inner voice and keep abreast of current outdoor basics. Even outdoor veterans can benefit from a refresher.

Preparedness

It's been said that failing to plan means planning to fail. So do take the necessary time to plan your trip. Whether going on a short day hike or an extended backpack, always prepare for the worst. You need to do your best to prevent the problem from arising in the first place. To stay reasonably comfortable, you need to concern yourself with the basics: water, food, and shelter. Don't go on a hike without having these bases covered. And don't go on a hike expecting to find these items in the woods.

Water. Even in frigid conditions, you need at least two quarts of water a day to function efficiently. Add heat and taxing terrain and you can bump that figure up to one gallon. Your metabolism and your level of conditioning can raise or lower that amount. Now, where do you plan on getting the water?

Preferably not from natural water sources. These sources can be loaded with intestinal disturbers, such as bacteria, viruses, and fertilizers. *Giardia lamblia*, the most common of these disturbers, can induce cramping, diarrhea, vomiting, and fatigue within two days to two weeks after ingestion. Giardiasis is treatable with prescription drugs. If you believe you've contracted giardiasis, see a doctor immediately.

The best and easiest solution to avoid polluted water is to carry water with you. If this isn't feasible, choose from the three methods of treating water: boiling, chemical treatment, and filtering.

Food. If we're talking about survival, you can go days without food, as long as you have water. But we're also talking about comfort. Try to avoid foods that are high in sugar and fat like candy bars and potato chips. These food types are harder to digest and are low in nutritional value. Instead, bring along foods that are easy to pack, nutritious, and high in energy (e.g., bagels, nutrition bars, dehydrated fruit, gorp, and jerky). Prepackage your food in heavy-duty resealable plastic bags to keep it from spilling in your pack. These bags can be reused to pack out trash.

First Aid

Outdoor adventures can be spoiled by sunburn, blisters, insect bites and stings, ticks, poison ivy/oak/sumac, and even snakebites. Also be aware of dehydration, heat exhaustion, hypothermia, and frostbite. Prevention is always better than treatment, but just in case, carry a first-aid kit with you. Many companies produce lightweight, compact first-aid kits. Whether you purchase one or make up your own, be sure it contains at least the following:

- adhesive bandages
- moleskin
- various sterile gauze and dressings
- white surgical tape
- an Ace bandage
- an antihistamine
- aspirin
- Betadine solution
- sunscreen
- a first-aid book
- Tums
- tweezers
- scissors
- antibacterial wipes
- triple-antibiotic ointment
- plastic gloves
- sterile cotton tip applicators
- syrup of ipecac (to induce vomiting)
- thermometer
- wire splint

Natural Hazards

Besides tripping over a rock or tree root on the trail, there are some real hazards to be aware of while hiking. Even if where you're hiking doesn't have the plethora of poisonous snakes and plants, insects, and black bears found in other parts of the United States, there are a few weather conditions and predators you may need to take into account.

Lightning. Lightning is generated by thunderheads and can strike without warning, even several miles away from the nearest overhead cloud. Keep an eye on cloud formation and don't underestimate how fast a storm can build. The bigger they get, the more likely a thunderstorm will happen. Lightning takes the path of least resistance, so if you're the high point, it might choose you. Ducking under a rock overhang is dangerous as you form the shortest path between the rock and ground. Avoid standing under the only or the tallest tree. Stay away from anything metal you might be carrying. Move to a low, treeless point and squat until the storm passes. If you have an insulating pad, squat on it. Avoid having both your hands and feet touching the ground at once and never lay flat. If you hear a buzzing sound or feel your hair standing on end, move quickly as an electrical charge is building up.

Bears. Black bears are plentiful. Most of all, avoid scaring a bear. Watch for bear tracks (five toes) and droppings (sizable with leaves, partly digested berries, seeds, and/or animal fur). Talk or sing where visibility or hearing is limited. Don't leave a trail of litter. Be especially careful in spring to avoid getting between a mother and her cubs. In late summer and fall, bears are busy eating berries and acorns to fatten up for winter, so be extra careful around berry bushes and oakbrush. If you do encounter a bear, move away slowly while facing the bear, talk softly, and avoid direct eye contact. Give the bear room to escape. Since bears are very curious, it might stand upright to get a better whiff of you, and it may even charge you to try to intimidate you. Try to stay calm. If a bear does attack you, fight back with anything you have handy. Unleashed dogs have been known to come running back to their owners with a bear close behind. Keep your dog on a leash or leave it at home.

Other considerations. Hunting is a popular sport, especially during shotgun season in October and November. Hiking is still enjoyable in those months in many areas, so just take a few precautions. First, learn when the different hunting seasons start and end in the area in which you'll be hiking. During this time frame, be sure to wear at least a blaze orange hat, and possibly put an orange vest over your pack. Don't be surprised to see hunters in camo outfits carrying bows or shotguns around during their season. If you would feel more comfortable without hunters around, hike in parks where hunting is not allowed.

Navigation

Whether you are going on a short hike in a familiar area or planning a weeklong backpack trip, you should always be equipped with the proper navigational equipment—at the very least a detailed map and a sturdy compass.

Maps. There are many different types of maps available to help you find your way on the trail. Easiest to find are New York–New Jersey Trail Conference maps. These maps can be obtained either from outdoor stores or the Trail Conference online.

Compasses. First off, the sun is not a substitute for a compass. So, what kind of compass should you have? Here are some characteristics you should look for: a rectangular base with detailed scales, a liquid-filled housing, protective housing, a sighting line on the mirror, luminous alignment and back-bearing arrows, a luminous northseeking arrow, and a well-defined bezel ring. Learn compass basics by reading the detailed instructions included with your compass; or sign up for an orienteering class or purchase a book on compass reading. Practice these skills before you head out.

You may want to check out a GPS (Global Positioning System) device. The GPS was developed by the Pentagon and works off satellites. The device is a handheld unit that calculates your latitude and longitude and provides nearly pinpoint accuracy (within 30 to 60 feet).

There are many different types of GPS units available and they range in price from $100 to $400. In general, all GPS units have a display screen and keypad where you input information. In addition to acting as a compass, the unit allows you to plot your route, easily retrace your path, track your traveling speed, find the mileage between waypoints, and calculate the total mileage of your route. Keep in mind that these devices don't pick up signals indoors, in heavily wooded areas, or in ravines, or in deep valleys.

Prickly pear cactus, New Jersey's only native cactus, grows on the sandy shores and the Coastal Plain, as well as on mountaintops, including Mount Tammany.

Pedometers. A pedometer is a small, clip-on unit with a digital display that calculates your hiking distance in miles or kilometers based on your walking stride. Some units also calculate the calories you burn and your total hiking time. Pedometers are available at most large outdoor stores and range in price from $20 to $40.

Trip Planning

Planning your hiking adventure begins with letting a friend or relative know your trip itinerary so they can call for help if you don't return at your scheduled time. Your next task is to make sure you are outfitted to experience the risks and rewards of the trail. This section highlights gear and clothing you may want to take with you to get the most out of your hike.

Day Hikes

- ❑ camera/film
- ❑ compass/GPS unit
- ❑ pedometer
- ❑ daypack
- ❑ first-aid kit
- ❑ food
- ❑ guidebook
- ❑ headlamp/flashlight with extra batteries and bulbs
- ❑ hat
- ❑ insect repellant
- ❑ knife/multipurpose tool
- ❑ map
- ❑ matches in waterproof container and fire starter
- ❑ Polar Fleece jacket
- ❑ rain gear
- ❑ space blanket
- ❑ sunglasses
- ❑ sunscreen
- ❑ swimsuit
- ❑ watch
- ❑ water
- ❑ water bottles/water hydration system

Overnight Trip

- ❑ backpack and waterproof rain cover
- ❑ backpacker's trowel
- ❑ bandanna
- ❑ bear repellant spray
- ❑ bear bell
- ❑ biodegradable soap
- ❑ pot scrubber
- ❑ collapsible water container (2–3 gallon capacity)
- ❑ clothing—extra wool socks, shirt, and shorts
- ❑ cook set/utensils
- ❑ ditty bags to store gear
- ❑ extra plastic resealable bags
- ❑ gaiters
- ❑ garbage bag
- ❑ ground cloth
- ❑ journal/pen
- ❑ nylon rope to hang food
- ❑ long underwear
- ❑ permit (if required)
- ❑ rain jacket and pants
- ❑ sandals to wear around camp and to ford streams
- ❑ sleeping bag
- ❑ waterproof stuff sack
- ❑ sleeping pad
- ❑ small bath towel
- ❑ stove and fuel
- ❑ tent
- ❑ toiletry items
- ❑ water filter
- ❑ whistle

Clothes. Clothing is your armor against Mother Nature's little surprises. Adequate rain protection and extra layers of clothing are a good idea. In summer, a wide-brimmed hat can help keep the sun at bay. In the winter months start with a "wicking" layer of long underwear that keeps perspiration away from your skin. Next, wear an "insulating" layer—like fleece— that will keep you warm and will "breathe" so you stay dry while hiking. The last line of layering defense is the "shell" layer some type of waterproof, windproof, breathable jacket that will fit over all of your other layers. It should have a large hood that fits over a hat. Don't forget to protect your hands and face. In cold, windy, or rainy weather, wear a hat made of wool or fleece and insulated, waterproof gloves.

Footwear. If you have any extra money to spend on your trip, put that money into boots or trail shoes. Buy shoes that provide support and are lightweight and flexible. A lightweight hiking boot is better than a heavy, leather mountaineering boot for most day hikes and backpacking. Trail running shoes provide a little extra cushion and are made in a high-top style that many people wear for hiking. These running shoes are lighter, more flexible, and more breathable than hiking boots. If you'll be hiking in wet weather often, purchase boots or shoes with a Gore-Tex liner, which will help keep your feet dry.

When buying your boots, be sure to wear the same type of socks you'll be wearing on the trail. If the boots you're buying are for cold weather hiking, try the boots on while wearing two pairs of socks. Speaking of socks, a good cold weather sock combination is to wear a thinner sock made of wool or polypropylene covered by a heavier outer sock made of wool. The inner sock protects the foot from the rubbing effects of the outer sock and prevents blisters. Once you've purchased your footwear, be sure to break them in before you hit the trail. New footwear is often stiff and needs to be stretched and molded to your foot.

Hiking poles. Hiking poles help with balance and, more important, take pressure off your knees. The ones with shock absorbers are easier on your elbows and knees. Some poles even come with a camera attachment to be used as a monopod. And heaven forbid you meet a bear or unfriendly dog, the poles can make you look a lot bigger.

Backpacks. No matter what type of hiking you do, you'll need a pack of some sort to carry the basic trail essentials. There are a variety of backpacks on the market, but let's first discuss what you intend to use it for: day hikes or overnight trips?

For short hikes or if you're an occasional hiker, consider a fanny pack to store just a camera, food, a compass, a map, and other trail essentials. Most fanny packs have pockets for two water bottles and a padded hip belt.

If you're more serious about day hikes, a daypack should have some of the following characteristics: a padded hip belt that's at least 2 inches in diameter (avoid packs with only a small nylon piece of webbing for a hip belt); a chest strap (the chest strap helps stabilize the pack against your body); external pockets to carry water and other items that you want easy access to; an internal pocket to hold keys, a knife, a wallet, and other miscellaneous items; an external lashing system to hold a jacket; and a hydration pocket for carrying a hydration system (which consists of a water bladder with an attachable drinking hose).

If you intend to do an extended or overnight trip, there are multiple considerations. First, decide whether you want the internal frame or the external frame. An internal frame pack rests closer to your body, making it more stable and easier to balance when hiking over rough terrain. An external frame pack is better for long backpack trips because it distributes the pack weight better and you can carry heavier loads. It's easier to pack, and your gear is more accessible. It also offers better back ventilation in hot weather.

The most critical measurement for fitting a pack is torso length. The pack needs to rest evenly on your hips without sagging. A good pack will come in two or three sizes and have straps and hip belts that are adjustable according to your body size and characteristics. If you go to an outdoor store, the salespeople should be knowledgeable in how to properly fit a pack. Test it by loading it with the approximate weight you plan on taking on the trail.

Cell phones. Many hikers are carrying their cell phones into the parks, forest, or woods these days in case of emergency. Be aware that cell phone coverage is often poor to nonexistent in valleys, canyons, and thick forest. And don't use the phone just because you're tired or lost. You are responsible for yourself. Use your brain to avoid problems, and if you do encounter one, first use your brain to try to correct the situation. Only use your cell phone, if it works, in true emergencies.

Hiking with Children

Hiking with children isn't a matter of how many miles you can cover or how much elevation gain you make in a day; it's about seeing and experiencing nature through their eyes. Kids like to explore and have fun. They like to stop and point out bugs and plants, look under rocks, jump in puddles, and throw sticks. If you're taking a toddler or young child on a hike, start with a trail that you're familiar with. Trails that have interesting things for kids, like piles of leaves to play in or a small stream to wade through during the summer, will make the hike much more enjoyable for them and will keep them from getting bored.

Use games to keep your child's attention and teach him or her about nature. Play hide and seek, where your child is the mouse and you are the hawk. Quiz children on the names of plants and animals. If your children are old enough, let them carry their own daypack filled with snacks and water. So that you are sure to go at their pace and not yours, let them lead the way. Playing follow the leader works particularly well when you have a group of children. Have each child take a turn at being the leader.

Always bring extra clothing for children, regardless of the season. In the winter, have your child wear wool socks and warm layers such as long underwear, a fleece jacket and hat, wool mittens, and good rain gear. It's not a bad idea to have these along in late fall and early spring as well. Good footwear is also important. A sturdy pair of high top tennis shoes or lightweight hiking boots is the best bet for little ones. If you're hiking in the summer near a lake or stream, bring along a pair of old sneakers that your child can put on when he wants to go exploring in the water. Remember when you're near any type of water, watch your child at all times. Also, keep a close eye on teething toddlers who may decide a rock or leaf of poison oak is an interesting item to put in their mouth.

From spring through fall, you'll want your kids to wear a wide-brimmed hat to keep their face, head, and ears protected from the hot sun. Also, make sure your children wear sunscreen at all times. Choose a brand without PABA, which can cause an allergic reaction to sensitive skin. Don't use sunscreen or insect repellent on infants younger than six months of age. Instead, protect their head, face, neck, and ears from the sun with a wide-brimmed hat, and be sure that all other skin is protected with the appropriate clothing.

Remember that food is fun. Kids like snacks so it's important to bring a lot of munchies for the trail. Stopping often for snack breaks is a fun way to keep the trail interesting. Raisins, apples, granola bars, crackers and cheese, cereal, and trail mix all make great snacks. If your child is old enough to carry her own backpack, fill it with

Trout lily is found in moist soils and bears yellow blossoms in early spring. Its name comes from the mottled, fishlike leaves that are its defining feature.

treats before you leave. If your kids don't like drinking water, you can bring boxes of fruit juice.

Avoid poorly designed child-carrying packs—you don't want to break your back carrying your child. Most child-carrying backpacks designed to hold a forty-pound child will contain a large carrying pocket to hold diapers and other items. Some have an optional rain/sun hood.

Hiking with Dogs

Bringing your furry friend with you is always more fun than leaving him behind. Our canine pals make great trail buddies because they never complain. Hiking with your dog can be a rewarding experience, especially if you plan ahead.

Getting your dog in shape. Make sure your dog's in shape for the trail by taking her with you on your daily runs or walks. If there is a park near your house, hit a tennis ball or play Frisbee with your dog. Swimming is also an excellent way to get your dog into shape. Gradually build your dog's stamina up over a two- to three-month period. A good rule of thumb is to assume that your dog will travel twice as far as you will on the trail. If you plan on doing a 5-mile hike, be sure your dog is in shape for a 10-mile hike.

Training your dog for the trail. Before you go on your first hiking adventure with your dog, be sure he has a firm grasp on the basics of canine etiquette and behavior. Make sure he can sit, lie down, stay, and, maybe most important, come. Another helpful command is the "get behind" command. When you're on a hiking trail that's narrow, you can have your dog follow behind you when other trail users approach. When you see other trail users approaching you on the trail, give them the right of way by quietly stepping off the trail and making your dog lie down and stay until they pass.

Equipment. The most critical pieces of equipment you can invest in for your dog are proper identification and a sturdy leash. If there is not a 6-foot restriction on leashes, Flexi-leads work well for hiking because they give your dog more freedom to explore but still leave you in control. Make sure your dog has identification that includes your name and address and a number for your veterinarian. Other forms of identification for your dog include a tattoo or a microchip. You should consult your veterinarian for more information on these last two options.

You can also purchase collapsible water and dog food bowls for your dog. These bowls are lightweight and can easily be stashed into your pack or your dog's. If you are hiking on rocky terrain or in the snow, you can purchase footwear for your dog that will protect his feet from cuts and bruises.

Always carry plastic bags to remove feces from the trail. It is a courtesy to other trail users and helps protect local wildlife.

Here is a list of items to bring when you take your dog hiking: collapsible water bowls, a comb, a collar and a leash, dog food, plastic bags for feces, a dog pack, flea/

tick powder, paw protection, and water. Your pet may encounter some of Nature's unpleasantries: bee and wasp stings, porcupines, heat stroke, heartworm, and poisonous plants. He could also suffer from paw injuries, sunburn, ticks and fleas, or mosquitoes and deer flies. Familiarize yourself with these potential hazards, and carry a first-aid kit that contains eye ointment, tweezers, scissors, stretchy foot wrap, gauze, antibacterial wash, sterile cotton tip applicators, antibiotic ointment, and cotton wrap. Carry water for your pet as dogs can get giardia, just like people. And make sure your dog doesn't sample mushrooms along the trail. They could be poisonous to him, but he doesn't know that.

When you are finally ready to hit the trail with your dog, keep in mind that national parks and many wilderness areas do not allow dogs on trails. Your best bet is to hike in national forests, BLM lands, and state parks. Always call ahead to see what the restrictions are.

How to Use This Guide

Each region begins with a section introduction, which provides a sweeping look at the lay of the land. After this general overview, specific hikes within that region are presented.

To aid in quick decision-making, each hike chapter begins with a hike summary. These short summaries give you a taste of the hiking adventure to follow. You'll learn about the trail terrain and what surprises the route has to offer. Next, you'll find the quick, nitty-gritty details of the hike: where the trailhead is located, the nearest town, hike length, approximate hiking time, difficulty rating, best hiking season, type of trail terrain, what other trail users you may encounter, trail contacts (for updates on trail conditions), and trail schedules and usage fees.

The approximate hiking times are based on a standard hiking pace of 1.5 to 2 miles per hour, adjusted for terrain and reflecting normal trail conditions. The stated times will get you there and back, but be sure to add time for rest breaks and enjoying the trail's attractions. Although the stated times offer a planning guideline, you should gain a sense of your personal health, capabilities, and hiking style, and make this judgment for yourself. If you're hiking with a group, add enough time for slower members. The amount of carried gear also will influence hiking speed. In all cases, leave enough daylight to accomplish the task safely.

The **Finding the trailhead** section gives you dependable directions from a nearby city or town right down to where you'll want to park your car. The hike description is the meat of the chapter. Detailed and honest, it's the author's carefully researched impression of the trail. While it's impossible to cover everything, you can rest assured that we won't miss what's important. In **Miles and Directions,** we provide mileage cues to key junctions and trail name changes, as well as points of interest. The selected benchmarks allow for a quick check on progress and serve as your touchstone for staying on course. At the end of each hike, **Hike Information** offers local information sources for learning more about the area and may suggest things to do nearby or places to camp.

Lastly, the **Honorable Mentions** section at the end of the book identifies hikes that didn't make the cut, for whatever reason. In many cases it's not because they aren't great hikes, but because they're over-crowded or environmentally sensitive to heavy traffic. Be sure to read through these. A jewel might be lurking among them.

How to Use the Maps

The overview map indicates major access roads to each trailhead and, possibly more important, the relative location of hikes to one another to help you plan a whole day or weekend of great hikes in one general vicinity.

For your own purposes, you may wish to copy the directions for the route onto a small sheet to help you while hiking, or photocopy the map and Miles and Directions to take with you. Otherwise, just slip the whole book in your pack and take it all with you. Enjoy your time in the outdoors and remember to pack out what you pack in.

The route map is your guide to each hike. It shows the accessible roads and trails, water, landmarks, towns, and key navigational features. It also distinguishes trails from roads, and paved roads from unpaved roads. The selected route is highlighted.

The included maps are not intended to replace more-detailed agency maps, road maps, state atlases, and/or topographic maps, but they do indicate the general lay of the trail and its attractions to help you visualize and navigate its course.

Trail Finder Chart

Number	Hike	Back-packing*	Beach & Coast Lovers	Waterfalls, Lakes, Rivers, & Streams	Children's/ Gentle Hikes	Views & Vistas	Industrial Archaeology	Rail-roads & Canals	History	Unique Environ-mental Features
1	Steenykill Lake and High Point			●		●			●	●
2	Lake Rutherfurd and the Appalachian Trail			●		●				
3	The Paulinskill Valley Trail			●	●	●	●	●	●	
4	Mount Tammany and Sunfish Pond	●		●		●				●
5	Culver's Gap and Stony Lake	●	●	●		●				
6	The Wallkill River Valley			●	●					●
7	The Pahaquarry Copper Mines	●		●		●	●	●	●	
8	Millbrook Village and Van Campens Glen			●					●	●
9	Buttermilk Falls and Rattle-snake Mountain	●		●		●				●
10	Pochuck Valley to Wawayanda Mountain	●		●		●				
11	Pyramid Mountain and Tripod Rock					●			●	●
12	Bearfort Mountain and Surprise Lake			●		●				

*These backpacking hikes, though not overnight backpacking trips, follow part of either the Appalachian Trail or the Batona Trail. As such they can be [...] backpacking trips. See Appendix: Backpacking Trips.

Trail Finder Chart

Number	Hike	Back-packing*	Beach & Coast Lovers	Waterfalls, Lakes, Rivers, & Streams	Children's/Gentle Hikes	Views & Vistas	Industrial Archaeology	Rail-roads & Canals	History	Unique Environ-mental Features
13	The Tourne					•		•		•
14	The Pequannock Highlands								•	
15	Saffin Pond and Headley Overlook			•	•	•	•	•	•	
16	Schooley's Mountain			•			•		•	
17	Terrace Pond			•		•				•
18	Wyanokie High Point			•	•	•				
19	The Black River			•	•		•	•	•	
20	Ken Lockwood Gorge			•	•		•	•	•	•
21	Wawayanda Lake		•							
22	The Great Falls of the Passaic			•	•	•	•	•	•	•
23	The Hudson Palisades			•		•		•	•	•
24	The Princeton Woods			•	•			•	•	
25	Jockey Hollow								•	
26	Watchung Reservation			•			•		•	
27	The Delaware and Raritan Canal—Millstone Valley			•	•		•	•	•	

Trail Finder Chart

Number	Hike	Back-packing*	Beach & Coast Lovers	Waterfalls, Lakes, Rivers, & Streams	Children's/Gentle Hikes	Views & Vistas	Industrial Archaeology	Rail-roads & Canals	History	Unique Environmental Features
28	The Great Swamp			•	•					•
29	The Delaware River Valley—Stockton to Bull's Island			•	•		•	•	•	
30	The Delaware River Valley—Stockton to Lambertville			•	•		•	•	•	
31	South Mountain and the Rahway River			•		•			•	•
32	The Hackensack Meadowlands			•	•		•	•	•	•
33	Lord Stirling Park			•	•					•
34	Belcoville and the South River			•	•	•	•		•	
35	Pakim Pond and Mount Misery	•		•			•		•	•
36	Parvin Lake		•		•					•
37	Bear Swamp Hill and the Pine Plains					•				
38	Wells Mills			•			•			•
39	Apple Pie Hill	•								•
40	Batsto Lake	•		•	•		•		•	•

*These backpacking hikes, though not overnight backpacking trips, follow part of either the Appalachian Trail or the Batona Trail. As such they can be expanded into overnight or multi-day backpacking trips. See Appendix: Backpacking Trips.

Trail Finder Chart

Number	Hike	Back-packing *	Beach & Coast Lovers	Waterfalls, Lakes, Rivers, & Streams	Children's/ Gentle Hikes	Views & Vistas	Industrial Archaeology	Rail-roads & Canals	History	Unique Environ-mental Features
41	Lake Nummy and East Creek Pond		●	●	●					
42	Cheesequake		●	●			●		●	●
43	The Maurice River Estuary		●	●	●	●	●			●
44	Higbee Beach		●	●	●			●		●
45	Cattus Island		●	●	●					
46	Sandy Hook		●	●	●	●				●
47	Finns Point		●	●	●	●			●	
48	Liberty State Park			●	●	●	●	●	●	
49	Island Beach		●	●	●					
50	Cape May Point		●	●	●	●				●

Map Legend

Transportation

Interstate Highway	95
U.S. Highway	9
State Road	31
County Road	583
Dirt Road	= = = = =
Railroad	+—+—+—+
Featured Trail	▬ ▬ ▬ ▬
Other Trail	- - - - - -

Hydrology

Lake/Reservoir	
River/Creek	
Marsh/Swamp	
Waterfall	

Land Use

State Park	

Symbols

Campground	▲
Point of Interest	■
Mountain/Peak	▲
Parking	🅿
Picnic Area	
Restroom	
Tower	
City/Town	○
Trailhead (Start)	❺
Bridge	
Boat launch	
Gate	•—•
Viewpoint	
Boardwalk	‖‖‖‖‖

Scale

0	Kilometer	1
0	Mile	1

True North
(Magnetic North is
approximately 15.5° East)

N

The Kittatinny Ridge and Valley

The Ridge and Valley province in the northwestern part of New Jersey is a link in the great Appalachian mountain-and-valley chain running between Canada and Tennessee. In New Jersey we recognize it as the Kittatinny Valley in Sussex and Warren Counties, and the adjacent Kittatinny Mountains to the west.

The Kittatinnies continue south into Pennsylvania, where they are called the Blue Mountains (as they once were in New Jersey) and north into New York State where

Scoping the Pocono Plateau just off the Appalachian Trail on the Kittatinny Ridge.

they become the well-known and much-loved Shawangunk Mountains. In places, the range is a lone ridge, in other places multiple ridges, and still elsewhere a wide plateau.

The Ridge and Valley province covers only about a twelfth of New Jersey's area yet includes some of its best-known natural landmarks. The level-crested Kittatinnies include Sunrise Mountain in Stokes State Forest, High Point to the north, and the awe-inspiring Delaware Water Gap. The famous Appalachian Trail runs the crest of these mountains for over 40 miles.

West of the Kittatinnies is the Delaware Valley, isolated from the rest of New Jersey by the mountains. This geographic factor, along with the establishment of the Delaware Water Gap National Recreation Area in 1965, lends the entire valley a unique aura of quiet and isolation.

Soft stones (limestone, shale, and sandstone) that eroded over the eons underlie these valleys. The mountain's backbone, in contrast, is the more resistant and concretelike Shawangunk Conglomerate, a mix of rocks and pebbles in a finer matrix. The Delaware River cuts a 2-mile path through this mountain-wall of rock, forming therein the Delaware Water Gap, a noted scenic landmark for two centuries. The valleys, with good soils and gently rolling landscape, first saw European settlement ca. 1700, and farming remains an important activity.

Railroads penetrated this region starting in the 1850s, shipping out all manner of agricultural goods, limestone, and iron ore. Today, abandoned railroad beds provide dozens of miles of easy hiking at both Kittatinny Valley State Park and the Wallkill River National Wildlife Refuge. The Kittatinny Mountains were home to both mountain farms, and later, resorts and camps. Since 1900, almost the entire mountain range in New Jersey has been preserved as a greenbelt of state parks and forests and the national recreation area. Beautiful and varied, the Kittatinny Ridge and Valley thus preserve the heritage of New Jersey's forest and farmland alike.

1 Steenykill Lake and High Point

This lollipop hike takes you into the "Golden Age of Parks" with trails, dams, and cabins built by the High Point Park Commission in the 1920s and by the Civilian Conservation Corps in the 1930s. The trail climbs and traverses the Kittatinny ridges with splendid views of the Pocono Plateau and the New Jersey Highlands, topping off at High Point Monument, the highest point in New Jersey, with a magnificent tri-state panoramic view. The hike encircles Dryden Kuser Natural Area, known for its Atlantic white cedar swamp. In addition to the mountain-valley scene, the trail also skirts the shores of Steenykill Lake, as well as Lake Marcia, with its designated swimming area (seasonal).

Start: Steenykill Lake boat launch parking lot, just off Route 23, north of park main entrance
Distance: 6.0-mile lollipop
Approximate hiking time: 4 to 5 hours
Difficulty: Moderate. Two climbs to the ridge
Trail surface: Mostly shale gravel with a few rocky sections
Seasons: Spring through fall
Other trail users: Hikers
Canine compatibility: Dogs permitted but must be on a leash no longer than 6 feet.
Land status: State park
Nearest town: South: Sussex Borough (7 miles); north: Port Jervis, NY (4 miles)
Fees and permits: None if you use our choice of trailhead; otherwise, there is a fee (higher on weekends) to drive into the park from Memorial Day weekend to Labor Day weekend.
Schedule: Dawn to dusk (from trailhead); main park entrance hours vary by season (call park office for hours)
Maps: *Kittatinny Trails Map 18: High Point State Park, Stokes State Forest, Delaware Water Gap NRA,* published by the New York–New Jersey Trail Conference; USGS Port Jervis South Quadrangle; also, a New Jersey Division of Parks and Forestry Map can be obtained at the High Point Park Office on Route 23. *DeLorme: New Jersey Atlas & Gazetteer:* p.19
Trail contacts: High Point State Park, 1480 Route 23, Sussex 07461-3605; (973) 875-4800; www.state.nj.us/dep/parksandforests/parks/highpoint.html. New York–New Jersey Trail Conference, 156 Ramapo Valley Road, Mahwah 07430; www.nynjtc.org
Other: Be aware that on nice weekends from spring through fall, the park can be very crowded. New Jersey state parks are pack-in pack-out; no trash cans available. It's worthwhile to stop in at the interpretive center and pick up handouts and materials on flora, fauna, and history.
Special considerations: Ticks have been known to be especially bad in this area in spring.

Finding the trailhead: From Sussex Borough, travel 8.3 miles north on Route 23, passing High Point State Park headquarters building on your left and the park entrance on your right. Continue north on Route 23 for 1.5 miles, descending the mountain. Turn right into the Steenykill boat launch area and travel 0.1 mile to the parking lot.

The Hike

The Steenykill Trail starts on Route 23 and skirts the boat ramp parking area, which is larger and quieter than the highway parking area. Crossing the lot and reaching the trail, you are immediately on the Steenykill Lake shoreline with an impressive view of High Point Monument. Looking across the lake on the east shore are two cabins built by the Park Commission during the 1930s, soon after the Civilian Conservation Corps (CCC) built Steenykill Lake, a former Atlantic white cedar swamp. (*Note:* You may consider staying in these fully furnished cabins, open from May 15 to October 15.)

Crossing the dam, you now walk on another CCC project, their largest in High Point State Park, if not the state. The construction of Steenykill Lake was begun by the state in the late 1920s but stopped due to the Great Depression. In 1935 the CCC re-started the project, a three-year effort that included the dredging of the lake and construction of the 1,200-foot-long, 45-foot-high dam. Make a mental note of the lake, so when you arrive at Dryden Kuser Natural Area you can compare the two white cedar swamps. Hiking up the trail, you are now on another project built by the CCC, reflected in the periodic stonework and the blue chip shale.

Once on the Monument Trail, there continues to be evidence of the CCC handiwork in rock cribs and stone steps. Once you climb up through the hardwoods, you are now experiencing scrub oak and pitch pine during your ridge walk. From various vistas looking west, views of the Delaware River, Pocono Plateau, and the city of Port Jervis and Matamoras lay out before you. Descending off the ridge, you will encircle the Dryden Kuser Natural Area, containing the highest elevation (1,500 feet) white cedar swamp in the world, with Atlantic white cedar, Eastern hemlock, and sphagnum moss. A nature guide, obtained from the park office, may enhance your experience.

▶ Steenykill Lake and the Dryden Kuser Natural Area could hardly be more different today, but a century ago they were the same. Both were cedar swamps, and cedar was valuable timber for shingles and siding. The Steenykill cedar swamp was clear-cut, but the Kuser cedar swamp was protected and preserved by the Kuser family's interest in nature and conservation.

Leaving this natural Shangri-La, emerge on the east ridge with periodic views (east) of the New Jersey Highlands. Impressive how much green still exists in the most densely populated state in the union. There will also be one vista looking west where most of the hike can be visually traced. Arriving at the High Point Monument complex, you will find bathrooms and a water fountain (seasonal). The 221-foot-tall monument was built in 1928–30 to honor New Jersey veterans of all wars and modeled after the Bunker Hill Monument. At the intersection with the Appalachian Trail, you stand on a footpath that connects with thirteen other states and runs 2,103 miles up and down the eastern seaboard. Pretty amazing, since this trail was built, managed, and maintained by volunteers.

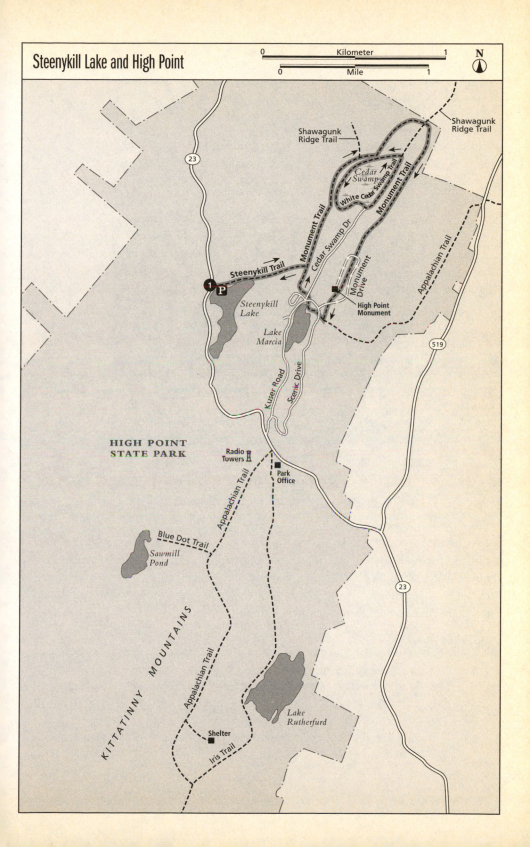

Steenykill Lake and High Point

0   Kilometer   1

0   Mile   1

N

Shawagunk Ridge Trail

Shawagunk Ridge Trail

Cedar Swamp Trail

White Cedar Swamp Trail

Monument Trail

Monument Trail

Cedar Swamp Dr

Appalachian Trail

Steenykill Trail

23

P
1

Steenykill Lake

Lake Marcia

Monument Drive

High Point Monument

519

Kuser Road

Scenic Drive

HIGH POINT STATE PARK

Radio Towers

Appalachian Trail

Park Office

Blue Dot Trail

Sawmill Pond

Appalachian Trail

23

K I T T A T I N N Y   M O U N T A I N S

Appalachian Trail

Lake Rutherfurd

Shelter

Iris Trail

High Point Monument (1,803 feet) viewed from the Kuser Mansion site.

The trail also passes Lake Marcia, the highest lake in New Jersey, as well as near the Interpretive Center. This handsome stone building has gone through many transitions. Originally built in 1930 as a restaurant for park visitors, it was later converted to the park Interpretive Center. From here, the hike goes back down the mountain to Steenykill Lake and dam, our starting point.

Miles and Directions

0.0 Start in the Steenykill Lake boat parking lot. Head 20 yards north to the boat ramp where Steenykill Trail (blue blazes) intersects. Turn left (east) onto the trail and skirt the north shore of Steenykill Lake.

0.3 Cross over the 1,200-foot dam into the hardwood forest and ascend the ridge.

0.7 Steenykill Trail dead-ends into the Monument Trail (red/green blazes). Turn left (northeast) onto the Monument Trail.

1.5 Shawangunk Ridge Trail (turquoise blazes) enters from the left (north) and becomes co-aligned with the Monument Trail. (**FYI:** The hike will weave back and forth over these two trails.)

1.6 Turn right (south) following the Shawangunk Ridge Trail for 20 yards to the White Cedar Swamp Trail. Turn right (west) onto the White Cedar Swamp Trail into Dryden Kuser Natural Area. (**FYI:** A self-guided booklet for this area can be acquired at the park office.)

2.3 Pass Cedar Swamp Drive (on the right) where it enters the Dryden Kuser Natural Area, marked by a stone and bronze plaque (on the left) honoring Dryden Kuser, the son of Colonel and Mrs. Kuser, and an ardent naturalist and ornithologist. Continue to circle the swamp counterclockwise.

2.7 Pass the departing Shawangunk Ridge Trail on the right (east), while the White Cedar Swamp Trail and the Shawangunk Ridge Trail co-align, crossing 100 yards of boardwalk.

2.9 Arrive back at the beginning of the circular. Turn right (north) onto Shawangunk Ridge Trail for 20 yards to an immediate junction with Monument Trail. Turn right (east) onto the Monument Trail.

3.3 The trail crosses Shawangunk Ridge Trail. Continue straight on the Monument Trail ascending (south) the ridge.

4.4 Pass through parking lot, staying to the right (west) side and heading (south) toward the restrooms. Pick up the trail on the southwest end of the restrooms.

4.6 Arrive at High Point Monument. Trail descends from the southwest corner of the monument.

4.7 Cross Monument Drive.

4.8 Arrive at junction with Appalachian Trail. Turn right (west) on Monument Trail and shortly cross Scenic Drive.

5.0 Trail skirts the north end of Lake Marcia and shortly crosses Kuser Road. Head up the driveway to the Interpretive Center.

5.1 The Monument Trail turns right (north) off the pavement and heads back onto the ridge.

5.3 Reach the Steenykill Trail intersection. Turn left (west) and descend on the Steenykill Trail.

5.3 Retrace 0.7 mile of the hike to the trailhead.

6.0 Arrive at parking lot.

Hike Information

Local Information
New Jersey Skylands Region Tourism Guide, www.njskylands.com

Local Events/Attractions
The New Jersey State Fair-Sussex County Farm and Horse Show, Route 206 in Augusta, runs from the first Friday in August for ten days; www.newjerseystatefair.org. In Port Jervis, Fort Decker and the Kleinstuber House, operated by the Minisink Valley Historical Society, preserve the history of the upper Delaware Valley. Minisink Valley Historical Society, 125–133 West Main Street, Port Jervis, NY 12771; (845) 856-2375; www.minisink.org

Lodging
High Point State Park operates Sawmill Lake Campground, with 50 tent sites, bathrooms, water,

and a telephone; open April 1 to October 31 (fee). Two cabins with full kitchen, bathroom, and fireplace may also be rented on the shore of Steenykill Lake, open May 15 to October 15 (fee).

Restaurants

The Elias Cole Restaurant on Highway 23 near Colesville is a local landmark famous for its grilled burgers, roast beef sandwiches, and pies (no credit cards accepted); (973) 875-3550.

Organizations

New York–New Jersey Trail Conference 156 Ramapo Valley Road (U.S. Highway 202), Mahwah 07430; (201) 512-9348; www.nynjtc.org

Other Resources

Dupont, Ronald J. Jr., and Kevin Wright. *High Point of the Blue Mountains*. Newton, NJ: Sussex County Historical Society, 1990. Scherer, Glenn. *Nature Walks in New Jersey*. Boston: AMC Books, 1998. Osborne, Peter. *Images of America: High Point State Park and the Civilian Conservation Corps*. Charleston, SC: Arcadia Publishing, 2002. Osborne, Peter. *We Can Take It! The Roosevelt Tree Army at New Jersey's High Point State Park, 1933–1941*. Bloomington, IN: 1st Books Library, 2002.

BUILDING A PARK: THE OLMSTED BROTHERS AND THE CIVILIAN CONSERVATION CORPS

When High Point Park was created in 1923, its commissioners knew they had to develop a plan for it, and they went to the creme de la creme of park designers: the Olmsted Brothers of Brookline, Massachusetts. The firm's founder, Frederick Law Olmsted, codesigned New York's Central Park, the U.S. Capitol grounds, and numerous other city and state parks; his sons continued the tradition. The Olmsteds proposed a broad development plan for High Point, but only a portion of it had been implemented by the early 1930s when the economic crunch caused by the Great Depression put an end to park development plans.

New hope came in 1933 with the administration of Franklin D. Roosevelt and the start of his program, the New Deal. One of his first plans was to give jobs to unemployed young men and undertake important conservation work. The program was called the Civilian Conservation Corps and was run jointly by the U.S. Army, the Department of the Interior, and the Department of Agriculture. Enrollees lived in camps set up near their project sites; they performed virtually all manner of outdoor work in state and national parks and forests, watersheds, and natural areas.

At High Point, the CCC operated from 1933 to 1941, working out of a huge camp located in the present Cedar Swamp picnic area. The National Park Service revised the Olmsted Plan, and the corps built it: New campgrounds, bathrooms, beaches, roads, trails, and lakes were constructed. The public benefited from all the new facilities, and the enrollees benefited, too. At a time when hunger was a genuine problem in America, CCC boys typically gained weight during their service; they were paid $30 per month, $25 of which went to their parents.

Improving economic conditions, and then the eruption of World War II, brought an end to the CCC, but the program was hardly forgotten. Today, tens of thousands of former "C-boys" recall with fondness their days working in the woods, and hundreds of state parks and forests are graced with the handsome and durable projects they constructed. The majority of High Point State Park's facilities were constructed during the CCC era, a tangible reminder of this heroic program from an epic time in American history.

IN ADDITION

The Kuser Legacy at High Point

High Point and Lake Marcia had been a popular picnic spot for surrounding communities since at least the 1850s, but in 1890 the site went commercial: Port Jervis newspaper publisher Charles St. John built the High Point Inn, a 300-foot-long hotel overlooking the lake. It was a popular resort for nearly twenty years, but a string of bad luck led to bankruptcy for St. John; the hotel property was sold at a sheriffs sale in 1908.

Two years later, it was bought by Anthony and John Kuser, twin brothers from Bernardsville, New Jersey, entrepreneur capitalists who had stakes in all kinds of businesses—brewing companies, ice companies, public utilities, railway companies, the Fox Film Company, and real estate. Anthony was known as "Colonel" Kuser (a state militia title). While they first viewed the High Point property as a business acquisition, the beauty of the site soon convinced Anthony Kuser and his wife, Susie Dryden Kuser, to use it as their summer vacation home. They had the wherewithal to do this—not only were the Kusers wealthy, but Mrs. Kuser's father was U.S. senator John F. Dryden, the founder of the Prudential Insurance Company of America.

Colonel and Mrs. Kuser tore down a third of the old hotel and remodeled the rest in Colonial Revival style with huge porticoes and porches as their summer "cottage." Land acquisitions by the Kusers and Senator Dryden soon created an estate that exceeded 10,500 acres. The Kusers used it for over a decade, but Mrs. Kuser is said to have lost her enthusiasm for the place upon finding a rattlesnake basking in the sunny drive in front of the mansion. Soon thereafter, the Kusers moved on to idea number two for the property: donate it as a state park. They did this in early 1923, conveying the mansion and all 10,500 acres to the state of New Jersey. High Point Park, as it was called, opened to the public on Memorial Day 1923. The Kusers' mansion became the park headquarters, museum, and visitor lodging.

The Kusers' interest in High Point did not end there: It had always been Colonel Kuser's intention to erect some kind of permanent tower or beacon atop High Point itself. In the aftermath of the First World War, there had been much debate about erecting a monument to honor New Jersey veterans. Colonel Kuser thought High Point was the perfect location, and in late 1927 he proposed to donate to the state of New Jersey a monument patterned after the one at Bunker Hill: a 221-foot-tall obelisk marking the highest point in New Jersey, and dedicated to New Jersey veterans of land, sea, or air, in all wars of our nation. The gift was accepted, and on Memorial Day 1930 High Point Monument was dedicated and opened to the public. It almost immediately became a New Jersey icon.

Colonel Kuser was not there to enjoy the festivities. He had died at his estate in Palm Beach, Florida, in February 1929, and never lived to see the monument.

The future held hard times for both Kuser's mansion and monument. The Kuser Mansion, as it came to be known, was showing signs of neglect by the late 1960s. Decades of debate, controversy, and state inaction over what to do about the building culminated in its tragic demolition in 1995. Today, only interpretive panels mark the site.

High Point Monument appeared to be headed toward a similar fate: Water damage and improper work left its joints cracked, its interior damp with mildew, its stairs rusted and unsafe; it was closed to the public for years. This necessitated a massive restoration project by the late 1990s, which was completed in 2004. Just in time for its seventy-fifth anniversary, Col. Kuser's monument escaped the fate of his mansion: It was rededicated and reopened to the public in the spring of 2005.

2 Lake Rutherfurd and the Appalachian Trail

This is definitely one of the classic hikes in New Jersey. The loop runs the rocky Kittatinny Ridge via the Appalachian Trail, providing grand views of the Pocono Plateau and the Great Valley before dropping down along the geological shelf to Lake Rutherfurd, a fabulous lunch spot. The adventure continues as it ambles back up the ridge, using a bridle path built by the Civilian Conservation Corps.

Start: Appalachian Trail parking lot on Route 23, just south of park headquarters
Distance: 5.5-mile loop
Approximate hiking time: 3 hours

Difficulty: Moderate with a few tougher sections
Trail surface: Woods roads and forested trails
Seasons: All, but best in spring, summer, fall

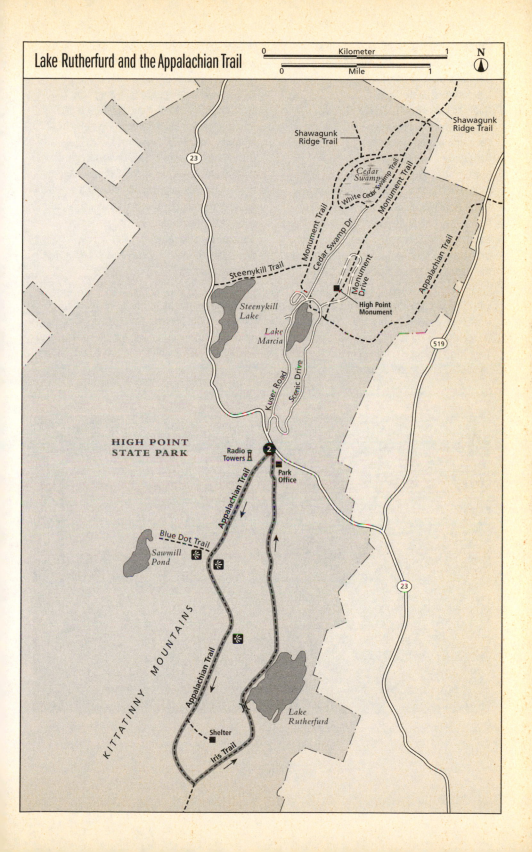

Lake Rutherfurd and the Appalachian Trail

0 Kilometer 1
0 Mile 1

N

Shawagunk Ridge Trail

Shawagunk Ridge Trail

Cedar Swamp

White Cedar Swamp Trail

Monument Trail

Monument Trail

Cedar Swamp Dr

Monument Trail

Monument Drive

High Point Monument

Appalachian Trail

Steenykill Trail

23

Steenykill Lake

Lake Marcia

Kuser Road

Scenic Drive

519

HIGH POINT STATE PARK

Radio Towers

2

Park Office

Appalachian Trail

Blue Dot Trail

Sawmill Pond

Appalachian Trail

KITTATINNY MOUNTAINS

Lake Rutherfurd

Appalachian Trail

Shelter

Iris Trail

23

Other trail users: Multiuse on the Iris Trail; hikers only on the Appalachian Trail

Canine compatibility: Leashed dogs permitted

Land status: State park

Nearest town: South: Sussex Borough (7 miles); north: Port Jervis, NY (4 miles)

Fees and permits: None

Schedule: Dawn to dusk

Maps: *Kittatinny Trails Map 18: High Point State Park, Stokes State Forest, Delaware Water Gap NRA,* published by the New York–New Jersey Trail Conference; USGS Port Jervis South Quadrangle; also, a New Jersey Division of Parks and Forestry Map can be obtained at the High Point Park Office on Route 23.

DeLorme: New Jersey Atlas & Gazetteer: p.19

Trail contacts: High Point State Park, 1480 Route 23, Sussex 07461-3605; (973) 875-4800; www.state.nj.us/dep/parksandforests/parks/highpoint.html. New York–New Jersey Trail Conference, 156 Ramapo Valley Road, Mahwah, NJ 07430; www.nynjtc.org

Other: While this hike goes through High Point State Park, Lake Rutherfurd itself and its immediate shoreline are off limits to the public (Sussex Borough Reservoir); trespassers are subject to prosecution.

Special considerations: This is a busy area in deer hunting season; wear some blaze orange, or stay home.

Finding the trailhead: From Sussex Borough, travel 8.3 miles north on Route 23, reaching High Point State Park. Just before reaching the park headquarters building (on your left) and the park entrance on your right, there is on the left a long-term parking lot (gravel) for the Appalachian Trail. This is located adjacent to the State DOT maintenance yard. Park here; the trail begins at the signboard near the end of the lot.

This ca. 1905 postcard shows the cabins of the Wantage Outing Club at Lake Rutherfurd. By the late 1920s, the club's lease expired and all the buildings were removed.

The Hike

This hike takes you through the heart of the Kittatinnies. Starting out on the historic Appalachian Trail, you will pass reminders of early history here: A large cliff/talus slope on your right soon after the hike begins is, in fact, a nineteenth-century stone quarry, later used to obtain stone by the Civilian Conservation Corps for its projects. Those projects included Sawmill Pond and Campground, which you'll see from an overlook.

This hike also provides a wonderful vista from the so-called Dutch Shoe Rock, looking east over the Kittatinny Valley, part of the Great Valley of the Appalachians. In few areas is it clearer why this is called the "Ridge and Valley Province." The woods and farmlands of Wantage Township below belie the common image of New Jersey.

You'll return via the Iris Trail. This broad path was part of the Olmsted Brothers' plan for High Point Park. Hiking along it, you'll perhaps expect to see irises in season, and you won't. So how did it get the name? High Point State Park headquarters (at the end of the trail) is located in a building built by the park in 1941 in the CCC–style of the era. Originally intended to be a visitor center and "tea house" (i.e., serving light refreshments), it was originally called the "Iris Inn," after the blue flag irises that grow (even now) in the pond in front of it.

A major highlight of the hike is Lake Rutherfurd, which is much like the famous "sky lakes" farther north along this range in the Shawangunks (Mohonk, Minnewaska, etc.). It was called "Sand Pond" in the 1800s. When John Rutherfurd, a wealthy businessman from Bergen County, started buying up tens of thousands of acres in the Kittatinny Mountains in the mid-1800s, it was perhaps inevitable that a lake should be named after him. "Sand Pond" became "Lake Rutherfurd" about the time it became Sussex Borough (formerly Deckertown) Reservoir ca.1897.

By the mid-twentieth century, most of the Rutherfurd family had changed the spelling to the more modern "Rutherford," and so too did the lake's name change, but we prefer the historical Rutherfurd. This is a natural lake raised by a dam in the late 1800s to supply extra waterpower to mills operating on Clove Brook in the valley below. Most lakes in these mountains were home to a summer colony or hotel, and this was no exception.

In 1893 a group of Deckertown residents formed the Wantage Outing Club, which took a thirty-year lease on the lake. Its members built cottages on the rocky eastern bluff overlooking the lake and enjoyed summers here. In this exposed location, extreme weather is common, and on several occasions, cottage owners came up in early spring to find their cottage had, quite literally, been blown off the mountain during the winter. Thereafter, most cottages were secured to their sites by heavy iron cables, the eye-rings of which can still be found here and there. Not surprisingly, the common name for the colony was "Camp Windy." The cabin colony operated even after the lake became a reservoir in 1897. In 1917 the Kuser family sold the land to Sussex Borough, and in 1924, its lease now expired, the Wantage Outing Club left the lake forever, and the cabin colony became a memory.

Miles and Directions

0.0 Proceed to the directory at the northwest end of the parking lot where you will find the trailheads to the Iris Trail (red blazes) and Mashipacong Trail (yellow blazes). Following this path immediately brings you to a T intersection. Turn left (southwest) onto the Appalachian Trail (white blazes) and the aforementioned trails (co-align). (**Side trip:** Turning right (northeast) onto the Appalachian Trail will take you to the lawn of the High Point State Park office, where there are bathrooms, water, maps, and displays.)

0.1 At the trail junction continue straight (southeast) on the Appalachian Trail, eventually climbing to the top of the Kittatinny Ridge. The Mashipacong Trail turns right, while the Iris Trail turns left. Take note of this spot! The hike will return via the Iris Trail.

0.8 Pass the Blue Dot Trail on the right. (**Side trip:** Traveling 150 feet on the Blue Dot Trail brings you to a secluded vista framed by pitch pine and backed by a Volkswagon-size glacial erratic. There are beautiful panoramic views directly over Sawmill Pond and campground and the Pocono Plateau.)

0.9 Arrive at an outlook (northwest) with a fabulous view: Sawmill Pond, Delaware Valley, and the Pocono Mountains.

1.4 Arrive at a series of outlooks (southeast) on the other side of the Kittatinny Ridge. It is quite apparent why this landform is called "Ridge and Valley." Overlooking Lake Rutherfurd, you can actually see all the way to the Jersey Highlands.

2.3 Pass the blue-blazed trail on the left leading to the Rutherfurd Shelter (0.4 mile).

2.9 At the trail junction with several woods roads, turn sharply left (east) onto the Iris Trail (red blazes), allowing the Appalachian Trail and Iris Trail (looping back on itself) to run jointly for a few hundred yards before they separate. (**Option:** The loop hike can be extended for 2.5 miles because the Appalachian Trail and the Iris Trail will cross paths again in about 1.2 miles.)

3.4 At the T intersection the Iris Trail turns left (west) onto a woods road, avoiding the private property. The trail will immediately pass a woods road on the left, which is an unofficial approach to the Rutherfurd Shelter.

3.6 The trail crosses a wooden bridge over the inlet to Lake Rutherfurd and ascends (north) to a ledge with natural benches over the lake. An ideal lunch spot!

4.0 Continue on the woods road while passing glacial erratics. Sing a few old summer camp songs, as this section gets a bit long on the heels. This portion of the Iris Trail reflects the handiwork of the CCC, which constructed it as a bridle path as part of the Olmsted Brothers' grand scheme loop road in High Point State Park.

5.4 At the intersection the Iris Trail turns right (northeast), running jointly with the Appalachian (white blazes) and the Mashipacong (yellow blazes) Trails.

5.5 Arrive back at the parking lot.

Hike Information

Local Information

New Jersey Skylands Region Tourism Guide; www.njskylands.com

Local Events/Attractions

The New Jersey State Fair/Sussex County Farm and Horse Show, U.S. Highway 206 in Augusta, runs from the first Friday in August for ten days. In Port Jervis, Fort Decker and the Kleinstuber House, operated by the Minisink Valley Historical Society, preserve the history of the upper Delaware Valley. Minisink Valley Historical Society, 125–133 West Main Street, Port Jervis, NY 12771; (845) 856-2375; www.minisink.org

Lodging

High Point State Park operates Sawmill Lake Campground, with 50 tent sites, bathrooms, water, and a telephone; open April 1 to October 31 (fee). Two cabins with full kitchen, bathroom, and fireplace may also be rented on the shore of Steenykill Lake, open May 15 to October 15 (fee).

Restaurants

The Elias Cole Restaurant on Route 23 near Colesville is a local landmark famous for its grilled burgers, roast beef sandwiches, and pies (no credit cards accepted); (973) 875-3550.

Organizations

New York–New Jersey Trail Conference, 156 Ramapo Valley Road (U.S. Highway 202), Mahwah 07430; (201) 512-9348; www.nynjtc.org

Other Resources

Dupont, Ronald J. Jr., and Kevin Wright. *High Point of the Blue Mountains*. Newton, NJ: Sussex County Historical Society, 1990. Scherer, Glenn. *Nature Walks in New Jersey*. Boston: AMC Books, 1998. Osborne, Peter. *Images of America: High Point State Park and the Civilian Conservation Corps*. Charleston, SC: Arcadia Publishing, 2002. Osborne, Peter. *We Can Take It! The Roosevelt Tree Army at New Jersey's High Point State Park, 1933–1941*. Bloomington, IN: 1st Books Library, 2002.

3 The Paulinskill Valley Trail

Amble down an old cinder railroad bed that meanders along the Paulinskill River through lush pastoral scenes. It doesn't get much better than this on a beautiful spring day with the water churning over rock. The trail transports you back in time by the old gristmills, over trestles, past picturesque Blairstown, and under the one-time world's largest viaduct. Traipse through farmland, a country airport, and small local parks. Overall, the hike hugs the Paulinskill River's edge down the Paulinskill Valley with the ever-present view of the Kittatinny Ridge and the Delaware Water Gap.

Start: East end: Kittatinny Valley State Park parking lot on Spring Valley Road, Marksboro; West end (end point): pull-off on Station Road Hainesburg
Distance: 9.5 miles, point-to-point
Approximate hiking time: 5 hours

Difficulty: Moderate due to distance
Trail surface: Old railroad bed; mostly cinder base
Seasons: All seasons, though spring may be best due to the rains making the Paulinskill River dance.

Other trail users: Mountain bikers, equestrians, joggers, cross-country skiers, and the occasional shopper near Blairstown

Canine compatibility: Pets permitted but must be on a leash no longer than 6 feet.

Land status: Kittatinny Valley State Park; Blairstown Airport: private

Nearest town: Blairstown, located on the trail 3.2 miles from the starting point

Fees and permits: None

Schedule: Dawn to dusk

Maps: *Trail Guide: Paulinskill Valley & Sussex Branch Trails,* published by the State Park Service. It may be obtained at the park headquarters, via park ranger, or possibly in a box attached to a trailhead directory. *Paulinskill Valley Rail-Trail* map published by the Paulinskill

Valley Trail Committee: www.pvtc-kvsp .org. *DeLorme: New Jersey Atlas & Gazetteer:* p.23. USGS Portland, PA, and Blairstown, NJ, quadrangles

Trail contacts: Kittatinny Valley State Park, PO Box 621, Andover 07821-0621; (973) 786-6445; www.state.nj.us/dep/parksand forests/parks/kittval.html

Other: This hike offers an excellent opportunity to explore the scenic and historic village of Blairstown, with bookstores, art galleries, churches, and Blair Academy Preparatory School.

Special considerations: Given the relatively smooth trailway, sneakers are a good option for this hike.

BACK IN TIME ON THE SUSIE-Q

Stand in the Paulinskill Valley Trail parking lot and imagine flagging down one of the five passenger trains that once ran daily over these cinders. Or smell the smoke of the milk-run train stopped at the Marksboro creamery. It's already picked up the milk cans at the creameries in Blairstown, Vail (the only one still standing today), and Hainesburg.

Approaching the deck girder bridge, you can almost hear the rattling of the rails from the two engines pulling twenty-five coal cars, racing at 30 miles an hour from the Pennsylvania coal fields to the Industrial Northeast. The coal trains rumbled across this railroad bridge five times a day to the tune of 1.5 million tons of anthracite per year.

As the trail approaches the thru-plate girder bridge, can you picture the ice train on its way to Jersey City? Or mightn't you be a vacationer on a special weekend express to Blairstown? Today, when you get there, imagine the ghost of a railway station, the freight yard, the water tanks, and the turntable, as you hike through the parking lot of cinders. On the other hand, could you be an employee of the New York, Susquehanna & Western who is on a special company excursion train to Lake Susquehanna at Blairstown Airport with your family for the annual employees' picnic?

And finally, are you onboard as the trail passes the site of the Hainesburg Station and under the colossal reinforced concrete Paulinskill? This behemoth structure over the Paulinskill River brings the "rail trip" to an end.

The Paulinskill Valley Trail

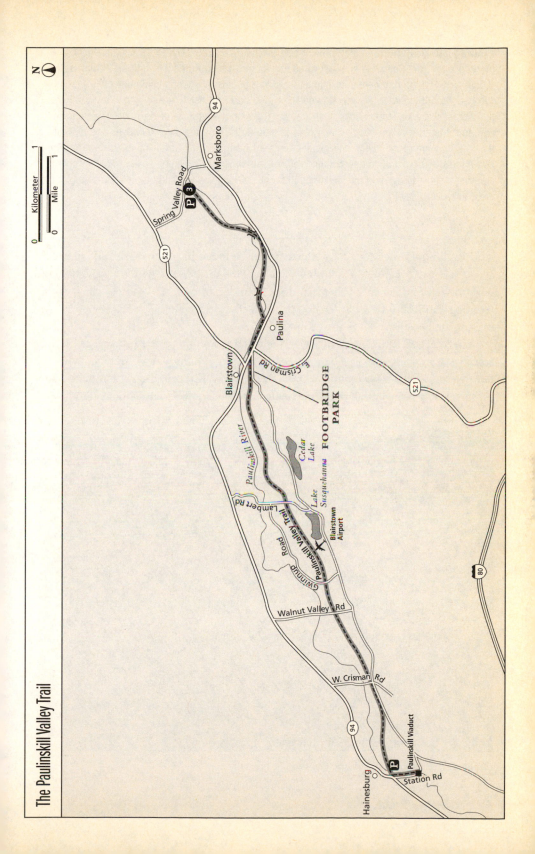

N

Kilometer
0   1
0   1
Mile

94

Marksboro

Spring Valley Road

P 3

521

Paulina

Blairstown

E. Crisman Rd

Paulinskill River

Cedar Lake

Lake Susquehanna

FOOTBRIDGE PARK

Blairstown Airport

Lambert Rd

Paulinskill Valley Trail

Gwinnup Road Trail

Walnut Valley Rd

W. Crisman Rd

521

80

94

Hainesburg

Station Rd

Paulinskill Viaduct

P

Finding the trailhead: A point-to-point hike takes a car shuttle. Directions for vehicle #1 (end car): Take the Columbia exit (exit 4) off Interstate 80 onto Route 94 north for 2.3 miles. In Hainesburg Station, turn right onto Station Road at a ONE LANE BRIDGE sign and immediately cross two bridges. At the end of the second bridge, you will find Paulinskill Trail coming in on your left and co-aligning with Station Road. Park your car there on the left side of the road. Directions for vehicle #2 (starter car): Retrace your trip on Station Road, crossing the two bridges and to Route 94 and turn right (east), following signs for Route 94 north. You will travel 9.5 miles through Blairstown to Marksboro. Turn left onto Spring Valley Road, driving 0.3 mile on a very twisty road. After crossing a stone bridge and the Paulinskill River, on your left you will find an official parking lot for the Paulinskill Valley Trail.

The Hike

The Paulinskill Valley hike begins next to an eighteenth-century gristmill and ends at the twentieth-century Paulinskill Viaduct. This former rail bed is a straight shot, without right or left turns. The trail does meander, of course; it loosely parallels the winding Paulinskill River as it flows through the Upper Delaware Watershed where it joins the Delaware River at Columbia.

The trail will wander off but eventually returns to the riverbank where the kill cascades over shelves of shale, dropping into long, straight, sleepy stretches where a family of mallards takes flight. The railroad bed travels through cuts, across fills, and on a shelf above the kill, all the while being canopied by 80- to 100-foot camouflage-

Paulinskill River and the majestic Paulinskill Viaduct.

colored, shaggy bark sycamores that thrive in damp, rich soil. The trail moves away from the river and is soon surrounded by farm fields. Here you may spot a red-tail hawk soaring above, making great circles as it searches for some unsuspecting mole.

The path comes back to the river and crosses it twice within the next 0.2 mile on railroad bridges. The trail skirts a pond formed by the Paulina Dam. Here at Paulina Park you may find a single swan, a beaver lodge, a trout angler, and most likely, a romantic couple. Crossing East Crissman Road, the trail passes a horse farm where they raise miniature horses. Don't be surprised if you see one being led down the path. The trail crosses another girder bridge and the Paulinskill River and works its way behind some backyards and approaches Highway 94. The sound of the automobiles is a bit distracting, but the trail drops below the highway and the noise fades.

As for the backyards, this will happen from time to time on this hike, and one might approach it as "European" in flavor. The trail comes into Blairstown, where you can take advantage of the facilities at the Foot Bridge Park. This municipal park has benches, a portable toilet, a picnic pavilion, and a playground. Back on the trail, you quickly leave the hubbub and enter a pastoral setting surrounded by farm fields and maybe a blue heron with its 6-foot wingspan heading down the Paulinskill.

The trail co-aligns with Lapert Road and turns into the Blairstown Airport, where you follow the airport road around the back of the Runway Café and along the edge of the runway, all the while marveling at the gliders taking off or landing. Here is another good place to picnic: shade, picnic tables, bathrooms, and a cafe serving super homemade pies. Take advantage of the wide-open northwest views down the runway of the Kittatinny Ridge and the Delaware Water Gap. As the hike continues, the landscape scene of the ridge and the gap reappear more or less like a Hudson River School painting; all the while the working farms and their rustic barns take on a New England feel. The trail shortly co-aligns with Station Road where the Paulinskill Viaduct looms overhead and the Paulinskill River continues its journey to the Delaware.

Miles and Directions

0.0   Start at Kittatinny Valley State Park parking lot on Spring Valley Road, Marksboro. Head west down the Paulinskill Valley Trail toward Blairstown.

0.8   Trail hugs the shelf above the Paulinskill River, passing milepost JC 80 (**FYI:** Railroad milepost indicates that you are 80 miles from Jersey City. The concrete mileposts are original and their triangular shape was only used in New Jersey.)

1.7   Cross over deck girder bridge #6 straddling the Paulinskill River.

1.8   Pass JC 81 milepost.

1.9   Cross the Paulinskill River on a thru-plate girder bridge #7 with 6-foot iron sides.

2.3   Pass through the Paulina Park, a township park with a scenic dam, and shortly cross East Crisman Road. This was a flag-stop station for the railroad (the train stopped only if flagged).

2.4   Cross over a girder bridge (#8) while crossing over the Paulinskill River.

2.8   Pass JC 82 milepost.

2.9   Proceed under the Route 94 overpass and head straight through a large parking lot (once a freight yard with a roundhouse).

3.2   Continue past Foot Bridge Park, which is to the right (north). (**Option:** Good place for lunch: picnic tables, pavilion, portable toilet, all under a canopy of hardwoods along the Paulinskill River. The footbridge takes you across the Paulinskill River to Route 94, where the Blairstown Diner and Dale's Market are located. Crossing Route 94 and taking Carhart Street north [0.1 mile] leads you to Main Street and the Old Mill [1825], Blair Academy [1903], and Blair Lake and Falls [1906], which are on the State and National Register of Historic Places. The town, with its bookstores, galleries, and eateries, is worth a look-see.)

5.1   Trail emerges onto Lambert Road. Walking along the shoulder, proceed straight ahead for 0.1 mile and turn right (north), following 2-foot-high signs that say trail into the Blairstown Airport.

5.2   Follow the airport driveway past the parking lot right (north) and proceed around the back of the Runway Café. (**Option:** Another great lunch spot. They serve delicious homemade apple pie. Picnic tables under large spruces provide a place to eat while watching gliders float above the Paulinskill Valley. Bathrooms and pay phone are available.)

5.3   The trail, running between the airport buildings and Lake Susquehanna, eventually swings out toward the taxi airstrip and jogs left (west) along the shoulder of the airstrip. The trail parallels the runway for 0.1 mile. Stay off the runway; otherwise, it's sure gonna hurt!

5.4   Look for the opening in the tree line at the left end of the strip and proceed on the cider railroad bed.

5.8   Pass JC 85 milepost.

6.5   Cross over Gwinnup Road.

6.8   Pass JC 86 milepost.

7.0   Cross Walnut Valley Road.

7.5   Cross private road to a farm.

7.8   Pass JC 87 milepost.

8.3   Cross West Crisman Road.

8.8   Pass JC 88 milepost.

9.3   Emerge onto Station Road. Walk past your vehicle and proceed straight (west) along the shoulder of the Station Road past Hainesburg Station (sign only) for 0.1 mile and under the Paulinskill Viaduct; upon viewing it, turn back and retrace your steps toward your vehicle.

9.5   Arrive back at your vehicle.

Hike Information

Local Information
Warren County, New Jersey, Visitor's Guide; www.visitwarren.org

Local Events/Attractions
Yards Creek Soaring: glider flights along the Kittatinny Ridge. Fee; yardscreeksoaring.com. Lakota Wolf Preserve: watch four packs of wolves interact; informal talk and photography. 89 Mount Pleasant Road, Columbia; (908) 496-9244; www.lakotawolf.com

THE PAULINSKILL VIADUCT: FLYING CONCRETE

In the late 1800s, the growing importance of Pennsylvania's coalfields, and the increasing coal consumption of the New York–New Jersey metropolitan area, led to increasing rail traffic in northern New Jersey. Moreover, rail lines, built in the pre–Civil War era, included winding curves, road crossings, steep grades, and tunnels. Junctions with other lines caused bottlenecks. These impediments were time-consuming and expensive. Rail traffic made it profitable to look for a solution—a railroad superhighway, if you will.

That solution came in 1908, when Lackawanna Railroad engineers commenced construction of the 28-mile Lackawanna Cutoff, a vast engineering project that would eliminate most of the curves and grades, and all the tunnels and road crossings, between Lake Hopatcong and the Delaware Water Gap. Massive cuts through hills provided the material for huge railroad fills, such as that across the Pequest River. Two river crossings, those across the Paulinskill and the Delaware, were carried on vast and graceful concrete bridges. In scale and complexity, it was a project akin to—albeit smaller than—the Panama Canal.

The Paulinskill Viaduct, which the Paulinskill Valley Trail (former New York, Susquehanna & Western Railroad) passes under here, was the largest of the concrete bridges. It includes nine spans (two abutments and seven arches), with each large arch supporting seven or eight smaller arches. It seems to soar with the grace of a Gothic cathedral. Built by contractor John Goll & Co. of Philadelphia (using mostly immigrant labor), it is 1,100 feet long with a maximum height of 115 feet. When it opened in 1911 it was the longest and largest concrete bridge *in the world*.

But not, alas, for long. Within a few years, the Clark's Summit–Hallstead Cutoff in Pennsylvania, likewise built by the Lackawanna, contained bridges that surpassed it in dimension. Though it paid for itself many times over, the Lackawanna Cutoff, became disposable. It saw its last passenger train in 1970 and, in the 1980s, was sold to a developer for $1 million; he intended to quarry it for fill-dirt. The state of New Jersey, a bit late, recognized the value of the Cutoff and purchased it a decade later for the "slightly" higher sum of $21 million. It is nevertheless a point of debate whether it will ever see another train. Recent discussions have raised the possibility of reactivating the line for commuter rail service, but it is unclear if the Lackawanna Cutoff hasn't indeed seen its sun set forever.

Lodging

Jenny Jump State Forest, State Park Road, PO Box 150, Hope 07844; (908) 496-9244 (22 tent and trailer sites open April 1 to October 31, 8 shelters open year-round; fee). Worthington State Forest, Old Mine Road, HC 62, Box 2, Columbia 07832; (908) 841-9575 (69 tent and trailer sites open April 1 to October 31; fee). Swartswood State Park, County Route 619, PO Box 123, Swartswood 07877-0123; (973) 383-5230 (65 tent and trailer sites; 8 yurts, open April 1 to October 31). Appalachian Mountain Club's Mohican Outdoor Center, 50 Camp Road, Blairstown 07825-9655; (908) 362-5670; www.mohicanoutdoorcenter.com (The Lodge, winterized cabins, tent sites, and dining hall available).

Restaurants

Runway Café, Blairstown Airport, Blairstown; (908) 362-9170. Pilots fly in for the homemade pies as well as for the Bonanza Burger. Open seven days a week. Blairstown Diner, Route 94, Blairstown. Open seven days a week. From the Paulinskill Trail, the diner is across the bridge at Foot Bridge Park, Blairstown. They serve a great breakfast and a hot cuppa joe, so it may be the place to stop during the car shuttle. Dale's Market serves prepared foods and has other grocery items.

Organizations

Paulinskill Valley Trail Committee, PO Box 175, Andover 07821; (908) 684-4820; www.pvtc-kvsp.org

Other Resources

Columbia Sport Shop, 27 U.S. Highway 46, Columbia; (908) 496-4410; has small selection of hiking and camping supplies; open seven days a week.

In Addition

John I. Blair: From Postmaster to Philanthropist

Sometime around 1820—so the legend goes—in the small town of Gravel Hill, a young storekeeper was settling a bill with a customer. The young merchant, hardly past twenty, was being asked to take a deed to a piece of land to settle the bill. Uncommon though the practice might be, the merchant took the deal, and the risk. It must have whetted his appetite, because for the young man—John Insley Blair— deals and risks became meat and drink: By the time of his death nearly seventy-five years later, he owned ironworks, mills, and businesses from coast to coast, and more miles of railroad than anyone else in the United States.

Born in 1802, John I. Blair came to business early, taking a post in a relative's general store at age eleven. By age eighteen, he was a partner in the store at Gravel Hill, and by age twenty-three he was the postmaster of the town. By that time, his dabbling in local real estate had extended to arranging the sale of nearby Oxford Furnace to two brothers, George and Selden Scranton, whose name would likewise gain renown. By the 1840s, he and the Scranton brothers were developing coal mines and ironworks in the Lackawanna Valley of Pennsylvania. Railroads were essential for the development of such an endeavor, and Blair built the Delaware, Lackawanna & Western Railroad as an adjunct of his Pennsylvania industries.

Blair's business and railroad holdings soon spread out across the growing nation, following the railroad west. He owned mills, real estate, mines (both iron and coal), furnaces, and of course, railroads, including a stake in the Union Pacific. Through all this, he still kept his job as postmaster at Gravel Hill, which in 1839 changed its name to honor its most important citizen: Blairstown.

By all accounts, Blair was an entrepreneurial machine—a ferocious and relentless competitor, and a cautious and sometimes-prickly ally and business partner. Yet he was also a world-class philanthropist, helping to build more than a hundred churches in the towns and villages served by his railroads across the United States. Towns in Iowa, Nebraska, Nevada, and Wisconsin also bear his name. He was a trustee of, and donated heavily to, Princeton University. His most notable philanthropy was his establishment of Blair Academy in 1848, a college preparatory school that remains a prosperous and elite institution more than 150 years later.

John I. Blair's life spanned the nineteenth century: Born just after it started, his prodigiously long and busy life ended with it, in 1899. At his death, the one-time shopkeeper from the hills of New Jersey had an estimated net worth of $60 million.

4 Mount Tammany and Sunfish Pond

This circuit takes you up Mount Tammany where it has been acclaimed "one of the finest views in the East." Continue on the Kittatinny Ridge, reflecting the healthy effects of forest fires on the environment, and pop down to one of New Jersey's Seven Natural Wonders, Sunfish Pond. Return down Dunnfield Hollow along the creek, by cascading waterfalls, and pools lined with rhododendron. There is also a fine option for a shorter, classic hike.

Start: Dunnfield Creek Natural Area parking lot

Distance: 9.7-mile loop

Approximate hiking time: 5 hours

Difficulty: Strenuous, with steep, 1,000-foot elevation gain

Trail surface: Grass fire roads and rocky hiking trails

Seasons: Spring through fall; the ascent of Mount Tammany is unsafe in winter.

Other trail users: Hikers only

Canine compatibility: Leashed dogs permitted

Land status: National recreation area, natural area, and state forest

Nearest town: Delaware Water Gap, PA

Fees and permits: None

Schedule: Dawn to dusk

Maps: New York–New Jersey Trail Conference, *Kittatinny Trails Map* 15; *DeLorme: New Jersey Atlas & Gazetteer:* p.22; USGS Portland, PA, quadrangle

Trail contacts: Delaware Water Gap National Recreation Area, River Road off Route 209, Bushkill, PA 18324; (570) 588-2451; www .nps.gov/dewa

Other: This can be a popular and crowded place to hike, especially on weekends. If you want quiet, go midweek or off-season.

Special considerations: Be aware of rattle-snakes, which are seen in this area.

Finding the trailhead: Take Interstate 80 west toward the Delaware Water Gap. Just past the 1.0 mile marker, take the exit for the picnic area and bear left at the fork. Continue past the underpass to the left and turn right into a parking area at the sign for Dunnfield Creek Natural Area. If you miss the exit, you can still take exit 1 and loop back and under I-80 to get here. The hike begins in the Dunnfield Creek parking area.

The Hike

By stepping away from your vehicle, you are immediately surrounded by a Natural Wonder of New Jersey, the Delaware Water Gap. Artists, hikers, and vacationers alike have marveled over the beauty of the gap. Its creation took hundreds of millions of years with the layering of sandstone, shale, and conglomerates at the bottom of a shallow seabed. Put this under pressure and give it a series of uplifts and folds, and a massive plateau forms with a stream flowing off it. Add more pressure, more uplifts, and more folds, and the region buckles like a pushed-up carpet. Meanwhile, the earth's surface continues twisting, sliding, and dipping, eventually fracturing at a unique geographical stress point. A determined stream takes advantage of this weakness and keeps slicing and flowing for millions of years. The result stands before you: an extraordinary 400-foot-wide gorge with thousand-foot walls, and a 390-mile river that trickles out of New York's Catskill Mountains and ends in the Delaware Bay.

The Delaware River is one of the cleanest rivers in the USA and the only major Eastern river that is free flowing.

Climb out of the bottomland under some massive tulip trees and begin to ascend, traversing the Bloomsburg Red ledges, highly resistant sandstones (red due to the oxidized iron and green because of low-grade copper). The Wisconsin Glacier's polishing action some 18,000 years ago gave the outcrop its smoothed appearance. If you look carefully, you might spot the striations made by embedded rock in the passing ice mass. As the climb continues, the gray Shawangunk conglomerate, consisting of quartz, tops the red beds.

Reach the top of Mount Tammany (1,527 feet), named for the Lenape chieftain Tamamend, who sold William Penn a tract of land. Through the pitch pines and scrub oaks, scramble down to the outlook where you can identify the Delaware River, Arrow Island, and Mount Minsi (1,463 feet) with its talus pile and folded strata complexion. A dramatic view!

Continue the loop, traversing the Kittatinny Ridge via the Fire Road through a chestnut oak forest, a high ridge environ consisting of dry, poor soil that is further affected by storms and fire. Looking down at the base of tree trunks, you find charred

Infamous Sunfish Pond was saved from industrialization by the likes of Supreme Court Justice William O. Douglass.

bark from the recent fires. In the past, the chestnut oak was the tree of choice for the tanning process. Other trees found in this forest besides the white pines and hickories are red, scarlet, and white oaks. The understory is beautifully carpeted in a broad sweep of sweet fern and lowbush blueberry.

Turn onto the Turquoise Trail, moving toward the center of the ridge, where you pick up the Fire Road around Sunfish Pond, the most southern glacial lake on the Appalachian Trail. The 41-acre, spring-fed lake, ringed by glacial debris, is the center of the 285-acre Natural Area. Due to its popularity, it is usually here that you meet the crowds. During the spring and the fall, timber rattlesnake (state endangered species) and copperheads, both venomous, have also been known to enjoy sunning themselves on the pond's rocky shores.

Descend on the Dunnfield Creek Trail into a hemlock-mixed hardwood forest. Sadly, the adelgid infestation has taken its toll on the hemlocks, but the tulips, the birches, and the beeches still stand tall. As you follow the creek into the cool hollow, observe the trail's mixed geology of the shale/sandstone layered grotto walls. In the spring the blooming rhododendron hangs over falls and edges the pools where native brook trout swim. You end this hike here within the magic of Dunnfield Creek Natural Area (1,085 acres).

Miles and Directions

0.0 Start at Mount Tammany Trailhead (red blazes; also known as the Red Dot Trail), found in the southeast corner of the parking lot, near the entrance. The path becomes stairs, which leads immediately to a fork. Veer left, following the red blazes. The right fork will lead to the rest area off I-80 that also claims to be Mount Tammany Trailhead.

0.5 Trail ascends to first vista, looking west over the Delaware River and across at Mount Minsi.

0.6 Trail swings away from the ledges, climbing the shoulder of Mount Tammany, only to meander back to a series of viewpoints.

1.2 Arrive at the crest of the Gap and turn right (west) for possibly the most dramatic view in New Jersey. Mount Tammany Trail ends and the Blue Dot Trail begins. Six feet beyond the crest (south), look for the triple blue blaze. The Blue Dot Trail (fire road) heads east on the south side of the ridge along the spine of Kittatinny Mountains.

1.5 Reach the true summit of Mount Tammany (1,549 feet) with a southern view of the Delaware River and the Great Valley. Continue straight along the Mount Tammany Fire Road (no blazes) while Blue Dot Trail on the left (north) departs. (**Option:** For a shorter hike, continue down the Blue Dot Trail onto the Appalachian Trail to the Dunnfield Creek parking lot [2 miles].)

2.2 Arrive at a clearing, New Jersey State Forest Fire Service Helispot 2, and continue straight on the Mount Tammany Fire Road. Just beyond the helispot pass a trail right (south) along with a sign: WATER GAP 2.2 M, YARDS CREEK 2.2 M.

4.4 At a small rock cairn, turn left (northwest) onto the Turquoise Trail. Continuing straight on the fire road leads to Upper Yards Creek Reservoir (private property and restricted area).

5.2 At the T intersection, the Turquoise Trail turns left (northwest) onto the Sunfish Pond Fire

Mount Tammany and Sunfish Pond

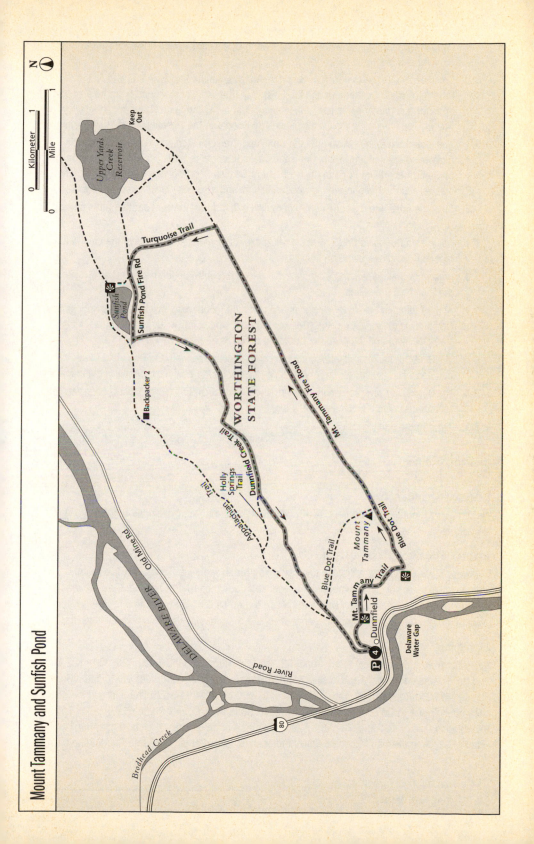

N

0   1 Kilometer
0   1 Mile

Upper Yards Creek Reservoir

Keep Out

Turquoise Trail

Sunfish Pond

Sunfish Pond Fire Rd

WORTHINGTON STATE FOREST

Backpacker 2

Holly Springs Trail

Dunnfield Creek Trail

Appalachian Trail

Mt. Tammany Fire Road

Blue Dot Trail

Mount Tammany

Blue Dot Trail

Mt. Tammany Trail

Dunnfield

P 4

Delaware Water Gap

DELAWARE RIVER

Old Mine Rd

River Road

Broadhead Creek

80

Road. A right turn onto the fire road will lead to Upper Yards Creek Reservoir (private property and restricted area).

5.3 Continue straight on the Sunfish Pond Fire Road, while the Turquoise Trail turns right (north). (**Option:** Continue on the Turquoise Trail [magnificent viewpoint from the east end of pond] onto the Appalachian Trail, heading west along the north shore [rough footway] of Sunfish Pond, rejoining the Sunfish Pond Fire Road and the Dunnfield Creek Trail [1 mile].)

5.9 Trail makes sharp left (west) onto the Dunnfield Creek Trail (green blazes) and ascends a rocky treadway heading south. One should take the time to travel 40 feet straight (north) on Sunfish Pond Fire Road to the west end of Sunfish Pond where a National Landmark plaque, an informational sign, a wooden bench, and a serene glacial pond await you.

6.5 Crest the ridge and descend from a ripraplike trail to forest-covered earthen path, arriving in Dunnfield Hollow.

7.1 Trail meets Dunnfield Creek, where it will snake its way along the banks of the creek with repeated crossings, some on bridges.

7.5 High Water Trail (green and white blazes) bears left (south) up the hill and shortly rejoins the Dunnfield Creek Trail.

7.9 At the T junction the Dunnfield Creek Trail turns left (southwest) while the Holly Springs Trail (red blazes) turns right (north). (**Option:** The Holly Spring Trail leads to the Appalachian Trail [0.4 mile] and the AT to the Dunnfield Creek parking lot [1.7 miles].)

9.0 The Blue Dot Trail on the left (south, blue blazes) converges with the Dunnfield Creek Trail and descends (splendid view of a waterfall and pools) to a bridge crossing of the creek.

9.6 The Dunnfield Creek Trail dead-ends into the Appalachian Trail (white blazes) here. Veer left (southwest) onto the AT, descending along Dunnfield Creek.

9.7 Arrive at the parking lot.

Hike Information

Local Information
Warren County Tourism Department; (800) 554-8540. Warren County Visitor's Guide; www.visit warren.org

Local Events/Attractions
Delaware Water Gap, PA, is a historic town with restaurants, cafes, bakeries, antiques shops, and world-class jazz at the Deerhead Inn (www.deerheadinn.com). The historic Shawnee Inn and Resort (Route 209, Shawnee-on-Delaware), once owned by C. C. Worthington and later by band-leader Fred Waring, offers recreational amenities and a famous golf course; www.shawneeinn.com.

Lodging
Jenny Jump State Forest, State Park Road, PO Box 150, Hope 07844; (908) 496-9244 (22 tent and trailer sites open April 1 to October 31; 8 shelters open year-round; fee). Worthington State Forest, Old Mine Road, HC 62, Box 2, Columbia 07832; (908) 841-9575 (69 tent and trailer sites open April 1 to October 31; fee). Swartswood State Park, County Route 619, PO Box 123, Swartswood 07877-0123; (973) 383-5230 (65 tent and trailer sites, 8 yurts, open April 1 to October 31). Appalachian Mountain Club's Mohican Outdoor Center, 50 Camp Road, Blairstown

07825-9655; (908) 362-5670; www.mohicanoutdoorcenter.com (The Lodge, winterized cabins, tent sites, and dining hall available).

Organizations

The New York–New Jersey Trail Conference, 156 Ramapo Valley Road (U.S. Highway 202), Mahwah 07430; (201) 512-9348; www.nynjtc.org

Other Resources

Bertland, Dennis, et al. *The Minisink.* 1975; reprinted by the Walpack Historical Society, Walpack, NJ. This book is an outstanding and richly illustrated history of the upper Delaware Valley. Brodhead, L. W. *Delaware Water Gap: Its Scenery, Legends, and Early History.* Philadelphia: Sherman & Co., 1870. Though out of print, this is a fascinating early guide to the Water Gap by a proprietor of one of its biggest hotels.

THE GROWTH OF A NINETEENTH-CENTURY RESORT

Long a landmark to Native Americans and early surveyors, few people ever saw the Delaware Water Gap up close in the 1700s. No road passed through it, and the only footpath that traversed its sheer walls above the Delaware River required hand-over-hand climbing in spots. Nonetheless, "civilization" began to make inroads. The first actual tourists came to marvel at the Delaware Water Gap around 1820, when the first hotel was started nearby. Note the following newspaper item from July 1845: "A writer in the *Newark Daily*, who has just returned from the Delaware Water Gap, describes in glowing terms the emotions excited by a view of that stupendous wonder of nature, and the scarcely less magnificent scenery which in every direction adorns the romantic region in which it is located. He talks like an enthusiast, yet every word is fully justified by the sublime realities of the mountain gorge and its adjunct displays of beauty and grandeur."

The writer goes on to wonder: "Why is this place so much neglected by citizens who devote the summer months to pleasure and recreation? Healthy, easy of access, and abounding in localities sacred to rural and sporting enjoyment, it ought to attract thousands of visitors yearly. 'Fashion,' however, the god who we all worship, has not yet given the 'approving nod,' and the Water Gap must awhile longer endure unmerited neglect and outlawry."

When the above account was written, the region was indeed semi-wilderness. But when the railroad penetrated the Gap in 1855, the floodgates of tourism opened. By the 1860s, the Gap was immensely popular with tourists and Hudson River School artists, as were the Catskills to the north. The Gap soon acquired a body of legends and romance, as well as hotels and saloons. All kinds of natural features were given names—not a creek, crag, or vista escaped. Within a decade of the railroad bringing "civilization" to the Gap, many were longing for the vanished days when it was still peaceful and unsullied. Kittatinny Point has been a popular recreational spot since the 1800s.

The Gap was scenic in winter, too: The *New Jersey Herald* reported in March 1868 that a huge ice dam in the Gap flooded the valley with ice and water as far back as Flatbrookville. It finally broke loose with a roar, creating "a scene of startling grandeur."

There were many hotels and boarding houses established up and down the Delaware Valley. The oldest and ultimately biggest was the Kittatinny House. Started in 1832 as a small boardinghouse run by Samuel Snyder, it grew over the years to become a colossal mountain hotel, serving 500 guests, including some famous ones (like President Teddy Roosevelt). It suffered a fire in the 1920s, and the ruins sat on the hillside for years; a scenic view area now occupies the site. Another landmark was the Water Gap House, built in the early 1870s. Every summer it was "filled to the roof with vacationists" from eastern cities; in the winter it closed. Just after closing one season, the Water Gap House met its end on October 31, 1931, when it burned to the ground. Firemen could only watch as the huge hotel—all wooden, and a firetrap, like so many other hotels of the era—went up in flames. In an hour and a half the hotel was a "mass of smoldering ruins."

The New Jersey side of the Water Gap is Mount Tammany. "Tamanend," according to tradition, was a benevolent and wise Lenape chieftain in the Pennsylvania–New Jersey region. He gained the admiration and respect of early eighteenth-century settlers because of his fairness and goodwill. By the time of the Revolutionary War, he was popularly established as "Saint Tammany." The Society of Saint Tammany in New York, initially a benevolent organization, soon became the focus of the Democratic Party. By the late nineteenth century, "Tammany Hall" was virtually synonymous with political corruption.

This general neighborhood where our hike begins was, in days of old (i.e., the late 1800s) the hamlet of Danfield or Dunnfield, a station on the Susquehanna Division of the Erie Railroad. It was home to the Delaware Water Gap Slate Company, owned and operated by the Browning Brothers and Company, featuring a slate factory, school, homes, and other structures, all now vanished. The railroad station was abandoned by 1930s. The railroad line that came through here was built in 1881 and ripped up in 1940. In a couple of decades another mode of transportation would daily deliver more people and material through the Water Gap than in all prior recorded history: Interstate 80.

5 Culvers Gap and Stony Lake

Again, one of those hikes that does it all. This circuit hike climbs the east side of Culvers Gap, providing panoramic views of the Pocono Peneplain. The trek continues along the top of the Kittatinny Ridge, passing the Normanock Fire Tower with views of the Delaware Valley before descending off the ridge alongside the bubbling Stony Brook, with its mini waterfalls, and arrives at the bottomlands where you travel a glacial lakebed with a possible swim in Stony Lake. The trip traverses mountain trails, woods roads, and Sunrise Mountain Road (built by the CCC).

Surveying the Kittatinny Ridge from scenic Stony Lake.

Start: Appalachian Trail parking lot just off County Route 636 and Sunrise Mountain Road
Distance: 5.9-mile loop
Approximate hiking time: 3.5 to 4 hours
Difficulty: Moderate due to 340-foot elevation gain
Trail surface: Hiking trails and grassy woods roads, with a few rocky stretches; a brief road walk
Seasons: All seasons good
Other trail users: Hikers only on the Appalachian Trail; other trails multiuse
Canine compatibility: Leashed dogs permitted.
Land status: State forest
Nearest town: Branchville
Fees and permits: None

Schedule: Dawn to dusk
Maps: *DeLorme: New Jersey Atlas & Gazetteer* p.18–19; New York–New Jersey Trail Conference *Kittatinny Trails Map 17;* USGS Culvers Gap quadrangle
Trail contacts: Stokes State Forest, 1 Coursen Road, Branchville 07826; (973) 948-3820; www.state.nj.us/dep/parksandforests/parks/stokes.html. The New York–New Jersey Trail Conference, 156 Ramapo Valley Road (U.S. Highway 202), Mahwah 07430; (201) 512-9348; www.nynjtc.org
Special considerations: Deer-hunting season is busy here, and hunting is allowed from the AT. Wear blaze orange or, better yet, stay home.

Finding the trailhead: Take U.S. Highway 206 approximately 10.8 miles north of Newton, passing Branchville and Culvers Gap. Turn right (north) onto CR 636 (Mattison School Road). Almost immediately turn left onto Sunrise Mountain Road. On your left is a parking lot for the Appalachian Trail; the hike begins here.

The Hike

This hike through Stokes State Forest takes us through some of the first land ever acquired in New Jersey for conservation purposes. It was established in 1907 as the Kittatinny Mountain Reservation. The governor at the time, Edward C. Stokes, was a strong proponent of land acquisition for timber and water resource management, and to demonstrate this he paid for the first 500 acres of the property. The forest was later renamed in his honor.

The Appalachian Trail, on which our hike begins, is one of the older footpaths in New Jersey. This particular path was built soon after the state of New Jersey acquired the tract and was used by rangers to access the fire tower lookout near the summit of the ridge. It was later adopted as a section of the Appalachian Trail.

The Culver Fire Tower, originally called the Normanock Lookout Tower, was part of a series of forest fire lookout towers established by the state of New Jersey early in the twentieth century. By 1928, the system consisted of nineteen fire towers across the state; at present, the system has twenty-one towers. There was an observation platform here as early as the 1880s. A wooden fire observation tower had been erected by 1919. The original wooden Culver Fire Tower had become a popular visitors' spot by the 1920s.

A visitor in 1928 noted that over a thousand people had signed the visitors' register by that time, most from New Jersey and New York, but some from as far away as

Culvers Gap and Stony Lake

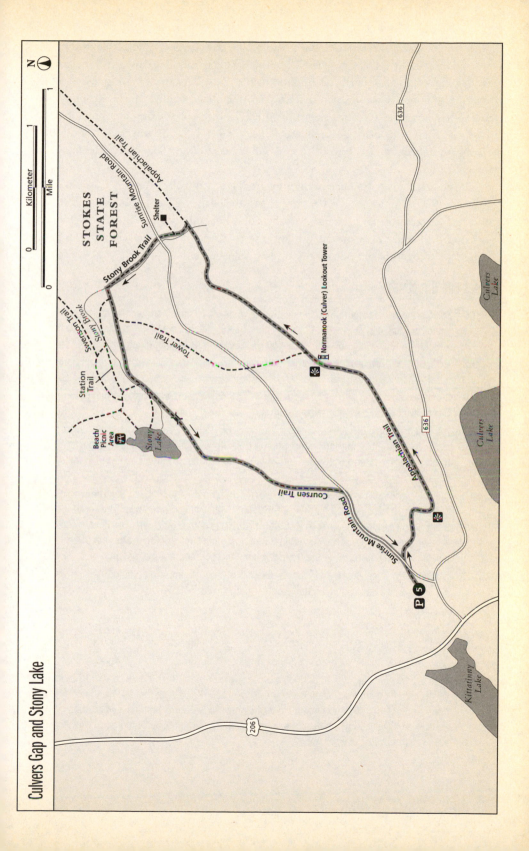

N

Kilometer
0 1
0 1
Mile

STOKES
STATE
FOREST

Swenson Trail

Station Trail

Beach/Picnic Area

Stony Lake

Stony Brook

Stony Brook Trail

Sunrise Mountain Road

Appalachian Trail

Shelter

Tower Trail

Coursen Trail

Normanook (Culver) Lookout Tower

Sunrise Mountain Road

Appalachian Trail

636

636

P 5

206

Kittatinny Lake

Culvers Lake

Culvers Lake

Florida, Colorado, Puerto Rico, and even Russia. The current 47–foot steel tower was erected in 1934 by CCC Camp S–51 in Stokes State Forest. The tower was originally located near the village of Blue Anchor, in the Pine Barrens of Winslow Township, Camden County. It was dismantled, trucked north, and hauled up the mountain to this spot where the "C" boys reassembled it. The Aermotor Company built the fire tower itself; their primary business was (and remains) building towers for windmills. For more information on forest fire lookout towers in New Jersey and elsewhere, go to www.firetower.org.

Stony Lake, now a popular swimming area, was originally home to Camp Madeleine Mulford, built for the Girl Scouts of Montclair in 1927. Mulford was a leader in Girl Scout activities; her husband, wealthy publisher and investor Vincent S. Mulford, donated the camp in her memory. It was the first real effort to develop Stokes State Forest for recreation, and not simply timber management.

Miles and Directions

0.0 Start in the Appalachian Trail parking lot 100 yards off Sunrise Mountain Road. The connector trail, located at the north corner of the parking lot, dead-ends immediately into the Appalachian Trail (white blazes). Turn right (northeast) onto the Appalachian Trail.

0.2 The trail zigzags across (east) Sunrise Mountain Road and begins to climb through hardwoods and mountain laurel.

0.6 Break into a clearing with views north and west. From here the trail runs the ridge (east) with a slight rise. Tree-framed view (south).

1.5 The trail, passing a cell tower, arrives at Normanook (Culver) Fire Tower. Site has a picnic table with incredible northern views. Shortly, pass the departing Tower Trail on the left (north) and a register box. (Feel free to sign the book. It helps with a count and in case of emergencies.)

2.5 Cross Stony Brook (rock-hop) and turn left (north) onto the Stony Brook Trail (brown blazes) which is co-aligned for the next 50 yards with side trail (blue blazes) where the Stony Brook Trail then departs to the left (north). Blue blazed trail leads 0.1 mile to the Gren Anderson Lean-to. The Stony Brook Trail descends through hardwoods with three magnificent tulip trees, while the treadway becomes soft and framed by ferns.

2.7 Cross (north) Stony Brook and immediately cross (north) Sunrise Mountain Road where the Stony Brook Trail continues to descend along the Stony Brook.

3.3 Reaching the valley, trail swings west, becoming a woods road, paralleling wetlands while under white pines and lined by stonewalls.

3.6 Pass Station Trail (right) and continue straight (west) by foundations.

3.7 Pass the Tower Trail (left), which co-aligns with the Stony Brook Trail, heading west.

4.1 Pass Stony Lake Trail (cream/turquoise blazes). (**Option:** Leads 0.2 mile [north] to Stony Lake. Open for swimming Memorial Day through Labor Day weekends, 10:00 a.m. to 6:00 p.m., so bring your suits and make it a multisport day. Seasonal bathrooms and bathhouses, along with picnic tables, playground, and waterfalls, are available here. Well worth the extra trek during any season.)

4.2 Stony Lake Trail loop rejoins the Coursen Trail.

5.1 The Coursen Trail ends at Sunrise Mountain Road. Turn right (southwest) onto Sunrise Mountain Road (one-way, coming at you).

5.6 The Appalachian Trail comes in on the left (east). After 125 feet turn right (north) onto the Appalachian Trail (white blazes) and follow it to the parking lot.

5.9 Arrive at the parking lot.

Hike Information

Local Information

New Jersey Skylands Region Tourism Guide; www.njskylands.com

Local Events/Attractions

The New Jersey State Fair–Sussex County Farm and Horse Show, US 206 in Augusta, runs from the first Friday in August for ten days; www.newjerseystatefair.org. Peters Valley Craft Center in Layton has a store and gallery selling fine arts and crafts made in the village and offers workshops and craft fairs. 19 Kuhn Road, Layton 07851; (973) 948-5200; www.pvcrafts.org

Lodging

Stokes State Forest offers inexpensive campsites, lean-tos, and family- and group-size cabins. Contact the park headquarters for current prices.

Restaurants

Dale's Market, 396 US 206, offers a variety of sandwiches and hot food to go; (973) 948-3078.

Organizations

The New York–New Jersey Trail Conference, 156 Ramapo Valley Road (U.S. Highway 202), Mahwah 07430; (201) 512-9348; www.nynjtc.org

Other Resources

Stokes Sport Shop, 29 US 206, Branchville, offers a variety of outdoor sporting goods; (973) 948-5448.

6 The Wallkill River Valley

"The Drowned Lands," also known as bottomland or flood plain, is the area explored on this loop hike. The farm lane path undulates between upland meadows and bottomland hardwood forest with an expansive view of the Wallkill Valley, framed by the Kittatinny Ridge and the Highlands. Walk out to the Wallkill River, one of the few rivers in the region that flows north. An excellent spot for birding, so bring your binoculars and enjoy the 225 species of birds that occur on the 4,200-acre refuge.

Start: Refuge parking lot on County Route 565
Distance: 2.7-mile loop
Approximate hiking time: 2 hours
Difficulty: Easy; gentle grades or flat
Trail surface: Old farm lanes and fields
Seasons: All seasons good
Other trail users: Hikers only
Canine compatibility: No dogs permitted
Land status: National wildlife refuge
Nearest town: Sussex Borough
Fees and permits: None
Schedule: Dawn to dusk
Maps: *DeLorme: New Jersey Atlas & Gazetteer* p.19; USGS Hamburg, NJ, and Unionville, NY, quadrangles; also, a trail map is available at refuge headquarters and at some kiosks throughout the refuge.
Trail contacts: Wallkill River National Wildlife Refuge, 1547 CR 565, Sussex 07461; (973) 702-7266; wallkillriver@fws.gov; www.fws.gov/northeast/wallkillriver
Other: Trail may be closed during hunting season (except on Sunday); call ahead.
Special considerations: An especially good hike in spring and fall when the migration along the Atlantic Flyway is in full swing; bring binoculars. The lower section of the hike may be wet or flooded during periods of high water. Ticks can be a serious problem on this hike, as can the lack of shade on some sections. Come prepared.

Finding the trailhead: Take Route 23 north past Hamburg approximately 2.7 miles. Turn right onto CR 565 (Glenwood Road). Take CR 565 for 1.5 miles; refuge headquarters and parking are on CR 565 on the left just past the turn for Lake Pochung Road.

The Hike

This hike leads you through both the uplands and the bottomlands of the Wallkill River valley. The valley has a long history of providing humans with what they need, going all the way back to the Paleo-Indian Period some 10,000 years ago. Archaeologists have discovered prehistoric chert quarries along the Wallkill, where Native Americans came to obtain the very fine-grained stone they used to fashion spear points, scrapers, knives, and arrowheads. Native American occupation of the Wallkill River valley was continuous up to the 1700s, when the first European-Americans started to settle in the valley. A number of prehistoric sites exist within the wildlife refuge.

Early settlers, too, utilized the chert deposits—not for arrowheads but for flints for their muskets and pistols. They also obtained fish from the river, using weir-nets to trap eels and other fish by the barrelful. They were then salted down and shipped out to the city for sale. The uplands were fine farming areas—good, deep, rich soils—and they were clear by the mid-1700s. But early farmers had a hard time farming this soggy bottomland: Though the earth was rich, it flooded both regularly and severely, which led them to give the area the mournful appellation "The Drowned Lands." The lower areas on this hike were routinely under 3 to 5 feet of water in the 1700s and early 1800s.

In the late 1700s, settlers tried to un-drown the land by digging drainage canals, but with minimal effect. It was not until the mid-1800s, with the construction of a huge drainage canal near Denton, New York, that the Wallkill was effectively drained. These flat farmlands then became a farmer's paradise, with the northern portion of the region, around Pine Island, New York, remaining a preeminent onion-producing region today.

▶ **It was the early Dutch settlers who gave the river here its name. It reminded them of their homeland's Waal River, hence Wallkill ("kill" is Dutch for "stream").**

Rich, prosperous farms dotted the Wallkill Valley, like the one occupied as Refuge Headquarters today. Though the large dairy barn burned in the 1990s, the farm-house—now headquarters—remains. Industrialist Gustav Nysélius, a Swedish émigré, owned the farm in the 1950s; an avid avocational farmer, he bottled and sold his own milk. He named the farm Dagmar Dale Farm after his wife, Dagmar Nyselius. A memento of the Nyseliuses' Scandinavian heritage is the handsome ceramic stove in the superintendent's office (check it out if you can!). Dagmar Dale Farm was the last farm in Vernon Township to bottle and deliver its own milk, and the history behind the name is preserved with the Dagmar Dale Trail.

Miles and Directions

0.0 Begin at the north side of the parking lot where there is a signpost for the Dagmar Dale Nature Trail, North Loop (blue blazes).

0.1 Continue straight (northeast) on the North Loop Trail along the hedgerow, passing the junction to the South Loop Trail on the left.

0.2 The trail arrives at a clearing with a north-northwest view, an interpretive sign, and a bench. (**FYI:** You can easily identify the Wallkill Valley, the Kittatinny Mountains, and High Point Monument. You can also trace today's hike.)

0.3 The trail turns left (northwest), bordering the tree line with grand views of Wallkill Valley and yonder hills.

0.6 The trail, crossing a stream, passes through the tree line with a zig and zag right, passing a bench. Continue northeast on the path along the edge of the field. Expansive views.

0.7 The trail turns left (northwest) with a gradual descent, bearing left and passing a bench on the way to the river's flood plain.

0.9 The trail turns left (southwest), continuing along the edge of the tree line and paralleling the Wallkill River.

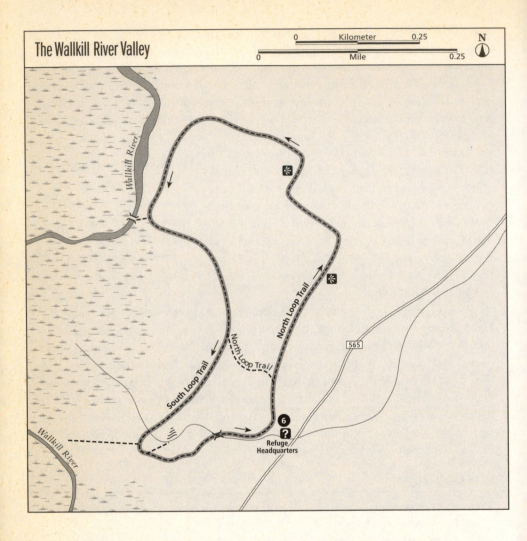

0   Kilometer   0.25

N

0   Mile   0.25

1.1 The trail turns left (southeast) with expansive views (northeast) of the flood plain.

(**FYI**: Just beyond the bench, there is a short side trail [west] to a bridge over Wallkill River.)

1.3 At the end of the field, the trail leads into the woods, crossing a stream, and begins to ascend.

1.5 At the fork and the bench, veer right onto the South Loop (yellow blazes) and continue to ascend. (**FYI**: The left fork will take you back to the parking lot [0.1 mile] on the co-aligned North Loop and South Loop Trail.)

1.8 After a descent the trail crosses a stream and reemerges out into the field, bordering the tree line. The trail makes a sharp U from heading west to heading southeast. (**Option**: At the bend in the U, an unmarked farm road leads straight [west] across the field toward an opening in the tree line, arriving in 0.3 mile at the Wallkill River. After passing over a culvert, you become up close and personal with the Wallkill River. The side trip ends at a sign that reads Enter By Permit Only. Retrace your hike back to the bend in the U.)

1.9 At the east corner of the field, a short side trail on the left leads to a small waterfall and a bench. Worth a look-see.

2.0 The trail turns left, passing through a fence row, and begins to ascend through cedars, leaving the flood plain.

2.1 Turn left (north) under a large sycamore tree and immediately after crossing over the bridge; turn right (southeast) and head for the pond.

2.7 The trail proceeds (north) through the fence opening, bringing you back to the parking lot.

Hike Information

Local Information
Vernon Township Chamber of Commerce, PO Box 308, Vernon 07462; (888) 663-9989; www .vernonchamber.com. New Jersey Skylands Region Tourism Guide; www.njskylands.com

Local Events/Attractions
The Appalachian Trail passes through the Refuge (Liberty Loop Trail); The D.A.R. Elias Van Bunschooten Museum is the 1787 home of a noted clergyman with period furnishing; tours available; 1097 Route 23, Sussex 07461; (973) 875-5335.

Restaurants
The Sussex Queen Diner, at the corner of Route 23 and CR 565, has been providing dependable diner fare for generations.

Organizations
U.S. Fish and Wildlife Service; www.fws.gov

Other Resources
Dupont, Ronald J. Jr. *Vernon 200: A Bicentennial History of the Township of Vernon, NJ,* published by the Friends of the Dorothy E Henry Library in 1992, provides information on the early settlement of the Wallkill River area and Vernon Township.

Wallkill River bottomlands from the upland meadow.

7 The Pahaquarry Copper Mines

This lollipop hike passes through a historical mining area while also moving past some of the most spectacular geological features in Jersey. From Old Mine Road and the Delaware River, steadily climb past the copper mines and up to the Kittatinny Ridge with a 180-degree view of the Great Valley. Run the ridge via the Appalachian Trail down to Catfish Pond Gap and descend along the Mine Brook with its fantastic cascading waterfalls, deep in the ravine. This is quintessential Delaware Water Gap National Recreation Area.

Start: Copper Mine Parking Area on River Road
Distance: 5.5-mile lollipop
Approximate hiking time: 3.5 hours
Difficulty: Strenuous due to steep climbs and elevation change
Trail surface: Steep woods roads and rocky hiking trails
Seasons: Best spring through fall; unsafe in winter
Other trail users: Hikers only
Canine compatibility: Leashed dogs permitted
Land status: State forest
Nearest town: Delaware Water Gap, PA
Fees and permits: None
Schedule: Dawn to dusk

Maps: *DeLorme: New Jersey Atlas & Gazetteer* p.22; USGS Bushkill, PA, and Flatbrookville, NJ, quadrangles; New York–New Jersey Trail Conference *Kittatinny Trails Map 15*
Trail contacts:. Delaware Water Gap National Recreation Area, River Road off Route 209, Bushkill, PA 18324; (570) 588-2451; www .nps.gov/dewa/. The New York–New Jersey Trail Conference, 156 Ramapo Valley Road (U.S. Highway 202), Mahwah 07430; (201) 512-9348; www.nynjtc.org
Other: This hike will be extra special after rainfall, when the waterfalls are running well.
Special considerations: The potential for icy conditions make this hike a no-go in winter.

Finding the trailhead: Take Interstate 80 west to the Delaware Water Gap. Take exit 1 (last in New Jersey) to River Road (Old Mine Road). Take River Road north approximately 7.8 miles to the Copper Mine Parking Area. **Note:** River Road is a one-lane road for roughly 0.75 mile, controlled by traffic lights at either end.

The Hike

"Greetings from Camp Pahaquarra." As you exit your car in the Copper Mine parking lot, you step onto what was once the Boy Scouts' parade ground with the postcard image: boys dressed in khaki-colored uniforms with a red triangular neckerchief, standing at attention, saluting Old Glory as the sun sets over the Delaware River and "Taps" echoes off the Kittatinny Ridge. Directly behind you depicted on another one-cent card are Scouts working on their swimming and boating merit badges in Oakley Cove. As you move out of the parking lot entrance, you walk on the original portion of Old Mine Road before it was relocated away from the river's destructive force.

Cross the paved road to the trailhead and pass through some more of the remains of Camp Pahaquarra, which stood here between 1925 and 1971. The camp, the first of six other Boy Scout camps in the Delaware Water Gap National Recreation Area, practiced the environmental slogan "Reuse. Recycle. Reclaim." They retrofitted the early-twentieth-century mining complex. The mill building that stood here became the mess hall, the boardinghouse changed into the staff dorm, the blacksmith shop was converted into the craftsmanship shop, the oil house transformed into the trading post, and the mining office (slightly altered) became the camp office. As you begin to climb away from Mine Brook, you pass the stone foundations of the Good Times Hall where "The bear comes over the mountain, the bear comes over the mountain . . ." could be heard sung after a scrambled-egg breakfast. As the Kaiser Trail ascends, cutting into the hillside, take a moment and look back onto the bottomland above the river. Can you spot the footprints of the Scouts' chapel site and the three circular tent sites?

Copper Mine boasts beautiful pools and colonial mines.

Sadly Camp Pahaquarra came to an end as a result of the federal government's Tock Island Dam Project. This camp, along with the other Boy Scout camps and the valley farms, homes, and lands, were purchased by the government from some reluctant sellers or condemned through eminent domain. The project's "talking points" were controlling floods, creating hydroelectric power, supplying water, and providing recreation. The location for the behemoth 160-foot-high dam would have been 2 miles downriver from the camp, flooding the entire Walpack Valley and your toes with a 37-mile-long lake.

The Delaware River Basin studies began in the 1930s and continued through the 1950s, with the big push by the Army Corp of Engineers coming in the 1960s with the Flood Control Act. Public action groups consisting of local residents, conservationists, and historians pushed back: *Pox on Tocks.* In the valley, clashes between federal marshals and the residents (some being squatters who made homes in the vacated buildings) became ugly. After more studies, more papers, more speeches, and more slogans ("Tax Island Dam"), the project began to die with the National Wild and Scenic Rivers System designation of the middle and upper Delaware River (1978) and the final blow coming when the dam project was officially de-authorized (1992). From these thunderstorms of razed homesteads, removed families, and physical confrontations, we can find a silver lining: the creation of the DWGRA and the preservation of this 70,000-acre natural public preserve.

Reach the top of the Kittatinny Ridge and join the thru-hikers on the Appalachian Trail. Enjoy the views south of the Great Valley of the Appalachians all the way to the Highlands. Directly below is the Lower Creek Reservoir, part of the Yard's Creek Generating Station. Using the concept of peak and low demand for electricity, water from the Upper Creek Reservoir is released and dropped 700 feet to the lower reservoir, passing through three generators and producing electricity. On off periods the generators act as pumps, sending the water back to the upper reservoir. All this accomplished with minimal pollution, and the water acting as stored energy. Not bad!

Come off the ridge at Catfish Pond Gap and descend into one of the most beautiful hemlock ravines in the state with a series of waterfalls and pools. You even get to pass the entrance to the Colonial Upper Mine, boarded up for your safety and the bats. When you reach the starting point, be sure to visit the banks of the Delaware River with its imposing view.

Miles and Directions

0.0 Travel back out through the entrance of the parking lot (south) and cross Old Mine Road, heading for the post with the hiker icon. The Coppermine Trail begins here, blazed with red. Within 100 yards the trail comes to a fork with a sign: LOWER MINE. Veer right, staying on the Coppermine Trail. (**Option:** The left trail takes you over a foundation of the mine's processing mill and up along the creek to the mine entranced and a small waterfall. A 300-yard detour worth a look-see.)

The Pahaquarry Copper Mines

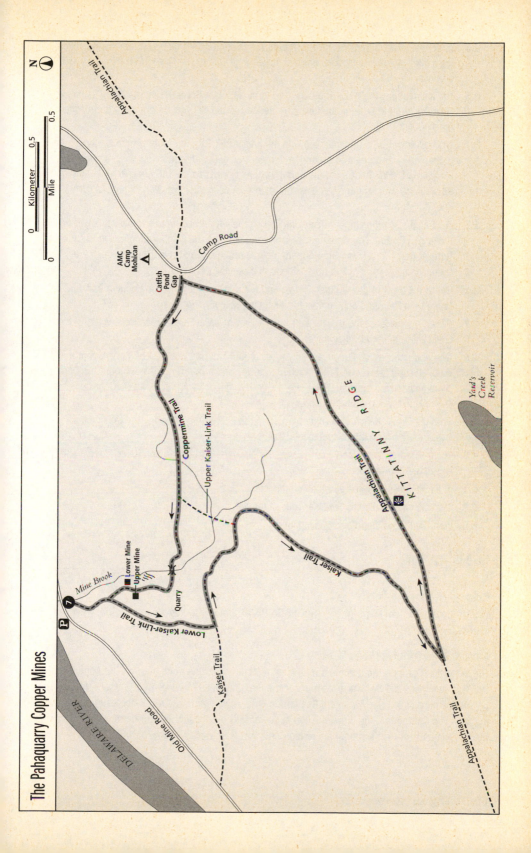

N

Kilometer
0   0.5

Mile
0   0.5

DELAWARE RIVER

Old Mine Road

Kaiser Trail

Appalachian Trail

Lower Kaiser-Link Trail

P   7

Mine Brook

Lower Mine
Upper Mine

Quarry

Upper Kaiser-Link Trail

Coppermine Trail

Lower Kaiser-Link Trail

Kaiser Trail

KITTATINNY RIDGE

Appalachian Trail

Yard's Creek Reservoir

Appalachian Trail

Camp Road

AMC Camp Mohican

Catfish Pond Gap

0.3 Prior to entering the ravine, turn right onto the Lower Kaiser-Link Trail (blue blazes), following a fairly steep woods road, which is cut into the side of the ridge. (**FYI:** This link was a gravity railroad!)

0.5 The trail reaches the base of a ridge and turns right (southwest), running along its base. (**FYI:** The red and blue mottled slate to the left [northeast] was an open-cut quarry site in the 1900s.)

0.7 The trail arrives at a T intersection with the Kaiser Trail. Turn left (south) onto the Kaiser Trail (blue blazes) and begin to ascend on a meandering (south-southeast-east) washed-out woods road. (**FYI:** The trail to the right [northwest] leads to the Old Mine Road.) The old Kaiser Road was an important over-the-mountain connector between Dimmicks Ferry and Blairstown.

1.2 The trail passes the Upper Kaiser-Link Trail on the left and continues to works its way up the ridge. (**Option:** The Upper Kaiser-Link connects with the Coppermine Trail in 0.2 mile. Turn left (northwest) onto the Coppermine Trail and descend for 0.9 mile through the ravine, bringing you back to the trailhead and parking lot.

2.1 Reach the crest of the Kittatinny Ridge and the junction with the Appalachian Trail. Turn left (east) onto the Appalachian Trail and begin a trek along the ridge.

2.7 Pass a major vista (south) with 180-degree view of Lower Yards Creek Reservoir and the Great Valley of the Appalachians.

3.9 Descend into Catfish Pond Gap. Fifty yards before crossing Yards Creek Bridge, spot a routered sign, COPPERMINE TRAIL, attached to a tree and turn left (northwest) onto the Coppermine Trail (red blazes). (**FYI:** From the bridge, AMC's Camp Mohican Outdoor Center is 0.3 mile left [east] on Camp Road.)

4.6 Pass the Upper Kaiser-Link (blue blazes) on the left (south), crossing the fall line and descending (west) into a spectacular ravine.

4.9 The trail swings down and crosses Mine Brook over a bridge and continues along a shelf edged into the gorge.

5.1 The trail passes a mine entrance on the left.

5.3 The trail passes the Lower Kaiser-Link on the left.

5.5 Arrive at the trailhead and parking lot.

Hike Information

Local Information

Warren County Tourism Department; (800) 554-8540. Warren County Visitor's Guide; www.visit warren.org

Local Events/Attractions

The Isaac Van Campen Inn, built in 1750, is an historic stone tavern located on Old Mine Road. The Walpack Historical Society gives tours of the inn. Phone: (973) 948-6671. Also farther north on Old Mine Road are the Watergate Recreation Area, a pleasant spot for a picnic lunch and strolling, and Van Campens Glen, a spectacular series of falls and cascades. For more information, visit the Delaware Water Gap National Recreation Area Web site, www.nps.gov/dewa/.

Lodging

Appalachian Mountain Club's Mohican Outdoor Center, 50 Camp Road, Blairstown 07825-9655; (908) 362-5670; www.mohicanoutdoorcenter.com (The Lodge, winterized cabins, tent sites, and dining hall available)

Organizations

The New York–New Jersey Trail Conference, 156 Ramapo Valley Road (U.S. Highway 202), Mahwah 07430; (201) 512-9348; www.nynjtc.org

Other Resources

Bertland, Dennis, et al. *The Minisink.* 1975; reprinted by the Walpack Historical Society, Walpack, NJ. This book is an outstanding and richly illustrated history of the upper Delaware Valley. The Water Gap Recreation Area also has excellent articles on the history of the copper mines and of the park in general on their Web site, www.nps.gov/dewa/.

WHOSE MINE IS IT, ANYWAY?

The Upper Delaware River valley was settled at a very early date; of this there is no dispute. Present-day Port Jervis probably saw its first European settler in ca.1699, and by ca.1701 the region southward to the Water Gap likewise saw farmsteaders. It is documented that the Pahaquarry copper mines were worked (unsuccessfully) by a group of investors in the 1750s; at the same time the valley nearby was seeing considerable settlement. All simple enough, right?

Then along comes Samuel Preston. Writing in Samuel Hazard's *Register of Pennsylvania* in 1828, Preston tells a very different story—the story of a conversation he had with one John Lukens some forty years before, in 1787. Lukens, says Preston, had been a member of a surveying team led by Nicholas Scull in 1730, checking old boundary claims in the valley for Thomas Penn. In the course of the surveying trip, Lukens talked with Samuel DePue, whose family was among the first to settle the Upper Delaware River valley.

In talking about the early settlement of the area, DePue relayed a story—he only knew the facts vaguely, from tradition. A company of miners from Holland had constructed the 100-mile Mine Road to Esopus (near Kingston) on the Hudson, and worked the mines at Pahaquarry, at some point during the Dutch reign of New Netherland (i.e., ca.1630 or so).

Of course, from the get-go, this "I was talking with a guy, who had talked with another guy, and *this* guy talked to a guy . . ." element makes one a trifle dubious. In fact, there was much to be dubious about regarding DePue's (and Luken's and Preston's) tale. An immediate red flag: The mines (supposedly) had been important enough to justify constructing a

100-mile road. Yet DePue didn't even know they contained copper, but thought it was either "lead or silver."

Still, the story was an interesting one, and most local historians through the 1800s regarded it with a mixture of interest and skepticism. Some repeated it without much comment; others cast doubt on it as a bit of questionable historical legend. Local historian Amelia Stickney Decker changed that. Writing first in *The Old Mine Road* (1932) and later in *That Ancient Trail* (1942), Decker pretty much stated Preston's assertions as fact: Old Mine Road had been built by the Dutch in the 1640s to transport copper ore from Pahaquarry to the Hudson River. She went on to champion another one of Preston's claims: that as such, Old Mine Road was the oldest road of any length in the United States.

Within a generation, what was once regarded as an interesting historical legend became enshrined as a fact. Even today, many—perhaps most—people regard the legend of Old Mine Road as established truth. It may be that local pride played a role in this. Having the "oldest" anything is a great claim to be able to make. Still, surviving facts fail to support this story. It's true the Dutch regarded their colony as a commercial venture and aggressively sniffed out any and all possible mineral resources. Yet no documentary records have been found to support the claim; there is no archaeological evidence of seventeenth-century activity at the mines; and the copper ore itself was of too low a grade to be profitably smelted even by far more sophisticated twentieth-century methods.

Arent Schuyler, traveling through the area in 1694, makes no mention of any road; and the Dutch government was, in any case, too parsimonious to build a proper 100-mile road through the rugged wilderness for a speculative mine. On top of this, the claim that it is the oldest road of any length in the United States—even if it could be documented—ignores New Mexico's Camino Real (Royal Road), in use by Europeans by the late 1590s and considerably longer.

It may be the truth lies somewhere in between. Did a group of adventurous prospectors from New Amsterdam make their way south from the Hudson along an old Native American footpath (later a public road), clearing their way here and there, and come across the Pahaquarry deposits? Did they start digging, fill up their sacks with samples, load them on their pack mules, and hack and clear their way back to the Hudson? Did this kernel of a story then reside among the later settlers, who embellished it out of pride? Possibly so. Until and unless more evidence comes to light, Old Mine Road will remain an interesting—and debated—historical legend.

8 Millbrook Village and Van Campens Glen

This adventure has Stephen King written all over it. The circular hike begins at a historic village, skirts cemeteries, and moves along abandoned roads. The trail drops down to the Delaware River, passing a limekiln, stone foundations, and vacated homes. At times it feels like you have arrived at the far reaches, and in some ways you have: the Jersey-Pennsylvania border. Returning via the Van Campens Glen, with its pools and falls, happens to be one of the most beautiful hikes in the state. Saunter over George Busch's former summertime estate before strolling the back "streets" of a 1900s village.

Start: Parking lot at Millbrook Village, Millbrook-Blairstown Road
Distance: 6.7-mile loop
Approximate hiking time: 4 hours
Difficulty: Moderate, with a few sections in the glen requiring care
Trail surface: Paved roads to hiking trails
Seasons: Spring through fall; the glen is too icy to negotiate in winter.
Other trail users: Multiuse trails
Canine compatibility: Leashed dogs permitted; use caution with pets in the glen and along the river.
Land status: National recreation area
Nearest town: Blairstown

Fees and permits: None
Schedule: Dawn to dusk
Maps: DeLorme: New Jersey Atlas & Gazetteer p.22–23; New York–New Jersey Trail Conference Kittatinny Trails Map 16; USGS Flatbrookville quadrangle
Trail contacts: Delaware Water Gap National Recreation Area, River Road off Route 209, Bushkill, PA 18324; (570) 588-2451; www.nps.gov/dewa/. Millbrook Village Society; www.millbrooknj.com
Special considerations: Be aware that Van Campens Glen can have unsafe icy conditions not just in winter but also in early spring and late fall.

Finding the trailhead: Take Interstate 80 west toward the Delaware Water Gap. Take exit 1 (last in New Jersey) to River Road (Old Mine Road). Take River Road north for 12 miles to Millbrook Village, at the junction of River Road and the Millbrook-Blairstown Road. *Note:* Narrow River Road is one-way for 0.75 mile, controlled at either end by traffic lights.

The Hike

This is a beautiful and melancholy hike—beautiful because it passes through some of New Jersey's nicest scenery; melancholy because it is a landscape scarred by controversy. Millbrook was one of a number of old hamlets that fell in the way of the proposed Tocks Island Dam and reservoir project of the 1960s. The Army Corps of Engineers bought all private homes and property in the Delaware Valley here. Some folks sold unhappily, while others had their property taken by eminent domain. Families whose roots went back 250 years had to vacate ancestral homes, many of which were demolished. All this, ironically, for a project that in the end was never built. The

Tocks Island Dam was shelved and ultimately scrapped, leaving behind a valley rich in scenery and history but tainted by the bitter memories of government takeover.

Such recent specters dot our walk, as well as reminders of the valley's more remote history. Lying above the waterline of the proposed lake, Millbrook was eyed early on for historic preservation. The village is today a historic site used to interpret the trades and crafts of the nineteenth century. It's part original and part ersatz—some historic structures that would otherwise have been demolished were moved here, while others were re-created. As such, it's not the Millbrook that the residents of 150 years ago would recognize, but similar.

Many other historic (and most nonhistoric) structures in the valley here had no such luck. When the government bought these lands, in the 1960s and early 1970s, scores and scores of homes were promptly and hastily razed. Others were mothballed, and others effectively abandoned, their derelict walls still haunting the landscape. We pass both the sites of destroyed houses and others still standing, waiting for the future—restoration, demolition, fire, or just slow decay? Old foundations and ruins pay mute testimony to many pleasant homes that met the bulldozer.

A cider press is one of the attractions during Millbrook Days.

The old farmlands and woods roads our walk follows are an important part of the scenery and history here. We follow part of the original Old Mine Road, the scenic (and controversial) road around which so much history is clustered. Passing an old limekiln, we are reminded of the days when farmers here burned their own lime to fertilize their fields. And while there are still active farmlands in the valley here (tilled under contract with the Department of the Interior), the many stone fences we pass document the time, in the mid-1800s, when the landscape was far more pastoral even than today. Passing the DePue Cemetery, we can visit the last resting place of some members of this notable family, one of the first European families to settle this valley in the first decades of the 1700s.

As our hike winds back toward Millbrook Village, we pass through the justly famous Van Campens Glen, a magnificent ravine with falls and cascades—a better place to spend a steamy summer day is not to be found. We also pass through the scenic and pleasant Watergate Recreation Area, named for the estate that stood here in the mid-1900s. It's a great spot for a picnic lunch or just plain relaxing. Those who recall the (coincidentally) same-name Washington scandal of the early 1970s will get a further laugh to learn that the "Watergate" estate here was owned by a man named George Busch. It's a welcome chuckle in a hike filled with some sad memories.

Miles and Directions

0.0 Depart from the north entrance of the parking lot. Cross (northwest) Old Mine Road where the Orchard Trail (orange blazes), an abandoned road, begins by a signpost. The trail, moving away from the village, ascends along a stone fence, eventually passing into a field in succession.

0.3 The trail bears left (west) through a woods line, passing a spring box just south of the trail and into another field. (**Note:** From the field there are seasonal views south of the Kittatinny Ridge.)

0.4 The trail swings back, heading up the hill (north) along a row of hemlocks, cedars, and a stone fence where eventually the stone fence lines both side of the trail.

0.6 At the T intersection turn left (west) onto the Hamilton Ridge Trail (blue blazes), an abandoned road (Hamilton Ridge Road) that the grass is taking back. The Orchard Trail ends here.

1.3 Beyond the crest turn right (northwest) onto the Pioneer Trail (orange blazes), a woods road under some serious Eastern white pine. Careful: You could easily hike past this trailhead. (**Option:** For a shorter, flatter hike, continue straight on Hamilton Ridge Trail, picking up the hike directions at the western endpoint of the Pioneer Trail.)

1.4 After the crest and slight descent, pass between a barely discernable stone fence and immediately turn right (northwest) onto a trail, leading off the woods road. Look carefully for this turn! As the trail drops down over an outcropping of shale, pass a limekiln on the right (east). (**Side trip:** The kiln is 40 feet off the trail and worth a look-see, especially from the top. The stonework is perfectly symmetrical.)

1.5 The trail bears left (west) onto a woods road above the Delaware Valley with the Delaware River far below. The trail becomes stitched by red shale fences here.

1.8 The trail descends steeply along a ravine, covered by cedars, hemlocks, pines, and oaks.

2.0 Turn right (northeast), following the orange blazes over the stone fence and along the old pasture.

2.3 Turn left (northwest) along a very old stone fence (grass covered), eventually crossing it and continuing to parallel it, passing through a phenomenal cedar grove.

2.4 Turn left (west) at the farmstead foundations and hike along the bluff above the Delaware River. The view from here gives you an awesome feeling, especially when you recognize that this area was continuously inhabited by humans for the past 10,500 years.

2.6 The trail at this point veers (southwest) away from the river on a woods road. (**Side trip:** At this junction there is an opening in the stone fence with a path descending to the Delaware River. If you are planning to visit the river, this is the easiest access point.)

3.0 Continuing straight (southwest) on the Pioneer Trail, the route passes a foundation and a road on the right (northwest). Again the hike takes place on an abandoned road (Lower Hamilton Road).

3.4 Pass through a series of abandoned farmsteads, a somber legacy of the area's recent past.

3.9 At the trail junction, the Pioneer Trail ends. Continue straight (southwest) and once again onto the Hamilton Ridge Trail (blue blazes), which enters from the left.

4.0 Pass the DePue Cemetery. (**Side trip:** To explore the cemetery, locate the end of the guardrail and turn right [northwest] onto a herd path, traveling along the embankment above the Van Campens Brook.

4.1 The Hamilton Ridge Trail dead-ends at Old Mine Road. Turn left (east) onto the road, traveling 400 feet along the shoulder. Following signs to Van Campens Glen Recreation Site, turn right (south) onto the entrance road to the parking lot. (**FYI:** There are picnic tables, the brook, and a portable toilet, making this an excellent lunch spot.)

4.2 Locate the Van Campens Glen Trailhead (yellow blazes) at the east end of the parking lot and left of the kiosk, and begin to edge up the northern bank of the glen, passing pools, grottos, and cascades.

4.7 The trail turns right (southeast) and crosses the Van Campens Brook bridge. Turn left (northeast) and travel along the water's edge, arriving at a magnificent pool and the Van Campens Falls. The trail climbs steeply up the fall's east side. This is a no-can-do situation during high water since this area would become an island.

4.8 From the top of the falls, the trail passes at least six dramatic drops in the brook as it carves its way from one grotto to the next.

5.0 At the head of the glen, the trail moves away from the brook and begins to ascend. Across the brook there appears to be the remains of the Van Campens mill built in the mid-1700s.

5.2 Cross over a brook and an abandoned road, continuing straight (east).

5.6 The trail drops to the floodplain, paralleling the southern bank of the Van Campens Brook, crossing over a driveway and under a power line. Alert: The yellow blazing disappears; therefore, you need to follow the path east.

5.7 Cross over Van Campens Brook via bridge and enter the Watergate Recreational Site (fee area), following the blue gravel path straight (east) ahead. To the left (north) and up the hill, you will find a directory, a pay phone, parking lot, water (seasonal), and restrooms (seasonal).

Millbrook Village and Van Campens Glen

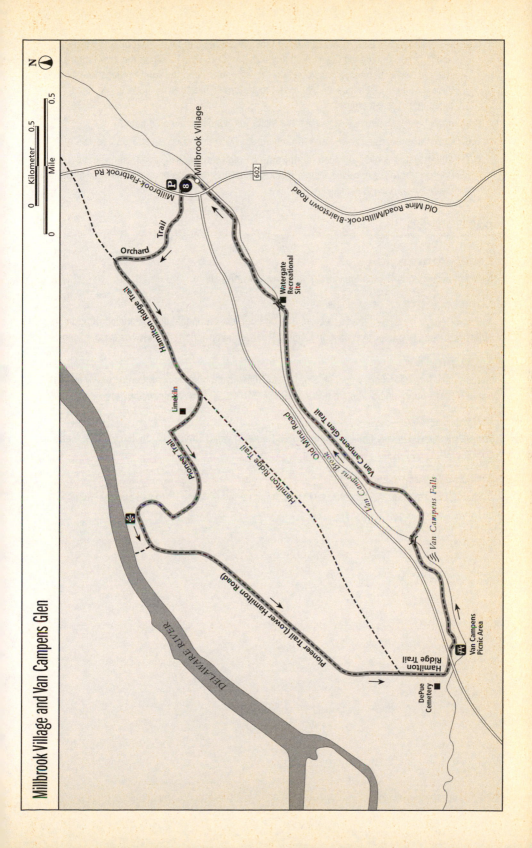

N

Kilometer
0   0.5

Mile
0   0.5

Millbrook Village
602
Old Mine Road/Millbrook–Blairstown Road
Millbrook-Flatbrook Rd
P
Orchard
Trail
Hamilton Ridge Trail
Limekiln
Pioneer Trail
Hamilton Ridge Trail
Old Mine Road
Van Campens Glen Trail
Van Campens Brook
Van Campens Falls
Watergate Recreational Site
Pioneer Trail (Lower Hamilton Road)
DELAWARE RIVER
DePue Cemetery
Hamilton Ridge Trail
Van Campens Picnic Area

5.9 The gravel path passes between two 50-foot evergreens and bears right between two ponds before turning left (east), reuniting with Van Campens Brook on the right (south). The trail travels between a large pond on the left (north) and the Van Campens Brook on the right (south). Continue straight (east) to Millbrook Village, while passing two roads entering on the left (south).

6.5 As you enter Millbrook Village, pass the Millbrook Schoolhouse on the left.

6.6 Cross Millbrook-Blairstown Road (County Route 602) and continue straight past the gate.

6.7 After traveling 1 block, turn left (north) onto an old road, passing a seasonal water source on the right (east). Traveling 1 more block and around the gate brings the hike full circle to the Millbrook Village parking lot.

Hike Information

Local Information
New Jersey Skylands Region Tourism Guide; www.njskylands.com

Local Events/Attractions
Millbrook Village Days, held the first weekend in October, are an annual demonstration of traditional nineteenth-century trades, skills, and industries. For more information, visit www.millbrooknj.com.

Restaurants
The Walpack Inn, open Friday through Sunday, on Highway 615 in Walpack Center, offers fine dining in a rustic atmosphere with great views; (973) 948-3890; www.walpackinn.com

Organizations
The New York–New Jersey Trail Conference, 156 Ramapo Valley Road (U.S. Highway 202), Mahwah 07430; (201) 512-9348; www.nynjtc.org

Other Resources
Bertland, Dennis, et al. *The Minisink*. 1975; reprinted by the Walpack Historical Society, Walpack, NJ

9 Buttermilk Falls and Rattlesnake Mountain

This lollipop hike climbs straight out of the Walpack Valley to the top of the Kittatinny Ridge, where it crosses over Rattlesnake and Bird Mountains and then heads back down again. You start the hike by climbing alongside the highest and possibly the most beautiful waterfalls in the Garden State. You will earn panoramic views of the Delaware River Valley along with the Great Valley of the Appalachians. While the Buttermilk Falls Trail is strenuous and the Appalachian Trail moderate, you will find the Woods Trail wonderfully easy.

Start: Buttermilk Falls parking lot on Mountain Road
Distance: 6.4-mile lollipop
Approximate hiking time: 4 hours
Difficulty: Strenuous due to steep mountain trails
Trail surface: Hiking trails and woods roads
Seasons: Spring through fall
Other trail users: Hikers
Canine compatibility: Leashed dogs permitted
Land status: National Recreation Area
Nearest town: Branchville
Fees and permits: None

Schedule: Dawn to dusk
Maps: DeLorme: New Jersey Atlas & Gazetteer p. 18; New York–New Jersey Trail Conference Kittatinny Trails Map 17; USGS Lake Maskenozha, PA, Culvers Gap, NJ
Trail contacts: Delaware Water Gap National Recreation Area, River Road off Route 209, Bushkill, PA 18324; (570) 588-2451; www.nps.gov/dewa/
Other: Rattlesnake Mountain didn't get its name for nothing; keep your eyes open!
Special considerations: This hike is not safe in icy conditions.

Finding the trailhead: Take U.S. Highway 206 roughly 11 miles north of Newton, past Culver's Lake and Stokes State Forest. Just past the forest entrance, turn left onto Struble Road. Struble Road becomes Dimon Road; follow both for a total of roughly 3.3 miles to Tillman Road. Turn right on Tillman Road, passing Tillman Falls parking area, until you reach a T intersection with Mountain Road. Go left on Mountain Road roughly 1.7 miles to Buttermilk Falls (falls on left, parking on right).

The Hike

The sound of plunging water cascading down the 75-foot waterfall begins this awesome hike. On the old maps the title *The Falls* was given to this, the highest waterfall in New Jersey. As you walk out of the parking lot, a former barnyard, spot the rubble, all that remains of the barn. Looking at the base of Buttermilk Falls, imagine a late-nineteenth-century two-story stone house with an adjacent stone mill. Attached to the mill is an overshot waterwheel, which is attached to a wooden sluice running from the upper section of the falls. The wheel, operating strictly by the weight of the water, is churning butter, hence the more "modern" name *Buttermilk Falls*. What a place to live and work, truly a cottage industry!

Traverse the falls by climbing the seventy-four steps, built by the Appalachian Mountain Club trail crew. Realize that the stairs preserve the resource while protecting the visitor. Be sure to take advantage of the two viewing stations, which provide bird's-eye views of the falls.

Cross the fall line and enter into a microclimate created by the Falls Brook's gouging action as it sliced through the plateau, leaving a deep, dark gorge that is further shaded by the hemlocks' canopy. Rhododendrons, ferns, mosses, and liverworts flourish in this light-deprived environ, and so will you on a hot summer day. Highly acidic soil produced from the carpet of hemlock nettles only further limits the understory growth. Within the ravine, the birches, beeches, and maples complete the hemlock-mixed hardwood forest. Their branches accommodate the ovenbirds, the warblers, the vireos, the tanagers, and the thrushes, just to name a few. As you climb onto the Kittatinny Ridge, the larger, exposed, drier chestnut oak forest acts as a strong contrast to the localized zone you have just departed.

Don't let the remoteness of the ridge fool you; you have just merged onto the Atlantic Flyway, a migratory corridor for birds. Using the updrafts coming off the Appalachian Mountains to conserve energy, our feathered friends may travel 240 miles a day from the Arctic to South America. From this ridge during the fall season, 15,000 to 20,000 raptor sightings have been recorded! On one given day, Hawk Watch reported 225 red-tailed hawks, 4 golden eagles, and 3 northern goshawks. Be sure to pack your binoculars, bird book, and silhouette guide. Get yourself a front-row ridge seat.

Enjoy the panorama of the Great Valley and the Pocono Plateau, believed by some to be the best views in the state. Rattlesnake Mountain (1,492 feet) is an ideal lunch spot. Just pick your spot carefully, since the mountain's name refers to the venomous timber rattlesnakes (state endangered species), which are known to sun themselves during the spring and fall along the rocky crags of the *entire* ridge. They are distinguished by their vertical pupils on a triangular head, sporting pits on either side, and ending with rattles on their tail. Colors vary between gray, yellow, and brown accented by black or dark brown blotches. Such beauty should be *avoided*!

Miles and Directions

0.0 From the Buttermilk Falls parking lot, pass through the entrance and cross Mountain Road to the base of the falls where you will find a kiosk. Locate the trailhead (blue blazes) on the left (east) side of the pool. Begin climbing seventy-four steps to the top of the falls with two viewing platforms. The Buttermilk Falls Trail crosses a bridge over the stream and immediately turns left (south) and parallels the stream through the hemlock ravine. (**FYI:** The extensive trail work may appear overkill but is needed to protect the fragile environment as well as Homo sapiens.)

0.1 After the first rise the trail bears right and sharply climbs away from the stream. Just before the sharp rise, if you continue 150 feet straight on an unofficial path, paralleling the right bank (southwest), you will arrive at a mine/cave, the Walpack Mine (ca.1770), which produced copper ore.

Buttermilk Falls and Rattlesnake Mountain

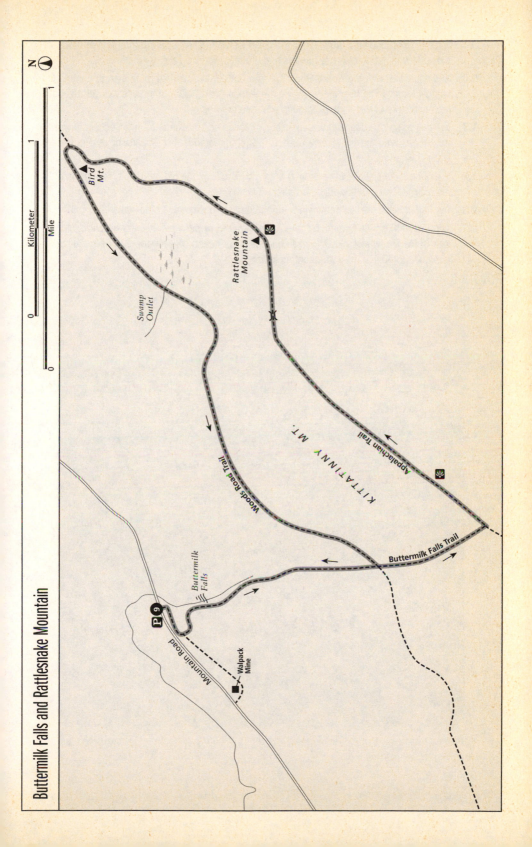

N

Kilometer
0   1

Mile
0   1

Bird Mt.

Swamp Outlet

Rattlesnake Mountain

Woods Road Trail

KITTATINNY MT.

Appalachian Trail

Buttermilk Falls Trail

Buttermilk Falls

P 9

Mountain Road

Walpack Mine

0.4 The trail rises along the ridge above the gorge with partial views north through the dead oaks. A combination of gypsy months and drought produced the dead stand.

0.9 At the junction with the Woods Road Trail, the Buttermilk Falls Trail (blue blazes) continues straight (south). The hike will return via the Woods Road Trail from the east, so get a good mental picture of this spot, preventing you from blowing by it.

1.3 The trail passes through some unofficial campsites and arrives at a T intersection. Turn left (northeast) onto the Appalachian Trail, following the famous "6 x 2" white blaze and an old grass-covered road.

1.5 The AT continues straight (northeast) onto a trail, leaving the old road as it dips down. You will meander atop of the ridge, passing two viewpoints.

2.3 The trail crosses over a stream via wooden bridge and ascends Rattlesnake Mountain.

2.7 Arrive at Rattlesnake Mountain (1,492 feet) rimmed by pitch pines. Enjoy a panoramic view of the Delaware Valley. The trail continues (northeast) over the top and descends on a rocky trail through oaks and mountain laurel.

In the vicinity of Rattlesnake Mountain, take in a rolling view across Walpack Valley to Pocono Plateau.

3.5 Arrive at Bird Mountain. Locate where Appalachian Trail runs into the woods roads and before it begins to descend, turn sharply left (west) onto Woods Road Trail. There are no official markings here except some debris strewn at the opening to the woods road, so AT hikers won't "go astray." Step around the branches and onto the clearly defined woods road. It will remind you of the Garden State Parkway without the traffic. (**Side trip:** Just beyond the trail junction [about 50 feet], take the AT north and before it begins to descend, turn left [north] onto a herd path that brings you to the end of the ridge with a sweeping view of Walpack Valley.

4.2 The Woods Road Trail edges a swamp, a former glacial lake that is lined with till, a product of the Wisconsin Glacier.

4.5 The trail crosses the outlet of the swamp. (**Side trip:** Before crossing the stream, turn right [northwest] and walk along the top of the bank for 0.1 mile, enjoying the series of cascades.)

5.5 After a series of damp areas, the trail begins to rise. Look for the ridge coming in from the right (north) and the junction with Buttermilk Falls Trail. Turn right (north) onto the Buttermilk Falls Trail (blue blazes) and retrace your trip to the parking lot.

6.4 Arrive at the parking lot.

Hike Information

Local Information

New Jersey Skylands Region Tourism Guide; www.njskylands.com

Local Events/Attractions

The Walpack Historical Society offers a variety of programs at Walpack Center; call or write for details. Walpack Historical Society, PO Box 3, Walpack Center 07881; (973) 948-6671. The Montague Association for Restoration of Community History (MARCH) operates the historic house museums in the Neldon-Roberts Stonehouse and the Foster-Armstrong House; MARCH, PO Box 1101, Montague 07827-0101; (973) 293-3106; www.montaguenj.org/march/march.htm

Lodging

Appalachian Mountain Club's Mohican Outdoor Center, 50 Camp Road, Blairstown 07825-9655; (908) 362-5670; www.mohicanoutdoorcenter.com (The Lodge, winterized cabins, tent sites, and dining hall available)

Restaurants

The Walpack Inn, open Friday through Sunday, on Route 615 in Walpack Center, offers fine dining in a rustic atmosphere with great views; (973) 948-3890; www.walpackinn.com

Organizations

The New York–New Jersey Trail Conference, 156 Ramapo Valley Road (U.S. Highway 202), Mahwah 07430; (201) 512-9348; www.nynjtc.org

Other Resources

Bertland, Dennis, et al. *The Minisink.* 1975; reprinted by the Walpack Historical Society, Walpack, NJ.

The Highlands Province

The Highlands are the rugged heart and spirit of northern New Jersey's mountains. Valued over the centuries for varying reasons, they are a southern extension of the New England Physiographic Province, embracing the great mountains of the northeast. This includes some of the oldest (600 million years) and most geologically complex rock in New Jersey. Broad, rounded, flat-topped parallel mountain

Resting atop Wyanokie High Point.

ridges (in some areas literally plateaus) are separated by narrow, deep, steep-walled valleys, generally running northeast–southwest. The mountains are swathed in dense forest, punctuated here and there by extensive swamps.

The Highlands also has a northern and a southern face. Ten thousand years ago, the Wisconsin glacier stopped about midway down the Jersey Highlands, roughly where Interstate 80 runs today. The mile-thick ice sheet retreated thereafter, leaving an indistinct pile of soil and earth it plowed up, what geologists called a terminal moraine.

South of this terminal moraine, the Highlands have a more gently rolling character and deeper soils; mountains might have farm fields on their very summit. To the north of the moraine, the ice sheet scoured the Highlands like a bulldozer, leaving behind such glacial features as bald peaks, deep valleys, steep rocky slopes, ponds and kettle lakes, and occasional huge boulders that hitchhiked south, called *erratics*. This post-glacial landscape can be both harsh (especially on the feet) and beautiful.

It was certainly harsh for the early settlers who farmed here. The soils are often thin and stony, and picking rocks was an endless job. The massive stone farm fences you'll find on even a short jaunt through the Highlands forests are reminders of these ghost farms of the hills—the by-product of clearing such stone and laying out farm fields.

The Highlands did have a hidden treasure, though: This is where most of New Jersey's mineral wealth lies, and mines (first iron, and later zinc) operated in this region from the earliest days of settlement right up through the 1970s. You will still find old mine pits and shafts, as well as the ruins of the furnaces that smelted the ore. The historic iron industry forms the backdrop for many of the state parks in the region, including Ringwood State Park, Long Pond Ironworks State Park, Allamuchy Mountain State Park, and Wawayanda State Park.

In the twentieth century, the Highlands became the area more and more people went to looking for a vacation place. First hotels and, later, lake communities and cabin colonies sprouted on the landscape. Summer houses with charming log architecture and stone fireplaces surrounded pretty (if artificial) lakes and ponds: New Jersey's commuting-distance version of the Adirondacks.

This onetime-industrial, oft-recreational region is now earmarked for preservation, with the passage of the Highlands Water Protection and Planning Act restricting or prohibiting future development in much of the scenic 1.2-million-acre area. The Highlands are valuable not just as scenery but also as a watershed for the Jersey cities and suburbs. The industrial history and recreational heritage embodied here will thus, with luck, be augmented by the preservation of much of the Highlands as valued open space.

10 Pochuck Valley to Wawayanda Mountain

Walk across Vernon Valley and climb the Stairway to Heaven to the top of Wawayanda Mountain, all on the Appalachian Trail. Meander on thousands of feet of boardwalk through wetlands; traverse a 150-foot suspension bridge; cross the Black, Pochuck, and Wawayanda Creeks, all the while keeping the Wawayanda Escarpment before your eyes. The traverse up the mountain is strenuous, but the scene from Pinwheel Vista (Shawangunk, Catskill, and the Kittatinny Mountains) may be one of the best panoramic views in the state! This is a shuttle hike with a partial out-and-back.

Start: Appalachian Trail crossing of County Route 517, south of Glenwood
Distance: 7.4-mile shuttle
Approximate hiking time: 5 hours
Difficulty: Valley portion is flat easy (flat), but mountain portion is strenuous (steep, with elevation change).
Trail surface: Hiking trail and boardwalk
Seasons: The valley portion is good year-round; the mountain is best spring through fall.
Other trail users: Hikers
Canine compatibility: Leashed dogs permitted
Land status: State park, national scenic trail
Nearest town: Vernon
Fees and permits: None
Schedule: Dawn to dusk
Maps: *DeLorme: New Jersey Atlas & Gazetteer* p.20; USGS Wawayanda, NJ, quadrangle; New York–New Jersey Trail Conference *North Jersey Trails Map 21* and *Appalachian Trail Map 4*
Trail contacts: Wawayanda State Park, 885 Warwick Turnpike, Hewitt 07421; (973) 853-4462; wsp@warwick.net; www.njparksand forests.org
Other: During periods of heavy rain or spring snowmelt, the entrances to the boardwalk section of this hike may be flooded.
Special considerations: Keep an eye out for rattlesnakes on the mountaintop. This hike passes through areas of botanical and archaeological sensitivity. Please stay on the trail; persons disturbing natural or historic resources are subject to prosecution by state and/or federal authorities. This section of the AT is heavily used, particularly on weekends; parking at trailheads can be scarce.

Finding the trailhead: From Route 23, get on County Route 515 (Vernon-Stockholm Road) at Stockholm. Take CR 515 north 8.5 miles to Vernon. At the traffic light at the Route 94 intersection in Vernon, continue straight, almost immediately turning left onto Vernon Crossing Road (County Route 644). Take this road for 1.4 miles, ending at a T intersection with CR 517 (McAfee-Glenwood Road). Turn right here, traveling 1.5 miles to the Appalachian Trail crossing of CR 517 (marked). Parking available alongside CR 517.

The Hike

This hike on the Appalachian Trail (AT) represents a figurative and literal change of pace for the historic trail. Most of the AT passes through the "green tunnel" of the mountains, but here you get to experience a genuinely pastoral walk through mead-owlands, farm fields, and pastures—mostly flat and easy. It begins on CR 517, known in the early 1800s as the Pochuck Turnpike. "Pochuck" was the name for most of this area in years gone by, though exactly where "Pochuck" was or what it means remains a subject of debate. There's Pochuck Mountain (immediately to the west) and Pochuck Creek (which we cross); most of the area between or around the two at one time was called "Pochuck." Some sources claim it's a Native American Lenape word meaning "an out-of-the-way place; a corner or recess," though what that might have referred to is unclear. Ask an old-timer around here where or what "Pochuck" is, and they'll say: Pochuck is a state of mind.

For the first sixty years of the Appalachian Trail's existence here, it followed old country roads across the Vernon and Wallkill Valleys between Wawayanda Mountain and High Point. But such roadwalks were not always safe and became less bucolic as the decades passed and housing development boomed. By the late 1970s, efforts were under way to move the AT to its own corridor. But this required massive trail rerouting. It was a cooperative effort involving volunteers and staff from the New York–New Jersey Trail Conference and the Appalachian Trail Conference working in conjunction with the land-managing agencies, the New Jersey Department of Environmental Protection, and the National Park Service. The old route up Wawayanda Mountain (a boulder scramble) was abandoned and a new, well-designed route laid out. The new trail up the mountain, dubbed "The Stairway to Heaven," was built in the late 1980s by volunteers and includes massive stone steps and carefully constructed switchbacks.

The valley route was even more difficult, involving the crossing of wetlands and rivers. The Pochuck Creek meadowlands were bridged in 1995 with a 150-foot

Pochuck Memorial Suspension Bridge spans the Pochuck Creek at flood stage. It's dedicated to the memory of Pete Morrissey, John Garcia, and Duane Bell.

suspension bridge, designed and built by volunteers with the assistance of General Public Utilities (GPU). The adjacent meadowlands were spanned with 1.5 miles of boardwalk built on nearly 900 metal piers sunk as deep as 20 feet into the muck. Begun in 1999, the boardwalk was dedicated in 2002. It involved some 9,000 hours of volunteer labor, and it's spectacular—more boardwalk, seemingly, than Atlantic City!

Near Canal Road, the hike passes through an area rich in Native American archaeological significance (a few miles north of here is the Black Creek Site State and National Prehistoric District, a major archaeological site now part of Wawayanda State Park). As near the Wallkill, the limestone rock here contains deposits of chert that the Native Americans quarried to make tools.

The trail also passes through active farm fields and pastures. The Rickey family has been farming near here since the Revolutionary War, and the Van Dokkenburg farm adjacent to it is likewise one of the oldest and most beautiful in the region. While it may mean dodging the occasional cow-pie (or even cow), this farming landscape is a rich part of our agricultural heritage and should be appreciated as such.

Miles and Directions

0.0 Leaving CR 517, proceed past the kiosk and onto the boardwalk, heading (east-southeast) into the "inlet." The entire hike will follow the infamous "6 x 2" white blazes of the Appalachian Trail with the exception of the blue blazes leading to Pinwheel Vistas.

0.2 The boardwalk swings northeast before entering the woods and earthen treadway.

0.5 The boardwalk begins again before crossing (south) a bridge over the Black Creek and continues to curve southeast.

0.7 Arrive at the 150-foot suspension bridge, crossing over the Pochuck Creek. Pick up the boardwalk on the opposite side. (**FYI:** The bridge makes for an excellent observation blind.)

0.9 As the boardwalk ends, pass over a gravel bed and a small bridge where you enter hard-wood forest and proceed up the trail through the limestone.

1.2 Pass through a series of stone fences and through fields in recession. At the end of the second field, the trail ducks into the tree line and bears left (east) along the top of the cliffs.

1.3 The trail swings right (south) and descends off the plateau through ash, tulips, and cedars.

1.4 Proceed through a bicycle gate and turn right (west) onto Canal Road and in 200 feet cross over Wawayanda Creek via a steel bridge and immediately turn left, passing through another bicycle gate, where the trail enters a field.

1.6 Cross over a wooden bridge spanning the Old Wawayanda Creek and bear right (south) along the tree line.

1.7 Pass through fence line, crossing stringer bridges and bog bridging.

1.8 Pass through a stone fence and ascend up the hill through a field in recession.

2.0 Cross over a stone fence via a stile and descend through the hardwoods.

2.1 After traversing a set of bog bridging, cross over a stile and immediately climb over the railroad tracks (active) and then over the second stile where the trail emerges into a field and onto more bog bridging. (**FYI:** These are real-life cows in this pasture, so we advise you: Don't tease the bull!)

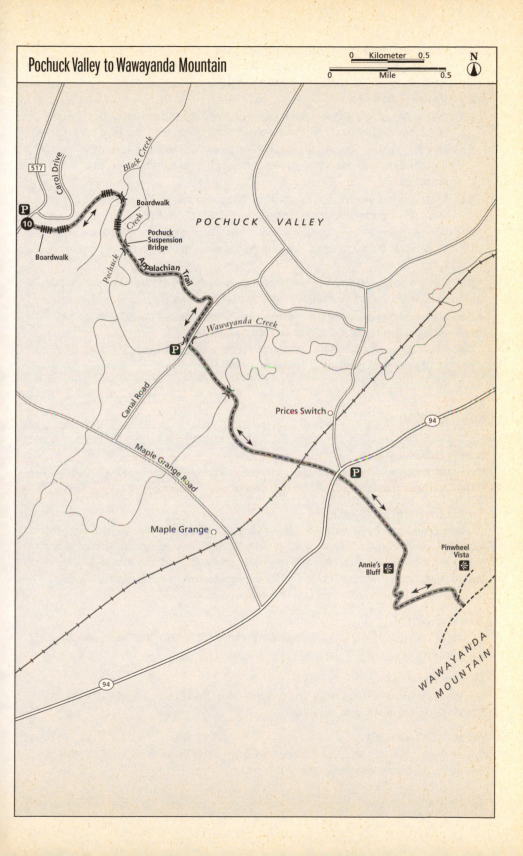

Pochuck Valley to Wawayanda Mountain

0   Kilometer   0.5

0   Mile   0.5

N

517

Carol Drive

Black Creek

P

10

Boardwalk

Boardwalk

Pochuck Creek

Pochuck Suspension Bridge

Appalachian Trail

POCHUCK VALLEY

Wawayanda Creek

P

Canal Road

Prices Switch

94

P

Maple Grange Road

Maple Grange

Annie's Bluff

Pinwheel Vista

94

WAWAYANDA MOUNTAIN

2.3 Climb over a stile and immediately cross (southeast) Highway 94 into the Appalachian Trail parking lot. Pass directly through the lot and up the stairs where a kiosk stands. The trail leads up through evergreens, before opening into a panoramic scene.

2.7 The trail enters the hardwoods.

2.8 The trail swings right (southwest) at the base of the escarpment and edges along the rock talus. Some people have been known to boulder on a few of these "bad boys."

2.9 After the last major boulder, the trail swings left (south) and begins to ascend the Wawayanda Plateau, called "The Stairway to Heaven": stone stairs and a series of switchbacks.

3.0 Following a steep switchback, reach Annie's Bluff, a view over Vernon Valley (more open in the winter). The trail continues to ascend along the side of the ridge.

3.3 Pass two massive oak trees known as Proudsman's Tree House, trees left standing when all others fed the iron furnaces. Alongside the trail within the boulders trickles a seasonal spring.

3.4 Before a boulder field the trail swings right (south-southwest) and climbs up through the rocks, where the trail turns left, running along the cliff's base.

3.5 After ascending a series of steep switchbacks, the trail runs in a "trough" where on the curve the blue-blazed trail to Pinwheel Vista emerges.

3.6 Turn left onto the side trail (blue blazes) and follow it out to the lookout. From this point, retrace your steps back to your car shuttle.

7.4 Arrive at parking lot.

Hike Information

Local Information
New Jersey Skylands Region Tourism Guide; www.njskylands.com. Vernon Chamber of Commerce, PO Box 308, Vernon 07462; (973) 764-0764; www.vernonchamber.com

Local Events/Attractions
Mountain Creek Water Park & Ski Resort offers a variety of recreational opportunities, including horseback riding; Route 94, Vernon 07462; (973) 827-2000; www.mountaincreek.com. Bobolink Dairy, close to the Appalachian Trail, offers gourmet cheese and breads made on-site; 42 Meadowburn Road, Vernon 07462; (973) 764-4888; www.cowsoutside.com. Wawayanda State Park offers swimming, boating, and hiking (see "Trail contacts" above).

Restaurants
The Vernon Inn Restaurant & Pub, 340 Route 94, Vernon 07462; (973) 764-9888; www.the vernoninn.com

Organizations
New York–New Jersey Trail Conference, 156 Ramapo Valley Road (U.S. Highway 202), Mahwah 07430; (201) 512-9348; www.nynjtc.org

Other Resources
Dupont, Ronald J. Jr., *Vernon 200: A Bicentennial History of the Township of Vernon, NJ* (1992), provides background information on the area.

11 Pyramid Mountain and Tripod Rock

Take an extraordinary jaunt through a natural sculpture garden created by the Wisconsin Glacier some 18,000 years ago. Pass some of the most amazing erratics: Bear Rock, possibly New Jersey's largest; Whale Head Rock, directly out of Moby Dick; and Tripod Rock, a balanced pedestal rock claimed by some to have links to the solstice and prehistoric congregations. Along with views of the Newark Basin and the New York Skyline, there are side trips to the Morgan Place foundations, Cole Farm Mine, and Lucy's Overlook. Just think: You are hiking on the edge of the Ramapo Fault!

Start: Pyramid Mountain Natural Historical Area parking lot on Boonton Avenue
Distance: 5.0-mile loop
Approximate hiking time: 2.5 hours
Difficulty: Moderate—a few rocky stretches
Trail surface: Hiking trails and woods roads
Seasons: All good
Other trail users: Hikers
Canine compatibility: Leashed dogs permitted
Land status: County park
Nearest town: Butler
Fees and permits: None
Schedule: Dawn to dusk
Maps: *DeLorme: New Jersey Atlas & Gazetteer* p. 25; USGS Boonton and Pompton Plains, NJ, quadrangle; a trail map of the park is also available from the Morris County Park Commission either at the visitor center, or online at www.parks.morris.nj.us/.
Trail contacts: Morris County Park Commission, 53 East Hanover Avenue, PO Box 1295, Morristown 07962-1295; (973) 326-7600; info@parks.morris.nj.us; www.parks.morris.nj.us. Pyramid Mountain Visitor's Center, (973) 334-3130
Other: It's worthwhile to stop in at the interpretive center and pick up handouts and materials on flora, fauna, and history.
Special considerations: The area is liable to be crowded on nice summer weekends and (no kidding) the summer and winter solstices.

Finding the trailhead: From the intersection of Route 23 and Boonton Avenue (County Route 511), travel southwest on Boonton Avenue 4.2 miles. Turn right (west) into the Pyramid Mountain Natural Historical Area parking lot.

The Hike

Two of the outstanding features of this hike through the Pyramid Mountain Natural Historical Area are Bear Rock and Tripod Rock, must-sees on any hike here. They are both amazing, but in different ways. Any way you look at it, a hike here is like a hike through a geological sculpture garden.

Bear Rock is alleged to be the largest boulder in New Jersey, and it could well be. Known early on as "Bare" rock, the origin of its name is unclear. Some say it looks like a bear; or perhaps a bear lived there; or perhaps it was bare. Whatever the case, Native Americans found a use for this colossal rock next to a stream and a swamp. Ancient Native American rockshelters existed on both sides of it, used as transient camps by hunting and foraging parties. Archaeologist Max Schrabisch excavated them in 1909.

Tripod Rock has a different story. The old wisdom says, "Don't bring up religion or politics unless you want to start a fight." In New Jersey hiking and history communities, you might add one more to that proscribed list: balanced boulders. Few things are both as fascinating and controversial as Tripod Rock.

As you will see visiting the site, Tripod Rock is a 160-something-ton boulder, roughly triangular, balanced at an angle on three smaller boulders, at a height of some 2 feet. Looking like a precarious joke left by an ancient race of giants, it is one of the great wonders of New Jersey. A geological wonder, most would say—the last ice age deposited untold glacial erratics across the mountains of northern New Jersey. It stands to reason that some of them would end up in unusual configurations. Tripod Rock is a monument to the power (albeit random) of natural geological forces.

▶ Nearby Lucy's Overlook is named for Lucy Meyer, the Kinnelon grassroots environmental activist who spearheaded the effort that led to the creation of Pyramid Mountain Natural Historical Area in 1987. She received a presidential award for her efforts.

Pshaw, says another camp. How can anything so obviously artificial be dismissed as a work of nature?

Over the past several decades, some researchers have advanced a belief that North America is filled with ancient, huge rock monuments—megaliths—placed by ancient cultures to mark important dates in the calendar—a

Tripod Rock reflects the capricious nature of the glaciers. The spot is believed by some to have spiritual significance.

summer or winter solstice, or a spring or fall equinox. Three boulders near Tripod Rock form a triangle that points (kinda, sorta) to the summer solstice. It is a calendar stone, an ancient astrological site, indeed, a spiritual energy vortex, they say.

"Phooey!" (accompanied by serious rolling of the eyes), say the geologists and historians. There's no archaeological evidence of any culture, Native American or otherwise, having been at Tripod Rock, and the notion that it points to the solstice requires wishful (and creative) thinking. It's a geological wonder—a natural one. Period!

A third camp represents a bit of a compromise and posits that while Tripod Rock may indeed be natural, it nevertheless could have attracted the attention of Native Americans, who could have worshipped there.

The difference of opinion will surely continue. Every year in June, Tripod Rock is a busy place to be for the summer solstice. Some come to enjoy the beauty of the scene, some come to ponder the mysteries of geology and ancient civilizations, and some are probably waiting for a call from the mother ship. Any way you look at it, Tripod Rock is a good place to ponder the imponderables.

Miles and Directions

0.0 Proceed to the kiosk found on the northwest side of the parking lot. The Blue Trail (blue blaze), also known as the Mennen Trail and the Butler-Montville Trail, begins directly behind the kiosk, heading north through the hardwoods.

0.1 Cross the Stony Brook via a wooden bridge.

0.2 At the fork with Yellow Trail, continue on the Blue Trail by bearing left (northwest) and begin to ascend, crossing under the power lines.

0.4 Pass the White Trail (white blaze) on the left (west) and continue to climb, paralleling the power lines.

0.5 After cresting the shoulder of the ridge, continue straight (northwest) onto the Red Trail South (red blaze), leaving the Blue Trail, which turns right (north). (**Note:** The hike will return via the Blue Trail, so make a mental note of this spot.)

0.8 The trail passes through the bottomland and is a bit tricky to follow; therefore, you must pay attention to the blazing.

1.0 Cross Bearhouse Brook via the bridge and immediately come to a T intersection. Turn right (north) onto the White Trail, a woods road, which rises above the bottomland and along some serious outcrops. (**Side trip:** To view the Morgan Place's foundations, turn left onto the White Trail and travel 50 feet for the first foundation and 200 feet for the second foundation. Supposedly during the late 1800s, the Morgans [Boonton bad boys] used it as a hideout.)

1.3 Arrive at a trail junction. Continue straight (north) on the woods road, passing Bear Rock on the left side and onto the Blue Trail, which comes in from the right (east). (**Option:** You can create a shorter loop to Tripod Rock and the visitor center by turning right [east] onto the co-aligned Blue Trail and White Trail.) (**Side trip:** If you are in the mood for adventure, bushwhack to the Cole Farm Mine. From Bear Rock, cross back over the stream and head due west for approximately 0.2 mile, avoiding the sheer outcropping. Ed Lenik, a local archaeologist, calls it "a keyhole-shaped exploratory trench." Look for a mound of mine tailings.)

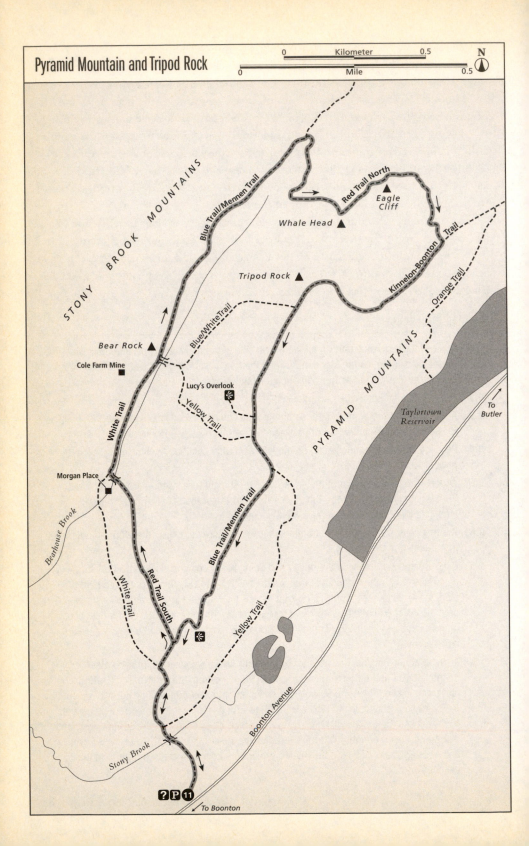

Pyramid Mountain and Tripod Rock

Kilometer
0   0.5
Mile
0   0.5

N

STONY BROOK MOUNTAINS

PYRAMID MOUNTAINS

Blue Trail/Mennen Trail

Red Trail North

Whale Head ▲

Eagle Cliff ▲

Kinnelon-Boonton Trail

Orange Trail

Tripod Rock ▲

Blue/White Trail

Bear Rock ▲

Cole Farm Mine ■

Lucy's Overlook

Yellow Trail

White Trail

Taylortown Reservoir

To Butler

Morgan Place ■

Bearhouse Brook

White Trail

Red Trail South

Blue Trail/Mennen Trail

Yellow Trail

Boonton Avenue

Stony Brook

? P 11

To Boonton

2.0 Turn right (east) onto a relocated Red-White Trail (red and white blaze), which snakes across the bottomland.

2.3 At the end of the relocation, emerge onto the Red Trail North and steeply ascend onto the ridge.

2.4 Just beyond the crest of the ridge, pass Whale Rock on the right (south). The Great Blue has a grin on its face.

2.6 The trail descends steeply off Eagle Cliffs and proceeds to cross a washboard of ridges.

2.9 At the T intersection the Red Trail North ends. Turn right (southwest) onto the White Trail (Kinnelon-Boonton Trail, white blaze), which will run the ridge before dropping down past Big Cat Swamp.

3.6 Arrive at Tripod Rock. Beside the glacial erratics, you may have a bit more company here, as it's a popular destination. There is also a nice view of the hollow (northwest) from this spot. The trail continues from the south side of Tripod Rock, crossing a stream on rocks.

3.7 At the trail junction proceed straight (southwest) onto the Blue Trail, leaving the White Trail, which was co-aligned with the Blue Trail, as it turns right (northwest) and heads for Bear Rock.

3.8 Pass on the right a trail (blue and white blaze) leading to Lucy's Overlook. (**Side trip:** The rocky 0.1-mile trail ends at a secluded view of the Highlands Region.)

3.9 At the fork bear left (southeast) continuing on the Blue Trail, which is now co-aligned with the Yellow trail. The Yellow Trail to the right (west) leads to Cat Rocks and Bear Rock.

4.0 Pass the Yellow Trail leaving left (east). Continue (south) on the Blue Trail, ascending the ridge.

4.3 Pass a vista on the left (southeast) with an impressive view of Turkey Mountain, Newark Basin, and the New York City skyline. It is also here that the trail turns sharply right (west), descending over a series of outcrops via switchbacks.

4.5 At the T intersection turn left (southeast) onto the Blue Trail and retrace the route back to the parking lot and visitor center.

5.0 Arrive back at the parking lot.

Hike Information

Local Information

Morris County Visitor's Center, 6 Court Street, Morristown 07960; (973) 631-5151; www.morris tourism.org

Local Events/Attractions

The historic town of Boonton has a museum, walking tours, restaurants, and shops; Boonton Town Hall; (973) 402-9410; www.boonton.org. Boonton Historical Society and Museum, 210 Main Street, Boonton; (973) 402-8840; www.boonton.org

Organizations

The Friends of Pyramid Mountain, Pyramid Mountain Home Page, www.kinnelon.com/htm/community/recreation/pyramidmt.asp

12 Bearfort Mountain and Surprise Lake

This Bearfort Ridge trek wakes up the body with an immediate 600-foot elevation gain. After the climb the ramble atop the ridge impresses you with its isolation, surrounded by pitch pine corridors and rhododendron "caves." The trail fluctuates between being nature's sidewalk and a roller coaster. Along the hike you will find a scattering of glacial erratics, bogs, and puddingstone outcrops before you arrive at Surprise Lake, a popular destination from the State Line Trail. Completing the loop via the Quail Trail, the fire road passes under and along some beautiful rock formations and through some damp areas, all fairly easy walking and secluded.

Start: Trailhead parking area on Warwick Turnpike
Distance: 5.6-mile loop
Approximate hiking time: 3.5 to 4 hours
Difficulty: Moderate, with a steep first ascent
Trail surface: Rocky trail and woods road, ledge
Seasons: Spring through fall
Other trail users: Multiuse
Canine compatibility: Leashed dogs permitted
Land status: State forest
Nearest town: Hewitt
Fees and permits: None

Schedule: Dawn to dusk
Maps: New York–New Jersey Trail Conference *North Jersey Trails Map 21*; *DeLorme: New Jersey Atlas & Gazetteer* p.20; USGS Greenwood Lake, NJ, quadrangle
Trail contacts: Wawayanda State Park, 885 Warwick Turnpike, Hewitt 07421; (973) 853-4462; wsp@warwick.net; www.njparksand forests.org
Other: Parking at the Greenwood Lake Turnpike trailhead may be limited, especially on nice weekends. Come early.

Finding the trailhead: From the intersection of Lakeside Road (County Route 511) and Greenwood Lake Road (County Route 513) in Browns, travel 0.2 mile west on Greenwood Lake Road (CR 513), passing a shopping mall on the left and Our Lady Queen of Peace on the right. At the fork, bear right (west) onto Warwick Turnpike and go 0.4 mile, crossing a concrete bridge. Immediately on the right is a parking lot for two cars. Do not park in the fire lane; there is a good chance you will get ticketed.

The Hike

Ascending through the hemlock-mixed hardwood forest and onto the Bearfort Ridge, you might notice the rock looks a lot like Ben and Jerry's Garden State, a blueberry-cranberry ice cream with chunky marshmallows. It's actually called *puddingstone* because someone else thought it looked like blood pudding, a concoction of blood, fat, and meat. Puddingstone is part of the Schunemunk Conglomerate, ". . . consisting of well-rounded quartz and red sandstone cobbles in a fine-grained red ironstone matrix . . ." explains the USGS. It's had various uses over the years: building material, especially foundations. Also monuments: a thirty-ton block honoring the 20th

Massachusetts Infantry at Gettysburg, another commemorating the Underground Railroad in Millington, and still another: a proposed 56-foot puddingstone bench on Morristown's Green. And names: Puddingstone Road, Puddingstone Heights, Puddingstone Publishing House, Puddingstone Resorts, Puddingstone Dam—even a musical group, The Puddingstones, which perform traditional and modern tunes. Need a trail name?

As you traverse the Bearfort Ridge, a pitch pine-scrub oak forest, you view one of the favorite subjects of leading Hudson River School artist Jasper Francis Cropsey (1823–1900). With his brushes, he depicted Greenwood Lake and its surrounding mountains. One such sunny landscape painting won him a membership in the National Academy of Design (1844). During this period, he also won the hand of his wife, Maria Cooley, a young woman from Greenwood Lake, and for a period they lived in neighboring Warwick. Over the next forty years, he returned and painted numerous works of this region. So as you reach various outlooks on Bearfort Mountain, picture yourself entering Cropsey's *View of Greenwood Lake, New Jersey* (1845) and experience all its "primordial essence."

Although the name "Bearfort" might seem apt given New Jersey's very real population of bruins (which are concentrated here in the Highlands), the name doesn't refer to them. Dating back to the mid-1800s, it is said to originate with a family named Beresford, who owned land on the mountain and had a home near its base. The name had a silent "s," which led to it later being corrupted to Bearfort. Still, there *are* plenty of bears.

Miles and Directions

0.0 From the parking space, cross the bridge over Green Brook and turn left (northeast) at the trailheads for the Bearfort Ridge Trail and Quail Trail (a fire road; therefore, *no parking*). Pick up the Bearfort Ridge Trail by following the white blazes into the rhododendron. (**FYI:** The hike will return via the Quail Trail.)

0.1 At the T intersection the Bearfort Ridge Trail turns left (north) onto the fire road (Quail Trail) and becomes co-aligned. Shortly, the Bearfort Ridge Trail turns left (northwest) and begins to climb through mountain laurel, hemlocks, and oaks while edging along a series of outcrops.

0.5 Pass on the left (southwest) the Blue Blaze Trail. Continue straight (northwest) while steadily climbing up through the puddingstone of the Schunemunk Conglomerate.

1.0 Don't pass up the vista on the left (west) even though you must scramble up to it. The impressive views of New York City, the Highlands, and Bearfort Mountain are worth it! From here the hike becomes a meandering ridge walk with sharp ups and downs and crossovers. Enjoy the pitch pine "caves" accented by stark standing glacial erratics.

2.2 The trail comes to a unique geological spot where the bedrock has split away from the core, creating a narrow wedge that stands alone overlooking a beautiful swamp. This is a good spot for food and hydration.

2.8 The Bearfort Trail ends at a spot where three white blazes are painted on the rock. The Ernest Walter Trail (yellow blazes) passes over the outcropping. Continue straight (northeast) onto the Ernest Walter Trail, descending steeply.

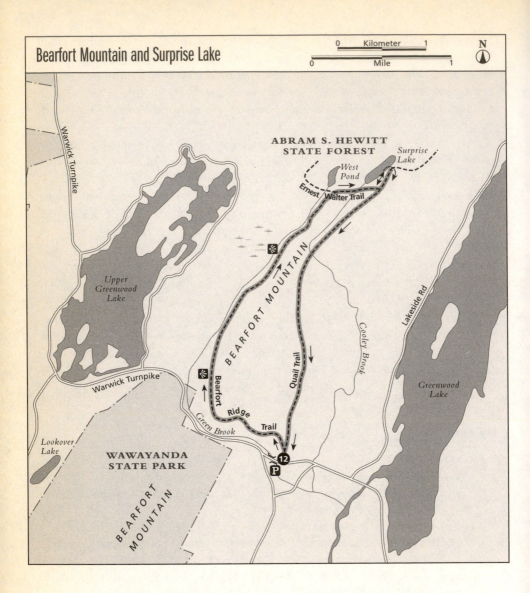

2.9 Rock-hop over a wetland and Cooley Brook (may be difficult during high water), the outlet to Surprise Lake and climb through a rhododendron "cave."

3.1 The Ernest Walter Trail merges with the Quail Trail (the fire road) and continues straight (northeast). (**FYI:** You will retrace this section on the return trip.)

3.2 Arrive at Surprise Lake, another footprint of glacial activity. This is one of the Garden State's five-star lunch spots. From Surprise Lake retrace your steps through the south end of the clearing and onto the Quail Trail (orange-blazed fire road). Pass the Ernest Walter Trail on the right. (**Side trip:** Continue [northeast] on the Ernest Walter Trail 0.2 mile up onto the ridge overlooking Greenwood Lake, Wanaque Wildlife Management Area, and Sterling Forest. From the vista retrace your steps back to Surprise Lake.

3.8 Continue straight on the woods road while the stream veers left, masquerading as the trail.

3.9 Rock-hop across Cooley Brook.

5.0 Continue straight (south) while passing a woods road leaving left (east) decorated with a series of painted arrows.

5.5 Pass the Bearfort Ridge Trail entering on the right (northwest). The Quail Trail and Bearfort Ridge Trail are co-aligned. Continue straight (south) while the Bearfort Ridge Trail leaves on the right (west).

5.6 Reach the trailheads of Bearfort Ridge Trail and Quail Trail on Warwick Turnpike. Retrace the hike back to the parking lot.

Hike Information

Local Information

Greenwood Lake tourism Web site: www.greenwoodlake.org; Abram S. Hewitt State Forest Web site: www.nj.gov/dep/parksandforests/parks/abram.html

Local Events/Attractions

Long Pond Ironworks State Park, south of Greenwood Lake, preserves the remains of an historic ironworking village that operated from the 1760s to the 1880s, including furnace ruins, water-wheels, worker's housing, and the former company store; www.longpondironworks.org

Organizations

New York–New Jersey Trail Conference, 156 Ramapo Valley Road (U.S. Highway 202), Mahwah 07430; (201) 512-9348; www.nynjtc.org

Bearfort Ridge with pitch pine, scrub oak, and a puddingstone erratic. Can you see the face in the boulder?

13 The Tourne

This undulating loop hike snakes through hill and dale, over terminal moraine, and around kettle holes dotted with puddingstone erratics. Strategically placed benches make for a relaxing tramp. Enjoy the impressive views of the Highlands, as well as the Manhattan skyline. Meander through the Wildflower Trail Area or along the banks of the lily-covered Birchwood Lake. Spend a quiet moment at a simple, sincere 9/11 memorial. This is a little prize of a park!

Start: Parking lot at west entrance to Tourne Park on McCaffrey Lane
Distance: 3.7-mile loop
Approximate hiking time: 3 hours
Difficulty: Moderate
Trail surface: Paths and woodland trails; some road walking
Seasons: All good
Other trail users: Multiuse
Canine compatibility: Leashed dogs permitted, but not in the wilderness trail area
Land status: County park
Nearest town: Boonton

Fees and permits: None
Schedule: Dawn to dusk
Maps: *DeLorme: New Jersey Atlas & Gazetteer* p.25; USGS Boonton, NJ, quadrangle; also, a park trail map is available at the park or online at www.morrisparks.org/aspparks/tournetr.asp
Trail contacts: Morris County Park Commission, 53 East Hanover Avenue, PO Box 1295, Morristown 07962-1295; (973) 326-7600; info@parks.morris.nj.us; www.parks.morris .nj.us/. Pyramid Mountain Visitor's Center; (973) 334-3130

Finding the trailhead: Traveling north on Interstate 287, take exit 43 for Intervale Road (Mountain Lakes). At the end of the ramp turn left and cross over I-287 to the traffic light. Turn right at the light onto Fanny Road. Proceed straight to the second stop sign. Turn right onto West Main Street. Bear left at the Y onto Powerville Road. Continue until the first road on the left, McCaffrey Lane. Turn left. A sign for Tourne Park marks the entrance.

The Hike

Like some other hikes in this book, this is a walk through a green oasis on the edge of the great megalopolis. The Tourne is just that: an island of forest at the edge of the great metropolitan sprawl of northeastern New Jersey.

"Tourne" is Dutch for "tower," and in the 1700s it was almost a generic term for a high promontory with a good view. The Boonton Tourne is particularly associated with Clarence A. DeCamp (1859–1948), the legendary owner of the property who spent his life developing it with roads and trails, and generally making it pleasant for public recreation. Everybody knew who DeCamp was: small, gruff, eccentric, outspoken, and often with an ax in his hand. He was a descendant of Morris County ironmasters, and he poured the same energy into his Tourne property that his ancestors did into mines and forges. It was a de facto public park, and DeCamp had frequent bonfire parties at the summit, where he built a tower. DeCamp kept hiking his beloved hill right up until the day before his death at eighty-nine.

Just as today this area is a tangle of highways, so too in the late 1800s was it a tangle of transportation systems, mainly the Morris Canal and railroads (the Delaware, Lackawanna, and Western, mainly). The Ogden Trail, which our walk follows for a bit, was originally a railroad spur that was to go from Boonton to Denville. Clarence DeCamp, in fact, worked on the construction of the railroad bed in 1898–99. But though the rail bed was built, no tracks were ever laid, mystifying both DeCamp and others—another failed business scheme, it seems.

The summit of the Tourne has excellent views of New York harbor and Manhattan, and the trails here are pleasant, easy walking. For these reasons, in recent years it has—like so many parks with a fine view of the city—become a memorial for those who died in the Twin Tower attacks on 9/11. The spot is adorned with photos, flowers, and other mementoes of those who lost their lives.

Miles and Directions

0.0 Walk (south) out of the parking lot entrance and cross McCaffrey Lane to the trailhead (right of the auto gate, which closes the lane to through traffic): next to the boulder with a red blaze. (You will follow the red blaze for the majority of the hike.) The red-blazed trail climbs (southwest) the hill. Avoid the mountain bike trails that crisscross this section.

0.2 Descending the rise, veer right off the main path, remaining on the red-blazed trail.

0.3 Cross a bridle path and continue to follow the red blaze up a slight rise.

0.5 Veer right (west) on the red-blazed trail and ascend to 711 feet, where a bench is placed for the weary.

0.7 Arrive at the high point.

0.8 After descending the hill, at the junction with an unnamed hiking trail, continue straight (red blazes) past a bench, which overlooks a vernal pool.

0.9 Shortly, the trail comes to a fork. Veer right, following the red blaze. The trail ascends pass the first of many kettle holes. (**FYI:** A kettle hole was formed when a large chunk of a glacier broke off and was buried by the till. When the ice melted, a depression was formed. You will find erratics, carried by the glacier, sitting in these holes.)

1.1 The trail descends to a junction with a large sign: MT. LAKES ONLY/TOURNE. Turn left (east) while staying with the red blazes.

1.3 The trail wraps around a bowl, while remaining on the ridge till you come to a fork with an unmark trail. Veer right, continuing to follow the contour of the ridge and the red blazes, shortly descending with views of Birchwood Lake.

1.4 At the trail junction, continue straight (east) uphill on a gravel road that overlooks the Birchwood Lake right (south), crossing the Ogden Trail left (north) and the Birchwood Loop right (south). The red-blazed trail is co-aligned with the Birchwood Loop. (**FYI:** The Ogden Trail [originally built in 1899 as a railroad spur but never actualized] is a direct route back via a left turn onto McCaffrey Lane to the start.)

1.5 In the middle of the climb and before the bend, turn left (northeast) by a bench onto the red-blazed trail now titled the Rattle Snake Trail. The trail passes through a bicycle stile and onto a footpath, which will traverse a large bowl. (**FYI:** There will be another kettle hole immediately after the turn on your right [south].)

1.8 The blue-blazed Swamp Trail enters from the left (north) and becomes co-aligned with the Rattle Snake Trail, ascending straight (east) up the rocky drift.

1.9 At the top of the hill, continue straight (northeast) on the red-blazed Rattle Snake Trail, while the Swamp Trail turns right (east-southeast).

2.0 A woods road enters from the right while the Rattle Snake Trail veers left (northeast) and merges with the woods road in a gradual descent. The forest to the right (east) has an unusual juxtaposition of glacial erratics and farmer's fieldstone fence. To the left (north) Rattlesnake Meadow appears through the trees. (**Warning!** The name of the meadow is aptly named for the *Crotalus horridus* who live here.)

2.2 Trail levels off and passes through a bicycle gate.

2.4 Junction with blue-chip stone road. The red-blazed trail continues straight ahead (northeast) and now also has a treadway of blue-chip stone.

2.5 At the fork the red-blazed trail veers right.

2.6 The red-blazed trail dead-ends at McCaffrey Lane. Located here are bathrooms (right), a directory, and a parking lot (cross the road). Turn left (northwest) and walk down McCaffrey Lane (paved).

2.7 After passing a bird sanctuary on the left and crossing the brook, turn right at the directory for wildflowers and pass through a hurricane fence gate and into the Wildflower Trail Area. The red blazes have reappeared; proceed to follow them. (Seasonal drinking water is located here.) (**Option:** Feel free to take a native wildflower/fern detour and wander the side paths through this delightful paradise. There are benches for sitting and Jack-in-the-pulpit for pondering. Many of the plants are identified with plaques.) No dogs are allowed in the Wildflower Trail Area, but 500 feet up McCaffrey Lane, you and your pet can rejoin the hike by turning right (east) onto DeCamp Trail.

2.8 The red-blazed trail passes out through the hurricane fence. Turn right (northeast) onto the DeCamp Trail, named for the man who built this trail with a pick and shovel. You are now leaving the red blaze and following the blue-chip stone path. (**FYI:** The red-blazed trail will take you back 0.4 mile to your car/parking lot, skipping the climb to the Tourne.)

2.9 The blue-chip stone path ascends, snaking its way up the Tourne, passing a series of strategically placed benches frequented by cozy bench sitters and a few readers.

3.0 The trail climbs up onto Hogback (yes, the official name), a geological feature where the stronger tilted stratum resists erosion while the weaker stratum erodes, therefore creating ravines. Worthy of a peek.

3.3 Just prior to the peak the trees open up with a background view of the Manhattan skyline and, in the foreground, a simple 9/11 Memorial Garden anchored by a large slab of puddingstone. Plaques with images of the Twin Towers (before and after), American flags, a teddy bear, a wreath, and a fresh bouquet of flowers make this a most moving tribute. The photos of individual firemen screwed to the trunks of trees only add to the poignancy. The Empire State Building (southeast) can be identified.

3.4 Arrive at the top of the Tourne. Picnic tables and a large open space with views to the southwest invite you to kick back. Bring a book, a lunch, or a Frisbee. Trail continues over the top, descending along the shoulder of the Tourne with panoramic views of the Highlands.

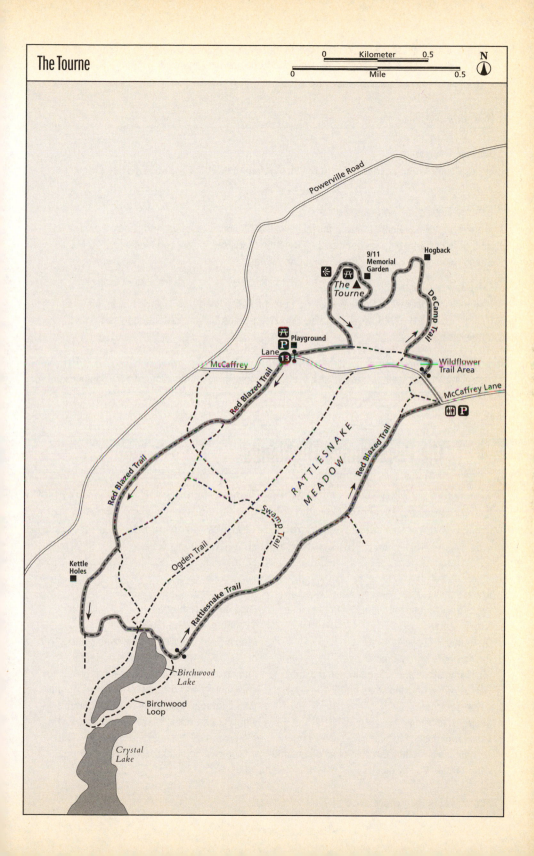

The Tourne

0 Kilometer 0.5
0 Mile 0.5

N

Powerville Road

9/11 Memorial Garden

Hogback

The Tourne

DeCamp Trail

Playground

Lane

McCaffrey

13

Red Blazed Trail

Wildflower Trail Area

McCaffrey Lane

Red Blazed Trail

RATTLESNAKE MEADOW

Red Blazed Trail

Swamp Trail

Kettle Holes

Ogden Trail

Rattlesnake Trail

Birchwood Lake

Birchwood Loop

Crystal Lake

3.5 At a triangular intersection cut back to the right onto the red-blazed trail, which winds its way back to the parking lot, passing picnic tales and a playground.

3.7 Arrive back at the trailhead parking lot.

Hike Information

Local Information

Morris County Visitor's Center, 6 Court Street, Morristown 07960; (973) 631-5151; www.morris tourism.org

Local Events/Attractions

The historic town of Boonton has a museum, walking tours, restaurants, and shops; Boonton Town Hall; (973) 402-9410; www.boonton.org. Boonton Historical Society and Museum, 210 Main Street, Boonton; (973) 402-8840; www.boonton.org

Organizations

New York–New Jersey Trail Conference, 156 Ramapo Valley Road (U.S. Highway 202), Mahwah 07430; (201) 512-9348; www.nynjtc.org. Mountain Lakes Environmental Commission, www .mtnlakes.org

Other Resources

"The History of the Tourne," by Jean Ricker, a great background introduction, at www.mtnlakes.org/ History/Histourne.htm

14 The Pequannock Highlands

This ramble in Silas Condict Park, with three short climbs, leads to a nice viewpoint looking over the Pequannock Valley. The hike abounds with glacial erratics and a small, charming lake. Stroll through the picnic groves and around the "Casino," allegedly a former speakeasy. This is a short hike that goes a long way.

Start: Parking lot off William Arthur Lewis Drive (first parking lot on left) in front of the Maintenance Center

Distance: 3.1-mile lollipop

Approximate hiking time: 2 hours

Difficulty: Moderate, with a few sharp climbs

Trail surface: Chipped stone paths and a few paved stretches

Seasons: All good

Other trail users: Multiuse

Canine compatibility: Leashed dogs permitted.

Land status: County park

Nearest town: Butler

Fees and permits: None

Schedule: Dawn to dusk

Maps: *DeLorme: New Jersey Atlas & Gazetteer* p. 25; USGS Newfoundland, NJ, quadrangle. A map is also available at the park or online at www.morrisparks.org/parks/trails/silastr.htm.

Trail contacts: Morris County Park Commission, 53 East Hanover Avenue, PO Box 1295, Morristown 07962-1295; (973) 326-7600; info@parks.morris.nj.us; www.parks.morris .nj.us/

Finding the trailhead: From the intersection of Route 23 and Kinnelon Road (County Route 618) in Butler, proceed west on Kinnelon Road. After passing the Mount Evergreen Cemetery and traveling 1.1 miles, turn right into Silas Condict County Park on William Lewis Arthur Drive. At 0.2 mile arrive at the parking lot on the left side for straight-in parking. The lot is just prior to the entrance to the county park's maintenance center.

The Hike

The glacial geology of the Highlands is everywhere in evidence on this walk. Exposed bedrock testifies to the force of the three glaciers that passed over these mountains during the last 100,000 years. Huge puddingstone boulders dropped here and there like toys similarly tell of the ice-age journey of the ice sheet, and the rocks it picked up like curios and left behind as it retreated a hundred centuries ago.

But the hike also tells of a more genteel history. Silas Condict Park was originally the Canty estate, one of many in this area of Morris County in the early 1900s. At that time, estates often featured a separate building just for entertaining. Such buildings were often architecturally ornate and included features like a dance floor or a bandstand. These entertainment buildings were in the tradition of the English banqueting hall, or the contemporary Italian custom of the "little house" near the main house, called the casina. In English, this was generally rendered "casino," even though gambling wasn't necessarily involved.

Savor the Pequannock Highlands from a scenic overlook.

The "Casino" at Silas Condict Park (which we pass on this hike) was one such structure, originally serving the Canty estate. With its mahogany bar, bandstand, murals, ornate woodwork, and mirrors, the handsome stone building radiated charm and fun (and still does). In the 1920s it became the site of one of the area's more famous Prohibition-era speakeasies. Restored to its historic splendor by the Morris County Park Commission in the 1990s, the Casino is a popular place for weddings and special events.

Perhaps the best part of this walk is the spectacular views of the Pequannock River valley. Route 23, the main artery through the valley, is an important commuter and commercial traffic road. Lots of people never see the Pequannock valley from any other perspective, but this hike changes all that. Like an eagle, you can rest in your aerie here and contemplate the scene far, far below.

Miles and Directions

0.0 Proceed (west) through the maintenance yard and head to the northwest corner of the lot where the woods road begins. The trail immediately ascends.

0.3 Trail crests, and to the left (west) are informal paths leading to bedrock viewpoint.

0.35 After a short descent, the trail passes a side trail on left (west), leading to picnic tables and another bedrock vista.

0.4 Pass another trail on the left (west), leading to picnic tables.

0.45 Trail descends into a parking lot. Head straight (north) through the lot with the lake on the left (west).

0.6 At the sign for the boat rentals, group shelter, restrooms, and ball field, turn left (west) and take the macadam road behind the stone building (The Casino), heading west toward the ball field.

0.7 Proceed between the backstop and the lake, heading out to center field where the trail begins at the opening in the woods line.

0.8 At the fork turn right (northwest) and begin to ascend.

1.1 Arrive at crest. Side trail leads to peak (1,012 feet) with seasonal views while a second trail leads east to a picnic grove.

1.2 During the descent (north), the trail makes a sharp right turn (east-southeast) and continues down.

1.3 Pass a trail on right, which leads to a picnic grove.

1.5 Trail ends at a large puddingstone boulder, a macadam road, and parking lot. Turn left (east) onto the gravel path, traveling 80 feet, veering left (northeast) and descend on a path through another picnic area.

1.8 The trail descends to viewpoint (920-foot elevation) sporting a bench. From here, retrace (southwest) the hike back to the puddingstone boulder at the edge of the parking lot.

2.1 From the puddingstone boulder, edge (south) the west side of the parking lot till, reaching stone steps midpoint at the edge of the lot. Turn right (west), climbing the stairs into the picnic grove.

2.2 Pass trail on right (north).

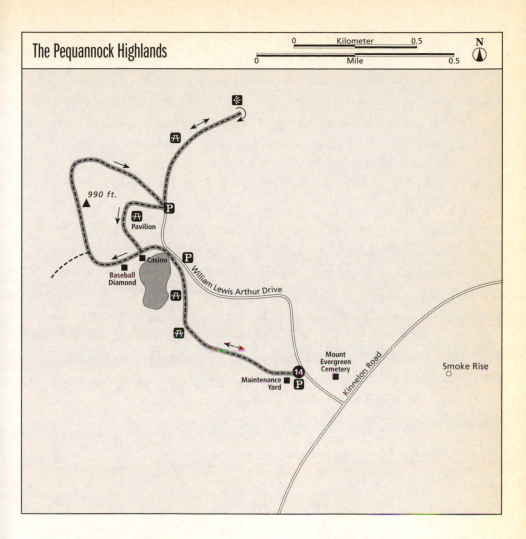

The Pequannock Highlands

990 ft.

Pavilion

Casino

Baseball Diamond

William Lewis Arthur Drive

Maintenance Yard

Mount Evergreen Cemetery

Kinnelon Road

Smoke Rise

2.3 Pass cedar block building on right (west). Pass trail on right (west) and descend on gravel path, ending at paved road. (**FYI:** Side trail leads to the 1,012-foot peak.)

2.4 Descend onto a macadam road, heading straight (south) for the back of The Casino. At The Casino turn left (east) onto the path between the water fountain (left) and the lake (right).

2.5 Arrive at the kiosk in front of The Casino and retrace the route from 0.6 back to trailhead.

3.1 Arrive in parking lot.

Hike Information

Local Information

Morris County Visitor's Center, 6 Court Street, Morristown 07960; (973) 631-5151; www.morris tourism.org

A WORKHORSE OF THE REVOLUTION

In times of war and turmoil, some people get to be heroes without ever dodging a bullet; Silas Condict was such a man. Born in Morristown in 1738, he was a farmer and surveyor, with large landholdings in Morris County. But he was an ardent patriot, too, and lent his hand to political causes. He was on the committee that drafted the state constitution, and in 1776 became his county's representative in the state legislature. In 1777–78, he served on the Revolutionary Council of Safety, and from 1781 to 1784 he was a member of the Continental Congress.

Condict's home in Morristown was the site of numerous meetings during the Revolution, and for his wisdom he was commonly called "Counselor" Condict. After the Revolution, he was elected to the New Jersey Assembly eight times, serving as speaker twice, as well as serving as Morris County justice of the peace and judge. He had no children of his own but adopted his deceased brother's sons. One of them, Lewis Condict (1773–1862), was a congressman and prominent physician who promoted early efforts at smallpox vaccination.

Silas Condict died in 1801, one of Morris County's busiest and most ardent patriots of the Revolution. His home in Morristown was torn down a century ago, but Silas Condict Park, dedicated in 1964, helps preserve his name and accomplishments.

15 Saffin Pond and Headley Overlook

This trek in Mahlon Dickerson Reservation is a typical Highlands hike through the ore belt. You will pass Saffin Pond twice, traverse the bottomlands, cross numerous brooks, and climb to Headley Outlook with views of Lake Hopatcong. Enjoy the variety of treadways: woods roads, rail beds, and mountain trails. There is also a good option to make the hike longer if you so desire.

Start: Saffin Pond parking lot on Weldon Road
Distance: 5.0-mile figure-eight
Approximate hiking time: 3 hours
Difficulty: Moderate
Trail surface: Treadways, woods roads, rail beds, and mountain trails
Seasons: All
Other trail users: Multiuse
Canine compatibility: Leashed dogs permitted
Land status: County reservation
Nearest town: Hurdtown
Fees and permits: None

Schedule: Dawn to dusk
Maps: *DeLorme: New Jersey Atlas & Gazetteer*, p.24; USGS Dover, NJ, and Franklin, NJ, quadrangles. A map is also available at the reservation or online at www.morrisparks.org/parks/directions/mahlondir.htm.
Trail contacts: Morris County Park Commission, 53 East Hanover Avenue, PO Box 1295, Morristown 07962-1295; (973) 326-7600; info@parks.morris.nj.us; www.parks.morris.nj.us/
Other: This is largest element of the Morris County park system.

Finding the trailhead: From Interstate 80 take exit 34 for Route 15 north and travel approximately 4 miles. Exit onto Weldon Road (leading to Milton) and travel north 3.0 miles to Saffin Pond parking lot located on the right (east) side of the road.

The Hike

This hike brings together a number of Highlands themes: iron, railroads, and canals. Thus it's no surprise that this park was named after Mahlon Dickerson, who was involved with all three. Dickerson (1770–1853) was a Morris County lawyer, writer, businessman, and politician. Few men in the history of the state filled as many roles as he, including virtually every office from legislator and Supreme Court judge to governor and U.S. senator. The family business was iron mines, and Dickerson named his hilltop Morris County estate "Ferromonte"—Iron Mountain.

Dickerson would probably be happy that the county park named after him includes some of the old Ogden Mine Railroad. Our hike starts out on the rail bed of this once-important railroad, built in 1865. It shipped iron and zinc ore from Sussex County to Nolans Point on Lake Hopatcong. Lake Hopatcong had been dammed and raised to feed the Morris Canal—with its numerous locks and inclined planes, it was a "thirsty" canal that needed a vast water supply. Loaded onto boats, the ore was tugged across the lake to the Morris Canal, where it was shipped out by canal boat.

A huge tonnage of ore was shipped this way (over 70,000 tons in 1873 alone). Dickerson would be happy about this, too: The construction of the Morris Canal was a project he advocated while governor. This unique system of shipping (railroad/lake/canal) worked for years.

But in 1881, the Central Railroad of New Jersey acquired and connected with the Ogden Mine Railroad, ending the canal use. The loss in revenue to the canal was but another blow in its long decline. In later years, the Ogden Mine Railroad shipped out the zinc briquettes produced by Thomas A. Edison's famous concentrating works near Ogdensburg. By the late 1940s, however, the line saw little use and was scrapped.

Today, the pleasures of Saffin Pond, the Highlands Trail, Headley Overlook, jungles of mountain laurel, and other rugged beauties of the Highlands make it easy to forget what a hotbed of transportation, industry, and commerce these now-peaceful hills once were.

Miles and Directions

0.0   Start in the Saffin Pond parking lot. Trail begins in the west side of the lot behind the directory. Turn left (southwest) onto the Ogden Mine Railroad Bed (yellow blazes), edging the western shore of Saffin Pond.

0.3   At the end of Saffin Pond turn left (east) onto the Highlands Trail (teal diamonds), leaving the railroad bed. The Highlands Trail crosses over the dam and the Weldon Brook spillway.

0.4   At the end of the dam, veer right (southeast) at the fork, following the Highlands Trail down a blue chip stone path, which will shortly begin to ascend through hardwood forest. (**FYI:** Trail veering left [teal with a black dot] returns to the Saffin Pond parking lot.)

0.6   Turn right (southwest) at the T intersection, continuing to follow the Highlands Trail while eventually hiking the edge of the uplands and the wetlands.

1.1   The trail veers left (east) at the fork, while an unofficial trail leaves right. (FYI: A 3-foot by 3-foot canal or channel runs the left side [north] of the trail. It's thought to have been used during times of drought to fill the millpond.)

1.6   Cross a brook on bridge and meander through the hollow.

1.8   The trail turns left (north) at the T intersection while the Beaver Brook Trail (white blazes) heads south. (**FYI:** This junction is not as clear as it could be; the intersection comes 80 feet after a massive glacial erratic topped by ferns.)

1.9   Cross brook on talus and continue trek through the bottomland.

2.0   Cross brook on "bridge" and begin to ascend onto the shoulder of hill (1,260-foot elevation) and above the hollow, passing split rocks and over talus.

2.2   Trail descends through boulder field just before crossing brook.

2.5   Trail crosses a yellow-blazed woods road. Continue straight (southeast) on the Highlands Trail, ascending out along the edge of the ridge. A series of short informal paths lead to viewpoints.

2.7   Trail descends into a saddle and ascends through cavernous mountain laurel and emerges onto the Headley Overlook with 180-degree view. To the east, Bowling Green Mountain (a former ski area) is visible. To the south is Weldon Brook Wildlife Management Area. To the

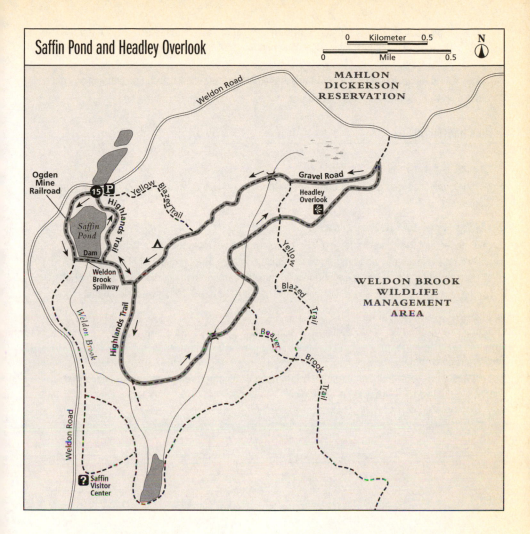

Saffin Pond and Headley Overlook

0   Kilometer   0.5

0   Mile   0.5

N

MAHLON
DICKERSON
RESERVATION

Weldon Road

Gravel Road

Headley
Overlook

Ogden
Mine
Railroad

15 P

Yellow Blazed Trail

Highlands Trail

Saffin
Pond

Dam

Weldon
Brook
Spillway

Weldon Brook

Highlands Trail

Yellow

Blazed

Trail

Beaver

Brook

Trail

WELDON BROOK
WILDLIFE
MANAGEMENT
AREA

Weldon Road

? Saffin
Visitor
Center

southwest is Lake Hopatcong (the largest lake in the Garden State). The trail leaves the northeast corner of the ledge, descending a woods road.

3.0 Make a sharp left turn (southwest) and descend onto a blue-chip stone woods road, leaving the Highlands Trail. The trail is "walled" by mount laurel.

3.4 The woods road dead-ends into the yellow-blazed trail at the fork. Take the right fork (northwest) and descend, passing the camp area.

3.5 Trail crosses bridge over brook and begins to ascend.

3.9 At the fork veer left (west), leaving the yellow-blazed trail. (**Option:** The yellow-blazed trail also leads to the Saffin Pond parking lot.)

4.3 Turn right (northwest) at signage to Saffin Pond and descend onto the Highlands Trail, retracing a short portion of today's trip.

4.5 At the southeast portion of the dam, turn right (northeast) onto the teal-black dot trail, which borders the east shore of Saffin Pond. The trail is rock-root rugged but with beautiful views of the pond.

4.9 Cross a bridge over inlet to pond and immediately pass yellow-blazed trail entering on right.

5.0 Arrive back at Saffin Pond parking lot.

Hike Information

Local Information

Morris County Visitor's Center, 6 Court Street, Morristown 07960; (973) 631-5151; www.morris tourism.org

Local Events/Attractions

Lake Hopatcong, New Jersey's largest lake, offers a variety of recreational, cultural, and dining opportunities, which can be found at www.lkhopatcong.com. The Sterling Hill Mining Museum offers tours of an actual zinc mine and related museum and equipment displays: Sterling Hill Mining Museum, 30 Plant Street, Ogdensburg 07439; (973) 209-7212; www.sterlinghill.org

Lodging

Camping is available in Mahlon Dickerson Reservation; call (973) 663-0200.

Organizations

New York–New Jersey Trail Conference, 156 Ramapo Valley Road (U.S. Highway 202), Mahwah 07430; (201) 512-9348; www.nynjtc.org

16 Schooley's Mountain

What a great hike! This circular trail allows you to climb nearly 400 feet before it ambles along woods roads. It edges George Lake and eventually crosses it on a 470-foot floating bridge. The ramble descends, steeply at times, along the cascading Electric Brook with its pools and marvelous waterfalls (seasonal). You'll climb back up along the Old Rock Quarry with its overlook, which provides a vantage point to view Long Valley. The multiple-trailhead parking lot was chosen so you would also be able to jump on the Columbia Trail if you need more to explore.

Start: Langdon Palmer Fishing Area parking lot off Fairview Avenue
Distance: 3.5-mile loop
Approximate hiking time: 2 hours
Difficulty: Moderate
Trail surface: Woods and mine roads, hiking trails, and a floating bridge
Seasons: Best in spring through fall
Other trail users: Multiuse
Canine compatibility: Leashed dogs permitted
Land status: County park
Nearest town: Long Valley
Fees and permits: None
Schedule: Dawn to dusk

Maps: *DeLorme: New Jersey Atlas & Gazetteer* p. 29; USGS Hackettstown, NJ, quadrangle; a map is also available at the park or online at www.morrisparks.org/parks/directions/ schooleysdir.htm
Trail contacts: Morris County Park Commission, 53 East Hanover Avenue, PO Box 1295, Morristown 07962-1295; (973) 326-7600; info@parks.morris.nj.us; www.parks.morris .nj.us/
Special considerations: The falls are icy and dangerous in winter; hence, this hike is not a good choice for cold weather.

Finding the trailhead: From the intersection of County Route 513 and Schooley's Mountain Road (County Route 517) in Long Valley, travel north on Schooley Mountain Road. After going 0.1 mile, turn right onto Fairview Avenue. After leaving the town and traveling 0.8 mile, arrive at the Langdon Palmer Fishing Access Area; parking is on the right.

The Hike

In the days when Saratoga Springs and Newport were the main playgrounds of the rich and famous, New Jersey had its own high-end resort: Schooley's Mountain. According to a nineteenth-century traveling Frenchman, the spa was "one of the most famous resorts in the United States." It was, at least, one of America's earliest summer retreats from the sweltering heat of Philadelphia and New York City. The Lenape Indians knew the mineral springs here as being healthful. Early settlers likewise found the mineral water a tonic, saying it cured many ailments (the water's main mineral ingredient is sodium bicarbonate!).

A resort hotel, the Alpha House, was built in 1795, but it wasn't until a turnpike was built over the mountain in 1806 that business took off. The mineral springs, fine mountain air, and splendid scenery led to construction of other hotels in the 1800s, including the Heath House and the largest of all, Belmont Hall. From June 1 until the leaves fell, it became a haven for writers, politicians, and scientists who cared to debate the ideas of the day. A stagecoach traveled once a day to Hackettstown station to meet the morning train, picking up the hotel patrons and the postage. Just imagine U.S. vice president George M. Dallas (1845–1849), for whom Dallas, Texas, is named, stepping out of a carriage. Or the founder of Chemical National Bank, Cornelius V. S. Roosevelt (Teddy's grandfather), fowling on the mountain. Or Ulysses S. Grant and his daughter strolling the promenade. Or the Vanderbilts and the Edisons watching an in-house theater production. They paid $14.00 to $28.00 a week for accommodations, but people like us, who are here for the day, would pay a fee of $2.50. Folks still flock to Schooley's Mountain for fresh air, great views, and recreation, but the resort hotels long ago vanished.

▶ **During the late Cretaceous period 65 million years ago, a level plain existed where the mountains and hills of New Jersey are now. Over millions of years, this plain eroded to form the current landscape of New Jersey. Geologists call it the Schooley Peneplain, because the largest surviving portion of it is the level summit of Schooley's Mountain here.**

Besides the mineral waters bubbling out from the crag, iron ore was another earthly treasure investors hoped to cash in on. Three ore belts ran northeast through Schooley's Mountain: the Marsh Mine, the Hurd Mine, and the Van Syckle Mine Belt. Starting ca. 1790 and operating intermittently for the next hundred years, prospectors dug more than fifteen mines and exploratory pits in and around the immediate area. The miners excavated 100-foot open pits, dropping 30 to 40 feet, while others created 60-foot shafts, all the while extracting 5,000 to 12,000 tons of magnetite. The state inspectors claimed, "None of the mines ... were what could be considered as large operations, most were prospect explorations at best." It has also been recorded that the magnetic attraction of the ore held onto the miners' tools, making a difficult job more difficult. So as you hike Schooley's Mountain, understand your compasses may go berserk, especially as you pass the two exploratory pits along the route.

Miles and Directions

0.0 Walk back through the entrance to the parking lot (southwest end) and directly cross (northwest) Fairview Avenue. There you will find the Patriots' Path and the Bee-Line Trail signpost. Just beyond the post, the trails split: The Patriots' Path (white blazes) turns left (northwest), and the Bee-Line Trail (no blazes) continues straight (north), the path of choice. The Bee-Line Trail rises up through beach, hickory, oak, and tulip trees.

0.1 At the T intersection turn right (east) onto a woods road, which continues to rise by traversing the slope.

0.3 Leaving the woods road, the trail turns left (north) at a spot with white arrows painted on the tree trunks. The trail eventually swings northwest.

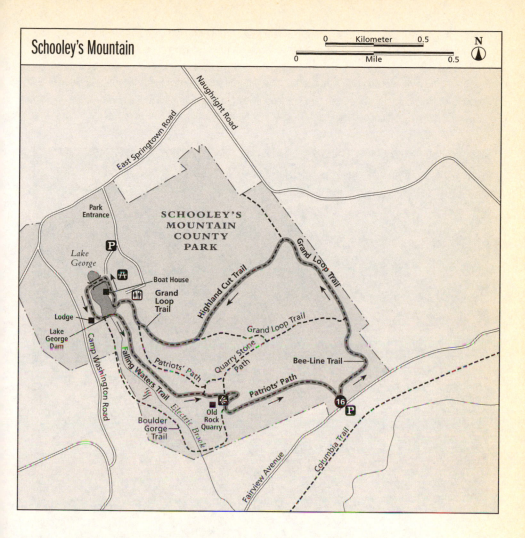

0.5 The trail turns right (east) back onto the woods road and continues to climb.

0.6 Bee-Line Trail ends at the trail intersection for the Grand Loop Trail (yellow blazes). Continue straight (north) onto the Loop, passing the signpost and the Loop segment that goes west. The trail meanders up the hill via a woods road, eventually curving toward the northwest, where you will pass on the right an exploratory iron mine pit.

0.9 Turn left (west) onto the Highland Cut Trail (red blazes), which runs along the edge of the slope, passing on the right another exploratory iron mine pit. The Grand Loop Trail continues to a picnic area.

1.4 Highland Cut Trail ends at the T intersection. Turn right (west) onto the Grand Loop Trail, a woods road.

1.6 Continue straight, passing the Patriots' Path on the left (west), which now becomes co-aligned with the Grand Loop Trail.

1.7 At the signpost, restrooms, and macadam road, turn left (west) onto a gravel road, which heads down to Lake George, passing an amphitheater (seasonally, a sledding area) on the left.

1.9 At the T intersection turn right (north) onto a gravel path and circumnavigate Lake George.

2.0 After passing the boathouse turn left (southwest), descending the steps and onto the boardwalk, which leads to the 470-foot floating bridge. Cross it and Lake George.

Electric Brook cascades off the shoulder of Schooley's Mountain.

2.1 After disembarking from the floats, proceed straight up through the row of trees and turn left (southeast) onto a grassy path across an open area, staying along the edge of Lake George.

2.2 After passing a trail on the right (west), which leads to the Lodge, the trail turns to gravel and descends to Lake George Dam. Cross (east) the bridge over the outlet to Electric Brook.

2.3 Turn right (south) onto the Falling Waters Trail (blue blazes), where the trail begins to descend along Electric Brook and a series of cascades and pools.

2.6 After scrambling down a massive outcrop, the trail arrives at the falls.

2.7 The trail swings left (southeast), leaving the quarry road to descend on the other side of a fence and private property signs. The Falling Waters Trail begins to climb to the top of the quarry.

2.8 Falling Waters Trail ends at the T intersection. Turn right (southwest) onto the Patriots' Path (white blazes). Within 50 feet you are above the overlook. (**Side trip:** Turn right again onto a herd path, which leads to a point over the quarry and the view of Long Valley and the Fox Hill Range.)

2.9 The Patriots' Path leaves the overlook by swinging east and then traversing southwest along the edge of the quarry with some awesome views of the cliffs. Be sure to look back.

3.1 As the trail gradually descends, pass the Boulder Gorge Trail on the right (south). (**Side trip:** If you need to see the falls from the other side of Electric Brook, take the Boulder Gorge Trail; this is a mile round-trip.)

3.5 At the junction with the Bee-Line Trail, turn right (south) and cross Fairview Avenue and into the parking lot.

Hike Information

Local Information
Warren County Tourism Web site: www.warrencountychamber.org. Washington Township Web site: www.washtwpmorris.org. Morris County Visitor's Center, 6 Court Street, Morristown 07960; (973) 631-5151; www.morristourism.org

Local Events/Attractions
The historic village of Hackettstown, the county seat of Warren County, offers a variety of shops and restaurants; www.hackettstown.net

Restaurants
Long Valley Brewery and Pub offers distinctive dining in a restored stone barn; longvalleypubandbrewery.com/index.shtml

Organizations
New York–New Jersey Trail Conference, 156 Ramapo Valley Road (U.S. Highway 202), Mahwah 07430; (201) 512-9348; www.nynjtc.org

17 Terrace Pond

There is one word to describe this outing: "treasure." This splendid loop hike has a glacial lake setting rimmed by pitch pine-scrub oak forest. After a moderate climb, passing through glacial bogs, the trail traverses open ridges (magnificent northern views), slabbing at times, and descending along a pipeline before ducking back into a hemlock-mixed hardwood forest. None of the ledges are more than 20 feet high, but they need to be negotiated. We also find the puddingstone, a sandstone conglomerate that looks like an ancient, crude version of concrete, a special feature of this trek.

Start: Terrace Pond Trail parking area on Clinton Road
Distance: 5.1-mile loop
Approximate hiking time: 3.5 hours
Difficulty: Strenuous, with some rocky ascents
Trail surface: Rocky hiking trail, ledge rock, and pipeline
Seasons: Spring through fall best; could be dangerous in winter
Other trail users: Hikers
Canine compatibility: Dogs not permitted in natural area
Land status: State park natural area
Nearest town: Upper Greenwood Lake
Fees and permits: None

Schedule: Dawn to dusk
Maps: *DeLorme: New Jersey Atlas & Gazetteer* p.20; USGS Wawayanda, NJ, quadrangle; New York–New Jersey Trail Conference *North Jersey Trails Map 21;* a hiking map is also available at the park office.
Trail contacts: Wawayanda State Park, 885 Warwick Turnpike, Hewitt 07421; (973) 853-4462; wsp@warwick.net; www.njparksand forests.org
Special considerations: Both of New Jersey's venomous snakes, the timber rattlesnake and the copperhead, live in this area. Keep your eyes open.

Finding the trailhead: From Route 23, take the exit for Clinton Road near Newfoundland. Take Clinton Road approximately 7 miles north, passing Clinton Reservoir on your left. The parking lot for the Terrace Pond North and South trails is on your left, while the trails are on the right. *Caution:* The parking area is easy to miss. If you start seeing signs of civilization (like houses and lakes), you've gone too far.

The Hike

Terrace Pond, a limpid jewel on the rock-ribbed summit of Bearfort Mountain, is part of the 1,325-acre Bearfort Mountain Natural Area in Wawayanda State Park. A natural glacial tarn, its beauty and isolation have made it a popular spot for decades. It makes for one of New Jersey's great hikes.

Perhaps because of its profound solitude, or perhaps because it's off the infamous Clinton Road, a body of folklore and legend has grown up around Terrace Pond. Clinton Road once went to the village of Clinton, which was destroyed to make way for Clinton Reservoir. In recent decades, a number of interesting sites along the road have attracted the adventuresome—at least those willing to trespass. Clinton Furnace, an historic iron furnace, and Cross Castle, the ruins of an old estate (since demolished) generated legends of "druid" temples and gothic ruins. Other legends followed: UFOs, ghosts, etc., all documented by the cult-hit magazine *Weird NJ*.

Terrace Pond shared in this rich body of baby-boomer mythology, which included tales of wild bonfire parties, swimming au naturel, sightings of ghostly park rangers and unexplained lights in the sky, and sundry other supernatural, psychedelic, parapsychological, or substance-abuse-related phenomena. But be warned: The rangers you'll see aren't spectral, but of the real, law-enforcing, summons-writing variety. The State Park Police and Pequannock Watershed Police both patrol frequently, and swimmers, campers, and other rule-breakers will get ticketed. For real.

In truth, Terrace Pond needs no bizarre mythology to make it worth visiting. It's magical and spectacular entirely on its own and is designated an official State Natural Area.

Miles and Directions

0.0 From the parking lot, cross (southeast) Clinton Road where the trailheads are located. There you will find triple blazing for both the Terrace Pond North (blue blazes) and Terrace Pond South (yellow blazes). Both trails are co-aligned for 20 feet. At the fork bear right (south) onto Terrace Pond South. The left fork will be the return route, so make a mental note.

Terrace Pond is held in winter solitude.

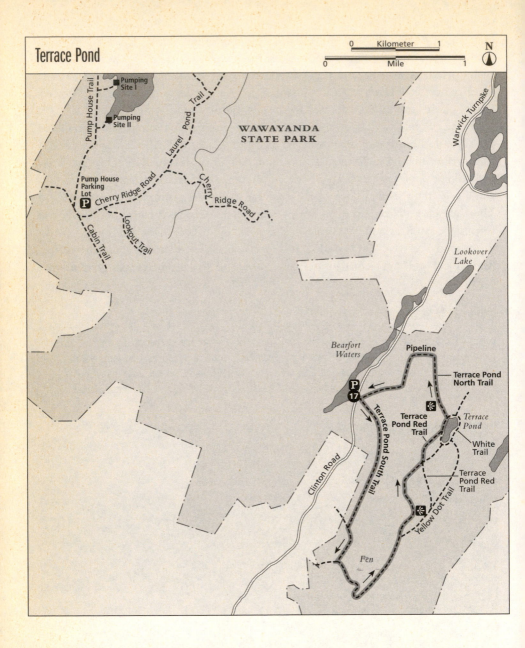

1.1 At the T intersection with a woods road, turn left (south) onto the road where the trail crosses through a series of stone fences.

1.6 At a junction with a woods road, turn sharply left (east) onto the road (yellow blazes) and descend through a fen. This section can be very wet due to beaver activity!

2.3 At the fork, bear left (north), remaining on the Terrace Pond South Trail. (**FYI:** The Yellow Dot Trail veers right, leading to the east side of Terrace Pond.)

2.9 Ascend and crest onto a ridge of puddingstone. Be sure to move to the very top (northeast) for a tranquil view (south) of the surrounding forest. The trail slightly drops to the north, staying on the ridge. Yellow blazes will be found on the outcrop.

3.1 Near the top of the ridge reach the junction with the Terrace Pond Red (red blazes). Turn left (northeast) onto it where it is co-aligned with Terrace Pond South (yellow). Within 70 feet arrive at a fork and bear left (northeast), remaining on the Terrace Pond Red. (**FYI:** Terrace Pond South veers right [east], leading to the south end of Terrace Pond.)

3.4 Arrive at a series of ridges where you will scramble up and down. Using your hands will be required.

3.5 At the T intersection with the White Trail (white blazes), turn left (northeast) onto it and ascend through the boulders to the top of the ridge.

3.6 Arrive at the outcrop 25 feet above picturesque Terrace Pond, an ideal spot for a break. The trail continues north, edging the pond and crossing a series of viewpoints overlooking the pond. (**FYI:** Be warned: It is a popular spot, so it could be crowded on weekends. Also, swimming is not allowed. In the 1960s and '70s, this was a natural swimming hole.)

3.8 At the northeast end of Terrace Pond, veer left (north) onto the Terrace Pond North (blue blazes), leaving the White Trail.

4.0 Arrive at one of the finest panoramic views in New Jersey. (**FYI:** Spot the Kittatinny, the Catskill, and the Shawangunk Mountains.) The trail continues to slab and scramble over a series of ridges. None of the ledges are more than 15 to 20 feet high, but they need to be negotiated.

4.3 At the junction with the pipeline, the Terrace Pond North turns left (west) onto the pipeline and descends in a free-for-all fashion down the loose rock.

4.5 After passing three unofficial paths leaving left, the Terrace Pond North turns left (southwest) onto a woods road by a massive 50-foot-tall eastern hemlock. The trail meanders through some fens and pine groves.

5.1 The Terrace Pond North converges with the Terrace Pond South and leads northwest directly to the trailhead and parking lot.

Hike Information

Local Information

New Jersey Skylands Region Tourism Guide; www.njskylands.com

Local Events/Attractions

For those with offbeat inclinations, a drive down Clinton Road is required—tales of witches, UFOs, and other oddities abound along this remote stretch of highway. Check out the stories at Weird NJ; www.weirdnj.com/stories/_roads02.asp. Be forewarned, however: Though the tales of mystery and terror may be figments of the imagination, the Pequannock Watershed police are very real and issue summonses for trespassing. Obey all laws.

Organizations

New York–New Jersey Trail Conference, 156 Ramapo Valley Road (U.S. Highway 202), Mahwah 07430; (201) 512-9348; www.nynjtc.org

18 Wyanokie High Point

Known as Little Switzerland, this loop in Norvin Green State Forest will surprise you! Some of the climbs are quite steep, but the views off Carris Hill and High Point are definitely worth the effort. Plan to sit by the Wyanokie and Chikahoki Falls. The circuit also skirts two nineteenth-century iron mines: the Blue and the Roomy; the latter one you can actually enter and explore. As the route borders the Wanaque Reservoir, there is a sense of "wilderness" about it. This is a long trek, so plan on an early start, which will allow you to explore the mine and enjoy the vistas.

Start: Weis Ecology Center parking lot on Snake Den Road
Distance: 6.8-mile loop
Approximate hiking time: 4 to 5 hours
Difficulty: Strenuous
Trail surface: Rocky trails and mine roads
Seasons: Spring through fall are best.
Other trail users: Multiuse
Canine compatibility: Dogs not permitted on Weis Ecology Center property; otherwise, leashed dogs permitted
Land status: State forest
Nearest town: Ringwood

Fees and permits: None
Schedule: Dawn to dusk
Maps: *DeLorme: New Jersey Atlas & Gazetteer* p.25; USGS Wanaque, NJ, quadrangle; New York-New Jersey Trail Conference *North Jersey Trails Map 21*
Trail contacts: Ringwood State Park, 1304 Sloatsburg Road, Ringwood 07456-1799; www.state.nj.us/dep/parksandforests/parks/norvin.html
Other: It's worthwhile to stop in at the interpretive center and pick up handouts and materials on flora, fauna, and history.

Finding the trailhead: From the intersection of Route 23 and Echo Lake Road (County Route 695) in Newfoundland, travel northeast on Echo Lake Road. At the T intersection turn left onto Macopin Road, passing West Milford High School (on right). After driving 1.5 miles, turn right (east) onto Westbrook Road and travel 5 miles. Turn right (south) onto Snake Den Road (Warning: You will have passed earlier a Snake Den Road, but these roads are no longer connected). At 0.3 mile, bear left (north) at the fork, staying with Snake Den Road. At 0.4 mile Weis Ecology Center's parking lot is on the right.

The Hike

This hike gives you the chance to do something pretty rare—explore a real, historic iron mine in safety. The Roomy Mine (probably named after a local family, originally spelled Roome) was also known as the Laurel or the Red Mine and operated from 1840 to 1857. With a flashlight, some protective headgear (or a hard head), and good boots, you can crawl through the opening and into a horizontal shaft cut 100 feet into the solid rock of the mountain. The only hazards you'll face are mud and the occasional bat (harmless). Drill holes visible in the rock testify to the hard work of mining by hammer, drill, and blasting powder. (*FYI:* The mine is closed [it's the law] between September 1 and April 30, while the bats hibernate.)

The nearby Blue Mine (aka the London, Iron Hill, or Whynockie Mine) is much older, having been opened by German iron entrepreneur Peter Hasenclever in 1765. It operated intermittently until 1905, when it closed for good. But unlike the Roomy Mine, the Blue Mine is today little more than a great flooded hole in the ground.

This hike may get you to thinking: Is it Wyanokie, Wanaque, Whynockie, or what? The original Native American Lenape name for the region was something like "Wah-NAH-kay" or "Why-hah-NAH-key." As with so many native words, there are variant opinions on its meaning: "rest and repose," says one source, "place of sassafras," say a number of others. It appears the first European to write down the name was a Frenchman, who rendered it phonetically in French: "Wa-na-que." Ever after, the name has frequently been pronounced "Wanna-cue," even though old-timers will insist it's "Wa-NA-key." And there are myriad other spellings: Wynokie, Wynocky, Wynoky, Wynockie . . .

Crawling out from the Blue Mine.

Miles and Directions

0.0 Exit the parking lot and turn left (east) and proceed along the shoulder of Snake Den Road. Just prior to Ellen Street (left), turn right onto Wyanokie Circular (red blazes) and the Mine Trail (yellow blazes), passing park signage. The trail leads down under spruce with backyards on either side.

0.3 As rock ledges build on the left, carefully look for the double yellow turn blazes on the tree. Turn right (southwest) onto the Mine Trail, leaving the co-aligned existence with the Wyanokie Circular.

0.4 Pick your way down off the ridge and rock-hop across the Blue Mine Brook, immediately ascending the ridge on the far side.

0.7 Rock-hop across Blue Mine Brook and the top of Wyanokie Falls.

0.8 At the intersection, cross (east) Wyanokie Circular and ascend the ridge, then swing north.

1.0 Arrive at the peak of Ball Mountain and enjoy the view west. The trail crosses the top and turns right (south), where it runs the ridge.

1.4 Cross a series of peaks with an impressive view west. At the end of the ridge turn sharply right (west), and descend (northwest).

1.5 At the trail junction with the Roomy Mine Trail (signage: MINE) our route continues straight. (**Side trip:** Turn right [northeast] onto the Roomy Mine Trail [orange blaze] and explore the Roomy Mine, one of the highlights of this hike! A 150-foot jaunt will take you to the mouth of the mine, one of the few in New Jersey that can be safely explored with caution.)

1.6 Arrive at the landing in front of the Roomy Mine and the junction with the Connection Trail (orange blazes). Turn sharply left (southwest) onto a rocky path, descending on the Mine Trail. (**Side trip:** Turn right [east] and explore the Roomy Mine.)

1.6 At the T intersection turn left (south) onto the Wyanokie Circular, a woods road. Note the route is co-aligned with the Mine Trail.

1.8 Turn right (southwest) and cross the wooden bridge over the Blue Mine Brook and ascend the bank and through a campsite. (**Side trip:** Continue straight on the mine road, paralleling the brook, and come to the entrance to the Blue Mine.)

2.0 At the fork bear left (west) onto the Wyanokie Circular. (**Bail-out:** Veer right onto the Mine Trail. Joined with the Otter-Hole-Trail (green blazes), it brings you back to the parking lot.)

2.1 Turn left (south) onto the Lower Trail (white blazes). (**Bail-out:** Continue straight [west] on the Wyanokie Circular and pick up the hike at High Point.)

3.4 Continue straight (south) on the Lower Trail, passing the junction with the Carris Trail (yellow blazes) on the right.

3.5 Turn right (northwest) onto the Post Brook Trail (white blazes). There is signage for Chikahoki Falls.

3.7 Arrive at the Chikahoki Falls and begin to ascend (northwest) above the falls.

3.8 At the fork veer right (north) onto the Hewitt Butler Trail and begin a steady climb.

4.8 Reach Carris Hill and bear left (northwest) off the peak, staying on the Hewitt Butler Trail (blue blazes). The Carris Trail comes in on the right (south).

5.6 At the junction, the Hewitt Butler Trail becomes co-aligned with the Wyanokie Circular. Continue straight (northeast), crossing a hollow and then ascending the shoulder of High Point.

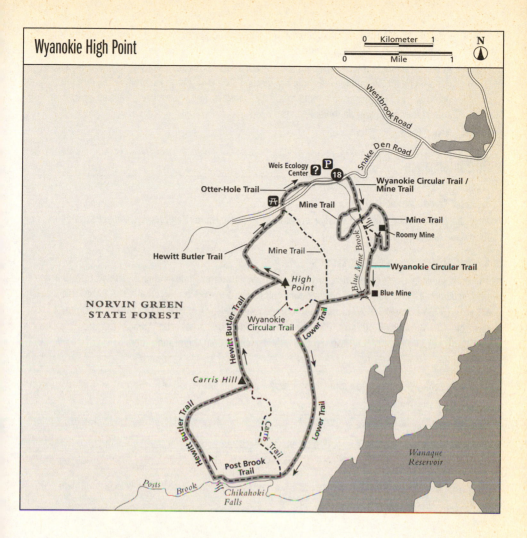

0 Kilometer **1**

0 Mile **1**

N

Westbrook Road

Snake Den Road

Weis Ecology Center

P 18

Otter-Hole Trail

Wyanokie Circular Trail / Mine Trail

Mine Trail

Mine Trail

Roomy Mine

Hewitt Butler Trail

Mine Trail

Blue Mine Brook

Wyanokie Circular Trail

High Point

Wyanokie Circular Trail

Blue Mine

NORVIN GREEN STATE FOREST

Hewitt Butler Trail

Lower Trail

Carris Hill

Carris Trail

Lower Trail

Hewitt Butler Trail

Wanaque Reservoir

Post Brook Trail

Posts Brook

Chikahoki Falls

5.7 At the fork bear left (north) solely onto the Hewitt Butler Trail, running the ridge with a northeast-facing vista. (**Side trip:** Veer right [southeast] onto the Wyanokie Circular and steeply climb to the bare top of High Point, one of the best views in New Jersey!)

6.0 At the fork veer right (north), continuing to follow the Hewitt Butler Trail, which climbs to an outlook before dropping down. The left fork is the Macopin Trail (white blazes).

6.3 At the trail junction, the Mine Trail, entering on the right (south), becomes co-aligned with the Hewitt Butler Trail. Continue straight (east) on the trail. (You are now on a relocated section.)

6.4 Arrive at a kiosk. Cross the woods road and onto the Otter-Hole Trail (green blazes), which in this final section is crisscrossed by numerous short trails.

6.5 Cross (northeast) over a wooden bridge and turn right (southeast), continuing to follow the Otter-Hole Trail, which parallels the brook for the rest of the trip.

6.6 Pass the Highlands Natural Pool on your right and the picnic grove on your left, as the trail proceeds under a stand of spruce.

6.7 At the T intersection turn right onto the entrance road to Weis Ecology Center and back to the parking lot where the Otter-Hole Trail ends. (**Side trip:** For the visitor center, turn left onto the road for less than a tenth of a mile. Displays, free maps, live creatures, nature store, restrooms, and an incredible staff await you.)

6.8 Reach the parking lot.

Hike Information

Local Information

AboutNewJersey.com, Ringwood page: www.aboutnewjersey.com/Regions/Gateway/Passaic/Ringwood/index.php

Local Events/Attractions

The Weis Ecology Center, operated by the New Jersey Audubon Society, has a variety of programs and activities as well as guided hikes; Weis Ecology Center, 150 Snake Den Road, Ringwood 07456; (973) 835-2160; www.njaudubon.orgcenters/weis/. The Highlands Natural Pool, an Olympic-size stream-fed outdoor pool, is open seasonally for a cool dip. Adjacent to the Weis Ecology Center and Norvin Green State Forest; www.geocities.com/highlands_pool

Lodging

The Weis Ecology Center offers both cabins and campsites for rental year-round. See their Web site or call (973) 835-2160.

Hike Tours

The Weis Ecology Center offers guided hikes. Contact the center for hike themes and schedules.

Organizations

New York–New Jersey Trail Conference, 156 Ramapo Valley Road (U.S. Highway 202), Mahwah 07430; (201) 512-9348; www.nynjtc.org

WHO WAS NORVIN GREEN?

Our public open spaces often bear the names of people whose significance has been forgotten. Such is the case with Norvin Green State Forest, as few Jerseyans could tell you who he was. In fact, Norvin Hewitt Green (1893–1955) was part of the great Cooper-Hewitt clan that resided at Ringwood Manor from the 1850s to the 1930s. His maternal grandfather was Peter Cooper, the great early inventor and industrialist. Cooper's daughter Sarah married Abram S. Hewitt. Aside from being his son-in-law, Hewitt was also Cooper's business partner in an array of iron-related industries in the region, not to mention mayor of New York City.

The Hewitts' daughter Amy (1856–1922) married Dr. James O. Green (1842–1924) at Ringwood in 1886. Green was himself descended from a notable family. His father Norvin Green (1818–1893) was an early entrepreneur in the telegraph industry. Green Sr. was responsible for organizing several smaller telegraph concerns into one large one, the Western Union Telegraph Company, in 1866. The elder Green was later the first president of the Edison Electric Light Company. His son, James O., was likewise president of Western Union in later years.

Norvin H. Green, born 1893, spent much time at Ringwood with his aunts and uncles, among them Erskine Hewitt, who deeded Ringwood Manor to the state of New Jersey in 1936. Norvin graduated from Columbia College in 1919 and served in the army in World War I. He was involved with a wide variety of business enterprises, including IBM. Locally, he served as both treasurer and mayor of Ringwood. He was also a noted collector of paintings and antiques. After Erskine Hewitt's death, Norvin Green donated the contents of the Ringwood Manor to the state as well, including antique furnishings, paintings, and other collections, ensuring that it would forever be seen as richly and uniquely furnished as it was when the Hewitts occupied it.

In later years, Norvin Green donated over 600 acres of land adjacent to Ringwood State Park, including some of the land that would later bear his name, as a state forest. For these good services, he indeed deserves to be remembered.

19 The Black River

From the nineteenth-century Cooper Mill, hike through Black River County Park, along the banks of the Black River into a hemlock ravine, accented by cascading falls and the romantic stone ruins of a summer cottage. Pass Kays Pond and peer into the gaping hole of the Hacklebarney Mine. This lollipop hike also climbs under hardwoods and loops through meadows, all on railroad grades, woods roads, trails, and the shoulder of a country road. Plan to visit the Kay Environmental Center as well as Cooper Mill.

Start: Cooper Mill and visitor center parking lot on Washington Turnpike

Distance: 8.2-mile lollipop

Approximate hiking time: 4 hours

Difficulty: Moderate

Trail surface: Railroad beds, farm roads, trails, and carriage roads

Seasons: All good

Other trail users: Multiuse

Canine compatibility: No dogs permitted in natural area

Land status: County park and state park

Nearest town: Chester

Fees and permits: Free permit available at the Mill or the Center is needed for the Natural Area.

Schedule: Dawn to dusk

Maps: *DeLorme: New Jersey Atlas & Gazetteer* p.30; USGS Gladstone, NJ, quadrangle; a basic directional map is also available online at www .parks.morris.nj.us/parks/directions/cooper milldir.htm.

Trail contacts: Morris County Park Commission, 53 East Hanover Avenue, PO Box 1295, Morristown 07962-1295; (973) 326-7600; info@parks.morris.nj.us; www.parks.morris .nj.us. Cooper Mill Visitor's Center, 66 Route 513 & State Park Road, Chester 07930; (908) 879-5463

Finding the trailhead: From the intersection of U.S. Highway 206 and Washington Turnpike (County Route 513) in Chester, travel west on Washington Turnpike (CR 513) for 1.2 miles. Turn left into the Cooper Mill and visitor center's parking lot.

The Hike

In the nineteenth century, the Black River Gorge must have been one noisy place. Above the gorge at the Cooper Mill, you would hear the rhythmic splashes of the waterwheel and the ever-present grinding of a 2,000-pound millstone upon the bed-stone. Can you catch the sweet scent of cornmeal as the mill produces 800 pounds an hour? Ready to make spoon bread or hush puppies?

Moving down along the Black River in 1872–73, the clank of picks and hammers rang out as the eighty immigrant Italians laid track for the Hacklebarney Branch of the Central Railroad, a spur connecting the mines with the Chester Branch. During the 1880s, thirty carloads a day rumbled over the very trail you are hiking.

As you continue down the line, the din from the Chester Iron Mining Company's operations could be heard echoing from the Hacklebarney Mine. For the time and place, it was a major iron producer, opening and shutting under the auspices of "supply and demand." From pre–Revolutionary War to 1896, it is estimated that 250,000 tons of ore came out of these hills, peaking at 20,000 tons a year. With about fourteen veins, running 0.5 mile long, there were approximately fourteen open cuts and shafts. The men (it was believed to be bad luck for a woman to be in a mine) worked for 50 cents to a dollar a day in shafts, ranging from 1 to 12 feet wide, 15 to 200 feet high, and 200 feet deep.

On April 24, 1881, the miners would have heard the beckoning knock, knock, knock of a lonely ghost (another miner superstition). The tragedy known as the "Hanging Wall Disaster" struck. A 300-ton roof collapsed, crushing six men and injuring two more. Had it not been Sunday, at least one hundred men would have been in the hole. Mining accidents were all too common.

Besides the mine's open pits (fenced in), the route will take you past tailing piles (mine refuse) and exploratory pits. You may want to refrain from whistling as the miners also felt that it was bad luck.

Entering into the Black River Gorge, the cascading water, pool to pool, should have a natural, soothing sound, especially after all the above "industrial clamor." The mixed oak forest gives way to the hemlock-mixed hardwood forest, becoming cooler as you descend along the cascading Allamatunk River, the Lenape name for the Black River, into the ravine.

Nineteenth-century Copper Mill along the Black River.

The second portion of the hike climbs back through mixed oak forest and traverses an open meadow full of singing purple martins, bluebirds, and starlings. After the Kay Environmental Center, retrace your steps along the rushing river's edge.

Miles and Directions

0.0 From the northwest end of the parking lot, pass through the gate onto a path heading toward the Cooper Mill.

0.2 At the south end of the mill, descend the stairs where the Black River Trail (blue blazes) runs north and south. Turn left (south) onto the trail before the Black River. The trail shortly crosses the mill's tailrace and a series of bridges while veering away from the river.

0.5 Heading south, the trail drops down onto a railroad bed of the former Central Railroad of New Jersey Hacklebarney Branch (1873–1900).

0.8 Arrive at Kay's Pond.

1.0 The trail turns left before the closed auto-bridges. (**Side trip:** Cross the bridge to view the dam, the mill [converted into an electric plant], and the arched supports for the flume.)

1.1 Fenced-in area to the left is the Hacklebarney Mine. (**FYI:** From 1873 to 1900, approximately 250,000 tons of iron ore were extracted from this site.)

1.2 The railroad, once crossing the Black River to the Langdon Mine, ends here and the trail veers left over mine tailings.

1.4 Cross a series of wooden bridges over feeder streams and ascend up through the hardwood forest.

1.8 At the fork, veer right (south) onto a woods road and gradually ascend. You are leaving the Black River Trail. (**FYI:** The hike will return via the Black River Trail, the left fork, so make a mental note of this spot.)

1.9 At the T intersection, turn right (west) onto a gravel road, passing a green-blazed trail leaving left, and descend toward the Black River. (**FYI:** This following section of the hike is an out-and-back.)

2.0 At the fork bear right (southwest) and cross the Black River on a wooden bridge. You have now entered the Nature Area. (A free permit is required to enter this space.) The route curves up and above Hemlock Ravine before descending back to the west bank of the river.

2.2 Pass stone steps on the left leading 200 feet down to the ruins of Kay's summer cottage, grotto, and dam.

2.5 After passing the foundation of a former dam and millrace, the path ends. Retrace the hike back to the T intersection: cross the bridge, turn left at the fork; pass the green-blazed trail, which merges, from the right.

2.6 Continue straight (southeast) on a gravel road (now with a green blaze), passing the trail (left) on which you hiked in from Cooper Mill. The trail rises above Hemlock Ravine, paralleling the east side of the Black River.

2.7 At the fork, the green-blazed trail dead-ends onto the Conifer Pass Trail (red blazes), which heads in both directions. Leaving the road, take the right (south) fork onto the Conifer Pass Trail that traverses the ravine.

3.1 The route moves back and forth between the trail and the road, zigzagging back down to the Black River, where it will edge the bank.

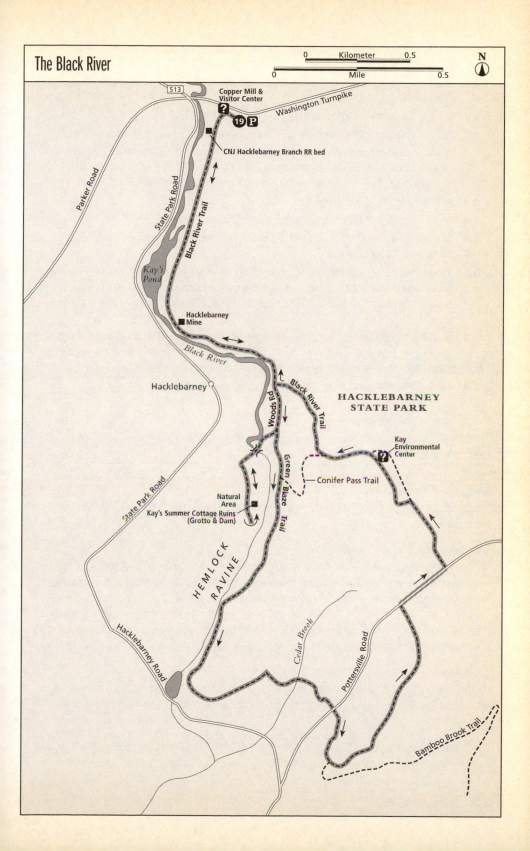

The Black River

0   Kilometer   0.5

0   Mile   0.5

N

513

Copper Mill &
Visitor Center

?

19 **P**

Washington Turnpike

CNJ Hacklebarney Branch RR bed

Parker Road

State Park Road

Black River Trail

Kay's
Pond

Hacklebarney
Mine

Black River

Hacklebarney

Woods Rd

Black River Trail

**HACKLEBARNEY
STATE PARK**

Kay
Environmental
Center

?

Conifer Pass Trail

Green Blaze Trail

State Park Road

Natural
Area

Kay's Summer Cottage Ruins
(Grotto & Dam)

**HEMLOCK
RAVINE**

Cedar Brook

Hacklebarney Road

Pottersville Road

Bamboo Brook Trail

3.4 The trail climbs away from the Black River through white pines and hardwoods, passing exploratory mine pits.

3.6 Reaching an outcrop, the trail proceeds to cross over a stone wall and through an evergreen grove.

3.8 The trail drops down and crosses (southeast) Cedar Brook.

4.0 The trail crosses (southeast) Pottersville Road and ascends though a hardwood forest.

4.3 At the T intersection turn left (east) onto the Bamboo Brook Trail (blue blazes), which runs along the ridge before descending on farmer's lane. (**FYI:** The route remains on the Bamboo Brook Trail until it reaches the Kay Environmental Center parking lot.)

4.9 At Pottersville Road turn right (east) onto the shoulder.

5.0 Turn left (north) onto the Kay Environmental Center entrance road.

5.4 Turn left (northwest) onto a dirt road and in 100 feet turn right (north) onto a grassy lane, which leads to the Center.

5.8 Passing the east end of the Center, cross (north) through the parking lot and turn left (west) onto a connector trail (red and blue blazes) for a number of trails. At this spot, there is a trail sign for the Cooper Mill. (**FYI:** A pay phone and directory are available in the parking lot.)

5.9 Continue straight (west) through the meadows till you come to a T intersection, where you turn right (north) onto a path. You shortly arrive at a four-way intersection, where you turn right again (northeast) onto the Black River Trail and down a grassy lane.

6.4 At the T intersection, turn right (northwest) and retrace the hike to the Cooper Mill parking lot.

8.2 Arrive at parking lot.

Hike Information

Local Information
Morris County Visitor's Center, 6 Court Street, Morristown 07960; (973) 631-5151; www.morris tourism.org

Local Events/Attractions
Cooper Mill, located here in Black River County Park, is a working 1826 gristmill where visitors can see grain being ground into flour; contact the park for hours of operation. Bamboo Brook Outdoor Education Center, a former estate, has formal gardens, fields, and woods; 170 Longview Road, Chester 07930; (973) 326-7600; www.morrisparks.net/parks/bbrookmain.htm. Adjacent to this is Willowwood Arboretum, a historic house surrounded by displays of native and exotic plants; 300 Longview Road, Chester 07930; (973) 326-7600; www.morrisparks.net/parks/wwmain.htm

Lodging
Camping is available at Voorhees State Park, 251 County Route Route 513, Glen Gardner 08826; (908) 638-6969; www.state.nj.us/dep/parksandforests/parks/voorhees.html#camp

Restaurants
The Publick House Inn, 111 Main Street, Chester 07930; (973) 879-6878. Food and lodging in a historic tavern, but beware—some say it's haunted!

20 Ken Lockwood Gorge

Stroll on a rail bed that runs along the shelf of the gorge and return by meandering along a lane on the floor of the ravine, all the while being shadowed by the scenic South Branch of the Raritan River. This spectacular lollipop hike pretty much stays within the Ken Lockwood Gorge Wildlife Management Area, running on the Hunterdon County Park's Columbia Trail. The road walk, part macadam (residential area), part dirt (management area), is quiet with a rural charm. You will be sharing the space with cyclists, serious fly anglers, and white-water enthusiasts, as well as the wildlife.

Start: Borough Commons Public Parking on Main Street
Distance: 8.1-mile lollipop
Approximate hiking time: 4 hours
Difficulty: Easy
Trail surface: Railroad bed, country lane
Seasons: Spring through fall
Other trail users: Multiuse
Canine compatibility: Leashed dogs permitted
Land status: State wildlife management area
Nearest town: High Bridge
Fees and permits: None
Schedule: Dawn to dusk
Maps: DeLorme: New Jersey Atlas & Gazetteer

p.29; USGS High Bridge, NJ, quadrangle; a map is also downloadable at www.njfishandwildlife.com/wmaland.htm, or can be obtained by calling (609) 984-0547 or e-mailing WMA MAPS@dep.state.nj.us.
Trail contacts: New Jersey Division of Fish and Wildlife, PO Box 400, 501 East State Street, third floor, Trenton 08625-0400; (609) 292-2965; www.state.nj.us/dep/fgw
Other: Please be mindful and respectful of the trout anglers using this area, for whom it was primarily acquired.
Special considerations: The hike along the bottom of the gorge is unsafe in icy conditions.

Finding the trailhead: From the junction of Route 31 and Interstate 78, travel north on Route 31 for approximately 1.7 miles. Turn right onto West Main Street (County Route 513) and drive 1.2 miles. Turn right (east) onto Bridge Street (CR 513) for 0.1 mile. At the T intersection turn left (north) onto Main Street (CR 513) and travel 0.2 mile to the edge of the commercial district. Turn left (west) into the Borough Commons Public Parking.

The Hike

Start this hike in the center of High Bridge, a former steel town. Beginning in 1742, the iron industry grew to become the major focus of the community, until the mills closed in the mid-1960s. The Taylor Iron Works provided cannonballs for both the American Revolution and the Civil War. The mills also created armaments for the Spanish American War, as well as World Wars I and II. During their more peaceful endeavors, they constructed railroad wheels, tracks, and, most notably, the teeth for the monster shovels that built the Panama Canal.

Cross Main Street and head on down the former Jersey Central High Bridge Branch, a 33-mile spur built in the 1860s, serving the iron mines of Morris County.

At its peak in the 1880s, 118 ore cars rambled down this road in one day, to the tune of 25,000 tons of ore in one month! On April 18, 1885, Engine #112, better known as the Columbia, came chugging down the tracks from the Chester Furnace. As it crossed the 260-foot-long wooden Gorge Bridge, the weight of the engine, 40 ore cars, 5 pig-iron cars, and caboose collapsed the structure, plunging all 80 feet into the South Branch of the Raritan and killing one brakeman. No fiddling with the NTSB in those days: The line was back up and running in a week!

The High Bridge Branch also had other purposes besides shipping ore. It had a milk run and ran a scheduled passenger train till 1935 and freight trains till 1976. Ice was shipped down to the city from Lake Hopatcong, while summer excursions ran up to the lake and its picnic grove. They even ran a Halloween Special at 11:15 p.m. from High Bridge to Somerville, where a celebration would take place: a parade, music, prizes, and fireworks. Makes you sorry that you missed October 31, 1910. But that is not the only spooky story that goes along with this hike. The legend of Hookerman also haunts this spur.

As the story goes, a railroad man lost his arm in a train accident, an all too common experience, especially for brakemen who got their appendages caught between the cars. Well, he lost his arm, which was replaced by an artificial limb with a hook—hence the name. And so at night you may spot a mysterious light—an orb—emanating from a swinging lantern, as Hookerman searches for his missing limb. Some

Approaching Lockwood Gorge and the 80-foot-high railroad bridge.

scientific explanations for the "burning orb" floating above the tracks have been put forth, but for our money, the jury is still out. It should also be noted that from local legend has sprung a local "Hookerman" record label.

Very real was the man for whom the gorge now takes its name. Ken Lockwood was a pioneering outdoor journalist, writing for the *Newark Evening News* from ca.1918 until his death in 1948. His column covered and promoted every aspect of outdoor life, especially hunting, fishing, and conservation. Among his many activities, he was a trustee of the New Jersey Audubon Society. His particular loves were fly fishing and the creation of state wildlife management areas. It was thus natural that this wildlife management area, an angler's heaven, was named in Lockwood's honor—it was purchased by the state the same year Lockwood died.

Miles and Directions

0.0 Head (east) out the entrance to the Borough Commons Public Parking lot (former rail yard) to Main Street and cross it onto a macadam-covered rail bed where you shortly cross Mill Street and Taylor Street.

0.2 Pass the kiosk for the Columbia Trail and travel under a boxed-pony-truss bridge (1937) onto a crushed stone treadway of the Columbia Trail, shortly passing the ¼ Mile Post.

0.5 Unofficial path leads to the Lake Solitude's dam. You hear the roar before you see it. A sign posted on the tree reads No Diving, No Jumping, No Swimming. You'll shortly pass the ½ Mile Post.

0.7 Cross Mine Road followed by a culvert with a stream 80 feet below. Lake Solitude is on the right (east), shortly passing the ¾ Mile Post. Below, right is the South Branch of the Raritan River.

1.0 Pass 1 Mile Post. On your right is the Boy Scouts' Camp Dill with its stone structures.

1.2 Just before the deck girder bridge over Cokesbury Road, you pass a path on the left, shortly thereafter passing the 1¼ Mile Post. (**FYI:** The hike will return via this path from Cokesbury Road.)

1.5 Pass 1½ Mile Post. The trail passes on a 50-foot fill above the Raritan River.

1.7 Pass 1¾ Mile Post. The trail enters Lockwood Gorge.

2.0 Pass 2 Mile Post, passing on a shelf and through a cut.

2.2 Pass 2¼ Mile Post.

2.5 Pass 2½ Mile Post.

2.7 Cross over the Lockwood Gorge on a steel deck, 120-foot-span structure, and 80 feet above the South Branch of the Raritan River. (**Bail-out:** At the north end of the bridge, turn right [east] and scramble down the herd path to Raritan River Road. Follow the directions found later in Miles and Directions.)

2.9 Pass 2¾ Mile Post, where there are excellent views of the ravine and the river.

3.0 Pass 3 Mile Post alongside a sheer drop to the river.

3.2 Just beyond 3¼ Mile Post, pass through a small cut.

3.5 Pass 3½ Mile Post.

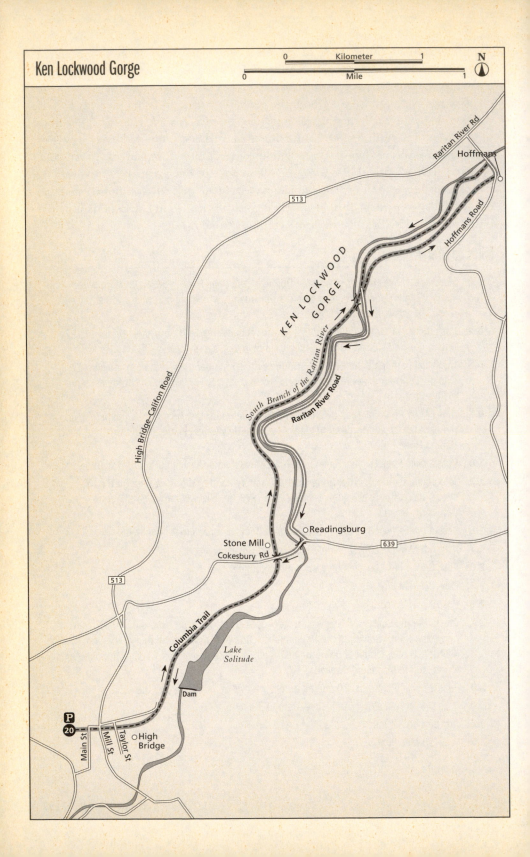

0   Kilometer   1

0   Mile   1

N

Raritan River Rd

Hoffmans

Hoffmans Road

513

K E N   L O C K W O O D   G O R G E

South Branch of the Raritan River

Raritan River Road

High Bridge-Califon Road

Readingsburg

Stone Mill

Cokesbury Rd

639

513

Columbia Trail

Lake
Solitude

Dam

P
20

Main St

Mill St

Taylor St

High
Bridge

3.8 At the junction with Hoffmans Road (Hoffman Crossing, Hoffman's Siding), turn left (north) onto Hoffman's Road, heading downhill.

3.9 At the intersection turn left (southwest) onto Raritan River Road. The macadam lane parallels the South Branch of the Raritan River. You will be going with the flow.

4.2 Pass a KEN LOCKWOOD sign and a parking lot for four cars. At this point the road becomes a dirt lane, snaking its way down the gorge.

4.9 Cross under the Lockwood Gorge Railroad Bridge and continue down the Raritan River Road, shortly passing a kiosk on the right and a monument to Ken Lockwood on the left. (**FYI:** If you took the bail-out, pick up the hike from this point.)

6.1 Pass a KEN LOCKWOOD GORGE sign as you emerge onto the macadam road with homes nestled on the ridge.

6.5 At the T intersection in Readingsburg, you turn right (southwest) onto Cokesbury Road, immediately crossing over the South Branch of the Raritan via road bridge, and begin to ascend.

6.7 Pass under the railroad bridge and immediately turn left (south) onto the entrance ramp, which after 50 yards intersects with the rail bed and the Columbia Trail. Bear right (south) and retrace your steps back to High Bridge and the Borough Commons Public Parking.

8.1 Arrive at the parking lot.

Hike Information

Local Information

New Jersey Skylands Region Tourism Guide; www.njskylands.com

Local Events/Attractions

Spruce Run Recreation Area offers a wide variety of activities, including hiking, camping, fishing, boating, swimming, and picnicking; 68 Van Syckel's Road, Clinton 08809; (908) 638-8572; www.state.nj.us/dep/parksandforests/parks/spruce.html. Voorhees State Park, built by the Civilian Conservation Corps in the 1930s, is home to the Paul H. Robinson Observatory of the New Jersey Astronomical Association. The Observatory's 26-inch-diameter telescope is available to the public during evening sessions; call for details; New Jersey Astronomical Association: (908) 638-8500; www.njaa.org

Lodging

Camping and shelters are available at Voorhees State Park, 251 CR 513, Glen Gardner 08826; (908) 638-6969; www.state.nj.us/dep/parksandforests/parks/voorhees.html. Camping is also available at Spruce Run Recreation Area (see above for contact information).

21 Wawayanda Lake

This is a journey around 255-acre Wawayanda Lake, traveling over rolling hills in mixed woodlands. Take advantage of mountain laurel and rhododendron, flowering throughout May and June respectively. Hike on nineteenth-century abandoned roads, skirting the forgotten hamlets of Cherry Ridge and Double Pond. Take side trips to the pump house sites and the secluded Laurel Pond. Skirt massive granite cliffs and gaze over the Wawayanda Plateau. Cap off the adventure by passing the iron furnace and edging Wawayanda Lake. On weekends during the summer, the park closes when it reaches capacity, so plan your hike accordingly.

Start: Wawayanda Lake beach parking area on park entrance road
Distance: 5.7-mile loop
Approximate hiking time: 3 hours
Difficulty: Moderate due to length
Trail surface: Hiking trails and woods roads
Seasons: All good
Other trail users: Multiuse trails
Canine compatibility: Leashed dogs permitted
Land status: State park
Nearest town: Upper Greenwood Lake
Fees and permits: Higher fees on weekends from Memorial Day through Labor Day
Schedule: Park hours vary by season; call park office for details.
Maps: *DeLorme: New Jersey Atlas & Gazetteer* p.20; USGS Wawayanda, NJ, quadrangle; New York–New Jersey Trail Conference *North Jersey*

Trails Map 21; a hiking map is also available at the park office.
Trail contacts: Wawayanda State Park, 885 Warwick Turnpike, Hewitt 07421; (973) 853-4462; wsp@warwick.net; www.njparksand forests.org
Special considerations: Summer weekends can be extremely busy at the beach and may result in the park being closed to further entrance. The first stream on this hike can be impassable during high water (no bridge); at such times, a good substitute hike is the circuit starting at the main dam of the lake: the Wing-dam Trail to Laurel Pond Trail, and back to the iron furnace and the main dam. Be aware also that the early part of this hike can be difficult to follow due to poor blazing.

Finding the trailhead: From Route 23, go north on Union Valley Road (County Route 513) near Newfoundland. Stay on Union Valley Road for 8.6 miles, passing the traffic light intersection with Marshall Hill Road (stay to the left here). Continue on Union Valley Road until it reaches Warwick Turnpike. Go left on Warwick Turnpike, traveling up through Abram S. Hewitt State Forest and passing Upper Greenwood Lake, for a total of 3.1 miles to the entrance of Wawayanda State Park (left-hand turn). Take the main park entrance road to the beach and boathouse day-use area, about 2 miles. The hike starts at the beach parking lot.

The Hike

This hike encircles Wawayanda Lake, a body of water that was created for industrial purposes, but soon became beloved for recreational pursuits. You'll get a flavor of both

Wawayanda Iron Furnace (1846) is just below Wawayanda Lake.

the deep forest that surrounds the lake, and the old woods roads, long-gone settlements, and onetime farmsteads that dot the landscape.

Wawayanda Lake was originally two smaller ponds called the Double Pond. First dammed in the 1790s to power a sawmill and gristmill, local forests fed the sawmill, and mountain farms grew grain for the mill. Small mountain farmsteads covered the landscape here, the settlers extracting a living from the steep, stony soils. One mountain settlement, the village of Cherry Ridge, was near the southern end of Wawayanda Lake. Between land acquisitions for state park and watershed, it's virtually vanished today. There was iron in these mountains, too, the first mines being opened during the Revolutionary War.

The Double Ponds were raised again in 1845. In that year, William L. Ames, a Massachusetts industrialist, bought the property and built an iron furnace, new gristmill and sawmill, and other structures, forming an industrial village (its site is a notable feature of our hike). Wawayanda Furnace consumed roughly an acre of timberland a day as fuel, with ore coming from the nearby mines. Ames, and later his family, owned the property until 1869, when it passed through a variety of other owners. These included the Thomas Iron Company of Pennsylvania, and briefly, the Standard Oil Company.

By 1900, most of Wawayanda's industry had faded away, but the property was becoming more and more popular as a place for recreation. This included one of the first YMCA summer camps in United States history. This was Camp Wawayanda, which operated here from the 1880s through 1918. The Wawayanda tract was later owned by the New Jersey Zinc Company, which harvested mine props here for the Franklin and Ogdensburg mines. Lake Wawayanda was for years ringed with summer cabins leased by the zinc company to its employees, torn down after it became a state park.

The property was purchased by the state of New Jersey in 1963, one of the first acquisitions of the Green Acres program. In the 1960s, Wawayanda's water resources were tapped by the city of Newark. Droughts in the 1960s led them to get permission to construct a pump house and pipeline, which drew water from Lake Wawayanda and deposited in streams feeding their Canistear Reservoir. Last used ca. 1980, the pump house sites and the pipeline remain interesting reminders of long-ago water emergencies. Similarly, the old furnace, stone foundations, and archaeological remains of Wawayanda Village are fascinating relics of the site's industrial heritage.

Miles and Directions

0.0 From the northwest corner of the bathhouse parking lot, locate the trailhead sign for Pump House Trail, which is to the right of the bathhouse on the edge of the paved lot and the grass. (The sign indicates the blazes are red, but actually they are orange.) Go through the opening in the wooden fence and cut across the grass, heading (west) to the right side of the bathhouse. Just before it, turn right (northwest) and cross a footbridge (a picnic area on the left) and onto a gravel path that ascends the hill.

0.2 At the top of the hill and just before Wawayanda Road, turn left (west) onto a woods road. There is a triple orange blaze placed on the tree indicating the trailhead of the Pump House Trail. The park staff is working to clear up the confusion.

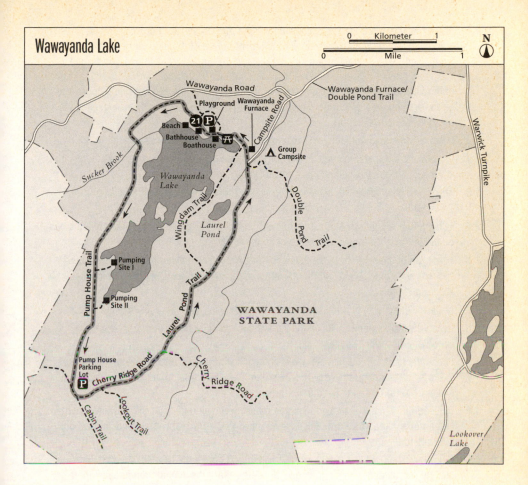

Wawayanda Lake

0.6 As the route begins to drop, turn left (south) off the woods road and onto a trail, which descends into the bottomlands where you cross a bridge and rock-hop.

0.8 Skirt (southwest) the edge of the swamp before swinging (south) away from it, climbing up through the mountain laurel and glacial moraine.

1.0 Heading south, reach the top of the ridge with seasonal views (east) of Wawayanda Lake. You have also entered a garden of massive glacial erratics. (**Side trip:** Bushwhack off the trail to explore these glacial phenomena.)

1.1 The trail becomes a woods road, eventually entering into a canyon of rhododendron. Be alert: The day we were here the blazing had been painted out.

1.5 Entering glacial till, an unmarked woods road enters (northwest) sharply from the right.

1.9 Pass a woods road and continue straight, passing vernal ponds on the left (southeast). (**Side trip:** Turn left [east] onto the woods road [tentatively slated for blue blazing], which drops down to Wawayanda Lake and the old pump house site. Beautiful place for a break, and you only add about 0.5 mile to the trip.)

2.0 At the junction of woods roads, continue straight and immediately cross a stream. There is a gravel quarry on the right as you ascend into a canyon of rhododendron and mountain laurel. (**Side trip:** At the junction turn left [east] onto a poorly maintained woods road. Less than a tenth of a mile, turn left [north] and descend through hardwoods and a thicket of rhododendrons before reaching the end of Wawayanda Lake and the pump house site. Be forewarned: This is not totally a pristine site, with all the pipes and decking. Trip adds about 0.5 mile to the trip.)

2.4 Cross over a stream and the pipeline and continue straight (southwest) on the woods road.

2.7 Pass by the kiosk and through the Pump House parking lot where the trail dead-ends. Turn left (southeast) onto Cherry Ridge Road, originally an old wagon road.

2.8 At the fork bear left (east), continuing on Cherry Ridge Road. The right road begins the Cabin Trail.

3.2 At the junction continue straight (northeast) on Cherry Ridge, passing a set of foundations on the left and a designated parking lot on the right.

3.5 At the top of the ridge, pass the trailhead for Lookout Trail on your right (southeast, easily missed) and continue straight (northeast) on Cherry Ridge Road, shortly passing around a steel auto gate.

3.6 At the trailhead sign turn left (north) onto the multiuse Laurel Pond Trail (yellow blazes).

4.0 Reach the grand granite cliffs on the right where local lore has it that they possess a Native American rock shelter.

4.3 Reach the crest (1,360-foot elevation) of the hill with a view of the Wawayanda Plateau to the right (east) and the Wingdam Trail (blue blazes) leaving to the left (west). Continue straight (north) on Laurel Pond Trail.

4.8 Proceed through a wall of rhododendron (passing two side trails on the left) and emerge into an open area. (**Side trip:** Take a jaunt down to the pristine Laurel Pond. Adds about 0.1 mile to the trip.)

5.0 Cross over the Double Kill on a wooden bridge and here ends Laurel Pond Trail. Continue straight (northeast) onto a gravel road, heading toward the 40-foot iron furnace. There are restrooms to the right in the open field.

5.1 Cross through the intersection and turn left (north) up the immediate diagonal gravel path with the Wawayanda furnace (1846) on the right (east). Cross over the raceway and through the foundations of Double Pond. (**Side trip:** Just beyond the juncture, arrive at the base of the iron furnace where there is an interpretive signage.)

5.2 The gravel road swings up, passing a small picnic area, the dam to Wawayanda Lake, and the trailhead of the Wingdam Trail. Continue straight (northwest) climbing above Wawayanda Lake.

5.5 Pass by a picnic area, a parking lot, the boathouse, and a turnaround, and continue straight (northwest) on a gravel road up the hill with the lake to your left and a restroom to your right.

5.6 The route cuts through a picnic area, arriving back at the beach area and the start of the hike.

5.7 Arrive at the parking lot.

Hike Information

Local Information

New Jersey Skylands Region Tourism Guide: www.njskylands.com. Vernon Chamber of Commerce, PO Box 308, Vernon 07462; (973) 764-0764; www.vernonchamber.com

Local Events/Attractions

High Breeze Farm State and National Historic District on Barrett Road, part of Wawayanda State Park, preserves a 160-acre mountain farmstead, owned by the Barrett family from 1860 until 1981. Two farmhouses, barns, outbuildings, and fields preserve a "Currier & Ives" landscape. Tours are given on select weekends or can be arranged by appointment; contact the park office for details. An adjacent museum run by the Vernon Township Historical Society/Friends of Wawayanda State Park has exhibits on the park's history as well as Vernon Township history.

Lodging

Group camping available at Wawayanda State Park

Organizations

New York–New Jersey Trail Conference, 156 Ramapo Valley Road (U.S. Highway 202), Mahwah 07430; (201) 512-9348; www.nynjtc.org. Vernon Township Historical Society/Friends of Wawayanda State Park, 173 Barrett Road, Highland Lakes 07422.

THE JERSEY PIEDMONT

The Piedmont Province is a gently rolling plain that slopes from the foot of the rough Highlands southeast to the flat and sandy coastal plain. It contains less than a quarter of New Jersey's area. But because of its geology, with much good soil, and its geography, running between New York and Philadelphia, it has historically contained the bulk of New Jersey's population and development.

From the Wickecheoke Creek Bridge, looking over the Prallsville Mill Complex

Mostly underlain with soft rocks—shale, siltstone, and sandstone—its undulating character is punctuated by dramatic cliffs and mountains, all of volcanic origin. In the north, diabase ridges form the famous Palisades of the Hudson, and to the south, the Sourland Mountains and others. Farther south, the columnlike cliffs and mountains of the Watchung Range were formed by volcanic basalt forced upward like toothpaste out of innumerable tubes. Paterson's Garrett Mountain and the Great Falls are other reminders of this volcanic past.

At the end of the last ice age, some 10,000 years ago, the receding glacier left behind three great lakes as it melted. One of them, glacial Lake Passaic, survives as the vast wetlands of the Great Swamp. Another, glacial Lake Hackensack, is today the Hackensack Meadowlands, while the third is now the Great Meadows, in Warren County.

The Piedmont contains some of the first land in New Jersey settled by Europeans. Its generally gentle terrain and rich soils encouraged farmers. By the Colonial era they were producing copious quantities and varieties of fruits, vegetables, grains, dairy, livestock, and related products, including cider and spirits. One account credits British soldiers passing through this richly cultivated farmscape during the Revolution as saying that New Jersey was like one big garden—one possible origin of our nickname, "The Garden State."

Always a travel corridor, much Revolutionary War history can be found here, most notably at Trenton, Princeton, Morristown, and Jockey Hollow. Later, industry took root, with the waterpower available at places such as Trenton and Paterson giving rise to an array of manufacturing enterprises, including ironworks, silk and textile mills, gun and locomotive works, and many others. Canals, such as the Morris Canal and the Delaware & Raritan Canal, aided this industry, as did later railroads.

In the twentieth century this region saw the greatest development and construction, with the corridor between New York and Philadelphia filling with highways and houses. As such, open space is precious in the Piedmont as nowhere else in New Jersey. Some of our earliest open spaces were established here, such as South Mountain and Watchung Reservations. These are green islands in a sea of industry and housing. The violence that 150 years of industrial activity did to the landscape is still visible in places, but fortunately recovery is under way, notably at places such as DeKorte Park in the Hackensack Meadowlands. All in all, the Piedmont is arguably the most "Jersey" part of New Jersey.

22 The Great Falls of the Passaic

An urban adventure! You'll scope out the second largest waterfall, by volume, east of the Mississippi. Ramble along raceways of the first planned industrial city in America. Marvel at the Valley of the Rocks and stroll along the Passaic River. All this is part of the 139-acre Great Falls National Historic District and a new 112-acre state park. *Caution:* Don't permit the bucolic moments along the hike to allow you to forget it's still an urban experience. Plans for the revitalization of this struggling area are in progress, and conditions are likely to change, so be aware of conditions and plan your walk accordingly.

Start: Overlook Park on McBride Avenue Extension, Paterson
Distance: 2.2-mile loop
Approximate hiking time: 2 hours
Difficulty: Easy
Trail surface: Sidewalks, paved trails, gravel paths, bridges
Seasons: All good
Other trail users: You name it.
Canine compatibility: Leashed dogs permitted
Land status: State park
Nearest town: Paterson
Fees and permits: None
Schedule: Dawn to dusk
Maps: *DeLorme: New Jersey Atlas & Gazetteer* p. 26; USGS Paterson, NJ, quadrangle; maps for walking tours are also available at the Great Falls visitor center.
Trail contacts: New Jersey Department of Environmental Protection, P. O. Box 402, Trenton 08625-0402; www.state.nj.us/dep/. Great Falls Historic District Cultural Center, 65 McBride Avenue Extension, Paterson 07050; (973) 279-9587; greatfalls@patcity.org; www.patcity.com/visitors_information/index.html
Other: At this writing, the New Jersey Department of Environmental Protection is in the process of taking over management of the Great Falls, which was declared a state park by Governor James McGreevey in 2004. A major rehabilitation and redesign of park facilities is planned, so conditions may change in future years.
Special considerations: This hike is in an urban area. Be aware of your surroundings. Also, for best viewing of the falls, visit after a significant rainfall.

Finding the trailhead: Take Interstate 80 to exit 57, toward downtown Paterson and Grand Street. Turn left on Grand Street. Shortly turn right onto Spruce Street. Turn right onto McBride Avenue Extension. Overlook Park is located nearly opposite the Great Falls Visitors Center at 65 McBride Avenue Extension.

The Hike

Stopped cold by that unmoving roar, fastened there: the rocks silent but the water, married to the stone . . . the cataract and its clamor broken apart . . . roaring . . . .
—William Carlos Williams, "Paterson: The Falls"

Gathering strength as it heads southeast, the Passaic River tumbles over the resistant basalt formations of the Watchung Mountains, and onto softer shales and sandstones. The softer stones below erode; the harder stone on top doesn't. The result (after some eons): a waterfall. Not just any waterfall: the Great Falls of the Passaic.

Often called Paterson Falls, this seems decidedly unfair: The Falls were known for a hundred years before the city of Paterson existed. Settlers in the 1600s noted their beauty, and in the 1700s picnic parties from as far away as New York came to see the massive waterfalls in the Jersey hinterlands. By volume, the only waterfall east of the Mississippi that's bigger is Niagara.

One such outdoor luncheon had enormous significance. In July 1778, two officers of the Continental Army took time off from fighting the British to enjoy some Madeira and provender whilst contemplating the thunderous foamy spray of the Great Falls. They were General George Washington and his aide-de-camp, Alexander Hamilton.

We look at a waterfall and think: *how pretty*. When the wheels of industry were turned by waterpower, a thinking man looked at the Great Falls and thought: money. It wasn't just water tumbling over the cliffs, it was liquid gold. That's what Hamilton thought, for sure. And there were iron ore and timber in the nearby mountains.

In 1791 Hamilton (now the first secretary of the U.S. Treasury) spearheaded the creation of a stock company to build a manufacturing city at the site. The Society for the Establishment of Useful Manufactures (SUM) was founded via a stock offering

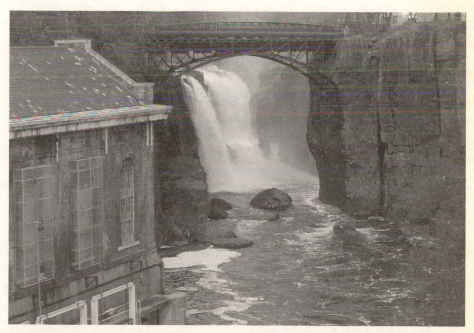

The Great Falls (second-largest waterfall east of the Mississippi River) and the SUM Hydro-Electric Plant

and a government-sponsored lottery. New Jersey governor William Paterson gave his approval and assistance; in return the new city was named in his honor.

The SUM acquired 700 acres around the Great Falls and set about building a three-tiered series of raceways to supply mill sites (the raceways are a notable part of our hike). As a manufacturing enterprise, the SUM quickly stumbled, and before long it became merely the glorified landlord of Paterson's waterpower resources.

There were ups and downs, but Paterson kept growing. Industrialist Peter Colt was among the first to operate in Paterson, making cotton cloth. In later years Paterson mills would produce something the Colt name is best known for: firearms. Paterson mills also made paper, machinery, locomotives, clothing, candles, soap, and chemicals. But its single most famous product was silk—for a generation, Paterson was known as "Silk City."

In spite of this industrial growth, the Great Falls of the Passaic—no longer in the wilderness and greatly hemmed in by factories—remained a famous natural landmark. It was probably New Jersey's most famous scenic landmark in the 1800s, painted by landscape artists, extolled by poets, and admired by all.

As an industrial city, Paterson's ascent continued, albeit with interruptions (mainly labor strikes and fires). In 1914 the SUM (now part of a larger water conglomerate) built the electric generating plant near the Falls to better supply Paterson with this new form of power. In the twentieth century, more modern enterprises, such as the Curtiss–Wright Corporation, joined Paterson's traditional industries. This aeronautics giant produced tens of thousands of aircraft engines here through the Second World War. Through it all, the Great Falls remained the wild and romantic heart of this historic American city.

Miles and Directions

0.0 Exit the entrance to the Overlook Park and turn right (southwest) along McBride Avenue Extension, passing the Great Falls Historic District Cultural Center on the left.

0.1 At the fork bear right (northwest) along Spruce Street, passing the Great Falls and the SUM Hydro-Electric Plant (1912–14).

0.2 At the intersection pass Mc Bride Avenue and continue straight (northwest) onto Wayne Avenue, crossing over a bridge spanning the Passaic River with a view of the SUM Dam (1838–40).

0.25 After passing Birch Street on the left, turn right (north) and proceed around the end of a cement wall and walk back (southeast) on a path toward the Passaic River, dropping down to a second, earthen trail. Immediately turn left (north), paralleling the riverbank. This earthen pathway has recently been cleared, but trash dumping still occurs here. If conditions aren't pleasant, retrace your steps and enter the park at mile 0.2, going to the right (northeast) and crossing the lot.

0.33 The trail merges with a macadam path coming in from the left (Maple Street) and continues straight (north) between two historic buildings: left, Steam and Boiler Plant (1876); right, Conduit Gate House (1906).

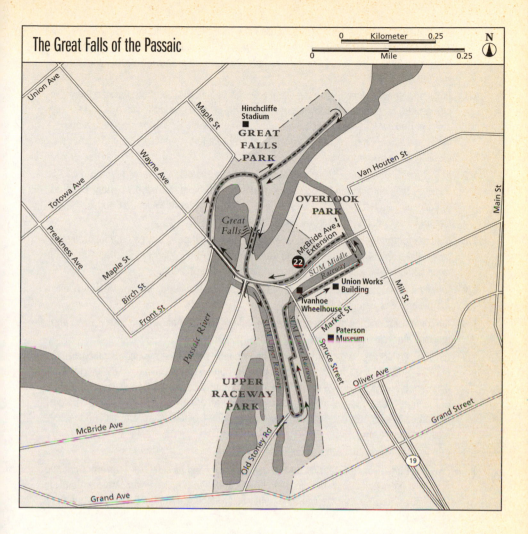

0 Kilometer 0.25

0 Mile 0.25

N

Union Ave

Maple St

Wayne Ave

Totowa Ave

Preakness Ave

Maple St

Birch St

Front St

Hinchcliffe Stadium

GREAT FALLS PARK

Van Houten St

Main St

OVERLOOK PARK

Great Falls

McBride Ave. Extension

22

SUM Middle Raceway

Union Works Building

Ivanhoe Wheelhouse

SUM Upper Raceway

SUM Lower Raceway

Market St

Paterson Museum

Passaic River

Spruce Street

Mill St

Oliver Ave

Grand Street

UPPER RACEWAY PARK

Old Stoney Rd

McBride Ave

19

Grand Ave

0.4 Turn right (southeast) after passing the Conduit Gate House and before the Hinchcliffe Stadium (1920). Pass the Pumping Station (1862) on the right.

0.45 At the fork before the Great Falls Park green, bear left (east), following the macadam bicycle path down the hill. If conditions here don't look great, you can skip this section and continue straight ahead.

0.5 As you descend, pass a path on the right (southeast).

0.7 Arrive at the Valley of the Rocks. At the foot of the magnificent cliffs (left) and Paterson Animal Shelter (right), turn around and retrace your steps back up to Great Falls Park.

0.9 As you ascend, pass a path on your left. (**Option:** Turn left [southeast] on the macadam path and climb down stairs leading to the Passaic River. Sadly, you might have to scramble over broken furniture and refuse, but the payoff is an impressive view of the basin at the foot of the falls. Retrace your route back up to the bicycle path and turn left [southwest].)

0.95 Reaching the top of the cliffs at Great Falls Park, take the far fork to the left (south) along the Passaic River and the Great Falls (right). (**Option:** Along the path and to the right there is an opening in the wrought-iron fence where stairs lead you to a bird's-eye view of the very top of the Great Falls!)

1.1 Cross a footbridge directly over the Great Falls with a primal view of the Passaic River plunging 80 feet through a 280-foot gorge. Shortly cross a second footbridge and through a cinder parking lot till you reach the intersection of Spruce Street, Wayne Avenue, and McBride Avenue. Cross (south) Spruce Street and turn left (southeast) onto the sidewalk, paralleling the upper raceway.

1.2 At the junction of Spruce Street and McBride Avenue Extension, turn right (south) into Raceway Park onto a path that parallels the lower and upper raceways. (**Option:** To return to trailhead turn left [north] crossing Spruce Street onto McBride Avenue Extension where Overlook Park will immediately be on your left [northwest].)

1.5 Before a footbridge over the upper raceway, turn left (northeast) onto a path following the curve of the spillway as it drops to the lower raceways. At this elbow in the path, there is a nice lookout of the race and the mills. The path now heads north.

1.6 Turn right (east) onto a footbridge crossing over the lower raceway. Immediately, turn left (north) onto the path.

1.8 Turn right (east) on the path before the backside of the Ivanhoe Wheelhouse (1865) and proceed alongside (north) the Wheelhouse.

1.9 Cross (east) Spruce Street and continue on the path, paralleling the middle raceway (1792–1802) on the left (north) and passing the Union Works Building (1890) on the right (south). Crosswalk is to the right (south) at Market Street. (**Option:** If you would like to visit the Paterson Museum [Rogers Locomotive Erecting Shop, 1871], turn right [south] and proceed along Spruce Street to Market Street for 1 block, where you will find the museum's entrance.)

2.1 Turn left (north) on the path as it follows the raceway.

2.15 Cross McBride Avenue Extension and turn left (west) along its sidewalk. (**Option:** Continue north along the raceway till it dead-ends [200 yards]. From up here you can view Colt Gun Mill [1836]. Retrace your steps on the path back to McBride Avenue Extension.) Turn right on the sidewalk.

2.2 Turn right (northwest) into the Overlook Park, back where the loop began.

Hike Information

Local Information

Passaic County Web site: www.passaiccountynj.org. Passaic County Administration Building, 401 Grand Street, Paterson 07505; (973) 881-4000.

Local Events/Attractions

The Paterson Museum has exhibits on the city's industrial and cultural heritage: Thomas Rogers Building, 2 Market Street, Paterson 07501; (973) 881-3874. The Botto House National Landmark and American Labor Museum was the focal point of a major 1913 mill workers' strike that played an important role in the early history of organized labor. 83 Norwood Street, Haledon 07508;

(973) 595-7953. Lambert Castle, former home of silk mill baron Catholina Lambert, overlooks the city from Garrett Mountain. Now home to the Passaic County Historical Society, it has exhibits on Passaic County history; Garrett Mountain Reservation, 3 Valley Road, Paterson 07503-2932; (973) 247-0085; www.lambertcastle.org

Restaurants

Paterson is full of great ethnic restaurants of all varieties; fast food is also available near the Paterson Museum.

Organizations

Paterson Friends of The Great Falls, Inc., 13½ Van Houten Street, Paterson 07505; (973) 225-0826; www.patersongreatfalls.com

DECLINE AND REBIRTH IN PATERSON

Paterson could not escape the urban and industrial decline that most American cities experienced after the Second World War—this is fairly evident around our hike. Cheaper labor and more modern facilities caused the textile industry to migrate south. And the middle classes, as everywhere in America, kept heading out to the suburbs. In 1945 the S.U.M. was dissolved, and its remaining assets were sold to the city of Paterson.

The early 1970s saw Paterson in decline, but soon to experience a rebirth. The importance of Paterson and the SUM in the history of American industry was being realized. During the U.S. Bicentennial in 1976, the Great Falls and 139 acres of surrounding factories were designated a National Historic Landmark. The historic factory buildings, dating from the late 1700s through the early twentieth century, reflect a huge span of American industrial design and operation.

Unfortunately, many historic mill buildings have been lost to fire and vandalism. Others have been restored and adaptively reused, converted to apartments, offices, shops, and cultural spaces. And through it all, the historic area of Paterson remains a place where important industry and manufacturing continue.

The Great Falls Historic District remains in need of substantial restoration and rehabilitation. Efforts at preservation got a boost, however, in October 2004, when the state of New Jersey designated the Great Falls as its newest state park. A national architectural competition is under way to rehabilitate the area around the falls. We can thus hope that the grandeur that entranced visitors in the eighteenth and nineteenth centuries will continue to awe those of the twenty-first century, as well it should.

23 The Hudson Palisades

This scenic loop hike traverses the top and bottom of the Palisades and beside the banks of the Hudson River. Due to its challenges, this adventure needs a heads-up approach. The trail fluctuates between serious stone steps, zigzagging dirt trails, wide meandering paths, abandoned highway (ghostly), and trailer-size rock talus. It should not be attempted in wet or icy weather, or if one is scared of heights. Children need to be closely in tow and pets left at home! The hike has its challenges, but the incredible views are some of the most unique in the nation and worth the effort.

Start: State Line Lookout, off Palisades Interstate Parkway
Distance: 4.2-mile loop
Approximate hiking time: 3 hours
Difficulty: Strenuous, with steep climbs, stairs, and boulders
Trail surface: Paved paths, stone steps, footpaths, boulders, and old highways
Seasons: Spring through fall
Other trail users: Multiuse on old highways
Canine compatibility: Leashed dogs permitted, but best left home on this hike of many cliffs and crevices
Land status: Interstate park
Nearest town: Alpine
Fees and permits: None

Schedule: Dawn to dusk
Maps: *DeLorme: New Jersey Atlas & Gazetteer* p. 27; USGS Yonkers, NY, quadrangle; New York–New Jersey Trail Conference *Hudson Palisades Trails—New Jersey Section;* also trail maps are available at the park or online at www.njpalisades.org/maps.htm.
Trail contacts: Palisades Interstate Park, New Jersey Section, PO Box 155, Alpine 07620-0155; (201) 768-1360; www.njpalisades.org
Special considerations: Inclement or icy weather cancels this hike, as many sections will be unsafe to negotiate. Think twice before bringing small children or pets on this potentially dangerous hike. The riverside area is copperhead habitat; keep your eyes open.

Finding the trailhead: State Line Lookout is about 1 mile south of the New York–New Jersey state line, and has its own unnumbered exit from the northbound Palisades Interstate Parkway about 2 miles north of exit 2 and immediately opposite the southbound-only exit 3. From the Palisades Interstate Parkway southbound, stay in the left lane after passing exit 3. Take the U-turn (well marked). *Use caution,* as you will need to get into the right lane immediately to exit for State Line Lookout. The hike begins at the State Line Lookout parking area.

The Hike

There are ghosts of people, but what about of places? Some places are so special they seem to have souls, harboring beautiful memories. Though later abandoned and forgotten, their hold on the human imagination survives. There are two such places on our hike along the base of the Palisades here: Forest View and Mary Lawrence Tonetti's waterfall and gardens. They make the walk a special one indeed.

The first ghost-place of the Palisades on our ramble is the huge, overgrown riverside area at the base of the steps down to the river. In the early days of the Palisades Interstate Park, when cars were less common, it didn't seem odd to have a recreation area you walked to, and this was one: Forest View. It included a pavilion, restrooms, water fountains, picnic areas, boat docks, marina, and a ball field. You got here either by walking the Shore Trail a few miles north from the Alpine Boat Basin, or by hiking down the stairs from the Women's Federation Monument above (or possibly by taking a boat). For decades, Forest View was happy with the sound of games, cookouts, swimming, and laughter. But two things were working against it by the late 1940s: River pollution made swimming less popular (and safe), and the centrality of the automobile to American life meant more people wanted to just drive and park—not walk—to their fun spot.

▶ This hike crosses the New York–New Jersey boundary. Station Rock, marked by a granite monument, marks the line atop the Palisades. It's on our hike and is worth a visit.

By the early 1960s, the park stopped maintaining Forest View, and in short order it was overgrown with weeds, vines, and poison ivy. Now only the stone-and-timber ruins of a few old picnic benches here and there, peering out under the brushlike Mayan ruins, testify to the happy days once enjoyed here.

Mary Lawrence came from an old New York family who established a summer home at nearby Sneden's Landing in the 1870s. The waterfall on our hike, sometimes

Author Ron Dupont on the Hudson River at the base of the Palisades is about to climb the "Giant Stairs."

called Peanut Leap Cascade or Half Moon Falls, was on the southern end of their property. Mary, born 1868, developed into a sculptor of considerable talent. By the early 1890s, she was an assistant to famed American sculptor Augustus Saint-Gaudens. While in his employ, she executed the statue of Columbus that stood in front of the Administration Building at the 1893 World's Columbian Exposition in Chicago.

Mary had visited Italy in the late 1880s and was particularly impressed by the Capuchin Monastery at Amalfi, whose columned pergola overlooks the Gulf of Salerno. Lawrence determined to create a similar structure at the waterfall on the Hudson. With the assistance of Saint-Gaudens and her associates, Stanford White and Charles F. McKim (of the famed architectural firm McKim, Mead, and White), she designed and constructed a terrace, bench, and columned pergola on the edge of the river, with a pool, grotto, niches, and gardens at the base of the waterfall. Decorated with sculpture, potted flowers, and shrubs, and lit with Chinese lanterns, the waterfall and gardens were the Lawrences' favorite spot for summer parties.

Mary and her husband, sculptor Francois Tonetti, had a large family and many friends. Their circle included a stellar array of those in the arts, architecture, and Broadway theater, including Noel Coward and the Barrymore family. They frequently held post-theater parties, arriving from Manhattan by boat up the Hudson. Sadly, in the years after Mary Lawrence Tonetti's death in 1945, the magical falls, pool, grotto, and pergola fell into decay. Now it's not an imitation ruin, but a real one—a sad reminder of a family's rich vision and imagination, yet remarkably compelling even in a state of vandalization and abandonment. Have lunch here, sit on the stone bench overlooking the Hudson, envision the statues, the pools, the flowers . . . imagine you are chatting with Mary about her latest sculpture, or schmoozing Ethel Barrymore about her new Broadway hit. Ah, those were the days . . .

The majesty and beauty of the Hudson and the Palisades are everywhere evident on this hike—small wonder that the preservation of these historic cliffs was one of the first great conservation victories in the region.

Miles and Directions

0.0 Begin in the Lookout Inn parking lot. Head east toward State Line Lookout and a retaining wall. Turn right (south) on the Long Path (blue blazes), which is old Route 9W, an abandoned highway.

0.2 Pass through boulders and proceed along the shoulder of the entrance road.

0.3 At a sign To Forest View Trail, the Long Path turns left into the woods, leaving the road.

0.4 Steep descent off the Palisades on stone stairs. Caution!

0.6 Cross stream and turn left (east) onto the Forest View Trail (blue/white blazes) and continue to descend off the Palisades on a series of switchbacks and steps.

1.1 At the T intersection turn left (north) onto the Shore Trail (white blazes), paralleling the Hudson River. (**FYI:** Area was known as Forest View Landing [see The Hike].)

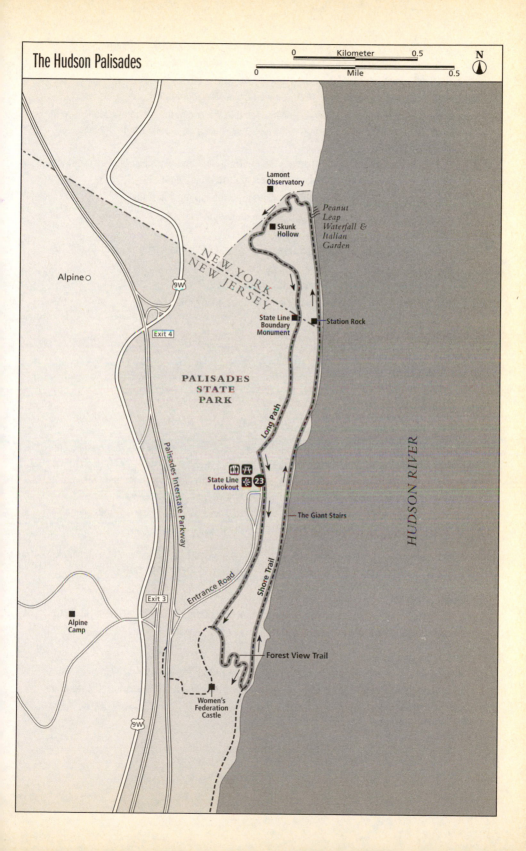

The Hudson Palisades

Kilometer
0   0.5

Mile
0   0.5

N

Lamont
Observatory

*Peanut
Leap
Waterfall &
Italian
Garden*

Skunk
Hollow

NEW YORK
NEW JERSEY

Alpine ○

9W

Exit 4

State Line
Boundary
Monument

Station Rock

PALISADES
STATE
PARK

Long Path

State Line
Lookout

23

The Giant Stairs

Palisades Interstate Parkway

HUDSON RIVER

Shore Trail

Entrance Road

Exit 3

Alpine
Camp

Forest View Trail

Women's
Federation
Castle

9W

1.6 The Shore Trail reaches "The Giant Stairs." Now begins the boulder-rock and roller scramble. *Caution!* Besides the boulders, the park warns that copperhead snakes are "relatively common here."

2.4 Pass through chain-link fence. (**FYI:** You are now in New York State.)

2.9 Cross stream and reach Peanut Leap Waterfall and the site of the "Italian Garden" (see The Hike). The trail turns left (west) up stairs and begins to zigzag up alongside the falls and alongside stream.

3.2 Reach Skunk Hollow. Turn left (south) onto the Long Path and cross two bridges over the stream. The trail leads up through the hollow to a set of stone stairs.

3.5 Reach the cliffs above Hudson River, Yonkers, and the Tappan Zee Bridge.

3.6 Pass open cliffs, up the stairs, and through a chain-link fence, reaching a 6-foot-tall State Line Boundary Monument (1882).

3.7 At fork bear left (south), continuing on the Long Path. (**FYI:** The right fork leads to old Route 9W.)

4.0 The Long Path goes from a woods path onto old Route 9W.

4.2 Back at State Line Lookout, Lookout Inn, and the parking lot.

Hike Information

Local Information

County of Bergen, One Bergen County Plaza, Hackensack, 07601, (201) 336-6000, www.co.bergen.nj.us

Local Events/Attractions

There are a number of attractions within the park itself, including the Kearny House, an eighteenth-century homestead, and Fort Lee Historic Park. For information call (201) 461-1776 or go to www.njpalisades.org. To the north is the historic town of Piermont, New York, which features restaurants, shops, cafes, and music venues. Also nearby is the Tenafly Interpretive Center, with trails and an interpretive center; 313 Hudson Avenue, Tenafly 07670; (201) 568-6093; www.tenaflynaturecenter.org

Restaurants

The historic Lookout Inn at State Line Lookout offers a selection of fast food along with snacks, drinks, books, maps, and gift items. Hours vary by season; call (201) 750-0456.

Organizations

Friends of the Palisades, Administration Building, Bear Mountain, NY 10911; (845) 786-2701; www.friendsofpalisades.org/home

Other Resources

Lots of good history and information on the park can be found at their Friends' Web site, www.njpalisades.org. For an excellent history of the Lawrence and Tonetti families, and their famous waterfall and garden, read Isabelle K. Savell's *The Tonetti Years at Snedens Landing* (New City, NY: The Historical Society of Rockland County, 1977).

24 The Princeton Woods

Roam the Revolutionary landscape at Princeton Battlefield State Park and the Institute Woods. Follow wide paths, sidewalks, pavement, and former trolley tracks, all linked, creating a loop loaded with interesting locals. The route skirts the Clarke House and the Friends Meetinghouse, the scene of a clash between the American and British forces. Stroll along the lanes that Einstein wandered. Traverse through upland forest festooned with giant oaks, hickories, and tulips. Amble along bottomlands under box elders, silver maples, and sycamores. Flow by the Stony Brook. Enjoy the beauty of the Institute's grounds with its modern sculptures. Migrate through the area like the notorious spring warblers.

Start: Princeton Battlefield State Park parking lot on County Route 583
Distance: 3.5-mile loop
Approximate hiking time: 2 hours
Difficulty: Easy, with gentle grades
Trail surface: Wide paths, sidewalks, pavement, and former trolley railbed
Seasons: All good
Other trail users: Multiuse
Canine compatibility: Leashed dogs permitted
Land status: State park and Institute for Advanced Study property
Nearest town: Princeton
Fees and permits: None
Schedule: Dawn to dusk

Maps: *DeLorme: New Jersey Atlas & Gazetteer* p.42; USGS Princeton, NJ, quadrangle; a trail map is also available at the park.
Trail contacts: Princeton Battlefield State Park, 500 Mercer Road, Princeton 08540-4810; (609) 921-0074; www.state.nj.us/dep/parks andforests/parks/princeton.html. Institute for Advanced Study, Einstein Drive, Princeton 08540; (609) 734-8000; www.ias.edu/
Other: A popular place during bird migratory season; bring binoculars.
Special considerations: Keep in mind that US 206 through Princeton is highly congested during morning and evening rush hours; you may want to schedule your visit accordingly.

Finding the trailhead: From the intersection of U.S. Highway 206 and Highway 27 in Princeton, travel 0.1 mile northeast on Highway 27. Turn right (southwest) onto Mercer Road/Princeton Pike (CR 583) and drive 1.4 miles. Turn left into Princeton Battlefield State Park. The parking lot will be on the right.

The Hike

This walk around Princeton Battlefield is on hallowed ground, but for more reasons than you might imagine. Following up his famous Christmas crossing of the Delaware River and surprise victory at Trenton in 1776, George Washington wanted one more punch at the British before entering winter quarters. Cornwallis had reestablished a large force at Trenton; using the same secrecy as before, Washington's army slipped past Trenton and attacked a smaller British force at Princeton on January 3, 1777. The battle spread over a wide area, from the park here all the way to Nassau Hall in

Princeton village. It was another victory for Washington, with 500 British killed, captured, or wounded. This huge morale boost was dampened only by the death of General Hugh Mercer from battlefield wounds. The oak under which Mercer lay while wounded was a landmark here for centuries, a massive living testimony to Revolutionary days. The "Mercer Oak" finally fell from old age in the year 2000.

▶ **Our hike passes two witnesses to the Battle of Princeton. The Thomas Clarke House (1772), now a state-owned historic site, stood amid the battle and was where General Mercer was brought afterward. The Stony Brook Friends Meeting House (Quaker) was built in 1760 and served as a field hospital for both British and American troops; it's still in use by the Religious Society of Friends.**

The growth of Princeton as a place of higher learning soon changed its reputation from military to intellectual. In 1930 the Institute for Advanced Study was established here as a center for worldwide theoretical research. Not formally affiliated with Princeton, the IAS has its own reputation as a home for stellar minds. These have included J. Robert Oppenheimer, the "father of the atomic bomb"; George F. Kennan, the Cold War diplomat, historian, and proponent of "containment"; John Von Neumann, who helped develop the modern digital computer; and not least, Albert Einstein, who lived in Princeton from 1933 until his death in 1955. The 800-acre Institute Woods (500 acres are permanently preserved) has been a place

Haning Bridge, a suspension bridge over Stony Brook, leads to "adventure island."

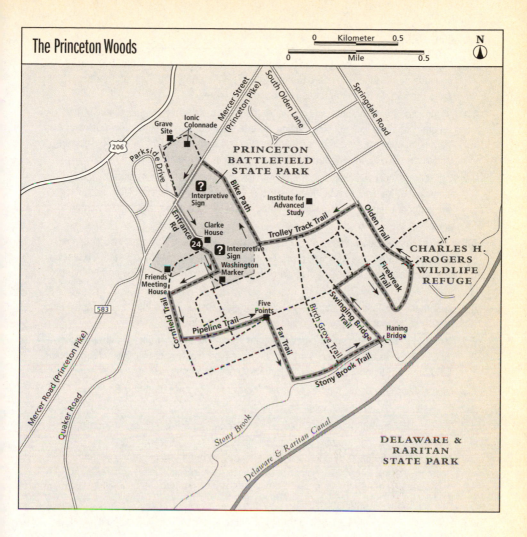

The Princeton Woods

Grave Site
Ionic Colonnade
Mercer Street (Princeton Pike)
South Olden Lane
Springdale Road
206
Parkside Drive
PRINCETON BATTLEFIELD STATE PARK
Interpretive Sign
Institute for Advanced Study
Entrance Rd
Bike Path
Clarke House
Trolley Track Trail
Olden Trail
24
Interpretive Sign
Washington Marker
CHARLES H. ROGERS WILDLIFE REFUGE
Friends Meeting House
Firebreak Trail
Cornfield Trail
Five Points
Swinging Bridge Trail
Birch Grove Trail
Haning Bridge
Pipeline Trail
Far Trail
583
Mercer Road (Princeton Pike)
Quaker Road
Stony Brook Trail
Stony Brook
Delaware & Raritan Canal
DELAWARE & RARITAN STATE PARK

for deep thinking and serious pondering for all of them. So Einstein strolled these same fields while thinking about unified field theory.

Between 1900 and 1939 the Trenton–Princeton Traction Company operated "Fast Line," or the trolley system, which ran on this trail. For one thin dime you could catch a ride every half hour between Trenton and Princeton.

As you stroll within these woods, see if you can spot a wood thrush with its flute-like song, or a scarlet tanager with its brilliant red plumage. Institute Woods is a bird-watcher's paradise! More than 40 species nest here and more than 200 species (special attention to the warblers) migrate through the woods. As the New Jersey Audubon Society says, "The name of Institute Woods and spring warblers are one." There is a maze of trails in this area. Don't worry if you get lost: You can't stray far, so enjoy it.

Miles and Directions

0.0 From the parking lot, walk back to the entrance lane and turn right (southeast) and continue up the lane toward the Thomas Clarke House. (**Side trip:** Turn left [northeast] and cross the lawn to Princeton Battlefield interpretive kiosks.)

0.1 At the end of the lane proceed south onto the lawn, passing the Thomas Clarke House and an outbuilding on your left side. Edging the tree line, you pass a marble trail post with a path coming on the right from the Meeting House. Continue straight (south), descending across the lawn to the woods line, where you will find an opening and a path.

0.2 Arrive at the Trolley Track Trail. At the marble trail post, turn right (west) onto the Trolley Track Trail. (**Side trip:** Explore the intersection, including an interpretive kiosk explaining the Institute Lands and an obelisk commemorating Washington's march from Trenton to Princeton.)

0.3 At the T intersection with the marble trail post, turn left (south) onto Cornfield Trail, a red shale road. (**Side trip:** Turn right [north] onto Meeting House Lane and travel 305 feet on the red shale road, leading to the historic Friends Meeting House [1724] and an interpretive kiosk.)

0.4 Before the cornfield veer left (east) off the Cornfield Trail and onto the Pipeline Trail, a large grassy swipe that eventually becomes a trail. Expect to cross two paths.

0.7 Arrive at a five-point intersection. Pass a path coming in sharply from the right and an open field. Pass a trail coming in on the left. Turn right (south) onto Far Trail after the open field. The Far Trail borders the cultivated field within the woods line.

1.0 Before the Stony Brook, the trail turns left (east) and becomes the Stony Brook Trail.

1.2 Pass the Birch Grove Trail on the left.

1.4 Arrive at Haning Bridge, a suspension bridge over the Stony Brook. Turn left (north) onto Swinging Bridge Trail, avoiding all trails leaving to the right. (**Side trip:** Cross over the bridge to explore the island. There is an unofficial trail that borders the Stony Brook, leading to some stepping-stones across a feeder stream, which brings you up onto the Delaware and Raritan Canal State Park towpath. [To the northeast is Carnegie Lake and to the southwest is Port Mercer.])

1.6 Come to a major intersection and turn right (northeast) onto the Pipeline Trail, a real wide red-shale lane, passing several trails.

1.8 One hundred and fifty feet before a culvert, turn right (south) onto the Firebreak Trail, a worn path leading into a magnificent pine grove.

2.0 The trail turns left (northeast), edging a marsh.

2.1 After crossing a bridge turn left (northwest) onto a path, which is also the Elizabethtown Water Company's pipeline. (Don't get confused; this is not the Pipeline Trail.)

2.2 At the intersection with the Pipeline Trail, cross through the tree line on some boards and onto the Olden Trail, a grassy path in a field between a red barn and a house.

2.3 Pass around an auto gate and through a cul-de-sac onto South Olden Lane (co-aligned with Olden Trail), a paved road, and heading northwest. (**FYI:** Some of the greatest minds ever either worked or resided on this lane: Einstein, Oppenheimer, Godel, Von Neuman, Beurling, and Woodrow Wilson.)

2.4 After Mailbox 330, turn left (west) onto Trolley Track Trail, a substantial cinder bed path. Ignore numerous trails entering from the left.

2.7 Pass the Institute for Advanced Study on the right with its vast lawn, towering buildings, modern sculptures, and serene pond.

2.8 Arrive at an intersection with a marble trail post and a sign reading BIKE PATH. Turn right (north) onto the paved Bike Path, which edges a tree line and meadow. (**FYI:** You are now looking over the Princeton Battlefield.)

3.2 Cross Mercer Street and turn left (southwest) onto the sidewalk, shortly passing an interpretive kiosk for the Colonnade. (**Side trip:** Turn right [north] and cross the lawn to visit the Ionic Colonnade, designed by the same man who later became an architect for the U.S. Capitol, and the gravesite for American and British soldiers killed at the Battle of Princeton.)

3.4 Cross Parkside Drive. Within 150 feet turn left (southeast) and cross Mercer Street and walk up the entrance road to Princeton Battlefield State Park and arrive back at the parking lot.

3.5 Arrive at the parking lot.

Hike Information

Local Information
Princeton Regional Convention & Visitors Bureau, 9 Vandeventer Avenue, Princeton 08542; (609) 924-1776; www.visitprinceton.org

Local Events/Attractions
The historic town of Princeton has a number of interesting sights, and Princeton University has a large historic campus. Tours available through the University: Princeton University, Princeton 08544; (609) 258-3000; www.princeton.edu/. The Princeton University Art Museum is first-rate and free to the public: www.princetonartmuseum.org

Lodging and Restaurants
Numerous options in town; see Princeton Online, www.princetonol.com

Organizations
Princeton Battlefield Area Preservation Society, PO Box 7645, Princeton 08543; (609) 921-0074; www.saveprincetonbattlefield.org

25 Jockey Hollow

This lollipop hike is a long hill-and-dale adventure through a unique portion of the Highlands. The Wisconsin Glacier stopped short of Jockey Hollow, leaving the terrain rounded, without jagged features. Mostly wide forested paths are well posted with mini-maps. March by the headwaters of the Passaic River and through Washington's winter encampment. En route visit the Wick House, a restored colonial farm. In contrast, skirt the Cross Estate and its gardens, once belonging to a wealthy member of the "mountain colony" of Bernardsville. Due to the web of trails, the route can easily be varied.

Start: The Scherman-Hoffman Wildlife Sanctuary parking lot on Hardscrabble Road
Distance: 9.7-mile lollipop
Approximate hiking time: 6 hours
Difficulty: Strenuous due to length
Trail surface: Wide forested paths
Seasons: All good
Other trail users: Horses on designated trails
Canine compatibility: No dogs permitted on Sanctuary property; leashed dogs permitted on National Park Service property
Land status: National Historical Park
Nearest town: Morristown
Fees and permits: Admission fee
Schedule: 9:00 a.m. to 5:00 p.m. year-round

Maps: *DeLorme: New Jersey Atlas & Gazetteer* p. 30–31; USGS Mendham and Bernardsville, NJ, quadrangles; a trail map is also available at the park.
Trail contacts: Morristown National Historical Park, 30 Washington Place, Morristown 07960-4299; (973) 543-4030; www.nps.gov/morr/
Other: Leave the metal detector home, if you were thinking of it: Artifact collecting is strictly a no-no. It's worthwhile to stop in at the interpretive center and pick up handouts and materials on flora, fauna, and history.
Special considerations: By starting at the Wick House, you can do a shorter version of this hike, or split it into two shorter hikes.

Finding the trailhead: From Interstate 287 in Van Dorans Mills (exit 30), turn north onto Maple Avenue and drive 0.2 mile to the intersection with U.S. Highway 202 (traffic light). Cross (northwest) the highway onto Childs Road, passing Van Dorans Mills on the right. After traveling 0.2 mile, turn right onto Hardscrabble Road. Go 1.3 miles to the Scherman parking lot (just past entrance to the Scherman-Hoffman Center).

The Hike

This hike requires imagination in summertime: You must pretend it's freezing cold. Revolutionary War winter suffering generally brings two words to mind: Valley Forge. The Continental Army's winter encampment there in 1777–78 was indeed fraught with hardship, but the fact remains a *harder* winter awaited them two years later, here at Morristown. Eighteenth-century armies didn't normally fight in the winter; they went to winter quarters, and fighting resumed in spring. As a winter encampment for the Continental Army for 1779–80, Washington chose Morristown. It was close enough to New York and Perth Amboy to keep an eye on the British, but it was protected by the Watchung Mountains. He couldn't have known this winter would be, by most accounts, the worst one of the eighteenth century, with 4 feet of snow on the ground by January.

Thirteen thousand Continental troops came to Morristown that winter. Over 1,000 log huts were built in Jockey Hollow, a few miles outside of town. The 14-by-16 foot huts had a fireplace and housed a dozen men each—we pass reconstructed huts on this walk. Washington and his entourage stayed in the Morristown home of the Ford family, the finest house in town.

Although Morristown's "hard winter" of 1779–80 surpassed that at Valley Forge, far fewer men died. In the intervening years the army became more competent at managing its affairs and acquiring provisions and supplies. But the winter at Morristown was hard enough—it fostered a mutiny of Pennsylvania soldiers. This gave birth to one of the more remarkable bits of New Jersey folklore.

According to legend, two Pennsylvania soldiers accosted a young Temperance Wick, on horseback. Wick's house (which you can visit on this hike) was nearby; "Tempe," as the girl was called, had gone to fetch a doctor for her mother; her father, an army captain, had died not long before. The mutineers wanted Tempe's horse; after first feigning surrender, she spurred the horse and charged for home. Knowing

American Revolutionary soldiers spent a horrific winter in Jockey Hollow, billeted in huts similar to this reproduction. The trail goes to the right of the huts.

the mutineers would give chase and look in all the customary places for her horse, Tempe—so the legend goes—brought the horse inside, put down a comforter to muffle its hoof-steps, and hid it inside the bedroom of the house.

This lovely bit of folklore is nonetheless only legend, possibly why the National Park Service makes scant mention of it. Instead they focus on the historical fact that the Wick House was the headquarters for General Arthur St. Clair—which is interesting, but no match for a horse hidden in a bedroom. Morristown National Historical Park preserves all these places—the Ford Mansion, Jockey Hollow, and the Wick House, as well as nearby Fort Nonsense. Local public-spirited citizens started acquiring the properties in the 1870s; in 1933 they were transferred to the federal government and became America's first National Historical Park (an honor not bestowed on Valley Forge until 1976). In the 1930s the Civilian Conservation Corps conducted archaeological investigations of the Revolutionary encampment at Jockey Hollow. It was crude by later standards, and much of the data was subsequently lost; yet this was some of the first historical archaeology conducted in the United States, and provided insights into that epoch of American history.

Miles and Directions

0.0 The trail leaves the northeast end of the parking lot and right of the kiosk, where it joins the Dogwood Trail (red blazes). Turn left (north) onto the Dogwood Trail and the Patriots' Path (white blazes with a tree design) and begin to climb.

0.1 At the fork, veer left (southwest) continuing on the Patriots' Path. The Dogwood Trail bears right (northeast), creating a loop within Scherman-Hoffman Wildlife Sanctuary.

0.3 Trail junction: signpost 64 with a map. Continue straight (southwest) downhill onto the New Jersey Brigade Trail where a series of historical kiosks are located. (**Side trip:** At the signpost, turn right onto the path where another set of historical kiosks are located, explaining archeological discoveries [trash pits and hearth remains].) (**FYI:** Throughout the national park, it seems at every intersection there is a numbered signpost [hike by numbers] with a map on it and a "You are here" arrow.)

0.5 Trail junction: signpost 63. With Indian Grove Brook before you, turn right (north), remaining on the New Jersey Brigade Trail.

0.7 Pass an unmarked trail on the right (south), which leads to the archaeological site and signpost 64.

0.9 Pass the Connecting Trail (white blazes) on the right (east), and continue straight (north).

1.0 A bridle path enters on your left (west), which leads directly to the Cross Estate and the public gardens.

1.1 Trail junction: signpost 62. Turn right (east), heading for Jockey Hollow. The trail entering on the left (west) leads to the Cross Estate. Shortly pass a trail entering on the left (northwest), which leads to a parking lot.

1.7 Cross over the Passaic River on a wooden bridge, which needs a little TLC.

2.4 Trail junction: signpost 58. Turn left onto the Grand Loop Trail (white blazes), skirting Blachleys Hill. (**Note:** The New Jersey Brigade Trail turns right and is co-aligned with the Grand Loop Trail, where our hike will return via this route.)

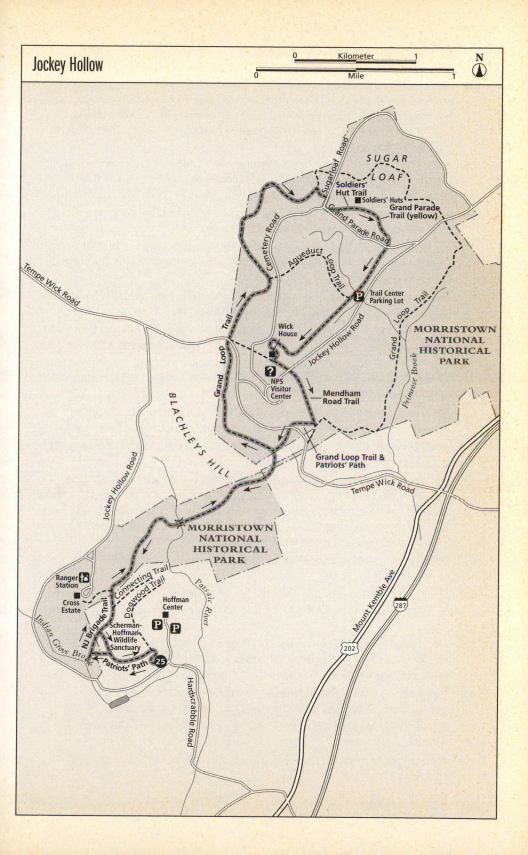

Jockey Hollow

0 Kilometer 1

0 Mile 1

N

SUGAR LOAF

Sugarloaf Road

Soldiers' Hut Trail

■ Soldiers' Huts

Grand Parade Trail (yellow)

Grand Parade Road

Cemetery Road

Aqueduct Loop Trail

Trail Center Parking Lot

Wick House

Grand Loop Trail

Jockey Hollow Road

Grand Loop Trail

NPS Visitor Center

Mendham Road Trail

MORRISTOWN NATIONAL HISTORICAL PARK

Primrose Brook

Tempe Wick Road

Grand Loop Trail & Patriots' Path

BLACHLEYS HILL

Tempe Wick Road

Jockey Hollow Road

MORRISTOWN NATIONAL HISTORICAL PARK

Connecting Trail

Passaic River

Dogwood Trail

Ranger Station

Cross Estate

Hoffman Center

NJ Brigade Trail

Scherman-Hoffman Wildlife Sanctuary

Patriots' Path

25

Indian Grove Brook

Hardscrabble Road

Mount Kemble Ave

287

202

3.1 Trail junction: signpost 59. Turn right (northeast) onto a gravel driveway, still following the white blazes of the Grand Loop Trail.

3.2 Pass around auto gate and cross (northeast) Tempe Wick Road. Bear left to signpost 1 and continue straight (northeast) on the Grand Loop Trail. There are a flurry of signposts and trails leading to the Wick House (0.2 mile) and Visitor Center (0.3 mile). (**Bail-out:** Take the Mendham Road Trail to the Wick House and pick up the hike from here [found in Miles and Directions].)

3.6 Trail junction: signpost 3. At the fork bear left (northwest) and continue to follow the Grand Loop Trail. The Aqueduct Loop Trail swings right (northeast), crossing Cemetery Road and eventually running along side Primrose Brook.

4.5 Trail junction: signpost 4. Turn right (east), leaving the Grand Loop Trail, once more back onto the Patriots' Path, and descend toward the soldiers' huts.

4.6 Trail junction: signpost 40. At the Soldier Hut parking lot and the intersection of Cemetery, Sugarloaf, and Grand Parade Roads, walk (southeast) along the shoulder of Grand Parade Road (Old Parade Road).

4.7 Arrive at the historical kiosks and turn left (east) between the three posts onto the Soldier Hut Trail (yellow blazes), climb across an open field toward the soldiers' huts.

4.9 Arrive at the soldiers' huts. The Soldier Hut Trail skirts the huts on the right side (south) and continues along the crest of the hill, passing historical kiosks and signpost 41.

5.1 At signpost 42 turn right (southwest) onto the Grand Parade Trail (yellow blazes). (**Note:** You will be following the Grand Parade Trail through a maze of signs and intersections, till you reach the Wick House.)

5.3 Just beyond signpost 43, come to historical kiosks where the trail crosses (southwest) Grand Parade Road to signpost 44 and continue on Grand Parade Trail down a hollow.

5.6 All within the next 0.1 mile pass signpost 45, a parking lot, and a directory, while heading southwest on the Grand Parade Trail.

5.7 Stay with the yellow blazes of the Grand Parade Trail through the maze of twists, turns, and trail intersections. After passing signpost 35, cross the Primrose Brook wooden bridge where the trail forks. Veer left at signpost 34, while the right fork begins the Aqueduct Trail. Pass around gate, and before Jockey Hollow Road, turn right (southwest), where the trail begins to climb between the road and the ravine.

6.1 At signpost 47 the Grand Parade Trail turns right (northwest) and parallels an orchard fence.

6.4 At signpost 48 the Grand Parade Trail ends. Turn left (south) onto Cemetery Road. Head toward the Wick House, which is clearly visible, walking by the barn and through the parking lot.

6.5 Arrive at the Wick House. From the back of the building, proceed around its left (east) side onto a stone walkway, leading to the front of the house and Mendham Road Trail. Turn left (southeast) onto the Mendham Road Trail, a red-shale-covered path.

6.6 Pass a walkway on the right, which leads to the visitor center: restrooms, water, and displays. There is a fee when entering from the parking lot side of the center.

6.7 Cross Jockey Hollow Road and continue heading straight (southeast) on Mendham Road Trail.

7.0 At the junction turn right (southwest) onto the Grand Loop Trail and the Patriots' Path and head down a gravel path.

7.1 At signpost 57 cross (south) Tempe Wick Road where the Grand Loop Trail climbs over the bank and drops into a hollow.

7.2 Cross over a wooden bridge, passing signpost 57.

7.3 At the junction and signpost 58, turn left (south) onto the New Jersey Brigade Trail and retrace the hike to Scherman-Hoffman Wildlife Sanctuary parking lot on Hardscrabble Road.

9.7 Arrive back at parking lot.

Hike Information

Local Information
Morris County Visitor's Center, 6 Court Street, Morristown 07960; (973) 631-5151; www.morris tourism.org

Local Events/Attractions
The Wick House at Jockey Hollow served as officers' quarters during the winters the Continental Army was encamped here (see above for contact information). Nearby on the outskirts of Morristown is Fosterfields Living Historical Farm, 73 Kahdena Road, Morristown 07960; (973) 326-7645; www.morrisparks.net. The Ford Mansion, Washington's headquarters at Jockey Hollow, is very much worth a visit: Ford Mansion, Morristown National Historical Park, 30 Washington Place, Morristown 07960-2016, ext. 210; www.nps.gov/morr

Lodging and Restaurants
Many options in the area; check Morris County Visitor's Center, 6 Court Street, Morristown 07960; (973) 631-5151; www.morristourism.org

Organizations
Jockey Hollow Historic Preservation Association, PO Box 1598, Morristown 07962-1598; www.jockeyhollow.org

THE CROSS ESTATE

In contrast to the harsh living conditions and the primitive log huts constructed by the New Jersey Brigade in 1779–80, you also pass on this hike the other end of the spectrum: the Cross Estate. At the turn of the twentieth century, the Mountain Colony, said to be the second wealthiest area in America, reached from your current location in Jockey Hollow all the way to Gladstone. The country estates, composed of forty-eight to a thousand-acre parks, were adorned with gardens, carriage houses, kennels, stables, and staff cottages. Names like Pierreponts, Ballantines, Whitneys, Kusers, Roeblings, Drydens, Pfizers, and the Dillons made their fortunes by speculating, merchandising, and financing: real estate and railroads, banking and insurance, minerals and chemicals, steel and the stock market.

John A. Bensel, an active member of the Mountain Colony, built this estate in 1905. He directed the construction of the infamous Chelsea Pier and later he became the state engineer for all of New York, supervising such projects as the Barge Canal. The estate ("Queen Ann Farm") was sold in 1929 to W. Redmond Cross, who had just lost his Morristown home to fire.

Mr. Cross, quite the wealthy unique character, seems to have made his fortune in the house of Redman Company, a New York City bank, which had strong ties with foreign financial institutions. While on the board of directors of various railroads, ironically, he belonged to the Early Birds, a fraternal order of select pilots who had soloed in vintage airplanes prior to World War I. Besides being a scholarly cartographer, this eclectic individual also had a naturalist streak; he became the president of the New York Zoological Society and a member of the American Committee for International Wildlife Protection, which reflected his concerns.

Mrs. Julia Newbold Cross was not to be overshadowed; she presided as the president of the New York Horticultural Society. Along with the renowned landscape architect, Clarence Fowler, they created a formal English garden with walls, walkways, and hanging wisteria from the pergolas. Today the Friends of Cross Estate and the Garden Conservancy maintain these refurbished gardens. They cherish volunteers!

In an effort to protect the New Jersey Brigade Encampment Site, the National Park purchased the Cross Estate in 1975, allowing us to experience the lifestyle of the rich and the famous, even if it's only for a moment. If time permits, take a side trip to the "Hardscrabble House," the name given to their home by the Cross family. Postscript: If you have "chump change" of six to nine million dollars, you too can purchase one of these estates on The Mountain.

26 Watchung Reservation

Journey through geological history, crossing sandstone and shale, or climbing the basalt of the First and Second Watchung Mountains. Edge the serene Blue Brook Valley and Lake Surprise. Follow the Green Brook to a waterfall. Ramble through the ruins of an old mill and a deserted village. Pass under the evergreens planted by the Civilian Conservation Corps. Visit the Nature & Science Center, the first such in New Jersey. This long loop hike on bridle paths, foot trails, and short stints on the roads has a few moderate climbs. Except for sections of traffic and quarry noises, the route is relatively tranquil.

Start: Watchung Reservation Trailside Nature and Science Center parking lot off New Providence Road

Distance: 10.5-mile loop

Approximate hiking time: 5 hours

Difficulty: Moderate, but lengthy

Trail surface: Footpaths, woods roads, and short roadwalks

Seasons: All

Other trail users: Horses on designated trails

Canine compatibility: Leashed dogs permitted

Land status: County park

Nearest town: Mountainside, but essentially surrounded by towns

Fees and permits: None

Schedule: Dawn to dusk

Maps: DeLorme: New Jersey Atlas & Gazetteer p. 31; USGS Chatham and Roselle, NJ, quadrangles; Watchung Reservation Trail Map, available at visitor center and Museum, as well as some park information kiosks.

Trail contacts: Union County Department of Parks and Recreation, (908) 527-4900; www .ucnj.org

Other: Paved roads that cross through the reservation are not just for park use—they are busy county roads used by commuters. Use care when crossing and keep your eyes open.

Finding the trailhead: From Interstate 78 west take exit 43. At the first traffic light, turn right onto McMane Avenue. Reaching the T intersection with Glenside Avenue, turn left. In 1.2 miles turn right onto W.R. Tracy Drive (County Route 645) entering the reservation. Reaching the traffic circle, take the first right onto Summit Lane then turn right onto New Providence Road. The parking area is to the right, where the road makes a sharp left turn.

The Hike

This hike takes us through the volcanic ridges of the Watchungs. Created during the Jurassic Era some 200 million years ago, the Watchungs sweep like a great crooked arm south and then west through the New Jersey Piedmont. Cradled deep within its embrace is the Great Swamp. Here, the Watchungs rise like a green, rocky wave above the surrounding sea of dense urban development.

The densely forested Watchung Reservation has an aura of untouched forest primeval in many areas. But like most places in New Jersey, it has a long history of industrial, agricultural, and residential uses, the traces of which can be found all along our hike. These stony ridges of the Watchungs in western Union County (originally part of Essex County) were not far from important eighteenth-century New Jersey tidewater cities like Newark and Elizabethtown. Such growing towns were a ready market for lumber; as such it's no surprise that the first settler in this area, Peter Willcocks, dammed the Blue Brook and built a sawmill here ca.1736. After the original forest was felled for timber, it was soon replaced with fields, pastures, and farmsteads.

The Willcocks family also exploited another natural resource here: copper ore. The Willcocks Mine, located below the Blue Trail in Copper Mine Ravine, was one of several copper mines that operated in the Watchung Mountains in the 1700s. As the original forests gave way to farmland, gristmills were added to the scene, using the waterpower of the Blue and Green Brooks to grind local grain into flour. The Willcocks family operated a gristmill on Green Brook starting ca.1760.

In the nineteenth century, a new industry was added to the economy here: paper-making. In the early 1800s, Edmund Seeley purchased the Willcocks gristmill on Green Brook and expanded it into a rag paper mill (so called because paper was then made from recycled cloth and rags, of which the nearby cities were a ready source). On the hill above the paper mill, Seeley built a beautiful Federal-style mansion. The ruins and foundations of both the paper mill and mansion can be seen along the Sierra Trail. The property was added to the reservation in the 1930s, and the ruins are being nominated to the State and National Register of Historic Places.

The Feltville general store and church, part of the Deserted Village of Feltville, are historic features of the Watchung Reservation.

The biggest story in the area's history came in 1844, when New York City businessman David Felt started buying up land from the Willcocks family. Felt was in the stationery business, and he soon built not just a paper mill but also an entire community for his works nearby. The industrial village on the hillside above Blue Brook came to be called Feltville.

Miles and Directions

0.0 From the south end of the Nature & Science Center's parking lot, locate the Sierra (or Nature) Trail (white blazes on an oak tree) and turn right (west) onto New Providence Road and immediately turn left (south) onto the trail (green blazes) and down the hill. (**FYI:** Except for a short section, stay on the Sierra Trail the entire hike.)

0.2 Within short order, the Yellow Trail (yellow blazes) comes in from the left and becomes co-aligned with the Sierra Trail. Immediately, they come to a T intersection; turn left (west) onto the Orange Trail (orange blazes), the Sierra Trail, and the Yellow Trail. At the fork, veer left (southwest), following the Sierra Trail and the Yellow Trail. Finally, turn right (northwest) onto the Sierra Trail. This maze plays out all within a tenth of a mile!

0.6 The Blue Trail (blue blazes) enters from the right and becomes co-aligned with the Sierra Trail. Cooper Mine Ravine is to the left.

0.8 At the bottom of the hill the Blue Trail turns right (north). Continue straight (west) on the Sierra Trail, shortly ascending above Blue Brook and the bottomland. Ignore the unmarked trails.

1.5 Cross a bridle path and begin to descend on the trail.

1.9 At the T intersection turn left (southwest) onto a bridle path. Shortly, turn left (south) onto a trail and ascend through a grove of red and white pines planted by the CCC. (**Option:** To avoid the road and quarry noise, continue straight [southwest] down the bridle path, picking up the hike at mile 4.9.)

2.4 Pay close attention to the white blazing as you approach the Sky Top Picnic Area. Turn right (southeast) before the pavilion and out the driveway. (**FYI:** Area also has picnic tables, water, and portable toilets.)

2.5 The Sierra Trail crosses (southeast) Sky Top Drive onto a bridle path.

2.6 At the T intersection, the Sierra Trail turns right (southwest) onto a bridle path, which begins to climb the First Watchung Mountain.

3.6 Arrive at Basalt Ledge, overlooking the quarry. Continue straight (south) along the ridge before descending. (**Option:** To avoid the road and quarry noises, take the trail that veers right [northwest] across the vista, picking up the hike at mile 4.7.)

3.7 Turn right (west) off the path and onto the trail behind the apartments (hideous trail design!). Shortly, the route improves, paralleling the Green Brook.

4.3 Pass through the ruins of a paper mill.

4.4 Turn right (north) and climb steeply in and out of the old millpond, passing old foundations and reaching an outlook over Green Brook. (**Side trip:** Continue straight [northwest] on a path leading to the falls, the lower pond, and a channel cut in the rock.)

4.7 Pass a trail on the right and shortly arrive at a T intersection. Turn left (northwest), following the Sierra Trail down the hill. (Trail to the right leads to the Basalt Ledge.)

4.9 At the fork veer left toward Sky Top Road, shortly turning left (southwest) onto its shoulder, crossing a bridge over the Blue Brook.

5.0 Before the intersection with County Route 527, turn right (north) and cross Sky Top Road onto the lawn. Pick up the woods line and the white blazes and enter (northeast) the woods on the Sierra Trail.

5.4 At the fork at the end of the boardwalk, veer left (northeast) on the trail over a series of rills.

5.8 Cross a trail and continue straight (east) onto a wide path framed by spruce. (Trail to the right leads to Hermit's Pond.

6.0 The Sierra Trail and Cataract Hollow Road (paved) become co-aligned for the next 0.5 mile, passing through the Deserted Village of Feltville.

6.5 At the end of the village, the Sierra Trail turns right (east) onto a bridle path. Shortly, turn right again (southeast) onto another bridle path.

6.7 Pass the Badgley/Willcocks family cemetery and at the fork, bear left (east) onto the trail.

6.8 At the fork bear left (northeast), moving away from the rim of the ridge. Ignore the numerous side trails.

6.9 At the T intersection turn right (east) and descend on a dirt road.

7.0 After a sweeping bend in the road, turn left (northeast) onto a path and immediately turn right (east) onto a footpath. If you miss these turns, you will come to a bridge too far.

7.1 The Sierra Trail edges Lake Surprise for the next 0.8 mile.

7.6 The Sierra Trail briefly encounters a bridle path.

7.8 At CR 645 (Tracy Drive) turn right (east) onto the shoulder. Traffic is fast and furious, so care must be taken.

7.9 Cross the bridge and turn left (east) onto a bridle path. Immediately turn right (south) onto a dirt road that heads up the hill, leaving the Sierra Trail. (**Option:** Continue straight on the Sierra Trail, which loops back onto this hike, adding 1.2 miles.)

8.1 From the left, the Sierra Trail joins the road, heading south. Once again you are following the white blazes.

8.4 The Sierra Trail passes (left) a bridle path, leading to the stables.

8.6 As you approach the traffic circle, the Sierra Trail turns left (southeast) off the dirt road and onto a footpath. Immediately reaching the traffic circle, turn left (east) onto the shoulder. At the outlet to the circle, carefully cross (southeast) Summit Lane and onto a foot trail.

8.8 At the T intersection, the Sierra Trail turns left (northeast) onto a bridle path, passing through a "deserted" picnic area from another era.

9.1 Arrive at the water tower with all its ghostly history. Walk around it, bearing right and onto a dirt road, heading southwest and passing a cell tower.

9.4 Pass an old pavilion.

9.6 After edging a parking lot, the Sierra Trail crosses (west) W. R. Tracy Drive and onto a bridle path.

9.9 Cross (northwest) Summit Lane onto a bridle path and immediately turn left (southwest) onto a footpath. The Sierra Trail is shortly crisscrossed by the Red Trail, which is to be ignored.

10.5 Passing a kiosk on the left, the Sierra Trail arrives at the northeast corner of the Nature & Science Center's parking lot.

Watchung Reservation

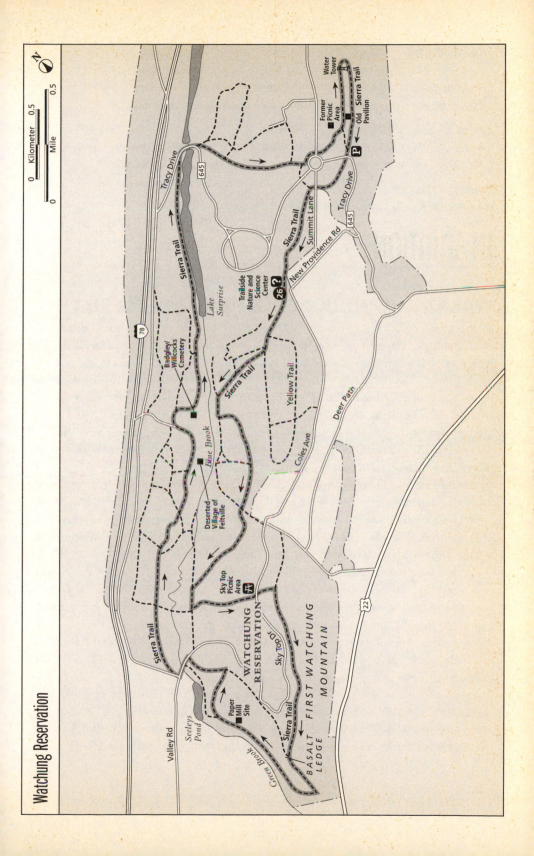

N

0   Kilometer   0.5

0   0.5
Mile

Tracy Drive

645

Sierra Trail

Lake
Surprise

78

Badgley/
Willcocks
Cemetery

Blue Brook

Sierra Trail

Deserted
Village of
Feltville

Yellow Trail

Coles Ave

Trailside
Nature and
Science Center

26 ?

Sierra Trail

Summit Lane

New Providence Rd

645

Deer Path

Tracy Drive

Former
Picnic
Area

Water
Tower

P

Old   Sierra Trail
Pavilion

Sierra Trail

Valley Rd

Seeleys
Pond

Paper
Mill
Site

Green Brook

Sierra Trail

Sierra Trail

Sky Top Dr

Sky Top
Picnic
Area

WATCHUNG
RESERVATION

BASALT   FIRST WATCHUNG
LEDGE   MOUNTAIN

22

Hike Information

Local Information
Union County has a Web site with lots of local information: www.ucnj.org/about

Local Events/Attractions
The park's Trailside Nature & Science Center is well worth a visit before or after your hike. A new visitor center is under construction nearby and promises to be equally worthwhile.

Organizations
The Friends of Feltville at www.groups.yahoo.com/group/FriendsOfFeltville

IN ADDITION

WALKING THROUGH THE PAST IN FELTVILLE

In the 1840s New York businessman David Felt bought land here for a paper mill and a worker's village. In addition to a large, three-and-a-half-story paper mill, which produced stationery, blank journals, and bound ledger books, Felt built at least eleven multi-family workers' cottages, an office, a general store/church, and a summer residence for himself. About 175 people lived in Feltville under the strict but good-hearted reign of "King David," as Felt was known. Felt ran a tight ship, as did most industrialists of the day. But he was also a Unitarian, and his religious convictions led him to provide a standard of living for his workers several notches better than that of their peers in larger industrial communities like Paterson.

David Felt sold the town and mill in its entirety in 1860, and was bankrupt little more than a decade later. Feltville changed owners six times in the next two decades, with various new manufacturing schemes—cigars, silk, and sarsaparilla—each proving unsuccessful. It was at this time, when the town was effectively vacant for periods, it gained the moniker it retains today: "the Deserted Village."

A new winning formula for Feltville was finally found in 1882. Warren Ackerman purchased the village, dropped any industrial plans, and reworked Feltville as a summer resort called "Glenside Park." As urban areas grew, rural summer retreats became ever more popular, and Glenside Park catered to those seeking to vacate the steaming hot summer streets of the nearby cities. The old village was dressed up and renovated in the then-popular Adirondack rustic style, with rough cedar porches, balconies, and railings; buildings were enlarged and improved.

Even this era of Feltville passed, as such rented summer cottage colonies lost their appeal to new resort areas and summer home developments at the Jersey shore and in the mountains—all now more accessible by automobile. Feltville might have become a mere footnote, absorbed into ever-growing Union County, but in the

1920s Union County established the Watchung Reservation. Feltville was one of the first big land purchases.

The Watchung Reservation got a big boost in the 1930s and early 1940s when two New Deal programs, the Works Progress Administration (WPA) and the Civilian Conservation Corps (CCC) set to work making improvements. The WPA built highway bridges over Blue Brook, and the CCC planted trees, built campgrounds, footbridges, picnic areas, pavilions, and the park's Nature & Science Center. Built in 1941, this was the first such museum in New Jersey.

As for the old "Deserted Village," the park commission rented out Feltville's houses. An outdoor education center operated there until the mid-1980s. By this point, the village was recognized as embodying important aspects of our architectural, industrial, social, and recreational history; it was added to the State and National Register of Historic Places in 1980. In 1992 a New Jersey Historic Trust grant funded the first architectural stabilization work in the village, which is an ongoing effort.

Important new insights into the history of Feltville came starting in 1998. In that year, the Feltville Archaeology Project began, a summer field school for students interested in pursuing the vocation. Under the direction of project director and senior archaeologist Matt Tomaso, the Feltville Archaeological Project worked for seven years mapping, excavating, and analyzing archaeological remains in the village. Over the years, the project investigated eighteenth-century homesites, workers' dwellings and associated privies, and the site of David Felt's summer home. Among the revelations produced: Felt's summer home, described in some sources as a "mansion," was in fact no larger than some of his workers' houses.

With archaeology providing new information, and grants helping to restore its buildings, it seems certain that Feltville—though forgotten and deserted in the past—will remain a much-visited and appreciated part of the Watchung Reservation's present and future. For further information, visit The Friends of Feltville at www.groups .yahoo.com/group/FriendsOfFeltville.

27 The Delaware and Raritan Canal–Millstone Valley

Skip like a stone down the Millstone River Valley and its floodplain. Stroll the Delaware & Raritan Canal towpath and return via the Camden & Amboy Railroad grade. This loop is a good level hike for a spring warm-up or a Sunday afternoon stroll. While sauntering under a canopy of trees, enjoy the rushing river on one side and the placid canal on the other. It's a favorite spot for joggers, cyclists, and canoeists, so you'll have company. The hike affords numerous interpretive kiosks and side trips to the historical sites. Easy to add more miles!

Start: Delaware & Raritan Canal State Park parking lot off Route 27
Distance: 3.8-mile loop
Approximate hiking time: 2 hours
Difficulty: Easy and flat
Trail surface: Towpath and railroad bed
Seasons: All good
Other trail users: Multiuse trail
Canine compatibility: Leashed dogs permitted
Land status: State park
Nearest town: Kingston
Fees and permits: None
Schedule: Dawn to dusk
Maps: *DeLorme: New Jersey Atlas & Gazetteer*
p. 42; USGS Hightstown and Monmouth Junction, NJ, quadrangles; maps are also available at the park. A variety of maps and charts are also available online at www.dandrcanal.com/maps.html.
Trail contacts: D & R Canal State Park, 625 Canal Road, Somerset 08873; (732) 873-3050; www.state.nj.us/dep/parksandforests/parks/drcanal.html. Delaware and Raritan Canal Commission, PO Box 539, Highway 29, Prallsville Mills, Stockton 08559; (609) 397-2000; www.dandrcanal.com/index.html
Special considerations: Lots of poison ivy here. Beware.

Finding the trailhead: From the intersection of U.S. Highway 206 and Route 27 in Princeton, travel 3.1 miles north on Route 27, where you will cross a bridge over the Millstone River. Turn right into the Delaware and Raritan Canal State Park parking lot (just before a bridge over the canal).

The Hike

This hike begins at the Crossroads of New Jersey. During the Late Woodland Period, the Lenape's Assunpink Trail took advantage of the Millstone Valley floodplain running between the Delaware and Raritan Rivers. This nearly flat terrain was not lost on the Dutch, who in the mid-1600s used it to travel between New Amsterdam and the Dutch settlements along the Delaware Bay. After the Dutch lost their bid for the New World, the Old Dutch Trail became the British Kings Highway, connecting New York City with Philadelphia.

It was also here that General George Washington passed on three separate occasions. After the successful Battles of Trenton and Princeton, Washington's nearly frozen army halted here, while Washington and his generals discussed whether to raid New Brunswick (and the British army's provisions) or to take the battle-weary troops to Jockey Hollow for the winter. Washington chose the latter. In June 1778 during a swelteringly hot period, he again brought his troops through here on their way to the Battle of Monmouth, possibly the longest and the largest battle of the American Revolution. Finally, General Washington, and for a time Martha, spent nearly three months in nearby Rockingham while the Continental Congress met in Princeton, all waiting for a signed Treaty of Paris, concluding the American Revolution. Imagine the likes of Thomas Jefferson, Alexander Hamilton, and Tom Paine hanging out with George along the Millstone River.

In 1913 the Kings Highway was designated as the Lincoln Highway, patching together other highways to create the first transcontinental route, thus promoting the use of the automobile . . . little did they know! The Lincoln Highway passed through twelve states from New York City to San Francisco.

Let us not overlook the obvious industrial crossroads before you: the Delaware & Raritan Canal (DRC). Opened in 1834, "The Big Ditch," primarily built by Irish immigrant labor, is a 75-foot-wide (top) by 60-foot-wide (bottom) by 8-foot-deep prism water route that uses fourteen locks to create a 36-mile shortcut between the Delaware and Raritan Rivers. It connected Philadelphia with New York City and the Pennsylvania anthracite-coal fields with Hudson Valley. The canal operations lasted nearly a hundred years, with canal barges being pulled by mules and eventually (for the first time on any canal) steam tugs, transporting mainly Pennsylvania coal and some local farm produce and products. The DRC's golden years straddled the 1860s to the 1870s, carrying more tonnage in a single year (1871) than the celebrated Erie Canal. Currently, the canal acts as a water supply for Central Jersey.

Your hike takes the towpath from Kingston to Rocky Hill. Crossing the bridge over the canal, your return route uses the other industrial road: the Rocky Hill Railroad, a branch of the Camden and Amboy Railroad (the first chartered railroad in the United States). The spur, built in 1864, along with the canal, connected the cities to tile, shrubs and nursery plants, and trap rock. The Atlantic Terra Cotta Company produced decorative tiles that adorn the Woolworth Building in New York City and the roof of the Philadelphia Museum of Art. The Trap Rock Quarry crushed rock for the streets of Newark and Jersey City. Finally, the Princeton Nursery, at one time the largest nursery in the world, grew shrubs for the entire country. In spite of these products, the rail met its demise in the early 1970s.

D&R Canal Lock #8, the lock tender's house, the toll house, and the basin are all listed on the State and National Register of Historic Places.

Today, your hike is officially on the National Recreation Trail as well as the East Coast Greenway, a crossroads of not only those who recreate but also the linear corridor for the migrations of plants and animals.

Miles and Directions

0.0 From the southwest end of the parking lot pick up the macadam path and pass (north) through the tunnel under Route 27, ascending onto the towpath. The Millstone River is on the left and the Delaware & Raritan Canal on the right. (**FYI:** Route 27's historical significance can be seen in its past names: Assunpink Trail, the Old Dutch Trail, Kings Highway, and the Lincoln Highway.)

0.3 Pass concrete milemarker. (**FYI:** The number 24 is the canal miles to New Brunswick, and the number 20 is the canal miles to Bordentown, for a grand total of 44 miles on the main canal.)

0.6 Pass along the spillway of the canal with a series of canal relative interpretive kiosks. (**FYI:** The spillway acted as flood prevention for the canal, sending the excess water into the Millstone River.)

1.9 At the junction with Georgetown-Franklin Turnpike (County Route 518), turn right (east) and cross the bridge over the canal; turn right again onto the rail bed of the Camden & Amboy Railroad, passing through a historical site. Just beyond it is a parking lot with restrooms. The infamous trap quarry can be seen and heard east of the rail grade. Plan on spending a little time among the "ruins" and reading the interpretive kiosks.

2.4 Pass a bench and a trail (blue blazes) on the left and continue straight on the rail bed. (**Side trip:** Take the blue-blazed trails [there are plans for two trails] left and ascend up the ridge for an eighth of a mile to historic Rockingham, the mansion where George Washington spent three months waiting for the Treaty of Paris to be signed, ending the American Revolution. Local lore says Washington gave his farewell address to his troops from the balcony of Rockingham.)

3.7 The trail swings away from the canal and into a picnic area. Pass through the parking lot till you arrive at Route 27. Cross it and turn right (west) into the park entrance and immediately cross the canal, arriving back into the parking lot. (**Side trip:** Continue south on the towpath, passing Lock #8, and arrive at Millstone Aqueduct, footbridge, and Carnegie Lake. Round-trip adds about 0.6 mile. This was the halfway point on the canal, and became a layover spot for canal traffic. This was also a busy place for the canal tender; he had to open and shut the locks, swing open or close the bridge, and collect the toll!)

3.8 Arrive back at parking lot.

Hike Information

Local Information

Princeton Regional Convention & Visitors Bureau, 9 Vandeventer Avenue, Princeton 08542; (609) 924-1776; www.visitprinceton.org

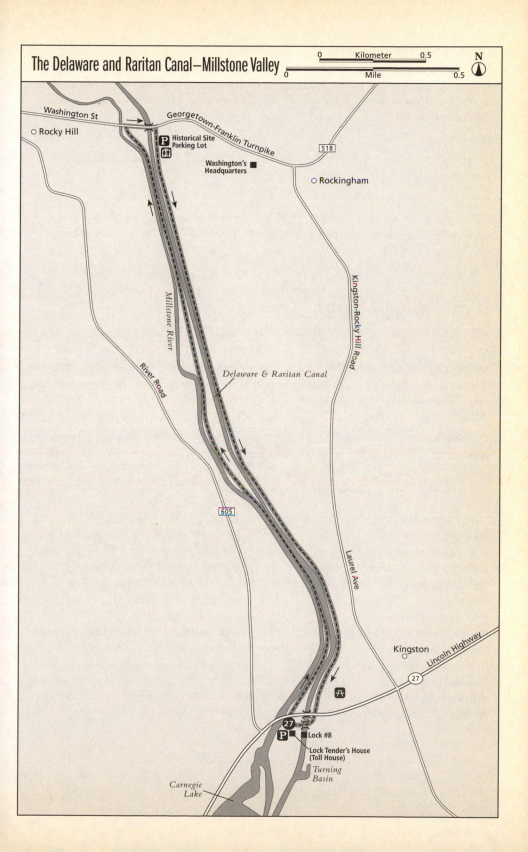

The Delaware and Raritan Canal—Millstone Valley

Kilometer
0 — 0.5
Mile
0 — 0.5

N

Washington St

○ Rocky Hill

Georgetown-Franklin Turnpike

P Historical Site Parking Lot

Washington's Headquarters ■

518

○ Rockingham

Millstone River

River Road

Delaware & Raritan Canal

Kingston-Rocky Hill Road

605

Laurel Ave

Kingston ○

Lincoln Highway

27

27

P ■ Lock #8

Lock Tender's House (Toll House)

Turning Basin

Carnegie Lake

Local Events/Attractions

The historic town of Princeton, with Princeton University its heart, makes for interesting visiting (see Princeton Woods, Hike 24). Historic Rockingham is a large eighteenth-century mansion that served as Washington's headquarters at the end of the Revolutionary War. PO Box 496, Kingston 08528; www.rockingham.net

Hike Tours

Guided walking, cycling, canoe, and kayak tours are all available at D & R Canal State Park; www.dandrcanal.com

Organizations

D & R Canal Watch, PO Box 2, Rocky Hill 08553-0002; (609) 924-2683; www.canalwatch.org. The Canal Society of New Jersey, PO Box 737, Morristown 07963-0737; (908) 722-9556; www.canalsocietynj.org

28 The Great Swamp

Pass some of the mightiest oaks in New Jersey while the route loops through the swamp's woodlands habitat. It's hard to believe that in the 1960s the largest airport in the world was planned here. Thanks to a grassroots effort to save the Great Swamp, you can experience this remote Wilderness Area 30 miles (as the heron flies) from the Big Apple. This flat, forested route periodically opens out into the swamp and marshes, passes ponds, and flirts with the Great Brook. Wildlife abounds! The trails may be mucky and buggy, especially in early summer; therefore, boots and repellant are the order of the day.

Start: The Blue Trail parking lot at Long Hill Road
Distance: 3.5-mile loop
Approximate hiking time: 2 hours
Difficulty: Easy, with mostly flat walking
Trail surface: Footpaths and some woods roads
Seasons: All
Other trail users: Hikers only
Canine compatibility: No dogs permitted
Land status: National Wildlife Refuge
Nearest town: Basking Ridge
Fees and permits: None
Schedule: Dawn to dusk
Maps: *DeLorme: New Jersey Atlas & Gazetteer*
p. 31; USGS Chatham and Bernardsville, NJ, quadrangles; a trail map is also available at the refuge.
Trail contacts: Great Swamp National Wildlife Refuge, 241 Pleasant Plains Road, Basking Ridge 07920; (973) 425-1222; www.fws.gov/ northeast/greatswamp/
Special considerations: Mosquitoes can be fierce in the spring and summer, especially in wet weather; come prepared.

Be aware that some trails may be closed due to flooding from seasonal snowmelt and/ or rain.

Finding the trailhead: From Interstate 287 in Van Dorans Mills (exit 30), turn north onto North Maple Avenue and drive 0.2 mile to the intersection with U.S. Highway 202 (traffic light). Turn right (north) onto US 202 and travel 1.8 miles to Glen Alpine. Turn right (east) onto Glen Alpine Road and travel 1.7 miles to the intersection (traffic light). Turn right (southwest) onto Lee's Hill Road. Passing the New Vernon School, at 0.4 mile turn left (south) onto Long Hill Road. After leaving a residential area at 1.0 mile, turn left (east) into the trailhead parking lot.

The Hike

Sometimes a disastrous situation turns out to be a stroke of luck. During the late 1950s, the Port Authority of New York and New Jersey (PANYNJ) deemed existing New York–metro area airports too small and hemmed in by urban areas for new, larger jet planes. A huge, empty tract was needed for a new, larger airport. PANYNJ looked at some seventeen sites, but their preferred one was in this location—the Great Swamp.

The Great Brook flows through the Great Swamp National Wildlife Refuge.

The PANYNJ planned to build a 10,000-acre jetport here, close to Interstates 78 and 287, then being planned. Some public opposition to the plan was anticipated but regarded as a minor factor. It appeared that nothing was going to stop this powerful entity, which runs the airports, tunnels, harbor, and bridges in the New York Harbor. What the PANYNJ did not count on was the mouse protesting in the corner growing into a thousand-pound gorilla.

The magicians preventing this natural landmark from becoming an airport were citizen-action groups, primarily the Great Swamp Committee. Supported by national environmental societies, local colleges, and wealthy, prominent, politically connected individuals, the committee sprang into action. When the PANYNJ came out with numerous reports, studies, and hearings, the savvy Great Swamp Committee organized smaller groups, created fact sheets, held coffee klatches, sought the media, and hired lawyers. The Friends crafted a three-pronged strategy: educate the public about the Swamp's unique habitat, prevent the PANYNJ from enlarging its legal domain in New Jersey, and pull the land out from under the PANYNJ.

The third plan was rather unique. The Great Swamp Committee secured donations of the land outright and sought financial donations to buy more land. A beautiful strategy: In turn, they would donate the land to the secretary of interior to create a Wildlife Refuge, if possible with a Wilderness Area designation.

The Great Swamp Committee raised a million dollars in all, which they used to buy 3,000 acres in the core of the Great Swamp. They donated this land to the Department of the Interior in 1960. Great Swamp National Wildlife Refuge, designated a National Natural Landmark in 1966, has since more than doubled in size. Helen C. Fenske, director of the Great Swamp Committee, later became commissioner of the New Jersey Department of Environmental Protection and remains the grande dame of the New Jersey environmental movement. From the initial 3,000-acre donation, the refuge has grown to nearly 7,700 acres, 40 percent having Wilderness status. Land saved!

So just what was such a fuss over? This was former Glacial Lake Passaic, formed when the Wisconsin Ice Sheet, approximately 18,000 years ago, stopped just short of what is today Interstate 80. As it retreated, the glacier melted, the runoff blocked by the Watchung Mountains (another one of our hikes), which in turn created a lake 30 miles long, 10 miles wide, and averaging 200 feet deep, draining through Paterson Falls (another one of our hikes). Over thousands of years, it eventually transformed itself into a marshland. The clay-bottom basin filled with debris and formed magnificent, diverse habitats: marshes, swamps, grasslands, and woodlands. Over the last 9,000 years, this terrain has been used for hunting (mink, muskrat, deer), lumbering (oaks, chestnut), farming (meadow hay, flax, fruit trees), and sadly, dumping (asbestos, lead, cars). It was ironically rather fortunate that the PANYNJ targeted the Great Swamp, since the local public needed an awakening to the treasure (hundreds of species of plants, birds, and animals) in their backyard before the Great Swamp was further ditched and drained, further cleared and developed, and further dumped and filled.

The Great Swamp

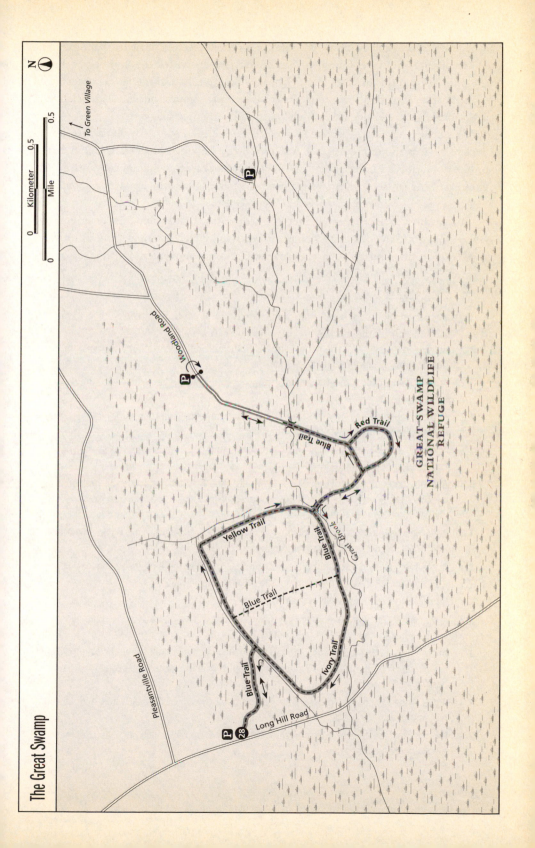

N

Kilometer
0   0.5
Mile
0   0.5

To Green Village

P

Woodland Road

Blue Trail

Red Trail

GREAT SWAMP
NATIONAL WILDLIFE
REFUGE

Yellow Trail

Blue Trail

Great Brook

Blue Trail

Ivory Trail

Pleasantville Road

Blue Trail

P   28

Long Hill Road

In addition to the National Wildlife Refuge, Morris and Somerset (another one of our hikes) County parks built environmental centers within the Swamp to educate the public about this unique setting. Miles of boardwalks and numerous observation blinds further provided access into the Swamp. Enjoy your wilderness experience in a National Natural Landmark, which was saved by people like you.

As you began your hike off Long Hill Road, picture this space before it was declared a Superfund Site in 1983. A school bus, a bulldozer, six cars, and 250 drums dumped into this area, alongside 29,000 square feet of lead-contaminated soil and 340 cubic yards of asbestos. After twelve years and $9.9 million for removal and capping, marvel at the power of restoration and recession.

And as for the jetport—well, Newark International got three new terminals and larger runways in the early 1970s. In many ways, the Great Swamp jetport controversy gave birth to the modern environmental conservation movement in New Jersey.

Miles and Directions

Creating somewhat of a loop hike, all the turns at trail junctions are to the left. (**Option:** The Blue Trail creates an out-and-back hike.)

0.0 Starting in the southeast corner of Long Hill Road parking lot, pick up the trailhead for the Blue Trail (blue blazes) inside the woods line.

0.2 At the T intersection turn left (northeast), staying with the Blue Trail and leaving the Ivory Trail Loop for the return route.

0.3 At the junction stay straight (northeast), following the Yellow Trail Loop (yellow blazes). The Blue Trail leaves right.

0.5 At a large maple tree, the Yellow Trail Loop curves to the right (south), first on a trail, but immediately opens onto a lane.

0.8 Arrive at the end of the Yellow Trail; turn left onto the Blue Trail, heading south and crossing the Great Brook on a 55-foot wooden bridge. (**Bail-out:** Follow the Blue Trail straight [west] back to the Long Hill Road parking lot.)

1.0 At the fork veer left (east) and continue to follow the Blue Trail, while leaving the right fork (Red Trail Loop, west end) for the return route.

1.1 At the T intersection turn left (north) and continue to follow the Blue Trail, while leaving the right turn (Red Trail Loop, east end) for the return route.

1.3 Cross 45-foot footbridge over a stream.

1.6 Arrive at the Woodland Road parking lot, your turnaround point. Retrace the route, using the Blue Trail, back to the Red Trail Loop.

2.1 At the east junction with the Red Trail Loop continue straight (south) onto the Red Trail (red blazes), leaving the Blue Trail. (**Bail-out:** Follow the Blue Trail back to the Long Hill Road parking lot.)

2.4 Arrive at the west end of the Red Trail Loop; turn left (west) onto the Blue Trail, and retrace the trek back to the bridge.

2.6 Re-cross the Great Brook and turn left (west) on the Blue Trail, which hugs the stream. Yellow Trail Loop leaves right.

2.8 Turn left (west) onto the south end of Ivory Trail Loop (ivory blazes), which parallels the Great Brook. The Blue Trail continues straight. (**Bail-out:** Follow the Blue Trail back to the Long Hill Road parking lot.)

2.9 The Ivory Trail passes an open area with a pond (part of a Superfund site) and enters a lane with magnificent hardwoods. It is here that the route swings right, away from the stream, off the lane, and onto a trail.

3.1 Arrive at the big ditch where the route bears right (northeast) along its edge.

3.2 Arrive at the north end of Ivory Trail Loop; turn left (northwest) onto the Blue Trail and retrace the route back to the Long Hill Road parking lot.

3.5 Arrive back at parking lot.

Hike Information

Local Information

Morris County Visitor's Center, 6 Court Street, Morristown 07960; (973) 631-5151; www.morris tourism.org

Local Events/Attractions

Nearby Morristown National Historical Park includes the Ford Mansion (Washington's headquarters) and Jockey Hollow, site of the Continental Army winter encampment. 30 Washington Place, Morristown 07960-4299; (908) 766-8215; www.nps.gov/morr/pphtml/contact.html.
The Museum of Early Trades and Crafts in nearby Madison features outstanding collections and exhibits in an equally impressive Richardsonian Romanesque building, the former Madison Public Library. Main Street at Green Village Road, Madison 07940; (973) 377-2982; www .rosenet.org/metc

Lodging

The Morris County park system offers camping in both Mahlon Dickerson and Lewis Morris Parks. (973) 326-7600.

Hike Tours

Friends of the Great Swamp offer tours (see below).

Organizations

Friends of the Great Swamp National Wildlife Refuge, 197 Pleasant Plains Road, Basking Ridge 07920; (973) 425-9510; www.friendsofgreatswamp.org

Other Resources

The Great Swamp Outdoor Education Center, part of the Morris County park system, is located off Southern Boulevard near Madison; (973) 635-6629; www.morris.nj.us/parks/gswamp

29 The Delaware River Valley—Stockton to Bull's Island

This hike and the next (Stockton to Lambertville) were designed so you can stay at a bed-and-breakfast and hike two spectacular loops on consecutive days from the same location. You can park your car and not move it for three days!

The serenity of the canals, the flow of the river, and the sunset from Centre Bridge make this and Hike 30 magnificent hikes. With its Old World charm, you amble along the Delaware River, Delaware Raritan Feeder Canal, and the Delaware Canal, passing the brownstone homes, backyard gardens, and canal-side cafes, but above all, bucolic scenes along the floodplain. Laden with historical railroad, canal, and mill structures, the loops are ripe for exploration. On Day One, you hike (north) on a soft rail bed from Stockton to Bull's Island Recreation Area. After crossing the Delaware River into Lumberville, Pennsylvania, you travel south on the towpath to Centre Bridge, re-crossing the river into Stockton.

Start: Public parking lot on Bridge Street
Distance: 7.5-mile loop
Approximate hiking time: 4 hours
Difficulty: Easy, with level walking
Trail surface: Canal towpath and railbed
Seasons: All good
Other trail users: Multiuse
Canine compatibility: Leashed dogs permitted
Land status: State park
Nearest town: Stockton
Fees and permits: None
Schedule: Dawn to dusk
Maps: *DeLorme: New Jersey Atlas & Gazetteer* p.40–41; USGS Stockton and Lumberville, PA, quadrangles; maps are also available at the park; a variety of maps and charts are available online at www.dandrcanal.com/maps.html.
Trail contacts: D & R Canal State Park, 625 Canal Road, Somerset 08873; (732) 873-3050; www.state.nj.us/dep/parksandforests/parks/drcanal.html. Delaware and Raritan Canal Commission, PO Box 539, Route 29, Prallsville Mills, Stockton 08559; (609) 397-2000; www.dandrcanal.com/index.html. Delaware Canal State Park, 11 Lodi Hill Road, Upper Black Eddy, PA 18972-9540; (610) 982-5560; www.dcnr.state.pa.us/stateparks/parks/delawarecanal.aspx
Special considerations: Spring flooding will close this hike.

Finding the trailhead: From the intersection of Main Street (Highway 29) and Bridge Street (leading to Pennsylvania) in Stockton, travel west on Bridge Street for 0.1 mile and at the former Bel-Del Station (now a market/deli) and just prior to the rail trail, turn left into the public parking lot.

The Hike

As you step onto the rail bed, you have entered the Delaware & Raritan Canal (D&R Canal) State Park, a 70-mile linear recreational paradise. While the main canal parallels the Millstone and Raritan Rivers, the feeder canal edges the Delaware River. Our hike today parallels the latter, sometimes along the towpath of the feeder canal and other times upon the rail bed of the Belvidere-Delaware Railroad (Bel-Del), both reflecting the nineteenth-century "modern" means of transportation.

Tramping along the Bel-Del route, transport yourself into the nineteenth century where 300,000 tons of coal yearly rumble down the tracks from the anthracite coal fields in Pennsylvania to New York City. Or iron from Sussex and Morris County mines, and building blocks from Hunterton County quarries, all come chugging south. Or during the harvest season, smell the rich, sweet scent of the boxcars loaded with peaches, blackberries, or strawberries, plucked locally and shipped to the urban areas. Or the ice cars dripping as they pass on their way to Philadelphia from Knickerbocker Ice Company, Lake Grinnel. Or the pleasant pungent odor of fifty carloads of evergreen trees, rattling over the rails to the cities during the holiday season.

Specials took the tourists to the Jersey Shore, Niagara Falls, and Gettysburg, as well as the Delaware Water Gap. Excursions carried the folks to the County, State, and World Fairs. The Bel-Del even put on a train from Lambertville to Belvidere, so fans could attend the local baseball games. Fight fans rode the rail to Bull's Island where boxing matches were held. As boxing was illegal in Pennsylvania, the Keystone fans crossed the Lumberville Bridge to Bull's Island to arrive at ringside.

At times presidents traveled the Bel-Del: Rutherford B. Hayes speaking at Lafayette College, Grover Cleveland fishing the Delaware River, Teddy Roosevelt and William Howard Taft campaigning, Woodrow Wilson vacationing, FDR secretly visiting

The Roebling Suspension Bridge spans the Delaware River from Bulls Island/Raven Rock to Lumberville, Pennsylvania.

Lucy Mercer, and Harry S. Truman returning to Washington, D.C. during the Berlin Crisis. To the delight of the children, a number of circus trains moved down the Bel-Del and into the towns, hauling hundreds of performers, roustabouts, and animals. Even the Liberty Bell made the Bel-Del trip twice: in 1904 traveling to the St. Louis World's Fair and in 1915 returning from the Panama Pacific Exhibition. Maybe the most prized subjects traveling the Bel-Del were the local youths commuting to their respected high schools in Frenchtown or Lambertville.

As you approach Prallsville Mill complex, the rail bed joins the canal, passing one of the two locks on this section. Built in the 1830s, the feeder canal was originally designed to maintain the water level in D & R Canal yet ended up transporting freight. In the 1840s improvements were made so the feeder canal could also transport coal barges from the Delaware Canal (Pennsylvania), which would lock out at the New Hope basin, cross the Delaware River via cable, and lock into the feeder canal at Lambertville. When you arrive at Bull's Island and cross the 700-foot Roebling suspension footbridge, look upriver at the wing dams, which direct the river's water into the canals: the Raritan Dam into the feeder canal and the Lumberville Dam into the Delaware Canal. As you exit off the bridge in Pennsylvania, climb onto the Delaware Canal towpath, another monument of the nineteenth-century Industrial Era. Stroll along the river and country homes, crossing back into New Jersey via the steel girder Centre Bridge. From the railings enjoy the tranquil panoramic views of the Delaware River Valley.

Miles and Directions

0.0 From the former Stockton Railroad Station (Errico's Market & Deli), head northwest on the old Belvidere & Delaware (better known as Bel-Del) rail bed, crossing Bridge Street.

0.1 Cross Ferry Street, continuing straight (northwest) on the rail bed.

0.4 Pass a historical site: interpretive kiosks and a milepost.

0.42 Pass around gate. Numerous interpretive kiosks are here along with one of the three locks found on the Delaware Raritan Feeder Canal. (**Side trip:** A must! Turn left [southwest] onto the road, crossing the canal, and immediately turn right [northwest], heading straight between the Delaware River and the D&R Canal with the Wickecheoke Creek and the spillway before you.)

0.54 Pass Prallsville Mill Complex on your right. As you leave the site, cross a deck-girder bridge over the Wickecheoke Creek and continue on the rail bed. (**Side trip:** Explore the Mill Complex.)

2.1 Cross over the Lochatong Creek on a deck-girder bridge. At this location the creek feeds the canal and the excess goes over a spillway, which leads directly to the Delaware River.

3.3 Arrive at Bull's Island Recreation Area and turn left (west) onto the entrance road, crossing the canal bridge.

3.4 On the right pass interpretive kiosks, park road, and the park office (restrooms). (**Side trip:** Take the park road [east side] through the campsite area to the end of the island where you will find the weir across the Delaware River, delivering water to the mouth of the feeder

The Delaware River Valley—Stockton to Bull's Island

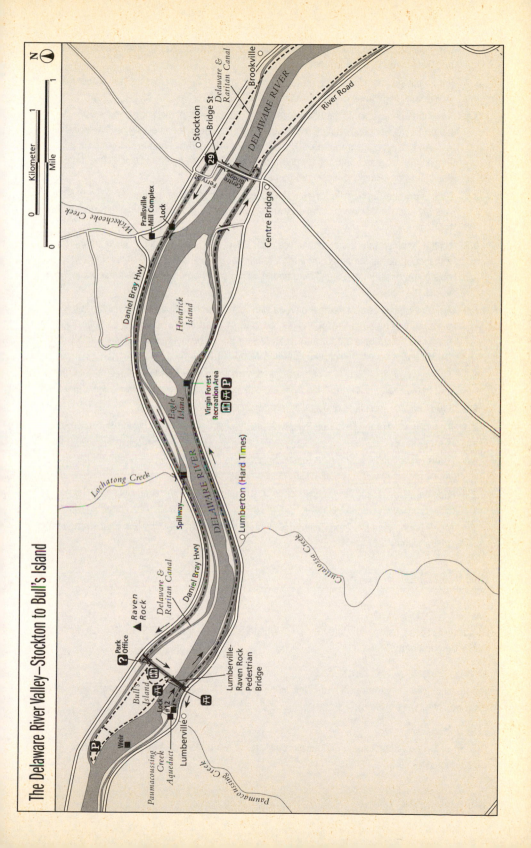

N

Kilometer
0   1
Mile
0   1

Brookville

Delaware & Raritan Canal

DELAWARE RIVER

River Road

Bridge St

Stockton

29

Ferry St

Centre Bridge

Centre Bridge

Prallsville
Mill Complex
Lock

Wickecheoke Creek

Daniel Bray Hwy

Hendrick
Island

Eagle
Island

Virgin Forest
Recreation Area

Lumberton (Hard Times)

DELAWARE RIVER

Spillway

Lochatong Creek

Cuttalossa Creek

▲ Raven
Rock

Delaware &
Raritan Canal

Daniel Bray Hwy

Lumberville-
Raven Rock
Pedestrian
Bridge

Park
Office

Bull's
Island

Lock
#12

Lumberville

Weir

Paunacussing Creek
Aqueduct

Paunacussing Creek

canal. Return by continuing the loop on the park road [west side] through the campsite and picnic area [1.5 miles round-trip].)

3.5 Pass a playground/picnic area on your right (northwest) before crossing the Lumberville-Raven Rock Pedestrian Bridge, built by John A. Roebling & Sons in 1947.

3.6 Arrive in Pennsylvania. To get down to the trail from the end of the bridge, you must perform a jug-handle. Turn right (northwest), traveling along the shoulder of River Road till you can turn right again (northeast), bridging over the spillway and the Delaware Canal. Turn right (southeast) onto the towpath. (**Side trip:** Located here are Lock #12 restoration, Paunacoussing Creek Aqueduct, and a picnic area.)

3.7 Pass under the Lumberville-Raven Rock Pedestrian Bridge, enjoying the Delaware River to your left and the Delaware Canal on your right. Be aware that you have limited exits off the towpath.

4.8 On the far side of the canal and across River Road, you pass a section called Lumberton with its Cuttalossa Inn and Lumberton Granite Company ("stone used to build Philadelphia"). You pass under a small auto bridge, which could be used as an emergency exit across the canal.

5.9 Arrive at Virginia Forrest Recreation Area with its bathrooms, picnic tables, kiosk, and maps; as well as a parking lot and access to River Road. At the southeast end of the Area, continue straight onto the towpath. (**FYI:** To your left in the Delaware River are Eagle Island [NJSP] and a second larger one, Hendrick Island [DCSP].)

6.7 On the left pass the remains of bridge abutments leading to Hendrick Island. Beyond the end of the island and across the river, you pick up a broad view of Prallsville Mill Complex.

6.8 Pass under a small auto bridge with private access to River Road.

7.1 Imposing view of the Delaware River with the steel girder Centre Bridge in the background.

7.2 Pass under the auto bridge and at the end of the abutment, turn left (east) and climb the stairs to the roadway. Turn right (east), crossing the Delaware River on Centre Bridge and its wooden sidewalk (a beautiful spot to be during sunset).

7.4 Upon arriving back in New Jersey, continue straight (east) on the sidewalk along Bridge Street, passing over the Delaware Raritan Feeder Canal and by the Stockton Post Office.

7.5 Arrive back to the Stockton Railroad Station (Errico's Market & Deli). Turn right (southeast) to the parking lot.

Hike Information

Local Information
Lambertville Area Chamber of Commerce, 60 Wilson Street, Lambertville 08530; (609) 397-0055; www.lambertville.org

Local Events/Attractions
The historic towns of Lambertville and New Hope are filled with antiques shops, cafes, and galleries (and sometimes crowds).

Hike Tours
Guided walking, cycling, canoe, and kayak tours are all available at D & R Canal State Park; www.dandrcanal.com

Organizations

D & R Canal Watch, PO Box 2, Rocky Hill, 08553-0002; (609) 924-2683; www.canalwatch.org. The Canal Society of New Jersey, PO Box 737, Morristown 07963-0737; (908) 722-9556; www.canalsocietynj.org

Lodging

Camping is available at Bull's Island State Park. For a fine B&B, try the Woolverton Inn, 6 Woolverton Road, Stockton 08559; (609) 397-0802; www.srinns.com/woolvertoninn. It's very close to the trailhead.

30 The Delaware River Valley—Stockton to Lambertville

This is the second-day expedition from the same starting point as the previous hike, Stockton to Bull's Island. On Day Two, you hike south, using the rail bed and the towpath into Lambertville. After crossing the Delaware River into New Hope, Pennsylvania, you travel north on the towpath to Centre Bridge, recrossing the river into Stockton. While moving through the communities and crossing the bridges, sidewalks are provided. In Lambertville you have a short road walk. These hikes allow you to kick back or pick up the pace; the choice is all yours. (Two obvious drawbacks to these hikes are the auto sounds from Route 29 and the possible crowds in Lambertville and New Hope.)

Start: Public parking lot on Bridge Street
Distance: 7.1-mile loop
Approximate hiking time: 4 hours
Difficulty: Easy
Trail surface: Towpath, railroad bed, some sidewalks, and a major bridge crossing of the Delaware
Seasons: All good
Other trail users: Multiuse
Canine compatibility: Leashed dogs permitted
Land status: State park
Nearest town: Stockton
Fees and permits: None
Schedule: Dawn to dusk
Maps: DeLorme: New Jersey Atlas & Gazetteer p.41; USGS Stockton and Lambertville, NJ, quadrangles; maps are also available at the

park; a variety of maps and charts are available online at www.dandrcanal.com/maps.html.
Trail contacts: D & R Canal State Park, 625 Canal Road, Somerset 08873, (732) 873-3050, www.state.nj.us/dep/parksandforests/parks/drcanal.html. Delaware and Raritan Canal Commission, PO Box 539, Route 29, Prallsville Mills, Stockton 08559, (609) 397-2000, www.dandrcanal.com/index.html. Delaware Canal State Park, 11 Lodi Hill Road, Upper Black Eddy, PA 18972-9540, (610) 982-5560, www.dcnr.state.pa.us/stateparks/parks/delawarecanal.aspx
Special considerations: Spring flooding will close this hike. It is also liable to be a crowded area on nice weekends.

Finding the trailhead: From the intersection of Main Street (Route 29) and Bridge Street (leading to Pennsylvania) in Stockton, travel west on Bridge Street for 0.1 mile and at the former Bel-Del Station (now a market/deli) and just prior to the rail trail, turn left into the public parking lot.

The Hike

This hike parallels the Delaware River, meandering along rail beds and towpaths and passing through river towns, reflecting the early growth of America's transportation industry. In the 1700s Colonial settlements sprang up on both sides of the river near ferry landings. By the early 1800s bridges replaced the ferries, funneling equestrian traffic through the growing villages. In the1830s boom years came to the hamlets with the arrival of Delaware & Raritan (D & R) Feeder Canal in New Jersey and the Delaware Canal in Pennsylvania. In the 1850s the Belvidere & Delaware Railroad in New Jersey and the Reading Railroad in Pennsylvania came chugging into area, furthering industrial growth. Just imagine the pungent odors produced by the paper mills, sawmills, sausage factories, breweries, potteries, cotton mills, iron works, and rubber factories (this was home of the "Snag-Proof Boot") that once operated here.

A unique historical feature of the river crossings was their locations: all a day's journey from New York City and Philadelphia via the stagecoach along the Old York Road. To provide the weary traveler lodging and grub, hostelries sprang up on either side of the river: Stockton Inn, Centre Bridge Inn, Lambertville House, and Ferry Tavern (today, Logan Inn). Still open for business and waiting for hungry, well-dressed trampers.

Our journey begins in Stockton, the site of the early-eighteenth-century Reading's Ferry. Originally worked by John Reading and family, it sold to other entrepreneurs and later sold to the Centre Bridge Company. In the spring of 1814, they opened the 950-foot wooden covered bridge across the river. Centre Bridge derived its name since it was equidistant between the Trenton and Phillipsburg bridges on the Delaware. The Pennsylvanian community claimed Centre Bridge (1851) for its name while the Jersey settlement took Stockton (1878) after Senator Robert Field Stockton, who came from good stock: his grandfather, a signer of the Declaration of Independence, and his father, a U.S. senator. Robert, as an accomplished naval officer, battled the Barbary Pirates, negotiated for the creation of Liberia, and annexed California from the Mexicans. As a U.S. senator, he introduced a bill to end flogging in the Navy. As a businessman, he promoted D & R Canal, eventually becoming its president.

Our hike's turnaround point occurs in Lambertville and New Hope, the Colonial site of Wells' Ferry, operated by John Wells and later by the Coryell family, hence the settlement name: Coryell's Ferry. The hamlet on the Jersey side became Lambertville when New Jersey state senator John Lambert persuaded "the powers that be" to open up a post office with his nephew as postmaster, hence, Lambertville (1810) . . . much to the chagrin of the local Coryells. Coryell's Ferry on the Pennsylvania side had a name-change after the 1790s, when fire destroyed three mills. When the owner rebuilt several mills, it gave "New Hope" to the Pennsylvanians and hence the new name.

The demise of the ferry service occurred in 1814 with the construction of the New Hope–Lambertville Bridge (N.H.–L.), a wooden covered bridge extending 1,050 feet over the Delaware. But like all the other bridges spanning this river, it came under yearly attacks by the natural elements: flooding, ice flows, debris, and lightning. As a prime example, in the Flood of 1841, Centre Bridge broke loose and floated off its piers. Traveling down the raging river, the toll collector was "onboard" the breakaway structure as it crashed into and removed the arches and piers of the N.H.–L. Bridge. The woebegone toll collector continued on his terrifying 13-mile odyssey until rescued amongst the flotsam in Yardleyville. Here is hoping that your journey along the Delaware River and across the rehabilitated steel-span bridges is far less arduous than the toll collector's and far more tranquil!

This towpath passes under one of the bridges along the Delaware Canal in New Hope, Pennsylvania. Notice the YIELD *sign.*

Miles and Directions

0.0 From the former Stockton Railroad Station (Errico's Market & Deli), proceed southeast on the rail bed, heading out of town. (**FYI:** There are picnic tables and informational kiosks here.)

0.6 Pass over a deck-girder bridge crossing over the Delaware & Raritan Feeder Canal into the section of town called Brookville. The rail bed has rejoined the canal, which is now on your left (east). (**FYI:** It was here in 1823 that the famous Deats plow was invented, which improved the scouring of the soil.)

0.9 Cross over a bridge, which passes over the wickets that allow for the drainage of the canal.

1.7 Coming in on your left and crossing the canal is the Mount Gilboa railroad siding, which leads to the quarry.

2.3 Pass under U.S. Highway 202 bridge and turn left (east), crossing a bridge over the canal. At the end of the bridge, turn right (south) onto the Delaware Raritan Feeder Canal towpath and continue straight. (**FYI:** Located here are a parking lot and the Jimison Farm.)

2.5 Proceed over the aqueduct and continue straight (south) along the towpath.

2.6 Pass under a railroad girder-bridge at Bum Junction and continue to parallel the canal. You are coming into the outskirts of Lambertville with numerous access points to the left: Elm Street, Buttonwood Street, Perry Street, Delevan Street, and York Street.

3.2 Cross Coryell Street and continue (south) on the towpath, passing on the right (west) a bridge over the canal.

3.4 At the junction with Bridge Street, cross the street and turn right (west) onto the sidewalk, paralleling Bridge Street, passing over the canal and passing by the former Lambertville Railroad Station on your left (south). You have arrived in Lambertville, the land of bistros, galleries, and boutiques.

3.5 Cross over the New Hope–Lambertville Bridge, built in 1904 and rebuilt in 1955 and 2004. (**FYI:** The bridge also functions as an artificial nesting area for the rare colony of cliff swallows.)

3.6 Upon reaching New Hope, proceed straight (west) along East Bridge Street upon the sidewalk 1 block till you hit Main Street. Cross over Main Street and onto West Bridge Street (Pennsylvania Route 179), continuing straight up the hill along the sidewalk.

3.7 Before the bridge over the Delaware Canal, turn right (north) and cross West Bridge Street and descend the driveway, which leads to the towpath. Pedestrians must yield to mules! This is no joke as this is a working canal in the summer. (**Side trip:** To explore the south end of the Delaware Canal, turn left [south] on the towpath, passing under the bridge. The Ingham Creek Aqueduct, restored locks, Lock Tender's House (exhibits), and backyard gardens are all part of a 1.5-mile out-and-back excursion.) (**FYI:** There are restrooms in the New Hope Information Center at the corner of Main and Mechanic Streets.)

3.8 Across from the canal, pass the former Reading Railroad Station. Heading out of town, the towpath will take you along the backyard gardens and several street accesses.

4.5 Pass under Rabbit Run Bridge (River Road) where the towpath becomes co-aligned with driveways.

4.8 Pass under US 202.

5.0 Pass over a pipeline.

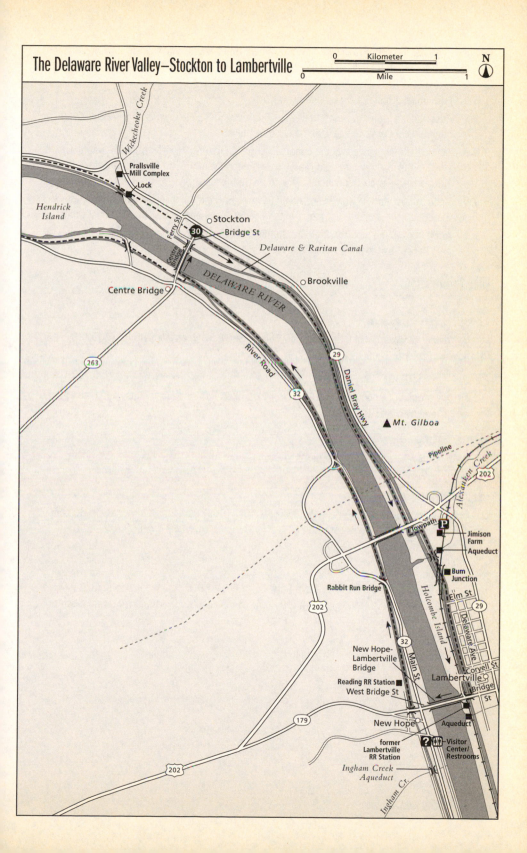

The Delaware River Valley—Stockton to Lambertville

0 Kilometer 1
0 Mile 1

N

Wickecheoke Creek

Prallsville Mill Complex
Lock

Hendrick Island

Ferry St
Centre Bridge

30
Stockton
Bridge St

Delaware & Raritan Canal

DELAWARE RIVER

Brookville

Centre Bridge

263

River Road

29

32

Daniel Bray Hwy

Mt. Gilboa

Pipeline

Alexauken Creek

202

Towpath

P

Jimison Farm
Aqueduct

Bum Junction

Elm St

29

Holcombe Island

Delaware Ave.

Coryell St

Rabbit Run Bridge

202

32

Main St

New Hope-Lambertville Bridge

Lambertville

Bridge St

Reading RR Station
West Bridge St

179

New Hope

former Lambertville RR Station

Aqueduct

? ♿ Visitor Center/Restrooms

Ingham Creek Aqueduct

Ingham Cr.

202

5.3 Pass under a bridge (a private driveway) where there is a historical kiosk. (**FYI:** Residing here in the 1900s, William L. Lathrop, member of New Hope's artist colony, would take his students by boat down the canal to sketch the town.)

5.9 Pass under a bridge (a private driveway).

6.3 Pass under a bridge (a private driveway). From this point, the towpath leads along the backyards of Centre Bridge with the canal in between.

6.8 Before the auto bridge over the canal at Centre Bridge, turn right (east) and climb the stairs to the roadway. Turn right (east), crossing the Delaware River on Centre Bridge and its wooden sidewalk (a beautiful place to be during sunset).

7.0 Upon arriving back in New Jersey, continue straight (east) on the sidewalk along Bridge Street, passing over the Delaware Raritan Feeder Canal and by the Stockton Post Office.

7.1 Arrive back at the Stockton Railroad Station (Errico's Market & Deli). Turn right (southeast) onto the rail bed to the parking lot.

Hike Information

Local Information
Lambertville Area Chamber of Commerce, 60 Wilson Street, Lambertville 08530; (609) 397-0055; www.lambertville.org

Local Events/Attractions
The historic towns of Lambertville and New Hope are filled with antiques shops, cafes, and galleries (and sometimes crowds).

Hike Tours
Guided walking, cycling, canoe, and kayak tours are all available at D & R Canal State Park; www.dandrcanal.com.

Organizations
D & R Canal Watch, PO Box 2, Rocky Hill 08553-0002; (609) 924-2683; www.canalwatch.org. The Canal Society of New Jersey, PO Box 737, Morristown 07963-0737; (908) 722-9556; www.canalsocietynj.org

Lodging
Camping is available at Bull's Island State Park. For a fine B&B, try the Woolverton Inn, 6 Woolverton Road, Stockton 08559; (609) 397-0802; www.srinns.com/woolvertoninn. It's very close to the trailhead.

31 South Mountain and the Rahway River

Climb the First Watchung Mountain to Washington Rock, where a 1780 bonfire signaled to the American forces "The British are coming!" Traverse rolling hills past three cascades (seasonal), the largest being Hemlock Falls with its 25-foot drop. Stroll along the Rahway River, passing ponds and wandering through bottomlands. The route fluctuates between trails and old carriage roads, some laid out by the Olmsted Brothers and built by the Civilian Conservation Corps. Wonder at the "turtle backs," geological phenomenons where the traprock fractured, creating hexagonal "plates." This 2,048-acre reservation truly preserves an amazing greenway among urban development.

Start: Locust Grove parking lot on Glen Avenue
Distance: 5.8-mile loop
Approximate hiking time: 3.5 hours
Difficulty: Moderate due to length
Trail surface: Woods trails and carriage roads
Seasons: All
Other trail users: Multiuse
Canine compatibility: Leashed dogs permitted
Land status: County par
Nearest town: Millburn

Fees and permits: None
Schedule: Dawn to dusk
Maps: *DeLorme: New Jersey Atlas & Gazetteer* p. 32; USGS Roselle and Caldwell, NJ, quadrangles; a map is also available at the park.
Trail contacts: County of Essex Department of Recreation & Cultural Affairs: (973) 268-3500; www.last-exit.net/essexcounty/index .php?section=dept/p/o
Other: The cascades may be seasonally dry.

Finding the trailhead: From Interstate 78 and exit 50B (Maplewood, Millburn), travel north on Vaux Hall Road for 0.7 mile. At the T intersection turn left (west) onto Millburn Avenue. Be aware: Millburn Avenue jogs right in 0.6 mile, becoming Essex Street (passes the Millburn railroad station). At 0.2 mile turn right (north) onto Lackawanna Place and go 0.1 mile to the T intersection with Glen Avenue. Turn right onto Glen Avenue and immediately turn left into the Locust Grove parking lot.

The Hike

We hike through one of America's first parks on this walk. Essex County was a pioneer in creating parks in New Jersey, and one of its first was South Mountain Reservation. This spot in the Watchungs is historic; Washington Rock here was the site of a signal beacon (one of a series) that warned the Continental Army of British approach while they were encamped in Morristown. The first park parcel here was bought in 1896, and land acquisition continued for over a decade.

At the same time, the Essex County Parks Department set about making plans for the reservation. While leaving it mostly natural, they wanted a series of romantic drives, paths, walks, and other features, all of which we use on our ramble. To design this they chose the best: Frederick Law Olmsted, designer of Central Park and many

▶ Turtle backs are a notable part of the local nomenclature—to the extent that the local zoo took the name. *Turtle back* refers to a geological phenomenon in which basalt fractured, leaving cracks to fill with minerals. When erosion took place, the softer basalt wore away while the harder minerals did not. This left the mineral deposited within the cracks extending above the basalt surface, creating hexagonal patterns resembling a turtle's back.

other notable American landscapes. Olmsted died before much could be done, but his sons' firm, the Olmsted Brothers, finished the plans in 1902. Reforesting the land was a priority, with over 3,000 rhododendrons planted in 1910 alone. The rest of the park design was built over time, the last significant work being done by the Civilian Conservation Corps in the 1930s.

Alas, some original park features (rustic shelters, bridges, and benches) have fallen to ruin and vanished, and much of the rest of the park is in varying stages of overgrowth and decay. Olmsted's Central Park once suffered the same fate but was reborn when the Central Park Conservancy was established to restore it to its original elegance. Thankfully, South Mountain Reservation is following the same route: The recently established South Mountain Conservancy is working hard to bring the reservation back to the elegance and charm of its glory days.

The "turtle back" geological phenomenon is found on the Rahway River outlook.

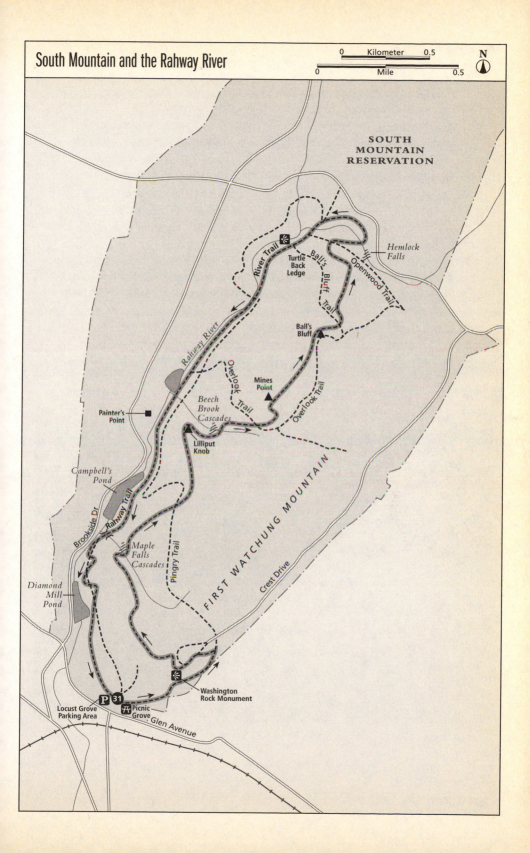

South Mountain and the Rahway River

Kilometer 0 — 0.5

Mile 0 — 0.5

N

SOUTH
MOUNTAIN
RESERVATION

Hemlock
Falls

Turtle
Back
Ledge

River Trail

Ball's
Bluff
Trail

Openwood Trail

Ball's
Bluff

Rahway River

Overlook Trail

Mines
Point

Beech
Brook
Cascades

Overlook Trail

Painter's
Point

Lilliput
Knob

Campbell's
Pond

FIRST WATCHUNG MOUNTAIN

Rahway Trail

Brookside Dr

Crest Drive

Maple
Falls
Cascades

Pingry Trail

Diamond
Mill
Pond

Washington
Rock Monument

P 31

Locust Grove
Parking Area

Picnic
Grove

Glen Avenue

Miles and Directions

0.0 At the far end (northeast) of Locust Grove Parking Area, locate the junction of the three carriage roads (which the park now calls trails). Take the right prong onto the Lenape Trail (yellow blazes) and ascend up a gravel path into the picnic grove.

0.1 Cross to the back left (east) corner of the picnic area on a grassy footpath, watching carefully for the yellow blazes. Enter the woods on a path and begin to climb the First Watchung Mountain.

0.3 Arrive at a chain-link fence. Turn right (east), continuing through a hardwood forest.

0.5 Just before the crest turn left (west) off the path and onto a forested trail.

0.6 At the T intersection turn left (southwest) onto paved Crest Drive (closed to vehicles). Yellow blazes are scarce, but one is found on an oak tree 50 yards up the road. Shortly pass a green-blazed trail on your left.

0.7 At the end of the stone guardrail, and before the Washington Rock Monument, the Lenape Trail leaves Crest Drive veering left. Continue straight along the Watchung ridge, descending to a lookout and eventually descending stairs. (**Side trip:** Explore the Washington Rock monuments and interpretive kiosks.)

0.8 Pass a series of unofficial trails to the left, leading to the top of the quarry (fenced).

1.0 Cross (north) Sunset Trail (bridle path) and ascend into a hardwood forest.

1.3 The Lenape Trail carves its way along a bowl, arriving at Maple Falls Cascades (seasonal).

One of the many bridle paths in South Mountain Reservation, designed by the Olmsted Brothers.

1.6 Cross (east) Pingry Trail (bridle path), passing some mighty tall oaks.

2.0 Arrive at Lilliput Knob, where the trail swings across a cobble field before descending.

2.2 Arrive at Beech Brook Cascades (seasonal), crossing two streams above the gorge. The trail swings away and parallels the brook.

2.4 Cross (east) Overlook Trail (bridle path) and ascend through rubble as the route rambles northwest.

2.5 Arrive at Mines Point. The top of the ridge has been devastated by gypsy moths.

2.9 Arrive at Ball's Bluff. The stone pillars are all that remain of a 1908 picnic pavilion. Beyond the ruins, the trail descends and turns left (north) before Ball's Bluff Trail (bridle path).

3.0 Cross (northeast) Ball's Bluff Trail (bridle path) and descend along a brook, which the trail eventually crosses.

3.4 At the T intersection with the Openwood Trail (bridle path) turn right (east) and ascend on the Lenape Trail. At the top of the rise, continue straight (northeast) on the Lenape Trail while the Openwood Trail turns right (southeast). Shortly the Lenape Trail veers right (south) off a point and into a hollow.

3.5 Arrive at Hemlock Falls and a stone pedestrian bridge. Cross the bridge and turn left (north) onto the Lenape Trail. (**Side trips:** Turning right brings you to the base of the falls. Continuing straight onto the Red Dot Trail brings you to the top of the falls.)

3.6 At the triangle veer left (west). At the T intersection at the base of the triangle, turn left (southwest) onto River Trail an old bridle path without blazing. The route immediately crosses a stone bridge, the Openwood Trail coming in on the left. (**FYI:** The Lenape Trail veers right at the triangle and, at the base of the triangle, brings you to the Rahway Trailhead.)

3.7 As the River Trail climbs out of the bottomland, arrive at a "turtle back" ledge 30 feet above the Rahway River, a good lunch spot. Continue heading south.

3.8 Pass Ball's Bluff Trail on the left (southeast).

4.0 Leaving the River Trail, turn right (north) onto a gravel road and walk 50 feet, stopping before the bridge abutment, turn left (west) onto the Rahway Trail (white blazes). The trail drops down along the Rahway River's bottomland. (**FYI:** Following the white blazes brings you back to the Locust Grove Parking Area.)

4.3 Cross woods road. Dam on right.

4.5 Pass a dam on right with a bridge leading to Painter's Point.

4.6 The Rahway Trail and the River Trail (bridle path) begin to crisscross, merge, and part more times than you want to count. Seems a little ridiculous. From the rhododendron grove, you can take either the River Trail or the Rahway Trail till you cross the stone bridge.

4.7 The brick plant and Campbell's Pond are below on your right; turn right (west) onto the Rahway Trail, following it back down toward the river. Stick with the white blazes.

5.0 Forty feet above the Rahway River, the trail traverses the bank before crossing a tributary on a beautiful stone bridge.

5.3 Crisscross River Trail three more time before passing Diamond Mill Pond/Dam on the right.

5.8 Arrive at the northwest side of Locust Grove Parking Area.

Local Information

New Jersey Tourism Commission, Gateway Region; (609) 777-0855; www.state.nj.us/travel/
regions_GWY_detail.shtml

Local Events/Attractions

The Turtle Back Zoo in South Mountain Reservation has over 500 animals, with a focus on native
New Jersey wildlife: Turtle Back Zoo, 560 Northfield Avenue, West Orange 07052; (973) 731-
5800; www.Turtlebackzoo.com. The Edison National Historic Site preserves the workshops of the
great New Jersey inventor of the electric lightbulb and numerous other innovations: Main Street
and Lakeside Avenue, West Orange 07052; (973) 736-0550; www.nps.gov/edis/home.htm.

Organizations

The South Mountain Conservancy, Box 273, South Orange 07079; www.somocon.org. New York–
New Jersey Trail Conference, 156 Ramapo Valley Road (U.S. Highway 202), Mahwah 07430; (201)
512-9348; www.nynjtc.org

Other Resources

USGS South Mountain Web site: www.3dparks.wr.usgs.gov/nyc/parks/loc42.htm

32 The Hackensack Meadowlands

If you want to visit the crossroads of environmental devastation and environmental
renewal, DeKorte Park is the place. This land has been diked, farmed, and lumbered;
crisscrossed by turnpikes, train tracks, power lines, and pipelines; and has the dubious
distinction of having been part of the largest dump in the world! But in the last three
decades, DeKorte has become a spot dedicated to restoring native vegetation, and
reclaiming wildlife habitation. This extraordinary hike travels through the middle of
impoundments and salt marshes along the Atlantic Flyway. Partial loop, partial out-
and-back, and the trails are built on floating boardwalks and dikes.

Start: Meadowlands Environmental Center
parking lot on Valley Brook Avenue
Distance: 3.7-mile loop
Approximate hiking time: 1.5 hours
Difficulty: Easy, though not always quiet
Trail surface: Gravel paths, floating and fixed
boardwalks, and dikes
Seasons: All, but potentially too hot in mid-
summer
Other trail users: Hikers only

Canine compatibility: No dogs permitted
Land status: New Jersey Meadowlands Com-
mission park
Nearest town: Lyndhurst
Fees and permits: None
Schedule: Monday through Friday 9:00 a.m. to
5:00 p.m., Saturday and Sunday 10:00 a.m. to
3:00 p.m.
Maps: *DeLorme: New Jersey Atlas & Gazetteer*
p.32, 78; USGS Weehawken, NJ, quadrangle;

a map is also available at the park or online at www.meadowlands.state.nj.us/EC/come_visit/DeKorte_Park_Map.cfm.

Trail contacts: Hackensack Meadowlands Environmental Center, 2 DeKorte Park Plaza, Lyndhurst 07071; (201) 460-8300; www.meadowlands.state.nj.us/ec/index.cfm

Special considerations: Mosquitoes can be serious here, and there is little shade along many portions of the walk, so be prepared. Large school groups, not to mention the proliferation of highway and jet traffic, means this may not exactly be a tranquil hike. But the birdwatching can be spectacular during migratory season, as you're smack in the Atlantic Flyway.

Finding the trailhead: From the New Jersey Turnpike, take exit 16W to Route 3 West. Take Route 3 west to Route 17 South (Lyndhurst exit). Follow around the ramp to the traffic light. Make a left onto Polito Avenue. Continue to the end of Polito Avenue. At the stop sign make a left onto Valley Brook Avenue. Follow this road to the end (approximately 1.5 miles). Cross the railroad tracks (keep to the left). Meadowlands Environment Center is the first building on the left after the tracks.

The Hike

Most natural landscapes in New Jersey—even the wildest ones—have undergone some degree of past alteration at the hand of humans. In this regard, few could hold a candle to our hike today through the Hackensack Meadowlands. This system of rivers and estuaries was once swathed in vast swamps of huge cedars, and its clear waters and wetlands were host to a wide array of wildlife.

But in the 1800s, the cedar forests here fell to the ax, and the rivers were rendered salty by upstream dams, restricting fresh water flow. Original flora and fauna left the newly inhospitable environment, and new, foreign ones filled the void. The now-omnipresent phragmites reeds monopolized the wetlands. The marshlands were diked, ditched, used as trash dumps and landfills, and crisscrossed by railroads, pipelines, power lines, and highways (routes used by some of our hiking paths today). Rivers flowed not with fish, but pollution. The

▶ New Jersey state assemblyman Richard W. DeKorte sponsored the legislation establishing the New Jersey Meadowlands Commission in the mid-1970s. Following his death from cancer at age thirty-nine in 1975, the park here was named in his honor.

landscape became the evil stereotype of New Jersey: a swampy, reedy wasteland—a place to be ignored and avoided, an abandoned, desolate, scary landscape: *Leave the gun. Take the cannoli.*

But with the growth of the environmental movement in the 1960s, the Meadowlands were recognized not as worthless but as a natural environment that was once magnificent and could be again. It was also recognized as an important wildlife habitat: Some 265 bird species make their home in the park. Dozens of others migrate through here, making it a major stop on the Atlantic Flyway. Some past damage can never be repaired, but after decades of concerted efforts, the Hackensack Meadowlands are now rebounding in a big way.

With land acquisition and restoration, the Meadowlands are poised to become one of the great wild urban greenways of the world—a green oasis in the shadow of the Manhattan skyline. Enjoy this walk through marshlands and reed–forests; at times, only the glimpse of the top of a skyscraper will tell you that you're practically next to Manhattan.

Miles and Directions

0.0 From the southwest end of the parking lot, locate the entrance to the Meadowlands Environmental Center. It's worthwhile to stop in at the interpretive center and pick up handouts and materials on flora, fauna, and history. Directly across from the entrance cross (north) the service road and climb a set of stairs. At the top, turn right (east) onto the Kingsland Overlook Trail.

0.3 The Kingsland Overlook Trail ends at the entrance road. Cross (southeast) it and proceed onto a brick walkway, which leads to the Marsh Discovery Trailhead. Take the Discovery Trail into Kingsland Tidal Impoundment via a floating boardwalk

0.8 At the T intersection turn right (northwest) onto the Transco Trail (yellow blazes). (**Side trip:** Turn left [southeast] onto the Transco Trail for an out-and-back. Opportunity to watch eighteen-wheelers migrating along the New Jersey Turnpike flyway.)

1.2 The Transco Trail intersects the Shorewalk (right) and the path leading (left) to Lyndhurst Nature Reserve. Continue straight (northwest).

1.8 The Transco Trail swings left (west) before a road and through a sitting area. At the junction, the Transco Trail terminates. Turn left (south) onto Saw Mill Creek Trail (blue blazes), passing through an elaborate wrought-iron gate, something out of *The Godfather*.

Tidal pool along the Hackensack River Estuary

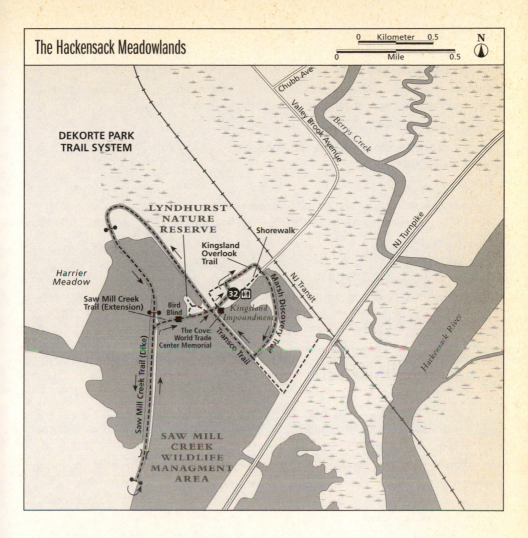

Kilometer 0.5

Mile 0.5

N

DEKORTE PARK
TRAIL SYSTEM

LYNDHURST
NATURE
RESERVE

Shorewalk

Kingsland
Overlook
Trail

Harrier
Meadow

Saw Mill Creek
Trail (Extension)

Bird
Blind

Kingsland
Impoundment

The Cove:
World Trade
Center Memorial

Transco Trail

Saw Mill Creek Trail (Dike)

Marsh Discovery Trail

NJ Transit

Chubb Ave.

Valley Brook Avenue

Berrys Creek

NJ Turnpike

Hackensack River

SAW MILL
CREEK
WILDLIFE
MANAGMENT
AREA

2.2 As the trail moves through a gate, pass the Saw Mill Creek Trail Extension to your left and continue straight. (**FYI:** The hike will return via the extension, so make a mental note of the spot.)

2.8 Cross over a bridge and arrive at a chain-link fence, your turnaround point. Retrace the hike back to the Saw Mill Creek Trail Extension, before the gate.

3.3 Before the gate turn right (east) onto the Saw Mill Creek Trail Extension (blue blazes).

3.4 Proceed through a bird blind and arrive at the Lyndhurst Nature Reserve. (**Side trip:** The two paths on the left create a loop into the reserve.)

3.5 The Saw Mill Creek Trail Extension terminates at the intersection with the Transco Trail and Shorewalk. Continue straight onto the Shorewalk, which is a stroll along the sidewalk, passing an impressive World Trade Center Memorial, a sculpture silhouette of the Manhattan skyline, and Meadow Commission courtyard.

3.7 Arrive back at the Meadowlands Environmental Center's entrance and the parking lot.

Local Information

Arts in the Meadowlands, www.njmeadowlands.gov/eco_tourism/Arts_In_The_Meadowlands.cfm.
Secaucus Web site: www.secaucus.org

Local Events/Attractions

City of Newark: www.ci.ne wark.nj.us/Guide_To_Newark/Guide_To_Newark.htm. Cuisine and
culture—no kidding!

Hike Tours

The Meadowlands Environmental Commission runs river cruises from the Carlstadt Marina; (201)
460-4640. Hackensack Riverkeeper runs an Eco-Cruise from Laurel Hill Park, Secaucus; (201)
968-0808.

Organizations

Hackensack Riverkeeper, Inc., 231 Main Street, Hackensack 07601-7304; (201) 968-0808;
www.hackensackriverkeeper.org. The Meadowlands Conservation Trust, 1 DeKorte Park Plaza, Lyndhurst 07071; www.njmeadowlands.gov/natural_resources/MCT/meadowlands_trust_fund.cfm

33 Lord Stirling Park

Visit the 18,000–year-old Glacial Lake Passaic, now called the Great Swamp. Designated a National Natural Landmark, it doesn't take long hiking this level loop to
know why. Within the 450-acre park's natural lands, the route meanders through
marshes, meadows, swamps, and woodlands, while hugging the Passaic River and a
series of ponds. While walking the paths and boardwalks, make use of the observation
towers and blinds to view the 215 species of birds recorded in the park. Depending
on the season, this serene hike could be interrupted by the mosquito.

Start: Somerset County Environmental Educa-
tion Center parking lot on Lord Stirling Road
Distance: 2.9-mile loop
Approximate hiking time: 1.5 hours
Difficulty: Easy
Trail surface: Paths and boardwalks
Seasons: All
Other trail users: Hikers
Canine compatibility: No dogs permitted
Land status: County park
Nearest town: Basking Ridge

Fees and permits: None
Schedule: Dawn to dusk
Maps: *DeLorme: New Jersey Atlas & Gazetteer*
p. 30–31; USGS Bernardsville, NJ, quadrangle;
a map is also available at the park.
Trail contacts: Somerset County Park
Commission, 355 Milltown Road, Bridgewater
08807; (908) 722-1200; www.somerset
countyparks.org
Special considerations: Beware of
mosquitoes.

Finding the trailhead: From Interstate 287 in Van Dorans Mills (exit 30), turn south onto North Maple Avenue, heading toward Basking Ridge. Travel 1.7 miles to a series of traffic islands where North Maple Avenue becomes South Maple Avenue. Bear left onto South Maple Avenue (avoiding the center of the town) and travel (south) 1.0 mile. Turn left (east) onto Lord Stirling Road and go 1.5 miles. Turn left into the Environmental Education Center and the parking lot.

The Hike

This hike takes us through rich bottomland meadows, once part of a glacial lake. It was prime farmland—and responsible for the park's name, indirectly. William Alexander, who lived here, was a lord who died creating a democracy. He was born in 1725 to a wealthy, well-connected family with a profitable provisioning business (they supplied the army in the French and Indian War). He married Sarah Livingston in 1748; his brother-in-law William Livingston was a future governor of New Jersey. Other relatives included the Stevens, Parker, and Rutherfurd families, a who's who of the time. He had long-standing land interests in the East Jersey Board of Proprietors, and in his spare time he became one of the founders of King's College in New York, now Columbia University.

There were some disputes over payment of army contracts, and Alexander went to England to claim payment in the late 1750s. At the same time he pursued another ambition: a claim to a lapsed Scottish earldom, which would have made him "Lord Stirling." A Scottish jury accepted his claims, but not the British House of Lords. This was still good enough for Alexander, who on his return to America in 1761 called himself "Lord Stirling." So did most everyone else, including George Washington.

With a lord's title (sort of) he decided to adopt a lord's lifestyle, which he could afford. Attracted by these rich meadows and grazing pasture here in Basking Ridge, he built a large mansion and estate, regarded at the time as one of the grandest in the colonies.

At the same time he expanded his business interests. He was heavily invested in the iron industry and owned mines and ironworks in northern New Jersey (at Hibernia) and at Sterling Lake, New York (named after him). Hibernia made cannon and grapeshot for the Revolutionary War effort, and Sterling Ironworks made part of the great Hudson River chain.

But all this investment absorbed more cash than it produced, and his finances grew dire. With the arrival of the Revolution, his status as lord did not prevent him from adopting the Patriot cause, which likewise drained his finances. First a colonel in the New Jersey Militia, he later served as a general in the Continental Army under Washington; the Hessians at Trenton surrendered to him. Descriptions of Alexander are complex. Some regarded him as flamboyant, vain, and pompous, with an excessive appetite for food and drink. Others who fought alongside him called him loyal, popular with his soldiers, and brave under fire—a reliable general, if not a brilliant one.

How would this lord fare in the new American democracy he helped create? No one knows—he died in January 1783, just as the war was winding down, from chronic gout, a virtual bankrupt. His property was sold to pay his debts. His grand estate fell to ruins soon after his death and was eventually forgotten.

But not forgotten forever—the site of his estate became Lord Stirling Park, and subsequent archaeological investigations of the site here proved that the grand descriptions of it were correct. Stirling's memory lives on in another way—his Sterling Lake and ironworks eventually gave their name (in modified spelling) to the surrounding property, today's Sterling Forest, New York State Park. Here, however, you can enjoy the lovely landscape that once attracted would-be nobility.

Miles and Directions

0.0 From the northwest corner of the parking lot and the east side of the Environmental Education Center veer right (northeast) onto the sidewalk, passing a boardwalk leaving left. Continue straight onto a gravel path, leading to the trail register. Park maps are available here. Crossing the causeway, you are on the Yellow and Red Trails: Esox Pond is on the right and Branta Pond on the left. (**FYI:** It's worthwhile to stop in at the interpretive center and pick up handouts and materials on flora, fauna, and history.)

0.1 Turn right (southeast) onto a grassy path. You are now solely on the Yellow Trail and will be till you reach Lenape Meadow (0.9 mile). It should also be noted that all turns will be to the right till you reach Earwig Bridge (2.0 miles). (**FYI:** Each intersection has a trail post with a map.)

0.2 At the fork (Yellow Trail leads both ways) veer right (south) onto a grassy lane with the meadow to the right, passing a kick-out to Esox Pond.

A tiger swallowtail visits Lenape Meadow in Lord Stirling Park.

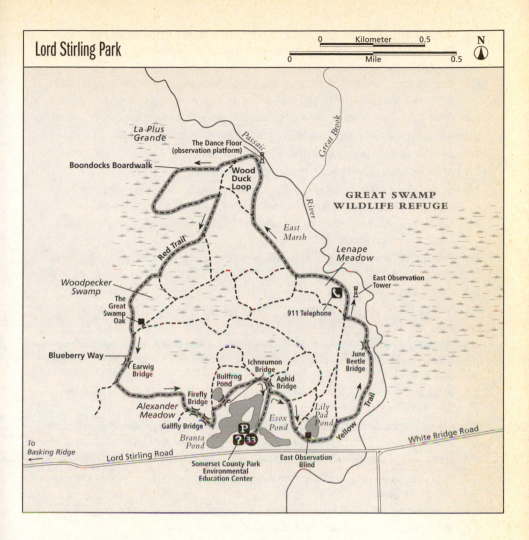

0   Kilometer   0.5

0   Mile   0.5

N

Lord Stirling Park

La Plus Grande

The Dance Floor
(observation platform)

Passaic

Great Brook

Boondocks Boardwalk

Wood Duck Loop

River

GREAT SWAMP WILDLIFE REFUGE

East Marsh

Red Trail

Lenape Meadow

East Observation Tower

Woodpecker Swamp

The Great Swamp Oak

911 Telephone

Blueberry Way

June Beetle Bridge

Earwig Bridge

Ichneumon Bridge

Bullfrog Pond

Aphid Bridge

Firefly Bridge

Alexander Meadow

Esox Pond

Lily Pad Pond

Gallfly Bridge

Branta Pond

Yellow Trail

White Bridge Road

To Basking Ridge

Lord Stirling Road

Somerset County Park Environmental Education Center

East Observation Blind

0.3 At the fork veer right (southeast) and remain with the Yellow Trail. Ignore the lane to Lord Stirling Road and the boardwalk to Esox Pond. To your left pass the East Observation Blind and Lilly Pad Pond.

0.4 At the fork veer right (east), staying with the Yellow Trail.

0.5 Pass fence and view of the Passaic River.

0.6 Cross June Beetle Bridge.

0.7 At the T intersection (Yellow Trail leads both ways) turn right (north) onto a path. Within a few hundred yards veer right (northeast) at the fork (Yellow Trail leads both ways) onto a path between the Lenape Meadow and swamp forest.

0.8 Arrive at the East Observation Tower, which overlooks the Passaic River and the Great Swamp National Wildlife Refuge. Just past this kick-out there is a 9-1-1 telephone.

0.9 At the T-intersection turn right (northwest) onto a grassy lane. The route leaves the Yellow Trail and turns onto an unmarked trail, passing another unmarked trail on the left. The trail eventually becomes a boardwalk.

1.1 At the junction turn right (northeast), remaining on the boardwalk. You are hiking the Wood Duck Loop with the East Marsh on your right.

1.2 Arrive at The Dance Floor, an observation platform above the Passaic River.

1.3 Turn right (west) on a boardwalk, heading toward the Boondocks Boardwalk.

1.4 Arrive at the Boondocks Boardwalk and the La Plus Grande.

1.5 At the triangle turn right (south), remaining on a boardwalk.

1.6 Turn right (west) onto the Red Trail, remaining on a boardwalk for a short while. (**FYI:** For the remainder of the hike, the route follows the Red Trail back to the parking lot.)

1.7 Turn right (southwest) onto a path, following the Red Trail. Eventually the path becomes a boardwalk, edging Woodpecker Swamp.

1.9 Arrive at The Great Swamp Oak. At the fork veer right (southeast), staying with the Red Trail through Blueberry Way.

2.0 Cross Earwig Bridge.

2.1 Turn left (southeast) (first left turn on this hike); the trail straddles the forest and the meadow.

2.2 Ignore the Blue Trail (from Alexander Meadow), which enters from the right, and continue straight (east), immediately crossing the Firefly Bridge. The Red Trail is co-aligned with the Blue Trail.

2.3 At the fork, veer left (east), remaining on the Red Trail, and immediately cross the Gallfly Bridge. The Blue Trail departs right.

2.4 Ignore an unmarked trail (from the Hidden Marsh loop) on left (north) and cross the Ichneumon Bridge, shortly passing Bullfrog Pond (left) and the West Observation Blind.

2.6 Ignore unmark trail (from the Hidden Marsh loop) on left (north) while the trail swings east.

2.7 At the T intersection, the Red Trail leads in both directions; you turn right (south) and cross the Aphid Bridge.

2.8 Ignore the Yellow Trail leaving left and continue straight on the co-aligned Red and Yellow Trails, retracing the hike from here to the parking lot.

2.9 Arrive back at the parking lot.

Hike Information

Local Information
New Jersey Skylands Region Tourism Guide, www.njskylands.com

Local Events/Attractions
While here, don't fail to visit The Raptor Trust, just nearby at 1390 White Bridge Road, with amazing exhibits of rescued eagles, owls, hawks, and other birds—great for kids: The Raptor Trust, 1390 White Bridge Road, Millington 07946; (908) 647-2353; www.theraptortrust.org. Morristown National Historical Park includes the Ford Mansion (Washington's headquarters) and Jockey Hollow,

site of the Continental Army winter encampment: 30 Washington Place, Morristown 07960-4299; (908) 766-8215; www.nps.gov/morr/pphtml/contact.html. Golf House, home of the United States Golf Association (USGA), has a museum on the history of golf in a landmark Georgian Revival mansion, as well as adjacent testing facilities: PO Box 708, Far Hills 07931; (908) 234-2300; www.usga.orghome/index.html

Organizations

The Lenape Meadow Archaeological Excavation is an ongoing archaeological field school run by the Somerset County Environmental Education Center. A public archaeological project (anyone can join in), it has uncovered remains of a Late Archaic–Early Woodland village area that once existed here in the Great Swamp: www.home.att.net/~briansnat/index.html

THE COASTAL PLAIN AND PINE BARRENS

The Coastal Plain comprises the biggest part of New Jersey, about three-fifths of the state. If the dramatic, mountainous variety of northern New Jersey is our yin, the flat, sandy, minimalist beauty of the Coastal Plain is definitely our yang. It's a seeming world apart, gently sloping from the Piedmont south to the Delaware Bay and the Atlantic Ocean shoreline.

The Skit Branch, which skirts the Batona Trail, is tea-colored due to its high iron and tannin content.

No boulders or cliffs here—this is the land of sand, clay, silt, and marl. The Piedmont and Coastal Plain meet on a line, running roughly from Raritan Bay near Perth Amboy southwest to Trenton, and from there down the Delaware. This is called the "fall line"—the change in geology creates numerous rapids and waterfalls, among them the rapids above Trenton, making that city the head of navigation on the Delaware, and hence leading to its historic commercial and industrial importance.

Though not as dramatic as other parts of New Jersey, the Coastal Plain nevertheless has a complex geology, comprised of three subareas. The Inner Lowland stretches from Perth Amboy to the Delaware River and Bay—largely the landscape of the southern New Jersey Turnpike. The Outer Lowland forms the landscape of the Jersey Shore.

Sandwiched in between these two lowlands is the Central Upland. This is higher in elevation and gently rolling, while the inner and outer lowlands are virtually flat. The region includes everything from dry, sandy plains of scrub oak and pitch pine, richly fertile farmland, and tea-dark rivers winding through endless pine forests.

Early settlers regarded the Pinelands as limited in value. Most of it wasn't inherently good farmland, and scrub pine wasn't the most desirable commercial timber. As such, the remote parts of the region developed a reputation early on as sparsely settled no-man's-lands of rustics and robbers. Abetted by a body of rich folklore (most significantly embodied in the legendary Jersey Devil), the region developed an aura of mystery.

Nonetheless, bog iron discovered in the Pinelands became an important Colonial industry at places like Batsto. When the bog iron gave out, glassmaking took its place as an important industry. Agriculturally, the lowlands proved to be ideal habitat for the cultivation of blueberries and cranberries, of which New Jersey is a major producer (we were the first producer of the commercial blueberry).

The pine and oak forests so long taken for granted gained new appreciation starting early in the twentieth century. The first state forest in New Jersey, Bass River, was established here in 1905. Not only is the region home to the oldest state forest, it is also home to the biggest: Wharton State Forest, at nearly 115,000 acres, dwarfs everything else in the New Jersey Park and Forest system. And while some parks, like Wharton, feature nearly endless expanses of wild land, others, like Parvin State Park, are little jewels, carefully developed with beaches, cabins, campsites, trails, and other facilities.

In the 1960s, a writer for the *New Yorker* penned a series of articles on the Pinelands. The tone of the articles, eventually published as a book, was nearly elegiac—an attempt to record this great, profoundly wild area tucked into the rapidly expanding megalopolis before it was gone.

But John McPhee's book, *The Pine Barrens*, ended up being not an obituary but a rallying cry. The importance of the million-acre Pine Barrens as both open space and aquifer became evident by the late 1960s, in large part because of McPhee's book. This ultimately led to the 1979 passage of The Pinelands Preservation Act. The Pine Barrens have since been designated a Biosphere Reserve by both the United States and the United Nations. Now, the Pinelands will forever remain one of the largest tracts of preserved open space in such proximity to urban development on the eastern seaboard.

34 Belcoville and the South River

This loop hike in Estell Manor Park is a hidden prize among oak–pine forests, white cedar swamps, and coastal ecosystems that border the South River and Stephen's Creek. The route takes you through Belcoville, a "ghost town," and the former Bethlehem Loading Company (1918), a World War I munitions plant, with foundations appearing along the way. The trail is made up of sand roads, abandoned railroad beds, and boardwalk. The route also passes the nineteenth-century Estell glassworks with much of the foundations still standing. Adding to the experience are a number of historical kiosks. As their brochure states, "Take time to enjoy and come back often."

Start: Warren E. Fox Nature Center parking lot in Estell Manor Park
Distance: 4.8-mile loop
Approximate hiking time: 3 hours
Difficulty: Easy, with level grades
Trail surface: Sand roads, railroad beds, and boardwalk
Seasons: All
Other trail users: Multiuse
Canine compatibility: Leashed dogs permitted
Land status: County park
Nearest town: May's Landing
Fees and permits: None
Schedule: 7:30 a.m. to dusk

Maps: *DeLorme: New Jersey Atlas & Gazetteer* p. 70; USGS Mays Landing, NJ, quadrangle; a trail map is also available at the park or online at www.aclink.org/PARKS/mainpages/ estell_trails.asp.
Trail contacts: Estell Manor Park, 109 Highway 50, Mays Landing 08330; (609) 645-5960; www.aclink.org/PARKS
Other: Some sections of this hike are barrier-free and suitable for wheelchairs, etc. Check park map for details. It's worthwhile to stop in at the interpretive center and pick up handouts and materials on flora, fauna, and history.
Special considerations: Beware of mosquitoes.

Finding the trailhead: From the intersection of U.S. Highway 40 and Route 50 in Mays Landing, travel 1.3 miles south on Route 50. Turn left (east) into the Atlantic County Park: Estell Manor (signage present). Go 0.1 mile to Warren Fox Interpretive Center's parking lot on your right.

The Hike

The Pine Barrens have a long and varied industrial history, and few places reflect it better than our hike in Estell Manor Park. It takes its name from John Estell, who acquired land here in the 1820s. Bog iron had long been profitable hereabouts, but the Estells switched over to the up-and-coming commodity in South Jersey, glass. Estell built a glassworks here in 1826; it was perhaps the first that could produce both bottle glass and window glass, which required very different processes. The glassworks here was built, unusually, of stone, and its ruins are thus still standing. The Estells also dabbled in timber, shipbuilding, and farming. They became wealthy landowners of huge tracts, built a fine mansion, and (so it was recalled) lived like lords. They treated their tenants, laborers, and neighbors accordingly—hence the "Manor."

Glass was a major industry in south Jersey, and the reason is everywhere underfoot on our hike: sand, the basic raw ingredient of glass. The Estell glassworks closed in 1877. Its ruins, including the glass furnace, walls and foundations of other industrial structures, and the sites of workers' housing, have in recent years been documented and stabilized. Any visit to the park should include this interesting site.

The next major phase in the park's industrial history was vastly bigger and remarkably shorter. The entry of the United States into the First World War in April 1917 signaled a need for greatly increased armaments production facilities. The Bethlehem Loading Company, in partnership with the federal government, quickly set about acquiring some 10,000 acres here, mostly old farmsteads and river landings. The area had several desirable features: rail access, river access, and relative isolation (the recent Black Tom explosion in New York harbor demonstrated that munitions plants were best built away from population centers).

Ground for the new munitions plants and related facilities was broken in May 1918, and by August, nothing less than a city had been built. It included a town hall, a school, a bank, a bowling alley, stores, cafeterias, a police headquarters, factories and plants, 24 miles of railroad siding, and barracks and housing for a total of 9,000 workers and their families. In honor of the Bethlehem Loading Company, it was dubbed Belcoville. Much of our walk follows the old roads and lanes of this onetime industrial plant/city.

The Swamp Trail Boardwalk edges the South River, part of the Great Egg Harbor Wildlife and Scenic River System.

But as a munitions plant, this remarkable new city had a short life. Production started in the fall of 1918, and by November of that year the war was over. Munitions production at Belcoville ended in 1919, and it was closed. Many structures were sold as scrap lumber or were jacked up and moved to nearby towns. Most steel and metal from the site was stripped for scrap. In 1923 the remaining houses and buildings of Belcoville were sold in situ and became the current town of Belcoville, north of Estell Manor Park. The park area was virtually all part of the Belcoville plant, primarily the manufacturing and administrative areas, and ruins and reminders of those days are still to be seen.

Our hike also goes by sites not to be missed. The Warren E. Fox Interpretive Center has outstanding exhibits on flora, fauna, and history, including both live animals and some of the finest mounted animal specimens you will find in New Jersey. And while you're on our walk, don't fail to appreciate the wonderful boardwalks through the wetlands and riverside environments that form an integral part of this beautiful area.

Miles and Directions

0.0 Leave the Fox Interpretive Center and turn right (east) onto Purple Heart Drive (loop), passing (left) the Shaw House (an 1825 farmhouse) and the maintenance yard.

0.1 At the fork veer left (northeast) off Purple Heart Drive onto a sandy lane. Pass around a chained gate and onto the North End Trail (road) and head north. (**FYI:** Purple Heart Drive veers right, but the sign reads, WRONG WAY.)

0.2 Cross Collins Lane (road).

0.3 Pass Sandhole Road (trail) on the right (east).

0.6 Pass TNT Road (trail) on the right (east).

0.7 Pass Eight Inch Road (trail) on the right (east). (**Side trip:** Stroll a few hundred yards down Eight Inch Road to get a feel of the ruins of the Bethlehem Loading Company, a World War I munitions plant 9 [see The Hike]. Within the next 0.1 mile, pass [right] interpretive kiosk pertaining to the Bethlehem Loading Company, pass [left] foundation of the water plant, and pass [right] an interpretive kiosk.)

0.8 Pass Frog Pond Road (trail) on the right (east) and continue straight (north). Warning: Ignore the arrow and sign to the North End Trail, which appears to point down Frog Pond Road. (**FYI:** Frog Pond Road was the main entrance to Bethlehem Loading Company, guard tower and all.)

0.9 Pass Storehouse Road (trail) on the right.

1.0 Pass around gate and along a parking lot.

1.1 At the intersection turn right (east) onto Artesian Well Road, leaving North End Trail. Boat trailers also use the cinder lane.

1.2 Pass Rabbit Square Trail on the right (south).

1.3 Pass Change House Trail on the right (south).

1.4 Pass Oak Ridge Trail on the right (south).

1.5 Pass a road and parking lot on the left (north).

1.6 At the cul-de-sac turn right (south) onto the Swamp Trail boardwalk. On your left are the remains of the artesian well (175 feet deep) and the Belco Powerhouse. (**Side trip A:** To view the South River and Weymouth Great Egg Harbor Wildlife Management Area, continue

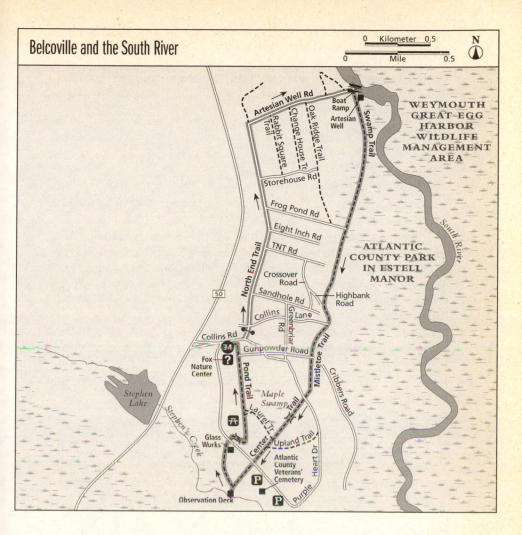

straight [east] down the road to the South River Boat Ramp. **Side trip B:** Once on the boardwalk, turn left [southwest] onto a path leading to the Smith/Ireland Cemetery [Veterans' Cemetery].)

2.0 Pass kick-out leading to the edge of the South River.

2.1 Pass kick-out leading to the South River.

2.3 Cross over Sand Creek.

2.4 Pass on the right (west) a kiosk and boardwalk: Frog Pond Road (trail), which leads to Oak Ridge Trail.

2.5 Pass bench and Cedar Swamp.

2.8 Pass on the right (west) Highbank Road (trail), Sandhole Road (trail), Collins Lane (trail), all coming at the same time.

3.1 Pass Cribber's Road (trail) on the left (southeast). It looks more like an unofficial path leading into the brush.

3.2 At the junction continue straight (south) onto the Mistletoe Trail, which drops down off the boardwalk and onto the former railroad bed. Alert: A sign on the edge of the boardwalk reads Center Trail, which means that Mistletoe leads to Center Trail. (**Bail-out:** The Boardwalk or Gunpowder Road [trail] exiting right [east] lead back to the Interpretive Center.)

3.3 Cross Purple Heart Drive (loop) and onto Center Trail, a former railroad bed. It is co-aligned with a fitness course.

3.4 At Maple Swamp cross over a 300-foot bridge.

3.5 Pass on the right (northwest) Laurel Trail.

3.6 Pass on the left (southeast) Upland Trail.

3.7 Cross Purple Heart Drive (loop) and continue on Center Trail.

3.8 Turn a sharp right (north) onto a sand road. (**Side trip:** Continue straight [southeast] 150 feet to the observation platform over Stephen's Creek.)

4.1 Arrive at the historical site of the Estellville Glassworks with the numerous interpretive kiosks. Take the sidewalk between the ruins of the Melting Furnace (right) and the Pot House (left) to Purple Heart Drive (loop). Cross Purple Heart Drive, heading north through the opening in the fence leading into the picnic area. Turn right (east), crossing a 75-foot wooden bridge, and turn left (north) at the far end onto the Pond Trail, which edges the former railroad bed.

4.3 Arrive at a trail kiosk. Laurel Trail leaves right (east). Continue straight (north) on the Pond Trail, crossing a 60-foot wooden bridge and immediately turn right (north) on the path, edging the railroad bed.

4.4 Pass a second link to Laurel Trail leaving right (east) while the Pond Trail drops down onto the former railroad bed.

4.5 Pass the pond on the left.

4.6 At the fork veer left (northwest) and continue on the Pond Trail. (**FYI:** The fork coming in on the right is the Boardwalk [Gunpowder Road] that concludes the bail-out. Sign on the boardwalk reads ARTESIAN WELL, which means that the Boardwalk leads to Artesian Well.)

4.8 Pass the back of Fox Interpretive Center where Pond Trail dead-ends at Purple Heart Drive. Turn left (west) onto Purple Heart Drive and arrive back at the parking lot.

Hike Information

Local Information

Greater Atlantic City Region Tourism; (800) VISITNJ; www.state.nj.us/travel/regions_GAC.shtml. New Jersey Commerce, Economic Growth & Tourism Commission, PO Box 820, Trenton 08625-0820. Atlantic County, New Jersey, Recreation & Leisure Web site: www.aclink.org

Lodging

Limited camping is available at Estell Manor Park; (609) 625-8219. Camping is also available at Belleplain State Forest, County Route 550, PO Box 450, Woodbine 08270; (609) 861-2404; www.state.nj.us/dep/parksandforests/parks/belle.html

Other Resources

Much history on the Bethlehem Loading Company is available at www.aclink.org/blc.

A POET ON JERSEY GLASSMAKING

In the following poem from *In Reckless Ecstasy* (1904), the great American poet Carl Sandburg gives just about the most evocative description of a south Jersey glassworks you're likely to find:

> Down in southern New Jersey they make glass. By
> day and by night, the fires burn on in Millville* and
> bid the sand let in the light. . . . Big, black flumes
> shooting out smoke and sparks, bottles, bottles of
> every tint and hue, from a brilliant crimson to the dud
> green that marks the death of sand and the birth of
> glass. From each fire the heat radiates on the
> 'blower," the 'gaffers,' and the carryin' boys. The
> latter are from nine to eighteen years in age,
> averaging about fourteen, and they outnumber the
> adult workers. . . . Their education has consisted
> mainly of . . . contact with 'blowers' and 'gaffers.' . . .
> The manufacturers have endowed a night school, but
> . . . the boys cannot keep their heads up and their eyes
> open during the sessions. . . . But the 'carryin' boys
> work from nine to ten and get two dollars and a half a
> week, sometimes three. Passing through, back and
> forth in the pale weird light these creatures . . . are
> grimy, wiry, scarmy, scrawny, stunted specimens,
> and I cuss-words and salacious talk, they know all the
> grown men know.

* Wheaton Village, formerly Wheaton Glass Works, in Millville, is located about 12 miles as the crow flies from Estell Manor.

35 Pakim Pond and Mount Misery

In this long loop through Brendan T. Byrne (formerly Lebanon) State Forest, you experience the Pine Barrens. The trail is relatively flat with a few rises along sand roads and trails. The route from Pakim Pond to Mount Misery travels through oak-pine forest, former cranberry bogs, and Atlantic white cedar swamps. The open space of the bog is startling after a day under the pines, while the coolness of the cedar swamps is refreshing after so much sun. One point of interest is the location of a former CCC bunkhouse along the side of the trail in Mount Misery, a town written up in Henry Charlton Beck's Forgotten Towns of Southern New Jersey.

Start: Pakim Pond parking lot on Cooper Road
Distance: 9.9-mile loop
Approximate hiking time: 5 hours
Difficulty: Strenuous due to length and potential sun exposure
Trail surface: Sandy woods roads and trail
Seasons: All
Other trail users: Multiuse
Canine compatibility: Leashed dogs permitted
Land status: State forest
Nearest town: New Lisbon
Fees and permits: None

Schedule: Dawn to dusk
Maps: *DeLorme:* New Jersey Atlas & Gazetteer p. 56–57; USGS Browns Mills, NJ, quadrangle; a trail map is also available at the park.
Trail contacts: Brendan T. Byrne State Forest, PO Box 215, New Lisbon 08064; (609) 726-1191; www.state.nj.us/dep/parksandforests/parks/byrne.html
Special considerations: Come prepared for heat, sun, and ticks, major problems in summer.

Finding the trailhead: From the traffic circle (near New Lisbon and Chatsworth) where Route 70 and Route 72 intersect, travel southeast on Route 72 for 1.0 mile. Turn left (northeast) into the entrance to Brendan Byrne State Forest (signage present) and travel 0.3 mile. (Park office is straight ahead.) Turn right (southeast) onto Shinns Road, crossing Four Mile Road in 0.2 mile, crossing an abandoned road in 0.6 mile, and arriving at intersection with Buzzard Hill Road in 1.4 miles (a total of 2.2 miles on Shinns Road). Turn left (east) onto Buzzard Hill Road. As you pass sandy Cooper Road on left in 0.5 mile, you immediately arrive at Pakim Pond parking lot located on your left. (Grand total of 3 miles within the park.)

The Hike

This hike is perhaps the quintessential New Jersey Pine Barrens, including a typically bizarre place name. In a world where names connoting peace, health, beauty, piety, or patrimony are often the norm, how does a place come to be called Mount Misery? The Pine Barrens are nearly chock-a-block with odd place names (e.g., Ong's Hat, Double Trouble), but this is one of the stranger ones. The answer seems to lie with Peter Bard, a French Huguenot who settled in the area in the early 1700s. The consensus is that he named the little rise of ground here Mont Miséricorde, or "Mount

Mercy." It's hardly a "mount," and the second half was rapidly corrupted to the similar-sounding but very different meaning "misery."

Life here was hardly miserable, though. For much of the eighteenth and nineteenth centuries, Mount Misery was a solid little settlement that derived its living from timbering, sawmills, and charcoal making. At its peak, it had perhaps a hundred homes, a school, a store, and a hotel. But it never had railroad access, and as the charcoal business faded away, so too did Mount Misery. By the 1930s, when Henry Charlton Beck visited the place and wrote it up in *Forgotten Towns of Southern New Jersey,* it was just the hotel and a few falling-down houses. A Civilian Conservation Corps camp later occupied the same

▶ **Lebanon State Forest was renamed Brendan T. Byrne State Forest in 2002, in recognition of the former New Jersey governor who signed the Pinelands Preservation Act into law in 1979.**

The northern pitcher plant, also known as adams-pitcher, is truly a flytrap. Using downward-pointed hairs, a numbing narcotic, and a "pitcher" of water, this seductive plant catches the unsuspecting bug, drugs it, and digests it with enzymes.

area, and a former CCC bunkhouse survives, relocated and repaired by the Mount Misery Retreat Center. But mostly the name Mount Misery is perpetuated by the legend of the vanished town. Not a merciful fate for a once-prosperous village.

In addition to Mount Misery, Henry Charlton Beck also wrote about another Forgotten Town: Lebanon. The hike passes just north of its general location. If you were here between 1851 and 1867, the resiny aroma of smoke, coming off the batch of charcoal, crushed shells, soda ash, and the white sand, would billow from the Lebanon Glassworks, the centerpiece of the hamlet. Inside the glass house, the name given to these factories, the gathers, gaffers (skilled glass blowers), and carrying boys produced green bottles, windowpanes, and glass canes. The later was a "must" accessory for the nineteenth-century fashionably dressed man, who carried a cane made of wood, bone, or (surprisingly) glass. They built the works here because of the abundance of wood supply within the Pine Barrens. When making glass, it took a 10-to-1 ratio of fuel (wood) to the batch, not necessarily an environmentally friendly process. The availability of white sand containing 90 percent silica played another important role in Lebanon's location. You will recognize this "sugar" sand as you slug through the "beach" in the middle of the Barrens. And the shells (lime) came from the Jersey coast.

With the depletion of the forest, and with coal and natural gas becoming the new source of fuel, the glass industry moved westward, and this glass house closed along with its post office. The two hundred villagers who supported the glass industry, the ". . . woodsmen, teamsters, sand-diggers, and glass-blowers . . ." and their families eventually moved on.

> *The righteous . . . shall grow like a cedar in Lebanon.*
> —Psalms 92:12

Ironically, the biblically named hamlet is gone like most of the cedars.

Miles and Directions

0.0 Proceed from the northeast end of Pakim Pond parking lot and locate the park sign listing permitted uses and trail blazes (pink, red, and white blazes). Pass through the opening in the guardrail and onto the gravel path, passing (northeast) through the picnic area.

Arrive (within 10 yards) at the trailhead sign for the Cranberry Trail (red blazes) and a blaze post (white, pink, and red). Turn left (north) onto the Cranberry Trail, following a gravel path out of the picnic area. Arrive (within 100 yards) at a trail junction. Turn right (southeast) onto the Mount Misery Trail (white blazes), which is co-aligned with the Batona Trail (pink blazes), crossing over a water gate between the bog and Pakim Pond. (**FYI:** The route remains on the Mount Misery Trail (white blazes) till it reconnects at mile 8.9 with the Cranberry Trail; hence, the trail to your left is your return route.)

0.1 At the fork bear left on the Mount Misery Trail. The Batona Trail veers right and continues around the east side of the pond. (**FYI:** The pond you initially pass on the hike is named for a Lenape chief, Pakimintzen. As the legend goes, he gave cranberries as gifts, and they in turn became symbols of peace. His name abbreviated becomes Pakim, hence the name for the pond. Pakim Pond acted as a reservoir, an integral part of cranberry farming. The fresh water, used to flood the peat bogs, keeps the vines moist in the summer and from freezing in the winter. Ditches and gates controlled the flow. When you hike through the former cranberry bogs, you might get the sense you are walking on a canal's towpath. Admire the insect-eating pitcher plants growing along the bog banks.)

0.8 At the intersection, the trail turns left (northeast) onto a woods road.

1.0 The trail intersects Muddy Road, a gravel road with yellow, green, and blue blazes, and continues straight on a woods road.

1.2 The trail turns left off the woods road onto a path. A blaze post is placed here as an aid.

1.9 The trail nears a paved road and veers away. The ATV trails crisscross this area, making the route difficult to follow, so it is suggested that you go from blaze to blaze in this section.

2.1 Reach Butterworth Road (paved) and turn left (northwest) onto the shoulder of the road and travel into an Atlantic white cedar swamp, crossing McDonalds Branch. (**FYI:** The culvert is one of the few cool places to sit and recoup from the sun. It also appears to be tick-free!)

2.2 Pass through an intersection, and immediately turn right (northwest) by the blaze post onto the ascending trail, leaving Butterworth Road. Follow the blazes carefully through the following section, as there is a patchwork of woods roads.

3.4 At the T intersection, stay to the right (north) onto the shoulder of Butterworth Road (paved).

3.5 At the trail sign MOUNT MISERY 2 MILES, turn left (west) onto a trail, leaving Butterworth Road.

4.3 Reach Woodmansie Road and turn left (northwest) onto the shoulder and shortly turn right (north) off the road onto a wide path.

Hiker in the vicinity of Pakim Pond with an "internal frame pack."

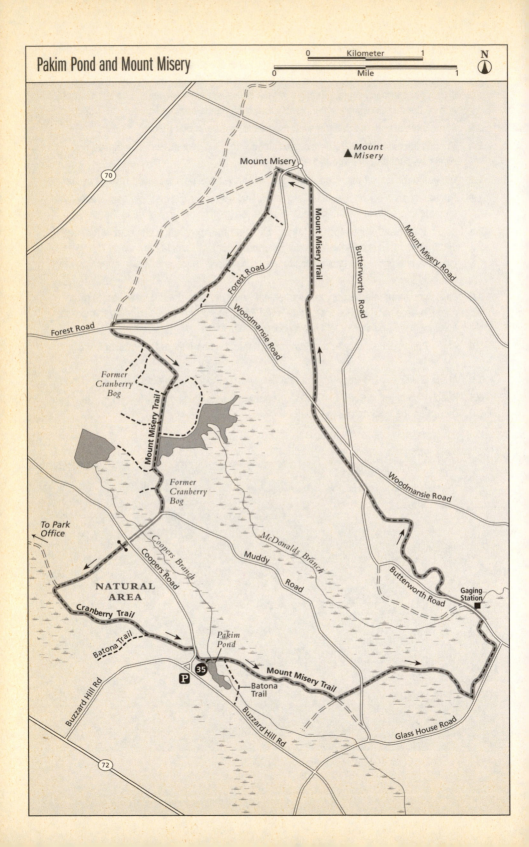

Pakim Pond and Mount Misery

Kilometer
0 — 1
Mile
0 — 1

N

Mount Misery ▲ Mount Misery

Mount Misery ○

70

Forest Road

Mount Misery Trail

Butterworth Road

Mount Misery Road

Forest Road

Woodmansie Road

Former Cranberry Bog

Mount Misery Trail

Former Cranberry Bog

Woodmansie Road

To Park Office

Coopers Branch

Coopers Road

McDonalds Branch

Butterworth Road

Gaging Station ■

NATURAL AREA

Muddy Road

Cranberry Trail

Batona Trail

Pakim Pond

P 35

Mount Misery Trail

Batona Trail

Buzzard Hill Rd

Buzzard Hill Rd

Glass House Road

72

5.5 Reach Mount Misery by crossing Forest Road onto a woods road and shortly turn left (west), popping in and out of fire breaks and onto the trail. You need to pay attention to the blazes. (**FYI:** To the right are the Mount Misery Retreat Center and the little hamlet of Mount Misery. The building alongside the trail is a historical structure from the CCC camp that was once located here in the 1930s.)

5.7 At the intersection, continue straight onto a woods road, which telescopes off into the distance. Don't get too zoned out and miss the next turn!

6.7 Turn right (west) onto a trail.

7.0 Cross Forest Road (paved) and continue straight (southeast) onto a woods road.

7.1 Pass through a bog and a white cedar swamp before turning left (east) off the sand road and onto a berm.

7.5 Emerge onto a sand road, bearing right (southwest). Enter the wide-open Controlled Area of wetlands, once a cranberry bog. Continue straight (south) on the berm, passing several sand roads on the right.

7.8 Continue straight (south), passing a sand road on the left and entering the second Controlled Area.

7.9 At the end of the wetlands, take the left (southeast) fork at the junction onto a road of sugar sand. Mount Misery Trail joins the red-, the yellow-, and the blue-blazed trails.

8.2 After the red-, yellow-, and blue-blazed trail leaves left (southeast), the Mount Misery Trail reaches a gravel road (Muddy Road). Turn right (southwest) and enter an Atlantic white cedar swamp, crossing Coopers Branch.

8.5 Cross (southwest) a gravel road (Coopers Road) and around an auto gate, entering the designated Natural Area.

8.9 At the fork veer left (west) onto the path. You are now on the Cranberry Trail, and shortly the Mount Misery Trail officially ends.

9.5 Continue straight (southeast), passing the Batona Trail (pink blazes) entering from the right and becoming co-aligned with the Cranberry Trail.

9.8 Cross Coopers Road, locating the trail behind the guardrail.

9.9 Arrive back at the trailhead sign for Cranberry Trail and Pakim Pond parking lot.

Hike Information

Local Information
Burlington County Tourism Web site: www.co.burlington.nj.us/tourism. Burlington County Office of Cultural and Heritage Affairs, PO Box 6000, Easthampton 08060; (609) 265-5068; www .co.burlington.nj.us/departments/resource_conservation/cultural/index.htm

Local Events/Attractions
The historic village of Whitesbog, now part of Brendan T. Byrne State Forest, was operated by the White family for many years, and played an important role in the development of commercial blueberry and cranberry culture in the United States. Whitesbog Preservation Trust, 120–13 Whitesbog Road, Browns Mills 08015; (908) 893-4646; www.whitesbog.org. Tours available on request.

Lodging

Camping, cabins, and yurts are available in Brendan T. Byrne State Forest (contact information in "Trail contacts" above).

Hike Tours

The Batona Hiking Club runs hikes (see below for contact information).

Organizations

Batona Hiking Club, 215 South Spring Mill Road, Villanova, PA 19085-1409; www.members.aol .com/Batona

Other Resources

Beck, Henry Charlton. *Forgotten Towns of Southern New Jersey.* New Brunswick, NJ: Rutgers University Press, 1961 (originally published 1936).

36 Parvin Lake

The trail begins at the park office/bathhouse complex, an exceptional example of the work accomplished by the Civilian Conservation Corps. This flat loop hike is partially in the Natural Area, so the route can be muddy and overgrown; otherwise, it is made up of beautiful sandy paths, a series of bridges, and a short road walk through the campground, all under mixed pine-oak forest, accented by Atlantic white cedar swamps. The route also plays tag with Parvin Lake and the Muddy Run, creating a feeling that you are south of the Mason–Dixon Line. Don't forget to bring your swimsuit!

Start: Parvin State Park boathouse and office

Distance: 5.7-mile loop

Approximate hiking time: 3 hours

Difficulty: Easy, mostly flat

Trail surface: Sandy paths, short roadwalks, muddy trails

Seasons: All

Other trail users: Hikers in natural areas; other areas multiuse

Canine compatibility: No dogs permitted

Land status: State park

Nearest town: Norma

Fees and permits: Higher fee on weekends from Memorial Day through Labor Day

Schedule: Varies by season; contact park office

Maps: *DeLorme: New Jersey Atlas & Gazetteer* p. 62; USGS Elmer, NJ, quadrangle; a trail map is also available at the park.

Trail contacts: Parvin State Park, 701 Almond Road, Pittsgrove 08318-3928; (856) 358-8616; www.state.nj.us/dep/parksandforests/ parks/parvin.html

Other: Bring your swimsuit if the weather's nice. Ticks can be a problem here.

Finding the trailhead: From Route 55, take exit 35 onto Garden Road (County Route 674), heading west (you are in the vicinity of Vineland). Travel 2.2 miles to Six Points intersection. Take the second right (southwest) onto State Park-Willow Grove Road (County Route 645) and go 2.0 miles. At the intersection turn right (west) onto Centerton–Norma Station Road, also called Almond

Road (County Route 540), and travel 0.3 mile. Parvin State Park bathhouse and office are on the left and the parking lot is to the right.

The Hike

This is a wonderful and enjoyable hike through the pinelands, never too far from civilization, and filled with the handiwork of the CCC. The Civilian Conservation Corps (CCC) was President Franklin D. Roosevelt's method of dealing with two Depression-era problems: high unemployment among young men, and the need for conservation-related work nationwide. Operating from 1933 until 1942, the CCC made enormous improvements to New Jersey's parks, forests, and historic sites (not to mention watershed acreage and even private lands).

Few places reflect the work of the CCC as thoroughly as Parvin State Park. Though at 1,137 acres it's one of New Jersey's smallest state parks, it's a CCC jewel. Parvin Lake, which our walk encircles, was created in the 1800s by damming the Muddy Run at the little crossroads hamlet of Union Grove. It powered a sawmill, but before long became a popular excursion spot for picnics, swimming, boating, and fishing.

▶ **The Island in Parvin Lake is one of the top ten places in New Jersey to get married.**

The state of New Jersey acquired the lake and some 900 acres around it in 1931. The advent of the CCC two years later made development of it as a state park possible. The Corps in the 1930s and early '40s built most of what you see here today. This includes the beach and pavilion, cabins, campgrounds, lean-tos, restrooms, paths, bridges, and other structures and features. While the CCC generally employed men in their late teens and early twenties, some Corps companies were designed to employ other "at-risk" groups. One such company, Number 2229V, constructed the cabin complex at Thundergust Lake (which we pass on our hike). The V stood for "veteran"—its members were all unemployed U.S. Army veterans of the First World War. One more reminder of how the CCC not only provided us with wonderful park facilities but also helped an entire generation get back on its feet.

Miles and Directions

0.0 From the entrance to the parking lot, cross (south) CR 540, arriving at Parvin State Park Office. Turn right (west) onto the sidewalk, where you will see a kiosk and a trailhead sign for Parvin Lake Trail. Continue heading west into the forest onto a sandy path of Parvin Lake Trail (green blazes).

1.0 At the intersection continue straight (northwest) onto the Long Trail (red blazes) and pass under a pavilion.

1.1 Pass the Nature Trail (white blazes) loop, which comes in on the right and now becomes co-aligned with the Long Trail. It will leave shortly on the right. You have entered the land of sporadic boardwalks and bridges.

1.9 Cross a 60-foot bridge over the Muddy Run. Shortly an unmarked path comes in on the left; continue straight.

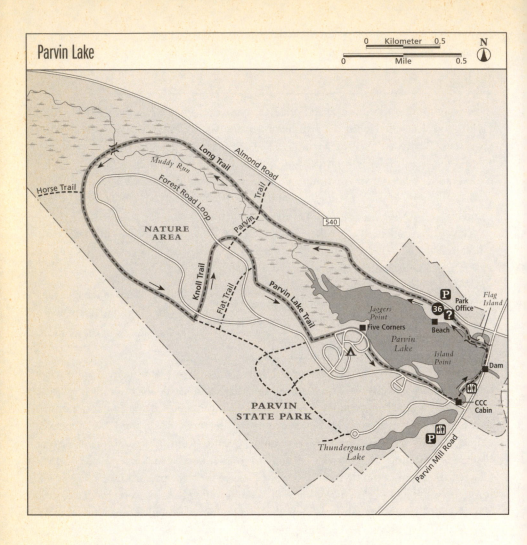

Parvin Lake

Kilometer 0.5
Mile 0.5

N

Long Trail
Almond Road
Muddy Run
Horse Trail
Forest Road Loop
Parvin Trail
NATURE AREA
Knoll Trail
Flat Trail
Parvin Lake Trail
540
Jaggers Point
Five Corners
Parvin Lake
Island Point
Beach
Park Office
Flag Island
36
P
?
Dam
CCC Cabin
PARVIN STATE PARK
Thundergust Lake
P
Parvin Mill Road

2.2 At the intersection with a horse trail, continue straight (southwest) under oaks, sassafras, and mountain laurel.

2.4 The Long Trail swings south by southeast under a pine-oak forest.

3.0 After a series of "holes" where the trail feels like its running on "dikes," look carefully for the trail junction, and turn sharply to the left (north) onto the Knoll Trail (orange blazes).

3.1 Cross (north) the paved Forest Road Loop (blue blazes). (**Bail-out:** Turn right onto the Forest Road Loop to the entrance where you can pick up the Parvin Lake Trail back to the park office.)

3.4 The Knoll Trail crosses the Forest Road Loop for a second time, continuing straight (northeast) onto a sandy road.

3.5 The Knoll Trail ends at the paved road. Cross (southeast) over onto the Parvin Lake Trail and into a pine-oak forest.

3.7 Pass Flat Trail (pink) coming in on the right (west).

4.1 After passing though an Atlantic white cedar swamp, arrive at a fork. Veer right (south-southwest) and continue to follow blue stone gravel and green "slap" blazing.

4.2 Continue straight, passing a sign that reads CAMPING AREA NO PETS and a trail on the right. (**FYI:** The trail to the right is an alternative route for those with pets around the campgrounds.)

4.3 At the intersection turn left (northeast) at the blaze post with an arrow. Continue to follow the blue stone gravel and the green "slap" blazing. The Parvin Lake Trail meanders through the campground, while a number of unofficial paths crisscross the route.

4.4 Arrive at Five Corners. Designate the corner in which you are standing as number 1. Starting on your left, corner 2 takes you to the lake. Corner 3 takes you to the playground. Corner 4 is the Parvin Lake Trail and the one you want! (Corner 5 leads you into a campsite.) Continue straight (southeast) on the gravel path where you eventually see a blaze post.

4.5 Zigzag around the end of the wooden fence and onto a paved road, heading south. A water fountain is located along the fence. The route passes a sign CAMPSITES 23-27. Look for the green "slap" blazing on the trees.

4.6 After passing Campsite 16 and at a blaze post (green), turn left (south) onto the path, leaving the campgrounds. Stay with the gravel path. (**FYI:** Directly across from the turn, you will find a water source.)

4.7 At the T intersection, turn left (east), eventually swing southeast, dropping down into an Atlantic white cedar swamp along a sandy-gravel path. The route begins to edge Parvin Lake. (**FYI:** The trail to the right is the alternative pet route rejoining the Parvin Lake Trail.)

4.8 Cross (south) a sand road leading to Island Point. The Parvin Lake Trail begins to drift away from the lake on a gravel path.

5.1 The trail turns left (east) and immediately crosses a bridge. The route edges Parvin Lake while many side trails lead to a parking lot. (**Side trip:** Before the turn, the CCC-built cabin stands to the right, up a short path and directly across Forest Road Loop.)

5.3 Along the east end of Parvin Lake, the route passes an observation deck, a boat ramp, and a dam. Continue on the gravel path.

5.4 Cross a bridge onto and off Flag Island.

5.5 After a grassy area dodge back into the forest.

5.7 Arrive back at the park office. Turn right (north) and cross CR 540 and enter the parking lot.

Hike Information

Local Information

Cumberland County's Web site has information on tourism, history, events, lodging, and dining: www.co.cumberland.nj.us/. Cumberland County Tourism Advisory Council, PO Box 472, Bridgeton 08302; (856) 455-0328.

Local Events/Attractions

Wheaton Village is a re-created nineteenth-century village preserving southern New Jersey's glassmaking heritage and culture. The village includes museum exhibits, galleries, shops, and live demonstrations of glassmaking: Wheaton Village, 1501 Glasstown Road, Millville 08332; (800) 998-4552; www.wheatonvillage.org

Lodging

Parvin State Park offers campsites and lodging in historic CCC-era cabins and lean-tos.

Organizations

Parvin State Park Appreciation Committee, 720 Almond Road, Pittsgrove 08318; (856) 358-5370; www.friendsofparvin.org

37 Bear Swamp Hill and the Pine Plains

Enter a unique ecosystem in Penn State Forest called the Pine Plains, where a community of genetically dwarfed pines grows to an average of 5 feet. This loop hike is on long, straight, sandy roads undulating up and down through a very remote and potentially hot environment. The hike tops out on Bear Swamp Hill, a former fire tower site, covered by mountain laurel and quartz pebbles of the Pliocene Beacon Hill Gravel. Don't be surprised if you get buzzed by some military aircraft.

Start: Sooey Road at the entrance to Bear Swamp Fire Tower site

Distance: 5.0-mile loop

Approximate hiking time: 2.5 hours

Difficulty: Moderate due to sun

Trail surface: Sandy roads

Seasons: All

Other trail users: Multiuse, including motor vehicles

Canine compatibility: Leashed dogs permitted

Land status: State forest

Nearest town: Jenkins

Fees and permits: None

Schedule: Dawn to dusk

Maps: *DeLorme: New Jersey Atlas & Gazetteer* p. 57; USGS Woodmansie and Oswego Lake, NJ, quadrangles

Trail contacts: Penn State Forest, c/o Bass River State Forest, PO Box 118, New Gretna 08224; (609) 296-1114; www.state.nj.us/dep/parksandforests/parks/penn.html

Special considerations: In summer this can be a very, very hot hike. Ticks are a serious problem. Don't expect peace and quiet: Military aircraft practice here.

Finding the trailhead: From the intersection of Chatsworth-Barnegat Road (County Route 532) and Chatsworth-Tuckerton Road (County Route 563) in Chatsworth, take Chatsworth-Tuckerton Road southeast for 8.4 miles. Turn left (east) onto Lake Oswego Road and drive 3.1 miles to the entrance of Penn State Forest (signage present). Pass a parking lot for Lake Oswego on the right and at fork bear left (northeast) onto Sooey Road. (You will remain on Sooey Road throughout this maze to the trailhead.) In 0.2 mile pass Lost Lane on the left (north). In 0.5 mile pass Deer Run Road on your right (southeast). In 0.9 mile, cross Penn Place (runs east-west). In 1.4 miles cross Cabin Road (running north-south) and in 1.8 miles arrive at the island (former entrance to the Bear Swamp fire tower) on the left (southeast) where the hike starts. From the entrance to Penn State Forest to the trailhead is 4.8 miles.

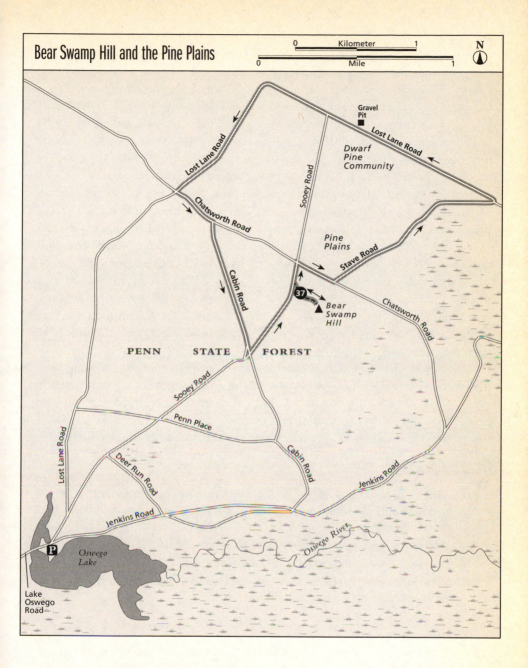

Bear Swamp Hill and the Pine Plains

0 Kilometer 1
0 Mile 1

N

Lost Lane Road

Gravel
Pit

Lost Lane Road

Dwarf
Pine
Community

Sooey Road

Chatsworth Road

Pine
Plains

Stave Road

Cabin Road

37

Bear
Swamp
Hill

Chatsworth Road

PENN STATE FOREST

Sooey Road

Penn Place

Cabin Road

Lost Lane Road

Deer Run Road

Jenkins Road

Jenkins Road

Oswego River

P

Oswego
Lake

Lake
Oswego
Road

The Hike

One of the remarkable features of this hike through Penn State Forest is the Pine Barren Plains, where one can stand and gaze over hundreds of acres of forest. This is because the dwarf pines reach a mature height of only some 4 to 5 feet. It's locally known as the "Pygmy Forest," and New Jersey has the world's largest concentration of this unique ecosystem. The reason these pines developed this diminutive stature may have been a response to the fires that are a standard part of the Pine Barrens ecosystem. Indeed, research has indicated that regular fires are a necessary part of the environment here, helping maintain plant diversity and assisting in the germination of certain plants. These types of Pine Barren Plains that evolved in response to forest fires occur elsewhere in the world, sometimes in similar areas (like the Pine Barrens of Long Island, New York) and sometimes on ridgetops (as at Sam's Point Preserve in the Shawangunk Mountains). It is, however, a globally endangered landscape.

As you ramble through this classic New Jersey Pine Barrens hike, you may stop for a minute and say: *Penn* State Forest? Most folks know that Pennsylvania was named after William Penn (1644–1718), the wealthy and well-connected admiral's son who converted to Quakerism. How did a New Jersey state forest get the Penn name, too? Penn was in fact almost equally involved in New Jersey affairs, beginning in the 1670s. He likely wrote "A Description of West New Jersey" in 1676 to promote colonization; it worked, as numerous Quakers came to south Jersey. Three generations of Penns were heavily involved in New Jersey land dealings; as members of both the East and West Jersey Proprietors, they owned substantial tracts of land. So it's only natural that New Jersey should name *something* after this distinguished family, if not the whole state.

Miles and Directions

0.0 From the island of Sooey Road and the approach road to the Bear Swamp Hill Lookout Tower site, head (north) onto Sooey Road (the opposite direction from which you drove into Penn State Forest).

0.13 At the intersection turn right (southeast) onto Chatsworth Road.

0.33 Turn left (northeast) onto Stave Road and enter the Pine Plains.

1.3 At the island veer left (northeast) at the fork, and at the base of the triangle, turn left (northwest) onto Lost Lane and the dwarf pine community.

1.5 Pass a road on the right.

2.1 Pass a sand/gravel pit.

2.2 At the intersection with Sooey Road, continue straight (northwest) passing a swamp on your left. (**Bail-out:** Turn left [south] onto Sooey Road, crossing Chatsworth Road and back to the endpoint.)

2.6 Lost Lane swings left (southwest) onto another long straightaway.

3.3 Turn left (southeast) onto Chatsworth Road.

3.6 Turn right (south) onto the Cabin Road, which begins to rise slightly.

4.3 At the T intersection turn left (northeast) onto Sooey Road.

4.7 Arrive back at the island where you parked your vehicle. Turn right (southeast) onto the old paved road and begin to climb Bear Swamp Hill.

4.8 Turn right (southwest) onto a mountain-laurel-lined path, only 50 yards long.

5.0 Arrive at the Bear Swamp Hill Lookout Tower site, just beautiful when the mountain laurel is in bloom. During the winter, there may be partial views. To return to your vehicle, turn left (northeast) at the site and walk through the opening in the mountain laurel till you arrive at a parking lot. Turn left (northwest) and head down the old paved road, passing the path on the right, which you climbed up.

Hike Information

Local Information

Burlington County Tourism Web site: www.co.burlington.nj.us/tourism. Burlington County Office of Cultural and Heritage Affairs, PO Box 6000, Easthampton 08060; (609) 265-5068; www .co.burlington.nj.us/departments/resource_conservation/cultural/index.htm

Lodging

Camping and cabins are available at Bass River and Brendan T. Byrne State Forests.

Organizations

Pinelands Preservation Alliance, 17 Pemberton Road, Southampton 08088; (609) 859-8860; www.pinelandsalliance.org. Outdoor Club of South Jersey, PO Box 455, Cherry Hill 08003-0455; www.ocsj.org

Other Resources

A great Web site on the Pinelands and its history and culture is www.NJPineBarrens.com.

WHEN "PRACTICE" BECAME SOMETHING MORE

Think of "plane crash" in the Pine Barrens, and the first thing that likely comes to mind is the 1928 crash of Mexican aviator Emilio Carranza near Tabernacle. There have, unfortunately, been many others.

One occurred here on Bear Swamp Hill in Penn State Forest. The 2,600-acre Warren Grove Gunnery Range near here started during World War II as a weapons research facility. By the early 1960s it was a practice bombing and gunnery range for New Jersey Air National Guard pilots. It remains a busy facility, with over 3,000 practice sorties flown annually (as you'll find out hiking here—don't forget to wave to the pilots!).

On January 16, 1971, an F-105 Thunderchief fighter-bomber piloted by Major William F. Dimas, thirty-six, took off from Warren Grove on a standard practice run. In civilian life Dimas was a pilot for United Airlines, married with three children. He was also flight commander with the Air National Guard 141st Tactical Squadron. With the war in Vietnam and Cambodia expanding, it was a busy time for the military, and Warren Grove.

For reasons never made clear, Major Dimas' jet clipped trees 100 feet from the Bear Swamp Hill Fire Tower. Losing control, it then struck the 40-foot fire tower, smashing it in half, and destroying a nearby generator building. Continuing its downward trajectory, the jet plowed through the pines, crashing 0.75 mile away.

The death of Major Dimas, combined with the damage done, made it a huge, headline-grabbing tragedy. In a bizarre twist, the Air Force refused to pay the state of New Jersey for damages, stating that as Major Dimas was a National Guard pilot and thus himself an employee of the state, the damages were not covered.

Nor was it the last accident at Warren Grove. An F-16 crashed in 2002, burning 11,000 acres. And in 2004 a fighter pilot accidentally strafed the roof of an Ocean County elementary school with his cannon (no one was injured.) Something to think about as the jets buzz overhead: It sometimes ends up being more than just practice. . . .

38 Wells Mills

This tramp dispels the impression that the Pine Barrens are flat; similar to a washboard, you traverse Raccoon Ridge, Penn's Hill, Laurel Hill, and The Island. On the other hand, a good portion is flat. The route travels through pine–oak forest and white cedar swamps. It meanders next to Wells Mills Lake with a chance of seeing a bald eagle. The various creek crossings become oases from the hot sun. The entire hike is on the Penn's Hill Trail with options to make it shorter.

Start: Behind the Interpretive Center at Wells Mills County Park
Distance: 8.5-mile loop
Approximate hiking time: 4 to 5 hours
Difficulty: Strenuous because of sand
Trail surface: Sand trails
Seasons: All
Other trail users: Hikers
Canine compatibility: Leashed dogs permitted
Land status: County park
Nearest town: Waretown

Fees and permits: None
Schedule: Varies by season; contact park office at (609) 971-3085
Maps: *DeLorme: New Jersey Atlas & Gazetteer* p.58; USGS Brookville, NJ, quadrangle
Trail contacts: Ocean County Department of Parks and Recreation, 1198 Bandon Road, Toms River 08753; (877) OC PARKS; www .co.ocean.nj.us/parks/wellsmills.html
Special considerations: Sun and ticks are your two concerns on this hike.

Finding the trailhead: From the Garden State Parkway northbound, take exit 69 (near Waretown) onto Wells Mills Road (County Route 532) west. Travel 2.3 miles to the entrance to Wells Mills County Park. Turn left and drive to the parking lot. From the Garden State Parkway southbound, take exit 67. Turn right (west) onto West Bay Avenue (County Route 554) and drive 4.5 miles to the intersection with Route 72. Turn right (northwest) onto Route 72 and shortly (0.4 mile) turn right (northeast) onto Wells Mills Road (CR 532). Drive 3.7 miles to the Wells Mills County Park entrance. Turn right and go to the parking lot.

The Hike

During the American Revolution, Elisha Lawrence, a Tory, had his property confiscated and auctioned off to James Wells. The Atlantic white cedar (AWC), the pine, and the oak growing on this tract made this a good investment. The lucky bidder proceeded to dam up the Oyster Creek and built a sawmill, hence the name: Wells Mills. From the Pine Barrens, they milled pine and the oak trees into building material or split it into cordwood, heating Philadelphia and New York City.

During the eighteenth century, the demand on the Atlantic white cedar was so great it was thought that the cedar would be clear-cut to extinction. After they depleted the cedar aboveground, they began to harvest it from below. Some of the fallen trees had remained under water for hundreds of years and surprisingly made for exceptionally fine timber. The cedar's unique properties made it an important commodity. It was

Milled in Wells Mills, the Atlantic white cedar shingled the colonial home.
COURTESY OF IAN BLUNDELL

water and rot resistant, while its long, straight grain made cedar easy to work. Coopers (barrel makers) used it to make barrels. Farmers pounded it into the ground as fence posts. Jersey cedar (another name for AWC) virtually shingled Colonial America.

Shipwrights found AWC especially ideal because steamed cedar bends. It was also strong and at the same time light. The 'wrights created ribs and frames using cedar, but especially used it for planking. Due to the abundance of Coastal Plain wood, shipyards dotted the Jersey coast from the Raritan Bay all the way around Cape May and up the Delaware Bay. They built schooners and sloops for coastal deliveries or for oystering. They also designed three Jersey originals: the Barnegat Bay sneakbox used for duck hunting, the garvey used for clamming and oystering, and Sea Bright skiffs used for fishing and launched directly from the ocean's beach (today, used for lifesaving). Instead of "planking out" a skiff today, hike out along the Penns Hill Trail, rambling through the Atlantic cedar swamps and the pine–oak forest.

Miles and Directions

0.0 From the south end of the parking lot and behind the restrooms take the sidewalk, passing the kiosk, and head toward the Interpretive Center.

100 yards Arrive at the front of the Interpretive Center and walk to the right (west) side of the building, crossing the lawn, where you will see the Penn's Hill Trailhead in the southwest corner of the lawn (directly above Wells Mills Lake). (**Side trip:** Explore the Interpretive Center exhibits: furry friends, boat building, forest fire management, and Estlow family history, just to mention a few. Open daily 10:00 a.m. to 3:00 p.m.)

150 yards From the Penn's Hill Trailhead (white blazes) follow (west) the trail down along the north shore of Wells Mills Lake, passing a gravesite, Cedar Lodge, and the boat ramp. (**FYI:** Take to heart *Tick Warning* signage at the trailhead; you'll run across the bloodsucking parasites during your visit!) (**Side trip:** Take a moment to walk down the boat ramp; you might spot a soaring bald eagle from this spot.)

0.3 The path dovetails into a trail under mountain laurel and Atlantic white cedar, crossing sets of narrow bridging, paralleling the lake. Feels like the Land of Oz.

0.4 Cross the Estlow Trail (green blazes) and continue straight (northwest) on the Penn's Hill Trail. (**FYI:** The additional yellow blaze you see indicates that certain routes are all-terrain bike trails.) Soon thereafter, cross Ridge Road (yellow blazes) and continue on Penn's Hill Trail where you cross a number of plow lines (fire breaks), an all-day occurrence.

Arrive on Raccoon Ridge, heading westward across the plateau.

1.85 Pass 2-mile marker.

2.5 Arrive at Penn's Hill (126 feet elevation). There is a short, steep climb to a bench at this point, and then the trail goes downhill.

2.8 Arrive at Laurel Hill (130 feet elevation), passing 3-mile marker.

3.0 Descend the stairs into the American cedar swamp.

3.2 Soon thereafter, arrive on Laurel Ridge with its rolling terrain.

3.5 At the T intersection, pass through a fence and turn right (south) where the Penn's Hill Trail is co-aligned with Ridge Road and Estlow Trail.

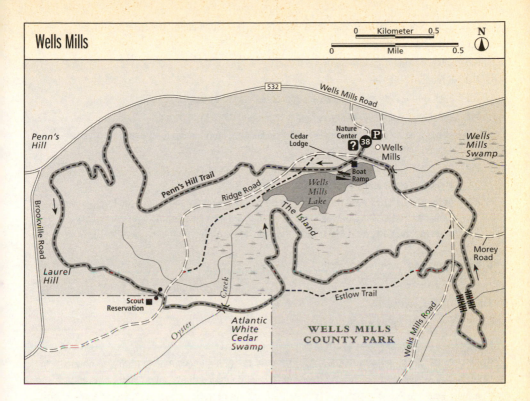

3.6 At the trail junction with signage: WELLS MILLS HIKING TRAIL, turn left (east) onto a needle-bed path, following the Penn's Hill Trail (white blazes), Estlow Trail (green blazes), and the all-terrain bike path (yellow blazes).

3.7 Pass mile marker 4.

3.8 Cross over Oyster Creek on a wooden bridge and under some magnificent Atlantic white cedars.

3.9 Climb up to an intersection with an unidentified woods road and turn left onto the sand road, following the white blaze of the Penn's Hill Trail.

4.0 The Penn's Hill Trail turns left (north) leaving the sand road and heading onto a trail. (**Bail-out:** Continue straight [east] onto the Estlow Trail, which takes you directly back to the Interpretive Center and parking lot. The Estlow Trail remains on the sand road and may be a bit shadier.)

4.5 Pass over The Island.

4.7 Pass 5-mile marker.

5.7 Pass 6-mile marker.

6.0 Cross southeast over Estlow Trail and the all-terrain bike trail, continuing on the Penn's Hill Trail. (**Bail-out:** Turn left [northeast] onto the Estlow Trail, which takes you directly back to the Interpretive Center and the parking lot.)

6.4 Cross (southeast) over Wells Mills Road (sand) and continue on the Penn's Hill Trail.

6.7 Pass 7-mile marker.

6.8 Cross a 65-foot boardwalk over a creek.

7.3 Re-cross creek.

7.7 Pass 8-mile marker, shortly crossing (northeast) Morey Road.

8.1 The Penn's Hill Trail runs above Oyster Creek and Wells Mills Swamp.

8.3 At the T intersection, the Penn's Hill Trail turns right onto a sand road and becomes co-aligned with Estlow Trail.

8.4 Cross north over Oyster Creek. Shortly thereafter, pass Cold Brook Trail (pink) on the right and continue heading northwest.

8.5 At the junction turn right (north) onto a path and walk up to the rear of the Interpretive Center and catch the sidewalk back to the parking lot. (**Side trip:** To your immediate left there are the dam, Wells Mills Lake, and benches provided for those weary feet.)

Hike Information

Local Information
Ocean County Web site: www.co.ocean.nj.us

Local Events/Attractions
Wells Mills County Park has an annual Pine Barrens Jamboree in October, featuring traditional south Jersey music, food, exhibits, and activities: www.co.ocean.nj.us/parks/jamboree.html. Nearby is Edwin B. Forsythe National Wildlife Refuge, one of New Jersey's outstanding bird-watching sites: Great Creek Road, Oceanville 08231; (609) 652-1665; www.fws.gov/northeast/forsythe

Hike Tours
Wells Mills County Park periodically offers guided nature hikes; contact the park office for schedule.

IN ADDITION

That Problem Kid of Mrs. Leeds

This legend is New Jersey's most-told tale, spun a thousand times; make this a thousand and one. In the small coastal town of Leeds Point in the 1730s, a Mrs. Leeds (some sources call her Mrs. Shourds—probably the sources coming from people named Leeds) has a baby. Not just any baby—her THIRTEENTH baby. Mrs. Leeds wasn't too happy about another mouth to feed, especially since Mr. Leeds was evidently an early-eighteenth-century version of Homer Simpson, spending all his time at Squire Moe's Ye Olde Tavern.

"MAY THIS ONE BE THE DEVIL!" shouted Mrs. L as the new lad entered the world. Today, you could get away with this, but in the 1730s, when there were witches, demons, etc., under every straw-filled mattress, it was asking for trouble, and Mrs. Leeds got it. Big time. Normal at first, the baby momentarily grew scaly skin, hooves in place of hands and feet, a serpentlike tail, batlike wings, and a face like a horse. It flapped and flew all over the birthing room, mauling all it encountered, before it crashed through the window and was gone forever. No doubt its Apgar score was just awful.

From then on, the Leeds Devil, as it was called, caused all manner of trouble in the Pine Barrens—devouring crops and livestock, wreaking havoc, and scaring the pants off the locals, even sober ones. Fortunately, along came a preacher who knew his Amos from his Ezekiel, and performed an exorcism, banishing the creature for a hundred years. It worked, for the Leeds Devil did not appear again until 1840, just in time for the Victorian fascination with horror, popular fiction, and the supernatural. How convenient.

In an apparent effort at rebranding the franchise for national consumption, it was no longer called the Leeds Devil, but the Jersey Devil, much to the relief of local hockey fans a century and a half later. The creature made regular appearances: Revolutionary War veteran and Commodore Stephen Decatur, testing cannons at the Batsto Iron Works, saw it and even got a shot off at it (passed through it harmlessly—rats!). But nothing prepared the populace for the month of January 1909, when the Jersey Devil showed up repeatedly, making headlines almost every day. Schools and businesses closed, folks were scared to leave their houses (well, some folks), and there was near mass hysteria. And so the stories go . . .

Could the Jersey Devil be something real, a prehistoric creature or a previously unknown species? Even dedicated cryptozoologists (those folk who hunt for Bigfoot and the Loch Ness Monster) seem to think not. A creature with horse's head and bat's wings? As described, the creature necessitates a belief in the supernatural. Or could it be a real creature simply mistaken for something supernatural and ferocious? The sandhill crane once made the Pine Barrens its home—a big bird, up to 5 feet tall, with a huge wingspan, a frightening unearthly croak, highly testy when encountered near its nest, and sometimes nocturnal. That could make for a decidedly Devil-like experience (combined with a sufficient mix of darkness, fear, imagination, and possibly alcohol).

Had the Jersey Devil legend not arisen, locals would probably have invented it. Every culture across the planet has its legends of the Boogeyman—the dark, fearsome creature that stalks the night and is *particularly* fond of eating tender, young children. Folks who grew up in the Pine Barrens will tell you that, as children, the Jersey Devil was routinely invoked to keep them on the straight and narrow. And in a region once known for some activities of questionable legality, the fearsome legend likewise no doubt kept meddling outsiders out of the Pine Barrens.

Today, the Jersey Devil is a high-camp cultural icon to some. Yet others who have spent their life in the Pines will tell you without a smile: Something is out there. If there is one fact about the Jersey Devil, it is this: Few legends draw such a mixture of fear and affection from their populace. So on your walk, keep your eyes open, and for Pete's sake, bring a camera!

39 Apple Pie Hill

The U.S. Geological Survey (USGS) calls Apple Pie Hill "one of the most amazing views on the East Coast." Begin this out-and-back hike in Wharton State Forest by exploring the Carranza Memorial, a monument for a Mexican aviator. Travel the sandy roads and paths through pitch pine forest, skirting a cedar swamp, and wetlands along the Skit Branch. Traverse a series of hills before arriving at Apple Pie Hill (209 feet), the highest elevation in the Pine Barrens. Experience a most unique and majestic panoramic view of the Coastal Plain's sea of green pines from a landing on the New Jersey Forest Fire Service lookout tower.

Start: Carranza Memorial parking lot
Distance: 8.0-mile out-and-back
Approximate hiking time: 4 hours
Difficulty: Moderate due to length
Trail surface: Sandy roads and paths
Seasons: All good
Other trail users: Multiuse
Canine compatibility: Leashed dogs permitted
Land status: State forest
Nearest town: Chatsworth
Fees and permits: None

Schedule: Dawn to dusk
Maps: *DeLorme: New Jersey Atlas & Gazetteer* p.56–57; USGS Chatworth and Indian Mills, NJ, quadrangles; a map is also available at the forest.
Trail contacts: Wharton State Forest, 4110 Nesco Road, Hammonton 08037; (609) 561-0024; www.state.nj.us/dep/parksandforests/parks/wharton.html
Special considerations: Ticks and sun exposure are serious considerations on this hike.

Finding the trailhead: From the Red Lion circle of U.S. Highway 206 and Route 70, take US 206 south for 1.2 miles. Turn left (southeast) onto Carranza Road (County Route 648). There is signage for Tabernacle and Carranza Memorial. Travel 2.2 miles to Tabernacle. At the stop sign, cross County Route 532 and continue south on Carranza Road (CR 648). Shortly you will enter Wharton State Forest. At 6.7 miles from Tabernacle, the Carranza Memorial and parking lot are located on the right.

The Hike

Leaving the Carranza Memorial, you begin the hike heading for Apple Pie Hill (APH), where stands another monument of sorts: Apple Pie Firetower. Fire plays an important role in the Pine Barrens, with the majority of the nearly 1,500 fires in New Jersey occurring here. This is due to the fuel surrounding you. The pitch pine, from which turpentine is derived, dominates the Pinelands. The pine needles, or green fuels, contain oils. The early settlers also gathered the pine knots from the same tree for illumination, because it burned long and bright. Add the flash fuels of huckleberry, blueberry, chokeberry, and sheep laurel and you have a hot, fast-moving fire! You might not realize it, but the sand also plays a role, as it is porous; therefore, the rain drains quickly, leaving the area tinder dry.

As you move along the trail, you see sections where the New Jersey Forest Fire Service (NJFFS) has waged war against the flames. They use terms like "battle," "direct attack," "outflank," and "suppression." They have created fire break-trenches, which have been cleared down to soil, so the fire will be deprived of fuel. They may have been constructed due to an approaching blaze or a controlled burn. To clear away flash fuels, the NJFFS performs controlled burns, which are planned forest fires under optimum wind, temperature, and humidity conditions. The fire lines can make following the trail tricky; therefore, at times you need to check for blazes fore and aft.

▶ **The Batona Trail takes its name from the Batona Hiking Club of Philadelphia, which blazed the first sections in 1961. "Batona" is derived from the club's original motto, "BAck TO NAture."**

Fire is also a productive part of this environmental system. The pitch pine needs an occasional burn to remain dominant over the oaks and to reproduce. From the thick, fire-resistant, scorched bark grow tufts, allowing for

Apple Pie Hill, a 209-foot-tall fire tower, highest point in the Pine Barrens, provides a phenomenal panoramic view.

quicker recovery. From the fires' intense heat, the cones open (serotinous), depositing their seed on the fire-improved soil. The Phoenix rises!

As you climb the 209-foot Apple Pie Hill covered with Beacon Hill Gravel (quartz pebbles also known as cap rock) left here when the ocean retreated, you arrive at the Apple Pie Hill Fire Tower No. 16. This was not the first lookout tower located here, nor was this the original location of the tower before you. When the NJFFS was established in 1906, lookout towers were part of the plan. The first tower on APH was a ca.1920s building with a series of steps running around its outside, each flight having a platform. On top sat a cupola for the NJFFS observer. A private auxiliary lookout built by Doctor White of the Pine Crest Sanitarium sat at the base of the hill, along with the Pine Crest Water bottling plant. It appears that he built the lookout to protect his investments.

Now for the Aermotor-built steel tower before you: It was originally constructed in 1923 on the neighboring Big Hill and called Retreat Fire Tower. In the 1950s, like an Erector Set, it was taken apart and reassembled on APH. It stands 60 feet high with a 7-foot-square metal cap, providing a vast view of a sea of green pitch pines and oaks. It truly is a phenomenal sight, which will catch you off guard. Descending the tower, you can't fail to notice the graffiti and the party trash. There needs to be a solution to the vandalism or the tower will be moved closer to civilization. It would be the end of the magnificent view from Apple Pie Hill, the highest point in the Pine Barrens.

Miles and Directions

0.0 From the north side of the parking lot, cross Carranza Road and proceed north on a sand road for a few hundred feet. At the junction with the Batona Trail (pink blazes), turn left (north) onto a sand road. (**FYI:** You will be on the Batona Trail for the entire out-and-back adventure.)

0.2 Arrive at the Batona Camp where the Batona Trail loops in and out of the site. Campsites (by permit only), water, and outhouse are located here. *Trail alert:* The trail proceeds (northwest) to periodically parallel, crisscross, or merge with the sand road for short spurts. It is easy to miss the route's departures from the sand road. The body of water to the left is Skit Branch.

1.0 Cross (west) over Skit Branch via an auto bridge and immediately turn right (north) onto the trail, leaving the sand road for the last time. (**FYI:** The route crosses Skit Branch and its tributaries via bridges three more times.)

2.7 Cross woods road.

3.3 Cross woods road.

3.8 Begin to climb the switchbacks on the shoulder of Apple Pie Hill.

4.0 Arrive at your turnaround point: Apple Pie Hill and the New Jersey Forest Fire Service fire tower. Enjoy the majestic panoramic view, which is quite unique for the Pine Barrens.

8.0 Arrive at the parking lot.

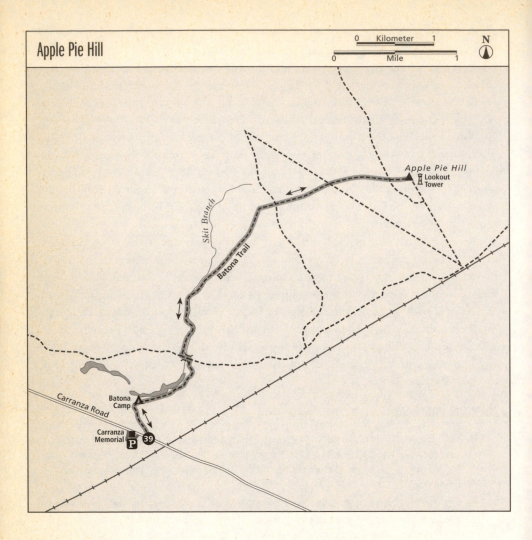

0   Kilometer   1

0   Mile   1

N

Apple Pie Hill

Lookout Tower

Skit Branch

Batona Trail

Batona Camp

Carranza Road

Carranza Memorial   P   39

Hike Information

Local Information

Burlington County Tourism Web site: www.co.burlington.nj.us/tourism. Burlington County Office of Cultural and Heritage Affairs, PO Box 6000, Easthampton 08060; (609) 265-5068; www.co.burlington.nj.us/departments/resource_conservation/cultural/index.htm

Local Events/Attractions

The Mullica, Batsto, Wading and Oswego Rivers provide excellent opportunities for canoeing; boats can be rented at the State Forest. The Carranza Memorial (see sidebar) honors Mexican aviator Emilio Carranza, whose plane crashed here in 1928. Web site: www.post11.org/carranza/carranza8e.html

Lodging

Camping and cabins are available in Wharton State Forest.

Organizations

Batona Hiking Club, 215 South Spring Mill Road, Villanova, PA 19085-1409; www.members
.aol.com/Batona

A MEXICAN HERO IN THE JERSEY PINES

South of Tabernacle, in a typically desolate stretch of the Pine Barrens, stands an incongru-
ous stone monument. Though erected less than a century ago, it looks like an ancient Aztec
pylon. It pays homage to the memory of a brave man and a mission of goodwill. Famed aviator Charles Lindbergh, in the aftermath of his historic transatlantic flight, made a goodwill
flight to Mexico City in 1927. Mexico reciprocated the gesture and selected a friend of Lindbergh's, Captain Emilio Carranza, to undertake a flight from Mexico City to Washington and
New York. Capt. Carranza, only twenty-three, came from a distinguished Mexican family and
was already a veteran of combat and crashes. The flight was the longest yet undertaken by
a Mexican aviator and generated both pride for Mexico and warm relations with the United
States. Flying his plane Mexico Excelsior (identical to Lindbergh's), Carranza was hailed as
"the Lindbergh of Mexico" upon his arrival in Washington and New York.

His return to Mexico City from New York, however, was repeatedly delayed by bad
weather. A telegraph from his superior, General Joaquin Amaro, strongly suggested that
further delay was unmanly. So on the evening of July 12, 1928, Captain Emilio Carranza
took off from New York in a roaring storm of thunder and lightning—never to be seen alive
again. The wreckage of his plane, and later his body, were found in the Pine Barrens here
the next afternoon. American Legion Post 11 of Mount Holly helped slash through the dense
vegetation to recover Carranza's body; more than eighty years later they still hold services
here annually. The monument isn't faux Mexican, but real: paid for by donations of Mexican
schoolchildren, designed and fabricated in Mexico, and reerected here. On the side, in bas-
relief, is an Aztec eagle, falling earthward.

40 Batsto Lake

This short hike, a circuit, moves through mixed pine-oak forest down into the Batsto Natural Area, including Batsto Lake. Atlantic white cedar, some very old pitch pine, and anglers in red canoes complete the picture. Some slight ups and downs on sandy trails and occasional boardwalk make for a varied outing. A portion of the route has interpretive kiosks, while a short section is co-aligned with the long distance, wilderness Batona Trail. A logical extension of the hike is the walking tour of the Batsto Historical Village.

Start: Batsto Village Center parking lot
Distance: 4.1-mile loop, not including village tour
Approximate hiking time: 2 hours
Difficulty: Easy
Trail surface: Sandy trails and boardwalks
Seasons: All
Other trail users: Hikers only (natural area)
Canine compatibility: No dogs permitted in natural area
Land status: State forest
Nearest town: Nesco
Fees and permits: None to hike; fee to visit Batsto Village from Memorial Day through Labor Day
Schedule: Dawn to dusk
Maps: *DeLorme: New Jersey Atlas & Gazetteer* p.64; USGS Atsion, NJ, quadrangle; a map is also available at the forest.
Trail contacts: Wharton State Forest, 4110 Nesco Road, Hammonton 08037; (609) 561-0024; www.state.nj.us/dep/parksandforests/parks/wharton.html
Other: Allow extra time for exploring Batsto Village, a 2-mile walk that can occupy most of the day.
Special considerations: Ticks can be bad.

Finding the trailhead: From the Garden State Parkway southbound, take exit 52 for New Gretna. Turn left (south) onto Greenbush Road (County Route 654) and go 1.3 miles to the junction with U.S. Highway 9. Turn right (west) onto US 9 south and travel through New Gretna. Just before US 9 swings south at 1.3 miles, bear right (west) onto County Route 542. Travel 13 miles to the entrance of Batsto Village (Wharton State Forest). Turn right and drive to the parking lot.

The Hike

Our walk here takes us alongside Batsto Lake, created as a waterpower source for Batsto Village, one of south Jersey's more remarkable historic settlements. Many quiet backwaters of the Pine Barrens were once bustling centers of early America's industrial prowess, and nowhere is this truer than at Batsto. Like most curious names in the Pines, the origin of Batsto is debated. Early Dutch or Swedish settlers or surveyors perhaps noted a Lenape sweat lodge along the river. They would have likely called it a "heat-bath" or "sauna"—in Dutch, "badstoof"; in Swedish, "bastu."

By 1766, Charles Read had acquired land here and started the Batsto Ironworks. The woods provided unlimited fuel; the creeks could be harnessed for power, and bog ore—a reddish brown oxide that collects along the perimeters of swamps and creeks—could be mined. Read was a genuine mover-and-shaker in Colonial South Jersey industry and politics, and also built furnaces at Etna and Atsion. But he over-extended himself financially, and by 1773 John Cox owned the Batsto works. They made a wide variety of goods—pots, pans, kettles, elegant firebacks, and other household goods, as well as pig iron.

By the Revolutionary War, the prospering Batsto works were producing cannon and shot for the Continental Army, and had become important enough to become a British target. In 1778 a British detachment attacked and burned a nearby river port, with the destruction of Batsto its next goal. But word of the attack spread, and a group of determined locals ambushed and repulsed the British; Batsto survived to continue supplying the patriot army. Joseph Ball became owner of Batsto in 1779, and his uncle William Richards took ownership in 1784. The Richards family was a dynasty of sorts, lasting three generations. William Richards turned the reins over to his son Jesse in 1809, and Jesse to his son Thomas H. in 1854.

These years saw the death of the bog iron industry, which eventually could not compete with the growing iron industry of Pennsylvania. Batsto made its last iron in 1848. Iron manufacture was replaced with glass production—the raw material of glass is sand, which the Pine Barrens had endlessly. But the glassworks were never entirely

White Trail rises above Batsto Lake through a mixed pine–oak forest with mountain laurel in bloom. Note: The trail and the firebreak are one.

profitable and finally shut down in 1867. The Richards family sold off more and more of their Batsto acreage to keep afloat, finally losing the village itself at sheriff's sale in 1876. There was little left standing, anyway: An 1874 fire ravished Batsto village, destroying most of the old Colonial structures, including the furnace.

Joseph Wharton and family owned Batsto for the next seventy-five years (see sidebar, below). The state of New Jersey pursued the purchased of the Wharton tract in the mid-1950s. A price of $3 million was agreed upon for the 110,000-acre tract. Thus in 1955, the state of New Jersey bought fully 2.5 percent of *itself*. It is likely the only time in United States history a state has done that. Today Wharton State Forest preserves the vast quiet green of the Pine Barrens, as well as dozens of historic sites and former settlements. Batsto Village is a famous New Jersey landmark, with ten major structures preserved, as well as the sites and archaeological remains of many other structures and features. Be sure to visit!

Miles and Directions

0.0 From the Batsto Visitor Center, head north on the sidewalk through the middle of the parking lot, locating the White Trailhead in the northeast corner. Here you will also find the picnic area. The White Trail immediately enters a rotary (this *is* New Jersey!). Bear right onto the sidewalk till you locate a blaze post for the White Trail where the trail leaves the circle and proceeds straight (northeast) amidst the picnic tables. The route is co-aligned with the Blue Trail (blue blazes) and the Batona Trail (pink blazes).

0.2 At the T-intersection (signage for the Batona Trail) turn left (northwest) onto the footpath, and shortly cross Washington Pike (sand road), continuing northwest.

0.6 Proceed straight (northeast) as the Blue Trail departs to the left. (Signage indicates that the White Trail is also co-aligned with the Batsto Lake Trail.)

1.8 Cross (northwest) a nondescript sand road.

2.0 Cross (northwest) a sugar sand road that appears to be used.

2.3 Turn left (south), staying with the White Trail and dropping into a firebreak. Again there is a sign for the Batsto Lake Trail. The Batona Trail continues straight ahead.

2.6 Arrive at a viewpoint, overlooking the Batsto Lake, where white cedars and pitch pines frame the scene. As the route proceeds, there will be other much closer lookouts.

3.2 Proceed straight (southwest) though sugar sand as the Blue Trail enters left (east) and once again becomes co-aligned.

3.6 At the junction with the Red Trail, turn right (southwest) onto a gravel path. The White Trail, the Blue Trail, and the Red Trail are co-aligned.

3.9 At the T intersection turn left (northeast) onto Washington Pike, a sand road, shortly passing the park's maintenance yard. (There appears to be no blazing in this section.)

4.0 Arrive at a fence. Zigzag through it onto a gravel path, picking up the Red Trail and heading for the picnic area.

4.1 Arrive back at the picnic area and the rotary. Circling right brings you back to the parking lot. (**FYI:** Restrooms and water will be found to your right.)

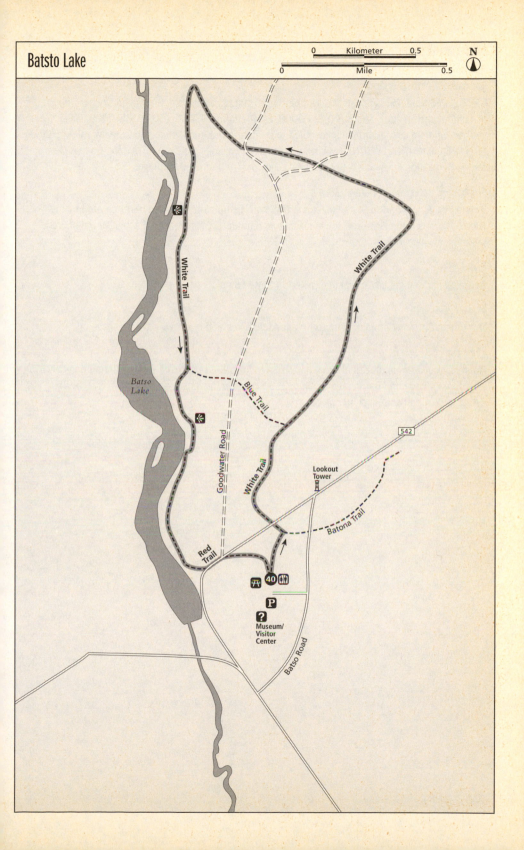

Batsto Lake

0 Kilometer 0.5
0 Mile 0.5

N

542

White Trail

White Trail

Batso Lake

Goodwater Road

Blue Trail

White Trail

Lookout Tower

Batona Trail

Red Trail

40

P

Museum/
Visitor
Center

Batso Road

Hike Information

Local Information

Burlington County Tourism Web site: www.co.burlington.nj.us/tourism. Burlington County Office of Cultural and Heritage Affairs, PO Box 6000, Easthampton 08060; (609) 265-5068; www .co.burlington.nj.us/departments/resource_conservation/cultural/index.htm. Greater Atlantic City Region Tourism: (800) VISITNJ; www.state.nj.us/travel/regions_GAC.shtml. Atlantic County, New Jersey, Recreation & Leisure Web site: www.aclink.org/webadmin/MainPages/Recreate.asp

Local Events/Attractions

Batsto Village in Wharton State Forest is a National Historic Site (see sidebar) operated by the Batsto Citizens Committee, Inc. Tours, hikes, and numerous other seasonal activities are offered; www.batstovillage.org

Lodging

Camping and cabins are available in Wharton State Forest.

Hike Tours

The Batsto Citizens Committee, Inc., gives periodic hikes and tours; www.batstovillage.org

Organizations

Batsto Citizens Committee, Inc, c/o Wharton State Forest, 4110 Nesco Road, Hammonton 08037; www.batstovillage.org. Batona Hiking Club, 215 South Spring Mill Road, Villanova, PA, 19085-1409; www.members.aol.com/Batona

MR. WHARTON'S WOODS AND WATERS

The Batsto tract was bought in 1876 by Joseph Wharton, born 1826, a Philadelphia Quaker and businessman of distinguished lineage; also an industrialist, metallurgist, philanthropist, poet, and all-around high-level factotum. Among his credentials: owner of numerous iron and zinc mines and manufactories in New Jersey and Pennsylvania, cofounder of Bethlehem Steel, cofounder of Swarthmore College, and founder of the first business school in the United States—the Wharton School of Finance and Commerce at the University of Pennsylvania, in 1881. In short, a serious nabob.

Wharton spent vast sums fixing up the old ironmaster's house at Batsto, transforming it into the magnificent Italianate mansion we see today (the Whartons spent occasional weekends there). He also removed old structures, improved forestry and agriculture on the property—and enlarged it. By the time Wharton was done buying, he owned 110,000 acres. He had a reason: His plan was to dam streams and create reservoirs on the property, making it a water supply for Philadelphia. The New Jersey Legislature got wind of the plans, didn't want to see New Jersey water pumped out-of-state, and put an end to the idea. Wharton died in 1909, and his heirs negotiated the sale of the property to the state of New Jersey in 1915 (New Jersey wanted it as a watershed, too). The purchase required a state referendum, which oddly failed; the state did not acquire the property until forty years later. The Wharton estate was retained by his heirs, which included the Lippincott publishing family. Today, Batsto's heritage is a mix of the early iron and glass industry, and the wealthy man who adopted the old village as his country home.

41 Lake Nummy and East Creek Pond

This healthy loop hike through Belleplain State Forest moves through mixed forest from oaks to pines, mountain laurel to holly. Most of the ramble is on flat sand roads and trails, accented by boardwalks and bridges. There are some muddy areas and another 0.3-mile section along a busy road that is a distraction, but the adventure is worth it. You will experience some magnificent white cedar swamps along with work completed by the Civil Conservation Corps. The hike skirts East Creek Pond with a chance of seeing a bald eagle and ends back at Lake Nummy, and a chance for a swim.

Start: Belleplain State Forest Interpretive Center on Meisle Road
Distance: 7.7-mile loop
Approximate hiking time: 3.5 to 4 hours
Difficulty: Strenuous due to length
Trail surface: Sand roads, trails, boardwalks, and bridges
Seasons: All
Other trail users: Multiuse
Canine compatibility: Leashed dogs permitted
Land status: State forest
Nearest town: Belleplain
Fees and permits: Higher fee on weekends

from Memorial Day through Labor Day
Schedule: Dawn to dusk
Maps: *DeLorme: New Jersey Atlas & Gazetteer* p. 72; USGS Woodbine and Heislerville, NJ, quadrangles; a map is also available at the park.
Trail contacts: Belleplain State Forest, County Route 550, PO Box 450, Woodbine 08270; (609) 861-2404; www.state.nj.us/dep/parks andforests/parks/belle.html
Special considerations: From January 15 to August 1, the East Creek Trail may be closed (endangered species zone).

Finding the trailhead: From the Garden State Parkway southbound, take exit 17 to its end and turn right onto Sea Isle Boulevard (County Route 625), heading for Ocean View (0.3 mile). In Ocean View turn right onto U.S. Highway 9 north and go 0.6 mile. Turn left (northwest) onto Woodbine–Ocean View Road (CR 550). Travel 6 miles to Woodbine. Turn left (southwest) onto Washington Avenue (CR 550/County Route 557). Go 0.4 mile and turn right (northwest) onto Webster Street (CR 550). Drive 1.4 miles to the entrance to Belleplain State Forest. Turn left (southwest) onto Henkin-Sifkin Road and shortly pass the forest office on the right. Go 0.6 mile and turn right (northwest) onto Meisle Road and shortly pass through the Contact Station. Travel 0.5 mile. Turn left just before the Interpretive Center with Lake Nummy on the right. Immediately on your left you will find parking. From the Garden State Parkway northbound, take exit 13 to its end and turn right onto Avalon Road (Cumberland County Route 601) and go 1.0 mile. At the intersection of US 9, turn right onto US 9 north. Travel 4.8 miles to Ocean View and turn left (northwest) onto Woodbine–Ocean View Road (CR 550) and follow the directions above.

The Hike

Most of New Jersey's great open spaces have witnessed a parade of change over the centuries since Europeans first settled on these shores. Once, Native American

Indians made this land their home, and the bear and bald eagle prospered. Yet within nearly a lifetime, all these became memories. Belleplain State Forest embodies this pageant of change as well as anyplace in the state.

Nummy was the last local chieftain of the Native American Unalachtigo tribe here. These local Lenape exploited the rich flora and fauna of this region. Nummy's ancestral home was somewhat south of here, around present-day Nummytown. But "King" Nummy, as tradition describes him, sold the last 16 miles of land along the bayshore some time prior to 1700, and then moved to an island in Hereford Inlet, still called Nummy Island. Soon, the natives who lived here for thousands of years were a memory.

In the 1700s and 1800s, this area was used for farming, timbering, and charcoal making, among other uses. As in much of the region, cranberries were an important crop here, with the Meisle family operating a large cranberry bog. But the exploitation of the forests and bogs took their toll, and by the early 1900s the state of New Jersey was looking to better steward its forest resources, both for improved timber production, preservation of water resources, and for recreation.

An early acquisition in this effort was Belleplain State Forest, the first 5,600 acres of which were purchased in February 1928. East Creek Lodge, a group cabin, was built on East Creek Pond. Vastly expanded recreational resources came in the 1930s, with the arrival of the Civilian Conservation Corps (CCC). The CCC operated three camps at Belleplain State Forest between 1933 and 1941, and much of the recreational resources we use today are their handiwork. Reforestation was a major CCC project, and you'll pass through one of their pine "cathedrals" toward the end of our hike.

Probably the biggest CCC project here was converting the old Meisle cranberry bog into a recreational lake. This little job, accomplished entirely with manual labor

Between 1933 and 1941, the Civilian Conservation Corps (CCC) played a solid role in the development of Belleplain State Forest.

(no bulldozers, etc.) took 10,456 man-days and resulted in Lake Meisle—soon re-dubbed Lake Nummy, in honor of the ancient Native American sachem. The CCC also built the Interpretive Center (originally Forest Headquarters), where you can stop at the beginning of your hike—directly across from Lake Nummy, it's the beginning and ending point of our hike.

Belleplain's service to the nation didn't end when the CCC left in 1941. With New Jersey's military installations, including Fort Dix, in full swing during the Second World War, Belleplain State Forest and its old CCC barracks became home to units of the 113th New Jersey Infantry, 44th Division. Troops occupied the old barracks, and tanks and soldiers conducted maneuvers in the state forest. The 113th New Jersey participated in the D-Day invasion of Normandy on June 6, 1944.

Belleplain State Forest returned to normalcy after the war and has grown in ensuing years. Its most recent addition occurred in 2003, when another 2,320 acres were added to the forest, which at some 20,000 acres is now nearly four times its original size. And more than a century after they vanished, the eagles have returned: Bald eagles have been nesting at East Creek Pond at Belleplain since the early 1990s. Our hike skirts East Creek Pond for part of its route, giving a prize opportunity to spot one of these amazing creatures. They are protected by an endangered species zone, which may limit access to the area at certain times of year—do not approach their nesting sites. It's a small price to pay to see this ancient winged inhabitant return to its ancestral nesting grounds here in the Pine Barrens.

Miles and Directions

0.0   Face the front of the nature center and proceed around its right side, picking up the trail cutting a swath through the woods, leading (west) to a gravel circle. (The back side of the maintenance yard is to your left.) Turn right (north) for 50 feet on the gravel road, and at the trailhead sign for East Creek Trail (white blazes), turn left (west) onto a sandy path. Follow the white blazes for the entire trip.

1.2   Cross Sunset Road (paved) and continue heading southwest on the trail.

1.5   Trail turns left (southeast), passing some old rotting bog bridging. Traverse (south) on boardwalk through the American cedar swamp.

3.5   At the T intersection, turn right (north) onto the shoulder of East Creek Mill Road (County Route 347), passing the entrance to East Creek Group Cabins on the right and the edge of the pond.

3.8   Turn right (northeast) into the boat launch area and cross it, reaching a series of interpretive kiosks and the East Creek Trail. Pick up (east) the trail as it skirts the pond. (**Note:** This stretch around the pond [within 10 feet] gives you an opportunity to spot a bald eagle. Do not approach any nest!)

4.6   At the T intersection turn right (east) onto a gravel road, following the white blazes.

4.7   At the fork veer left (east) onto a sand road and within 100 feet turn left (north) onto the trail. There is a blaze post, but it is easily missed.

4.8   Cross (northwest) the gravel road (Tom Field Trail) and head back into the mountain laurel, pine, and holly.

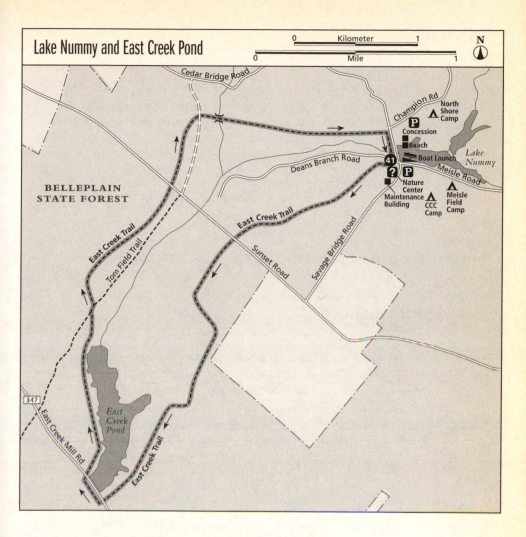

Lake Nummy and East Creek Pond

0 — Kilometer — 1

0 — Mile — 1

N

Cedar Bridge Road

Champion Rd

North Shore Camp

P

Concession

Beach

Boat Launch

Lake Nummy

Deans Branch Road

41

?

P

Meisle Road

Nature Center

Maintenance Building

CCC Camp

Meisle Field Camp

BELLEPLAIN STATE FOREST

East Creek Trail

East Creek Trail

Tom Field Trail

Sunset Road

Savage Bridge Road

347

East Creek Mill Rd

East Creek Pond

East Creek Trail

5.7 Cross (northeast) Sunset Road (paved) and onto the trail.

6.2 Cross (east) the gravel road (Tom Field Trail West) and into a mixed forest.

6.4 Cross (southeast) the gravel road (Tom Field Trail East) and descend into wetlands area, shortly crossing a wooden bridge (tributary of the Savages Run) and into an Atlantic white cedar swamp.

6.6 Cross (southeast) the sand road and onto the trail through mixed forest, leading into a spectacular stand of white pine.

7.0 Cross (southeast) paved road and back onto the trail, modulating between a mixed forest and Atlantic white cedar swamp, which parallels the Savages Run.

7.7 At the T intersection turn left (north) onto a sand road, which meanders around to Champion Road where the East Creek Trail ends. Turn right (south) onto the shoulder of Champion Road, passing Lake Nummy on your left and the nature center on your right. You are back where you started.

Hike Information

Local Information

Cape May County Department of Tourism, PO Box 365, Cape May Court House 08210; (800) 227-2297; www.beachcomber.com/Capemay/tourism.html. Cumberland County Cultural & Heritage Commission, 800 East Commerce Street, Bridgeton 08302; www.ccculturalheritage.org/contact.html

Local Events/Attractions

The Sam Azeez Museum of Woodbine Heritage preserves the history of the nearby town of Wood-bine, founded as a philanthropic endeavor for immigrating Russian Jews. 610 Washington Avenue, Woodbine 08270; (609) 646-9400; www.thesam.org/contact/contact.htm

Lodging

Campsites, a group cabin, lean-tos, and yurts are available at Belleplain State Forest.

42 Cheesequake

As close as this hike is to the Garden State Parkway and the metropolis, the terrain here in Cheesequake State Park is pleasantly diverse and rather remote. Journey past historic clay pits along with an array of ecosystems: saltwater marshes, freshwater swamps, white cedar swamps, hardwood forests, and the Pine Barrens. Where else can you find this much diversity in one park? Bring your binoculars and spy on the snowy egrets, the northern harriers, and the nesting ospreys. A bit hilly, the loop hike is made up of trails, stairs, boardwalks, and park roads. Be aware that the park has a limited capacity and closes when full.

Start: Trailhead parking lot on left just beyond park office

Distance: 4.5-mile loop

Approximate hiking time: 2.5 hours

Difficulty: Moderate

Trail surface: Trails, stairs, boardwalks, and park roads

Seasons: All

Other trail users: Hikers only on trails; roads multiuse

Canine compatibility: Leashed dogs permitted

Land status: State park

Nearest town: Cheesequake

Fees and permits: Higher fee on weekends from Memorial Day through Labor Day

Schedule: Dawn to dusk

Maps: *DeLorme: New Jersey Atlas & Gazetteer* p. 38; USGS South Amboy, NJ, quadrangle; a map is also available at the park.

Trail contacts: Cheesequake State Park, 300 Gordon Road, Matawan 07747; (702) 566-2161; www.state.nj.us/dep/parksandforests/parks/cheesequake.html

Other: This park fills up early on nice week-ends. Likewise, be aware that Sunday night gridlock is common on the Garden State Parkway.

Finding the trailhead: From Garden State Parkway southbound, take exit 120 to Laurence Harbor/Matawan, Cheesequake State Park. In 0.3 mile keep bearing right (south) onto Matawan Road/Laurence Harbor Parkway (County Route 626). In 0.2 mile turn right (west) onto Morristown Road (County Route 689). In 0.3 mile turn right (north) onto Gordon Road and drive 0.6 mile to the Cheesequake State Park Contact Station. Passing the park office on the right, travel 0.1 mile on the park road to the trailhead parking lot on the left.

The Hike

This hike through Cheesequake State Park highlights how different centuries see value in different things. For us, the area is a beautiful, amazing transition zone: from the hilly, forested Piedmont to the sandy pine barrens of the Coastal Plain—also from the saltwater bay and marshes to the freshwater swamps and creeks. But Colonial craftsmen saw something else—rich yellow clay in the riverbanks that's abundant and superior for stoneware pottery. Central New Jersey played an important role in Colonial American pottery manufacture. It had good transportation, skilled labor, and an entrepreneurial climate. These wouldn't have meant much without this band of clay

Within Cheesequake State Park, Atlantic White Cedar Swamp is just one of the varied ecosystems.

deposits running from Perth Amboy to Trenton. With this geological leg-up, potteries sprang up throughout the region.

An important pottery was here in the Cheesequake area (then South Amboy) established by Captain James Morgan ca. 1770. The Morgan Pottery produced a variety of handsome and decorative kiln-fired household stoneware, including bowls, jugs, crocks, jars, beer mugs, plates, colanders, and other goods. Morgan died ca. 1784, and the pottery works were taken over by his son-in-law Thomas Warne, who later joined with his son-in-law Joshua Letts. The Warne & Letts Pottery became even better known than Morgan's. Warne & Letts ceased production about 1827. Gone, but hardly forgotten today: Cheesequake-area stoneware produced by Morgan and Warne & Letts is now highly collectible. Indeed, most surviving Morgan pieces are in museums, and the rare ones that come up for sale fetch four and five figures. Could the farm wives of long ago have dreamt that the cider jug in their hands, bought for a dollar, would someday be worth $15,000? Probably not, or they wouldn't have dropped so many . . .

Cheesequake's clay industry didn't end there—Harry C. Perrine & Sons Co. of South Amboy continued to mine clay in the twentieth century, from ca. 1900 to 1918, and again in the 1940s and '50s. This legacy is reflected in place names along our hike—Perrine Road, and Perrine Pond, a former clay-mining pit now filled with water. Cheesequake State Park opened in 1940.

Miles and Directions

0.0   Locate the trailhead kiosk at the southwest corner of the parking lot. Head west onto the Yellow, Green, Red, Blue, and White Trails. Shortly, before a set of stairs, veer right onto the Yellow Trail (loop, yellow blazes), which runs the crest of the knoll.

0.3   Before reaching the bottom of the stairs, turn left (south) onto a trail (yellow blazes) with the salt marsh on the right.

0.7   Turn right onto the Red Trail, which is now co-aligned with the Blue and Green Trails. Immediately cross a wooden bridge and ascend a steep grade, heading toward the Interpretive Center.

0.8   Arrive at the Interpretive Center. Pick up the Blue Trail to the right (west) of the front of the building and head southwest. (The Blue Trail is co-aligned with the Red and Green Trails.) (**Side trip:** Explore the local displays in the center.)

0.9   At the T intersection at the top of the stairs, turn right (north) onto the Blue Trail, leaving the Red and Green Trails. Run the ridge before dropping onto bridging and stairs.

1.1   Cross a 325-foot boardwalk above the salt marsh.

1.2   Pass a clay pit on the left.

1.3   At the T intersection, turn right (north) onto Perrine's Road. Shortly you encounter a fork in the road, veer left (west) onto a sandy road, continuing on the Blue Trail.

1.5   Arrive at Perrine Pond and a bird blind. (**FYI:** The pond was formerly a clay pit.)

1.8   At the T intersection turn right (southeast) onto Perrine's Road (blue blazes) and into some shade.

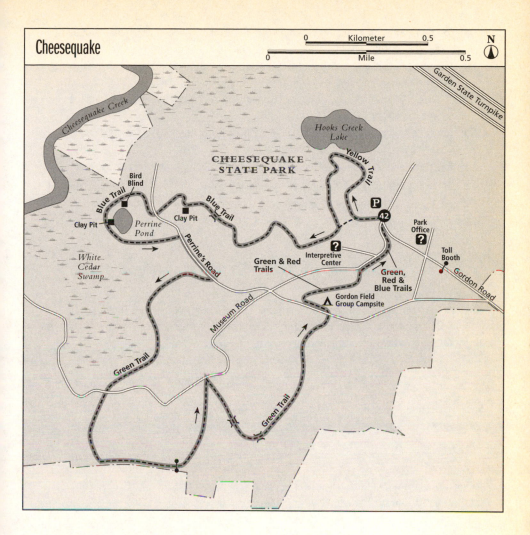

0   Kilometer   0.5

0   Mile   0.5

N

2.0   At the trail junction make a sharp right turn (west) onto the Green Trail (green blazes). (**Bail-out:** Continue straight on Perrine's Road. Turn left [east] onto Museum Road and back to the parking lot [0.8 mile].)

2.3   Arrive at a freshwater swamp. Continue along the boardwalk (can be super slippery).

2.5   Arrive at a magnificent Atlantic white cedar swamp.

2.7   Cross (south) Museum Road and move under some impressive white pines. (**Side trip:** Turn right onto Museum Road then right onto Dock Road, bringing you to the former steamboat landing and views of Cheesequake Creek [round-trip: 1.4 miles].) (**Bail-out:** Turn left onto Museum Road and back to the parking lot [1.1 miles].)

2.8 The Green Trail bears left (southeast) and begins climbing through pines and hardwoods, crossing a series of bridges.

3.0 Before a gate, the trail swings left (northeast) and passes a vernal swamp on the right before descending through a trench.

3.3 The Green Trail swings right (east), descending unto the flood plain. The trail skirts the swamp, passing under a grand stand of tulip trees.

4.0 At the T intersection turn left (north) onto Perrine's Road, passing Gordon Field Group Campsite just beyond the "Comfort Station."

4.1 Turn right (northeast) onto the Green Trail and the Red Trail, skirting the campground.

4.3 At the T intersection, turn right (east) onto Museum Road (the Blue, Red, and Green Trails).

4.4 Pass (left) the entrance to the Interpretive Center, continuing on Museum Road.

4.5 Arrive at the parking lot.

Hike Information

Local Information

Middlesex County Cultural and Heritage Commission, 703 Jersey Avenue, New Brunswick 08901-3605; (732) 745-4489; www.co.middlesex.nj.us/culturalheritage/index.asp. Monmouth County tourism Web site: www.visitmonmouth.com

Local Events/Attractions

Monmouth County has a number of historic lighthouses worth visiting; www.visitmonmouth.com/lighthouses

Lodging

Camping is available at Cheesequake State Park.

Organizations

New York–New Jersey Trail Conference, 156 Ramapo Valley Road (U.S. Highway 202), Mahwah 07430; (201) 512-9348; www.nynjtc.org

THE JERSEY SHORE AND BAYS

I f there is a single word wedded to "Jersey" in the slang lexicon, it must be "Shore." For millions, both in New Jersey and beyond, the shore is the quintessential Jersey experience. The Jersey Shore occupies, geologically, the Outer Lowland. This includes the coastline from the southern Delaware Bay east to Cape May and north up the Atlantic Coast to Sandy Hook. The flat coastline itself is a mixture of barrier islands, bays, estuaries, marshes, and meadowlands.

Climb the Cape May Lighthouse for a spectacular view of the point.

Making the trek to the shore is far from a modern fascination. Archaeological evidence indicates that ancient Native Americans made visits to the shore, or maintained trade links with it, as seashells can be found at ancient sites far into the interior. The landmarks of the shore were some of the first noted by European explorers. Giovanni da Verrazano visited Sandy Hook in 1524, as did Henry Hudson in 1609—on maps in the 1600s they called it "Sant Punt," or Sandy Point. Dutch captain Cornelius Mey was the first to note the southern cape, in 1620, which was thus named after him (with altered spelling), Cape May. For generations, the shore region sustained itself on traditional enterprises: shipbuilding, saltwater farming, fishing, whaling, and timbering.

The shore became an important resort area in the mid-1800s, when vacationers could reach it by railroad (trains first came to Absecon Island—now Atlantic City—in 1854). The iron horse brought the throngs to the ocean, and they've never stopped coming. To this day, summertime traffic jams are a classic part of the "down the Shore" experience. Though Atlantic City is our most famous oceanside town, it was Cape May that first gained renown as America's original seaside resort. By 1800 it was attracting visitors, and it had scores of hotels when many other future seaside resorts were nothing but saltwater farms. By the early twentieth century, however, Cape May became a faded Victorian valentine, supplanted in popularity by Atlantic City. But this bypassing of popularity preserved it as the Victorian jewel it is.

With its historic Convention Center and Boardwalk, saltwater taffy, and (until 2005) Miss America Pageant, Atlantic City saw its star rise and fall as the premier resort of the Atlantic Coast. Casino gambling and a revived tourist trade have helped it regain and retain its place as the queen of the Jersey Shore. Other resorts retain their own unique charm, like Wildwood, now nationally famous for its 1950s "doo-wop" architecture.

With important harbor entrances at both its northern and southern ends, the Jersey shore was improved early on with lighthouses and forts. One of the earliest lighthouses in the nation, and the oldest still in operation, was built at Sandy Hook in 1764. Many others along the coast built in the 1800s remain both important navigational beacons and beloved historic landmarks—to the point, even, of having affectionate nicknames, like "Old Barney" (Barnegat Light).

While our lighthouses have served long and important duty, the fortifications that ring the coast were built for invasions that never came, save for the German U-boats that lurked the coastline during the First and Second World Wars. Ironically, the greatest war-related destruction came not to any of these military fortifications but to present-day Liberty State Park.

There, in July 1916, German saboteurs blew up the Black Tom Island munitions depot in the middle of the night. The explosion destroyed the works and spewed shrapnel for miles; many windows in lower Manhattan were blown out, and the blast woke people up in Philadelphia. As a terror attack, it was an eerie precursor to one that looms even larger at Liberty State Park: September 11, 2001, which played out in full view right across the river.

In contrast to those horrific memories, Liberty State Park is for millions of Americans the best place in the world to see the Statue of Liberty and Ellis Island, a short boat trip away. The ancestors of tens of millions of Americans passed through the Central Railroad of New Jersey Terminal here on their way from Ellis Island to their final home. This is literally America's front porch, the "Golden Door." From glittering casinos to secluded beaches, horrific history and scenic landmarks: like the rest of New Jersey, the Jersey Shore and Bays are landscapes of both beauty and contrasts.

43 The Maurice River Estuary

Don't let the name "Commercial Township Restoration Area" fool you! This out-and-back hike takes place in a PSEG (Public Service Electric & Gas) wetland restoration site, 4,200 acres of open space running along the Delaware Bay and the Maurice River. The salt marshes are former sites of commercial salt hay farming. Enjoy the 360-degree view of the horizon, the perfect spot for spotting bald eagles and cloud watching. The path, made up of sand and shells, primarily runs along the top of a dike with side trips into the bay on elevated boardwalks to viewing platforms. Dull hums of refrigerator trucks, smells of the packing plant, and the docking of the *Jersey Devil* all add to this coastal ambience

Start: Commercial Township Wetland Restoration Site parking lot just off Warren Street
Distance: 3.2-mile out-and-back
Approximate hiking time: 2 hours
Difficulty: Easy, level walking
Trail surface: Sand and shells
Seasons: All good
Other trail users: Multiuse
Canine compatibility: Leashed dogs permitted
Land status: PSEG restoration project, open to public

Nearest town: Bivalve
Fees and permits: None
Schedule: Dawn to dusk
Maps: *DeLorme: New Jersey Atlas & Gazetteer* p. 66; USGS Port Norris, NJ, quadrangle
Trail contacts: Public Service Enterprise Group (PSEG), www.pseg.com. No staffing at site.
Other: This hike is best during bird migration season.
Special considerations: There is zero shade on this hike; be prepared for sun.

Finding the trailhead: From the intersection of Main Street (County Route 553) and North Avenue (County Route 649) in Port Norris, travel west on Main Street for 0.9 mile to Strawberry Avenue and turn left (south). In 0.2 mile the road forks; bear right onto Warren Street. In 0.1 mile you enter the Commercial Township Wetland Restoration site. Go 0.1 mile to the dead end and to the parking lot.

The Hike

Hiking the dikes above the marsh and along the Maurice (pronounced "morris") River could be a maddening experience from June through September: The greenhead flies, gnats, and mosquitoes want their pound of flesh. During any other month, you might be attacked by a gentler, friendlier ear bug created by the late Tom Rowe of the folk trio Schooner Fare:

> Salt water farm, my salt water farm, / A little bit of heaven, just a house and a barn. . . . / And later I would take you in my arms, / And listen to the sounds of our salt water farm.

There is a sense of awe as you break through the tree line and encounter the salt marsh: Big Sky Country ... open in all directions, but this is New Jersey. Walking the banks, imagine the early Dutch and English Quakers ("ditchers") building trapezoidal dikes from 4-foot base by 8-foot base to 12-foot base by 30-foot base around the marshes and meadows, so they could attempt to control the flooding and the high tides of the brackish waters. The farmers found the marsh's rich sediment grew salt-tolerant grass or salt hay, a much-needed feed for their livestock. If the soil became depleted or rainwater flooded the banked meadow, they could open the tide gates and replenish the soil for another season or simply drain it. Bringing in hay became a community affair; the farmers joined each other scything, raking, stacking, and stowing the hay aboard scowls, which were pulled or poled, canal style, or even sailed.

▶ **The correct pronunciation of "Maurice" (as in the river) is "Morris"—just a heads-up!**

The harvested salt hay had various uses besides livestock feed or bedding. Due to its rot resistance and insulation properties, it was used in icehouses, over fresh cement, or around plants. Reflecting South Jersey's former industries, salt hay packed glassware, bricks, ceramics, and fruit. Butcher paper made from salt hay wrapped meat, fish, and fowl. You may have even colored on it in art class. Salt hay was even turned into rope.

Since the dikes successfully held back the brackish water, flax, hemp, and vegetables grew in the banked meadow. Unwittingly, it also allowed for invasive plants such

Maurice River Estuary and Basket Flat are seen from the third observation platform. Side-trips to the other two platforms are not to be missed!

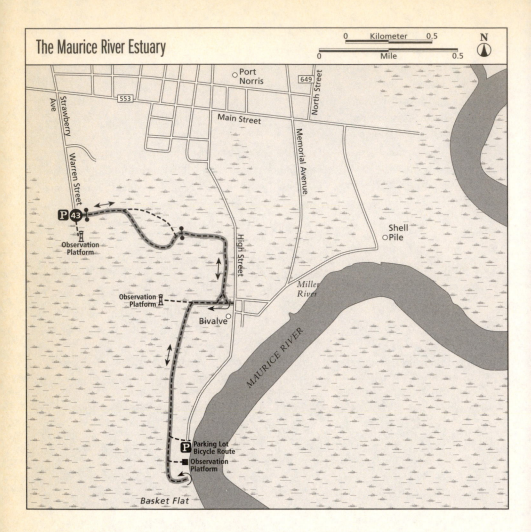

The Maurice River Estuary

as phragmites to prosper, eventually dominating the drained marsh. In short, what the dikes destroyed is now being restored by this reclamation project of The Nature Conservancy of New Jersey and Public Service Electric and Gas Company. With the opening or removal of dikes, normal tide circulation reestablishes the habitat and the food web. Salt-tolerant plants have returned along with fish, which spawn, grow, and feed. Migratory birds along the Atlantic Flyway stop and dine while others, like the bald eagles, take up residency. In addition the salt marsh acts as a buffer from coastal storms while naturally filtering the runoff.

It must also be noted that salt hay wasn't the only crop harvested here. Shell Pile and Bivalve refer to areas that once bore the title "The Oyster Capital of the World." In the late 1880s more than 365 ships harvested 2.4 million bushels of the shellfish, shipped in eighty train cars a day from two separate rail lines for a profit of $6 million.

Up through the 1950s the local oyster industry employed more than 4,500 people, working at twenty-nine processing plants. Throughout the country, oyster parlors, houses, and cellars served stewed, fried, baked, or raw oysters. Vendors on the streets, like hotdog stands, sold raw oysters for 6 cents a gulp.

Tragically, in 1957 and again in 1990, protozoan parasites attacked the oyster beds, nearly eliminating the industry. Today only thirty boats dredge for 100,000 bushels while employing 150 for one processing plant: Bivalve Packing. It is a far cry from the peddlers who sang out through the city streets, " Aysters for sale! Fresh aysters!"

Miles and Directions

0.0 From the southeast corner of the parking lot and left of the boardwalk, walk past the post and head east onto a shell-covered road. There is a sign here that reads, WARNING ABSOLUTELY NO MOTORIZED VEHICLES. (**Side trip:** Surrounded by the salt marsh, a 200-yard walk on the boardwalk puts you on an observation platform, looking over this unique habitat. You just might want to leave the side trips for the return.

0.2 The road swings right (southeast) toward the bay and then swings back (east) along the water and a dead stand of trees. It is important to follow the white shell road, forsaking all other roads and paths.

0.5 Proceed through the wooden guardrail and up onto the dike, providing an open view of the salt marsh. Shortly pass as interpretive kiosk. (**FYI:** Once up on the dike, the route continues to follow it and it alone.)

0.7 The trail turns right (south) along the top of the dike and parallels High Street.

0.9 Before a trail island veer right (west) onto a paved path. (**FYI:** If you continued straight, it would bring you to interpretive kiosk and access to High Street.)

1.0 At the second observation platform, turn left (south) onto the cinder path on top of the dike. (**Side trip:** Take the boardwalk out to the observation platform and amidst the marsh.)

1.5 Pass the Bike Path leaving to the left (northeast) and continue straight (south-southeast) back onto the white shell path and out into the marsh.

1.6 Arrive at the third observation platform and the turnaround point. (**FYI:** From the platform you have an extraordinary panoramic view: east, Maurice River; southeast, Basket Flat; southwest, Berrytown State Wildlife Management Area; west, Sanitary Ditch; north, Bivale section of Port Norris.) (**Side trip:** The white shell path continues another 210 feet through the salt marsh and to the edge of the Maurice River.)

3.2 Arrive back at the parking lot.

Hike Information

Local Information

Cape May County Department of Tourism, 4 More Road, Crest Haven Complex, Cape May Court House 08210; (800) 227-2297; www.thejerseycape.net/. Cape May Tourism Web site: www.njsouthernshore.com/membership/member_pages/Cape_May_County_Tourism.html. And another Cape May Web site: www.beachcomber.com/Capemay/tourism.html. Cumberland County tourism Web site: www.co.cumberland.nj.us/tourism

Local Events/Attractions

New Jersey's official "Tall Ship," the schooner *A.J. Meerwald,* is berthed at nearby Port Norris. A project of the Bayshore Discovery Project, the schooner can be visited, and sailing trips can be reserved: (800) 485-3072; www.ajmeerwald.org/index.htm

Lodging

Camping is available at Belleplain State Forest.

Organizations

Delaware Riverkeeper, PO Box 326, Washington Crossing, PA 18977-0326; (215) 369-1188; www.delawareriverkeeper.org. The Nature Conservancy, Delaware Bayshores Program Office, 2350 Route 47, Delmont 08314; (609) 861-0600.

Other Resources

New Jersey Coastal Heritage Trail Web site: www.nps.gov/neje/cumberla.htm

BE "SHORE" TO VISIT THIS TRAIL!

Because of its significance in wildlife migration, the Commercial Township Restoration Area is part of the 300-mile New Jersey Coastal Heritage Trail, created in 1988. A joint undertaking of the National Park Service, the state of New Jersey, and numerous other private and public organizations, it's an automobile-oriented trail linking natural and cultural sites of the Jersey shore. It's divided into five regions—Delsea (Delaware Bay), Cape May, Absecon, Barnegat Bay, and Sandy Hook—and five themes: maritime history, coastal habitats, wildlife migration, historic settlements, and relaxation and inspiration. Helping to both educate the public and promote tourism, the trail is a rich resource for exploring the Jersey shore. For lots of information, photos, news, maps, and links, visit its Web site at www.nps.gov/neje/home.htm.

44 Higbee Beach

Stroll along the Delaware Bay, edging the coastal dunes while hunting for Cape May "diamonds." Travel through secondary dunes and thickets. During the spring and fall, enjoy the variety of species of songbirds and raptors that stop by this Atlantic Flyway rest area before their epic journey south. This hike is a partial loop, a partial out-and-back, and mostly on the sand and in the sun. As one Cape May native stated, "It's the best place in the world to watch the sunset!"

Start: Higbee Beach Wildlife Management Area parking lot off New England Road
Distance: 2.5-mile partial loop
Approximate hiking time: 1.5 to 2 hours
Difficulty: Easy walking
Trail surface: Beach, sand roads, and sand trails
Seasons: All good
Other trail users: Bathers, and cars on the sand roads
Canine compatibility: Leashed dogs permitted
Land status: Wildlife management area
Nearest town: West Cape May
Fees and permits: None
Schedule: Dawn to dusk

Maps: *DeLorme: New Jersey Atlas & Gazetteer* p.73; USGS Cape May, NJ, quadrangle; a map is also downloadable at www.njfishandwildlife.com/wmaland.htm, or can be obtained by calling (609) 984-0547 or e-mailing WMAMAPS@dep.state.nj.us.
Trail contacts: New Jersey Division of Fish & Wildlife, NJDEP, PO Box 402, Trenton 08625-0402; www.njfishandwildlife.com/ensp/higbee.htm
Special considerations: There is limited shade on this hike, so sun exposure is a consideration. Be prepared. Also, while nude bathing is illegal, it is known to happen here. Wear beach shoes; broken glass is present.

Finding the trailhead: From the south end of the Garden State Parkway, take Route 109 west for 0.7 mile. Bear right onto Sandman Boulevard (U.S. Highway 9). In 0.1 mile, bear right again, continuing on Sandman Boulevard and travel (west) 0.3 mile. Turn left (south) onto Seashore Road (County Route 626) and go 0.1 mile. Bear left on Seashore Road (Route 162, CR 626) and cross the Intracoastal Waterway. In 0.5 mile turn right (northwest) onto New England Road (County Route 641) and travel straight to the end, where access parking to the beach is located within Higbee Beach Wildlife Management Area.

The Hike

Most likely you came via the Garden State Parkway to arrive here at the trailhead. Standing in coastal dune forest and about to pass through thickets from the beach to the bay, you arrive at another superhighway: the Atlantic Flyway. This runs along the Atlantic Coast. In fall and spring, millions of birds, as well as butterflies, dragonflies, and some bats, funnel their way through the Cape May Peninsula, heading south in the fall and north in the spring. Their trip may range from the Arctic to South America, exiting anywhere in between. Crossing the large, open stretch of Delaware

Bay, Higbee Beach Wildlife Management Area acts as a "rest area" along this migratory route. (Besides Cape May Peninsula, New Jersey Audubon lists other stopover sites, corresponding to our book's hikes. In the spring: Wallkill River Valley, Highlands, and Delaware Bay. In the fall: Sandy Hook and Island Beach State Park.)

The forest of red cedar, black cherry, American holly, and the thickets of green brier, bayberry, beach plum, Virginia creeper, and poison ivy here provide shelter for the winged weary travelers, as well as a flyway food court. This avian banquet reaches its peak in the fall and lasts through winter. Cedar waxwings gorge on the fruit of the red cedar. Flickers and sapsuckers dine on the hackberry. Tanagers and towhees feast on the blueberry. Woodpeckers and warblers snack on the bayberry, while the mockingbird and thrushes sup on the beach plum. Virginia creeper is the favorite choice of the bluebird, and the warblers and flickers relish poison ivy. Sassafras provides a meal for sparrows and the catbirds, while the black cherry, also known as whisky cherry, can leave the grosbeaks and the thrushes quite inebriated if the berries have aged. It also happens to be a major food source for 200-plus kinds of butterflies and moths.

For the shore birds, seafood may be more to their liking. In the spring under a full moon, the ancient horseshoe crabs invade the Delaware Bay beaches to spawn. In the past they would arrive by the millions; currently, their number is in the hundreds of thousands, laying billions of eggs! This spectacle is not lost on the shorebirds, especially the red knot, the ruddy turnstones, and the tourist. These birds may double or triple their body weight before flying off to the Arctic. As for refreshments, the wildlife area serves up two freshwater ponds, a creek, and a freshwater marsh. Concerning the flight schedule, shorebirds, hawks, ducks, and geese take to the air during the day, while the songbirds travel during the night. During migration, a special time to be here is before dawn to 10:00 a.m., watching the flocks land in this coastal dune forest.

Coming to the north end of the hike, you arrive at the Cape May Canal, another Atlantic Coast route, but this time for boaters and freighters on the Intracoastal Waterway. Built during World War II by the U.S. Army Corps of Engineers, it was a reaction to Operation Drumbeat, the German strategy by which U-boats attacked the United States. The sinking of nearly 200 ships and killing of thousands promoted the building of this 3-mile-long, 100-foot-wide, and 12-foot-deep canal, allowing Allied shipping to bypass the mouth of the Delaware Bay, where the U-boats lurked. It's interesting to note that at the end of World War II, the first German warship (U-858) to surrender to the United States did so at Fort Miles in the Delaware Bay.

Miles and Directions

0.0 From the parking lot, head north onto a gravel road, under swamp magnolias, holly, and honeysuckle.

0.2 Pass an observation platform on your left. (**Side trip:** Climb the platform for a view over the freshwater marshes and the Delaware Bay.)

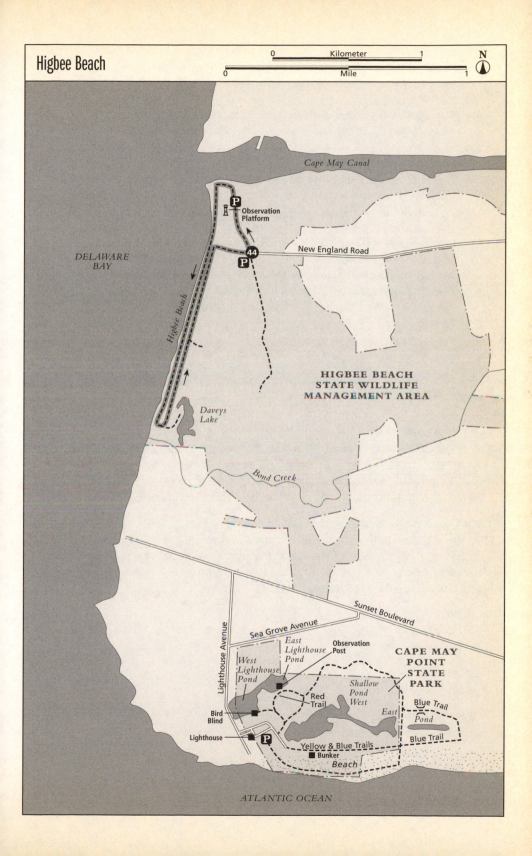

Higbee Beach

0 Kilometer 1
0 Mile 1

N

Cape May Canal

DELAWARE BAY

P

Observation Platform

New England Road

44

P

Higbee Beach

Daveys Lake

Bond Creek

HIGBEE BEACH STATE WILDLIFE MANAGEMENT AREA

Sunset Boulevard

Sea Grove Avenue

Lighthouse Avenue

West Lighthouse Pond

East Lighthouse Pond

Observation Post

Shallow Pond West

East Pond

CAPE MAY POINT STATE PARK

Blue Trail

Red Trail

Bird Blind

Lighthouse

P

Bunker

Yellow & Blue Trails

Blue Trail

Beach

ATLANTIC OCEAN

0.3 Pass through a parking lot and turn left (west) onto a sandy path (possibly a yellow blaze), paralleling the Cape May Canal.

0.4 Arrive at the entrance to the canal and Higbee Beach. Turn left and rove the beach, heading south.

0.7 On the left (east) pass the path leading back to the Higbee Beach parking lot. The hike will return via this path, so make a mental note. Continue south on the beach.

1.0 On the left (east), pass an opening in the dunes, solely indicated by a steel post. Sunbathers have a tendency to cluster here. (**Side trip:** Turn left [east] and onto the sandy trail [orange/blue blazes], which meanders through the coastal and inland dunes. Broken glass makes footwear a must.)

1.5 Arrive at the estuary to Daveys Lake (a stream across the beach) and the turnaround point. (**Side trip 1:** Turn left [east] and take the trail to the side of the stream, toward Daveys Lake. From the top of the dune, take a look out over the freshwater marsh and contrast it with the view over the bay. The trail is difficult to follow for lack of blaze posts and eventually blocked by poison ivy. **Side trip 2:** Wade across the estuary and continue down to Sunset Beach across from the sunken remains of the SS *Atlantus,* a World War I experimental concrete ship that foundered here in 1926.)

2.0 On the right, pass the opening in the dunes and the trail leading into the thickets.

2.3 Turn right (east) onto a wide sandy path.

2.5 Arrive back at the parking lot.

Hike Information

Local Information

Cape May County Department of Tourism, 4 More Road, Crest Haven Complex, Cape May Court House 08210; (800) 227-2297; www.thejerseycape.net. Cape May Tourism Web site: www .njsouthernshore.com/membership/member_pages/Cape_May_County_Tourism.html. And another Cape May Web site: www.beachcomber.com/Capemay/tourism.html

Local Events/Attractions

Cape May Point State Park is a popular spot for a variety of recreational activities and a bird-watching mecca (see the Cape May Point hike). The historic town of Cape May is a magnificently preserved Victorian seaside resort; for a twentieth-century experience, go north and visit Wildwood's bright, candy-colored doo-wop architecture.

Lodging

Innumerable bed-and-breakfasts, hotels, and motels to fit a variety of budgets are to be had in both Cape May and Wildwood.

Restaurants

Many options in both Cape May and Wildwood

Organizations

Conserve Wildlife Foundation of New Jersey, PO Box 400, Trenton 08625-0400; (609) 292-1276

CAPE MAY DIAMONDS

The last coastal dunes here on the bayside are strewn with "treasures." Starting out as debris from the Pleistocene Ice Age, alluvial trash containing quartz traveled down the Delaware Valley, acting as a giant tumbler powered by water, wind, and wave. This polishing removed the yellow limonite stains from the quartz, leaving a clear pebble resembling a diamond (carbon). Today, these semiprecious gems (silica dioxide) are a "pocket treasure" used for earrings, pendants, tie tacks, key chains, and yes, rings. Lore connecting Cape May diamonds with mystical powers swirls around the Lenape Chief Kechemeche, who gave the stones as a charm. Legend has it that the possessor holds good fortune. Have fun beach combing and good luck!

45 Cattus Island

This park correctly refers to itself as an "ecological gem." Our level, circular hike traverses uplands, crosses freshwater wetlands, and saunters through spectacular salt marshes with panoramic views. Flora and fauna abound! Numerous, strategically placed interpretive kiosks, along with the Environmental Center, add to the enjoyment of this trek. Travel on sandy roads, boardwalks and woods trails, and, if you choose, along the shoreline of Silver Bay. Take note: You must come prepared for ticks, chiggers, and mosquitoes.

Start: Cattus Island County Park parking lot off Cattus Island Boulevard
Distance: 4.8-mile loop
Approximate hiking time: 2.5 to 3 hours
Difficulty: Easy
Trail surface: Sandy roads, boardwalks, and woods trails
Seasons: All
Other trail users: Multiuse, including wheelchairs
Canine compatibility: Leashed dogs permitted
Land status: County park
Nearest town: Bellcrest Park

Fees and permits: None
Schedule: Dawn to dusk
Maps: *DeLorme: New Jersey Atlas & Gazetteer* p.50; USGS Seaside Park and Toms River, NJ, quadrangles; a map is also available at the site or online at www.co.ocean.nj.us/parks/c.p.128.pdf.
Trail contacts: Cattus Island County Park, 1170 Cattus Island Boulevard, Toms River 08753; (732) 270-6960; www.co.ocean.nj.us/parks/cattus.html
Other: The roads can be busy on summer weekends. Beware.

Finding the trailhead: From the Garden State Parkway exit 82 in Toms River, travel Route 37 east for 4.5 miles, heading toward Seaside Heights. Using a jughandle, turn left (north) onto Fischer Boulevard (County Route 549 Spur) and go 2.1 miles to the third traffic light. Turn right (east) onto Cattus Island Boulevard and turn immediately left into Cattus Island County Park. Travel 0.5 mile to the park's parking lot.

The Hike

Sometimes a hike gives us the opportunity to enjoy a landscape once accessible to only the privileged few. This is one of those hikes! Lots of us dream about buying an island of our own to vacation on. But John Cattus actually did it.

The history of this not-quite-an-island (more of a peninsula, really) goes back to the 1700s, when Joseph Page acquired it. He settled there in 1763, engaging in salt-water farming. His son Timothy was born there, and during the Revolutionary War he was probably a privateer—a pirate, basically, but an officially licensed one, preying on British ships. The island passed to Lewis Applegate in 1842, who built a sawmill and a dock for lumber boats. For much of this era it was known as Applegate's Island.

It was sold in 1867 for resort development, but the Crash of 1873 put an end to those plans. By the 1880s, it was known as Gillmore's Island.

Enter John V. A. Cattus. His father, John Cattus Sr., had come from Germany to the United States in 1859 and built up a lucrative business as a tobacco broker, exporting to Europe (Germany in particular). The import-export business remained a Cattus specialty. His son, John Van Antwerp Cattus, was born in 1867. Son, like father, engaged in the import-export business, this time in the Far East, which brought the family to the highest levels of wealth, comfort, and social acceptance. John V. A. Cattus's passion, however, was the water: He was an Olympic-class oarsman, and an avid sailor.

It was undoubtedly the love of water that led Cattus to acquire Gillmore's Island in the early 1900s, making it his summer retreat. The sailing in the area was excellent, and Cattus was a member of the Bay Head Yacht Club and the Manasquan River Golf and Country Club. He died in 1945, and the island passed to his son, Charles Baber Cattus. Charles Cattus died in 1964, and the family sold the island to developers. However, new environmental regulations made development difficult, and the plans fell through. In 1973 the property was acquired as a county park for all to use— not just privateers and millionaires. Enjoy it!

This Cattus Island boardwalk contours Crossway Creek through the wetlands.

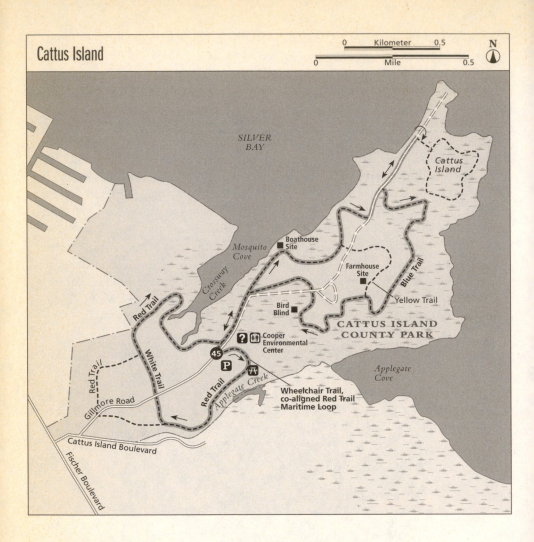

Cattus Island

SILVER BAY

Cattus Island

Mosquito Cove

Boathouse Site

Crossway Creek

Farmhouse Site

Red Trail

Blue Trail

Bird Blind

Yellow Trail

Cooper Environmental Center

CATTUS ISLAND COUNTY PARK

Applegate Cove

White Trail

45

P

Red Trail

Red Trail

Gillmore Road

Applegate Creek

Wheelchair Trail, co-aligned Red Trail Maritime Loop

Cattus Island Boulevard

Fischer Boulevard

0   Kilometer   0.5

0   Mile   0.5

N

Miles and Directions

0.0   From the northwest end of the parking lot, locate the map kiosk. Facing it, turn right (northeast) onto the paved Wheelchair Trail, passing a series of interpretive kiosks. Shortly, turn right (south) onto a boardwalk. The Wheelchair Trail becomes co-aligned with Red Trail (Maritime Forest Loop, red blazes). (**FYI:** The Cooper Environmental Center is straight [northeast] ahead on the paved path, providing restrooms, maps, programs, and a museum.)

0.2   Pass a kick-out with views of the marsh and an osprey-nesting stand.

0.3   Continue straight (southwest) on the Red Trail while the Wheelchair Trail turns right (north) into the picnic area. The trail runs (southwest) along Applegate Creek and passes a wood chip path on the right (northwest), moving into pitch pines and behind some houses. In this next section, there are two quick right and left turns.

0.8 At the intersection with the White Trail (Swamp Crossing Short Cut, white blazes); turn right (north) onto the path, temporarily leaving the Red Trail.

0.9 Shortly before the paved road, the White Trail appears to fork; take the left fork. Cross the paved road and continue straight (north), shortly entering freshwater wetlands with a stand of Atlantic white cedar.

1.2 At the junction the White Trail (Swamp Crossing Short Cut) ends. Continue straight (north) onto the Red Trail, which has entered from the left (west).

1.3 After crossing over an easement (open area), a sandy path leads to views of Crossway Creek and Mosquito Cove. There are a number of paths in this tight section, so there is a need to focus on the red blazes.

1.7 Red Trail ends at Gillmore Road (shell covered). Turn left (northeast) and immediately enter the causeway with open views of the salt marshes. (**FYI:** The Center is just across the road as well as the starting point.)

1.8 After the bend in the road locate the Blue Trail (Island Loop, blue blazes) and turn left (north) onto a trail under pitch pines.

2.0 Arrive at the Boathouse Site and views of Mosquito Cove and Silver Bay. The trail shortly passes a bird blind.

2.4 Continue (north) on the Blue Trail, passing the Yellow Trail (Cedar Line Short Cut, yellow blazes) on the right.

2.7 At the junction with Gillmore Road, turn left (northeast) onto the road and enter into the salt marshes, leaving the south side of Island Loop and the Blue Trail for the return trip.

3.0 Arrive at the end of Gillmore Road and the Beach Bay Area. From here you have an impressive view of Silver Bay. Retrace the route via the road back to the junction with Blue Trail. (**Side trip:** Continue to walk along the shoreline to the end of Page's Point and back [0.5 mile round-trip].)

3.3 As you leave the salt marshes and enter the uplands, immediately locate the junction with the Blue Trail and turn left (southeast) onto the trail and into mixed holly forest.

3.9 Continue to follow the Blue Trail through a maze of sandy roads as you approach the Farmhouse Site, passing the Yellow Trail on the right.

4.3 Pass a bird blind.

4.5 The Blue Trail crosses Gillmore Road and continues north, swinging northwest, till it parallels Gillmore Road.

4.6 Arrive once again back at Gillmore Road. Turn right (west) onto the road, shortly passing the original point on the Island Loop and where you begin to retrace the route back across the causeway.

4.8 On the right pass the Red Trail and on the left pass by the driveway leading to the Center. Continue straight (southwest) onto the paved road. Shortly, turn left (southeast) onto the path leading back to the parking lot and your vehicle.

Hike Information

Local Information

Ocean County Web site: www.co.ocean.nj.us/. Ocean County Chamber of Commerce, 1200 Hooper Avenue, Toms River 08753; (732) 349-0220; www.oc-chamber.com

Local Events/Attractions

Historic Double Trouble Village in Double Trouble State Park preserves a traditional south Jersey cranberry farm and packing plant, as well as history related to the timber industry. Fourteen historic structures can be visited. Double Trouble State Park, PO Box 175, Bayville 08721; (732) 341-6662; www.state.nj.us/dep/parksandforests/parks/double.html

46 Sandy Hook

An extraordinary adventure! Explore the thickets, the dunes, and the shore of the Sandy Hook section of Gateway National Recreation Area. Amble through Fort Hancock, marching along Officers' Row and the Parade Ground. Climb the Sandy Hook Lighthouse. Stroll along the Atlantic Ocean and Sandy Hook Bay, especially at sunset. This flat route is a loop with a short overlap, using a multiuse pathway, a sandy trail, a sidewalk, and the beach. Be forewarned: Crowds, mosquitoes, ticks, and poison ivy are part of the summertime fun; you might want to consider the off-season. If the park would knock back the poison ivy, this would be one of New Jersey's most exciting hikes.

Start: Fort Hancock parking area off Hartshorne Drive
Distance: 6.9-mile figure-eight loop
Approximate hiking time: 4 hours
Difficulty: Moderate, due to length
Trail surface: Pathways, sandy trails, sidewalks, and beach
Seasons: All good
Other trail users: Multiuse
Canine compatibility: No dogs on beach between March 15 and Labor Day; otherwise, leashed dogs permitted
Land status: National recreation area
Nearest town: Highlands
Fees and permits: None
Schedule: Dawn to dusk
Maps: *DeLorme: New Jersey Atlas & Gazetteer* p.39; USGS Sandy Hook, NJ, quadrangle; maps

are also available at the recreation area or online at www.nps.gov/gate/shu/shu_maps_directions.htm.
Trail contacts: Sandy Hook Visitor's Center, Gateway National Recreation Area, PO Box 530, Fort Hancock 07732; (732) 872-5970; www.nps.gov/gate/shu/shu_home.htm
Other: Be aware that on nice days in the summer (especially weekends) the recreation parking areas may fill up and entrance gates be closed; come early!
Special considerations: Poison ivy can be a problem on this walk, as can be ticks. There is little shade, particularly on the bike path. Be prepared. You might consider parking a bicycle at one end of this hike and doing a hike-and-bike.

Finding the trailhead: From Route 36 in Highlands, get on Ocean Avenue. Take Ocean Avenue for 0.3 mile to the Entrance Plaza; it becomes Hartshorne Drive. Inform the plaza attendant you are going to Fort Hancock for free parking. Stay on Hartshorne Drive for 5 miles. Follow signs for the Fort Hancock Parking area, where our hike begins.

The Hike

Some of our most precious parks and historic sites might be termed "accidental" ones—places that for most of their existence weren't valued for culture or recreation but for very practical reasons. A perfect example is Sandy Hook, the location of this hike. European sailors first entered New York harbor some five centuries ago. The great sandy point that extends north from the mainland across the harbor entrance— Sandy Hook—has always been a barrier. The bay is wide here (Brooklyn's Coney Island is a good 5 miles north), but the historic shipping channel required a treacherously close squeeze against Sandy Hook—you could toss a biscuit from a ship and hit it, so it was said.

The dangers of this harbor entrance led Colonial New York shipping and mercantile interests to lobby for the erection of a lighthouse here. Sandy Hook lighthouse was built and first lit in 1764. The unique flat-sided structure is now the oldest lighthouse in America and still in use. Originally located near the tip of the point, shifting sands have now increased that distance to a mile. In the 1840s, another effort to safeguard shipping was made with the creation of a U.S. lifesaving station here. These stations were charged with rescuing passengers from foundering ships off the coast. One of these lifesaving stations is now the park visitor center.

These efforts made the harbor entrance safer for ships, but not all ships are friendly. Sandy Hook also had military importance. Both British and American troops were,

Sandy Hook Lighthouse (built 1764) and Keeper's Quarters, the oldest lighthouse in America.

at different times, stationed around the lighthouse during the Revolutionary War, but it wasn't until the War of 1812 that this strategic point saw construction of a military installation. Fort Gates, a temporary fortification, was built to guard New York against the British Navy. In 1817 the federal government bought Sandy Hook peninsula in its entirety and, in 1859, started construction of a permanent fort made of granite. But the development of the rifled-bore cannon, which could punch through the thickest masonry, made such forts obsolete, and it was never finished. However, in 1874 the U.S. Army did establish a weapons proving ground here.

In 1890 gun batteries were added to protect New York shipping channels. These and later gun batteries at Sandy Hook were built within low-profile earthworks, providing both camouflage and protection. In 1895 facilities for a garrison of 400 soldiers and officers were added, making the installation a full-fledged fortification. It was dubbed "Fort Hancock" in honor of Major General Winfield Scott Hancock, whose distinguished career included repulsing Pickett's Charge at the Battle of Gettysburg. Fort Hancock became the outermost point of defense in a ring of fortifications that surrounded New York harbor.

In keeping with the camouflaged, low-profile philosophy of the fort's design, its guns were mounted on retracting carriages of several varieties. These were commonly called "disappearing" guns, since they only rose above the earthworks for firing, and then lowered down for reloading. They ranged in bore from 3 to 12 inches. The weapons proving ground left Fort Hancock for Aberdeen, Maryland, in 1919, but the rest of the fort stayed active. Indeed, it reached its zenith during World War II, when as a troop staging area its population reached some 12,000 men. But technology was rapidly making such forts obsolete. By the 1950s, it was clear that any attack would come not from an armada of ships, but via jet fighters and bombers. Fort Hancock accordingly added a Nike missile base in the early 1950s.

In the 1960s and 70s the focus of defense shifted yet again from jet aircraft to nuclear missiles, and Fort Hancock once again found itself outmoded. In 1974 the Army deactivated Fort Hancock. Happily, the history and scenery here at Sandy Hook were readily appreciated, and the property was almost immediately transferred to the National Park Service to become part of the new Gateway National Recreation Area. The entire peninsula was designated a National Historic Landmark in 1982. As an historic site, it reflects an array of military technology from the 1850s through the 1950s, and is rich in architectural treasures; as a natural site, it is both serene and spectacular. All in all, a happy accident indeed.

Miles and Directions

0.0 From the west side of the parking lot, walk out the entrance and cross Magruder Road onto a sidewalk. Turning right (north), head up Magruder Road, passing Hudson Drive veering off right.

0.1 At the T intersection turn left (west) toward the bay onto Hudson Road and a sidewalk (different from Hudson Drive). Immediately pass the park headquarters on your left. (**Side trip:** Directly across Hudson Road is Sandy Hook Lighthouse. Also across from the lighthouse and Hudson Drive is the Mortar Battery.)

0.2 Cross (west) an island with Kearney Road coming in on the right. (**Side trip:** Fort Hancock Museum is two buildings down Kearney Road on the right.)

0.3 Cross (west) Kessler Road and shortly Hartshorne Drive at a traffic island, and turn left (south) onto the paved Multi-Use Pathway. (You remain on the Pathway till you reach Sandy Hook Visitor Center.) On the right is Sandy Hook Bay and on your left is Officers' Row.

0.6 Pass on your left (east) an island created by entrance roads to a parking lot. (**FYI:** The hike will return via these roads, so make a mental note.)

0.7 On the left pass the New Jersey Audubon Society Observatory, Pemmington Road, traffic island. (**FYI:** Restrooms and a telephone are located up Pemmington Road and directly behind the Observatory.)

0.8 The Multi-Use Pathway turns left (east) and crosses Hartshorne Drive into Guardian Park (a picnic area, historical kiosks, and missile monument). Immediately cross Magruder Road and turn right (south), remaining on the Multi-Use Pathway and heading south.

1.1 At the fork veer right, staying with the Multi-Use Pathway, avoiding Randolph Drive (north end), a service road.

1.3 Cross Randolph Drive (south end).

1.4 Cross parking lot entrance.

1.5 Pass the Halyburton Monument.

1.6 Pass Nike Missile Radar Site (1950 to1974), on the left, and parking lot.

1.7 Pass the South Beach Dune Trail coming in on your left at mile marker 3.4. There is *no* trailhead sign. (**FYI:** The hike will return via this trail, so make a mental note of this spot.) Shortly cross Atlantic Drive (paved).

2.4 Cross the Fishing Beach Road.

2.5 Cross a road leading to South Maintenance (former Nike Base). To the right and across the Harthsorne Drive is a parking lot and a historic Ajax Nike Missile.

2.7 On the right pass the Ranger Station.

3.0 Cross the Old Dune Trail, while the South Beach Area E is on the left. Cross entrance to lot.

3.4 Arrive at the Sandy Hook Visitor Center parking lot. Leaving the Multi-Use Pathway, turn right (west) before the lot onto a paved path and immediately turn right (north) onto the Old Dune Trail, a sandy path. Trailhead sign is apparent. From this point, you are heading north, back up the Hook. Due to poison ivy, ticks, and mosquitoes, this may be a good time to don long pants and a long-sleeve shirt. (**FYI:** To your left [east] a path leads up to the Sandy Hook Visitor Center, with restrooms and exhibits [10:00 a.m. to 5:00 p.m.]. The Center, once a Duluth style lifesaving station [1894], is a National Historical Landmark.)

3.5 Cross (north) the entrance road to South Beach Area E, passing through the thicket. Shortly, cross (east) Multi-Use Pathway (Old Dune Trail sign post apparent) onto a sandy trail, heading east.

3.6 Arrive at the interpretive kiosk, "Old Salty Survivors," and continue straight (north).

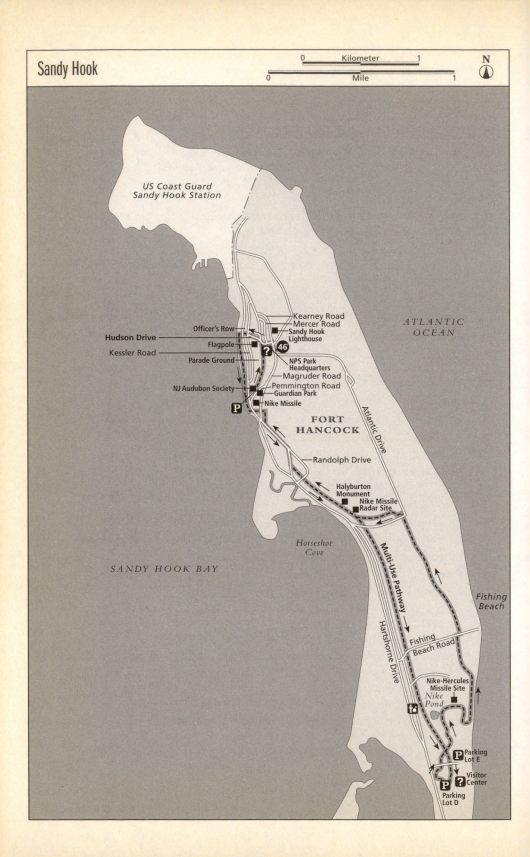

Sandy Hook

0 Kilometer 1
0 Mile 1

N

US Coast Guard
Sandy Hook Station

*ATLANTIC
OCEAN*

Kearney Road
Mercer Road
Officer's Row
Hudson Drive
Flagpole
Kessler Road
Parade Ground
NPS Park Headquarters
Magruder Road
NJ Audubon Society
Pemmington Road
Guardian Park
Nike Missile

Sandy Hook
Lighthouse

46

P

**FORT
HANCOCK**

Atlantic Drive

Randolph Drive

Halyburton
Monument
Nike Missile
Radar Site

*Horseshoe
Cove*

SANDY HOOK BAY

Multi-Use Pathway

Hartshorne Drive

*Fishing
Beach*

Fishing
Beach Road

Nike-Hercules
Missile Site
*Nike
Pond*

P Parking
Lot E

Visitor
Center

P
Parking
Lot D

3.7 Arrive at the Observation Platform. (**Side trip:** Left of the platform, take a short journey via path and boardwalk to a blind looking over Nike Pond, a freshwater pond.)

3.8 Pass the abandoned Nike-Hercules missile site behind the fence. The trail curves south.

3.9 The trail swings east, crossing the primary dunes.

4.0 Arrive at the Atlantic Ocean. Turn left (north) and head up the beach.

4.3 Keep your eye on the missile-site fence to the west. One hundred yards beyond the last fence pole, by a nondescript trail post, and prior to Fishermen's Beach, the trail turns left (west) though the primary and secondary dunes. There will be a series of guiding trail posts, but even so, it is a bit of a maze through the dunes and thickets.

4.6 Arrive at Fishing Beach Road with a cement-block structure to the right. Cross (north) the pavement, picking up the trail by the SOUTH BEACH DUNE TRAIL sign. Continue to follow trail posts with arrows through the maze of trails.

5.3 Pass around cabled gate and arrive at Atlantic Drive. Cross by zigzagging west then north, picking the trail up by the sign SPEED LIMIT 35. (**Option:** If the trail is poison ivy–choked, you may opt to take Atlantic Drive west to the Multi-Use Pathway, turning north on it where you can pick up the hike again.)

5.5 At the junction with the Multi-Use Pathway, turn right (north) and retrace the hike back to the New Jersey Audubon Society Observatory and Officers' Row.

6.6 Passing the New Jersey Audubon Observatory and before Officers' Row (site of the Post Hospital), turn right (east) and cross Hartshorne Drive, passing through a traffic island into the parking lot. With Kessler Road on the left and the parking lot on your right, locate the brick sidewalk underneath the sycamores, directly before you, and continue straight (east). The promenade curves between the Parade Ground and the Barracks.

6.8 Follow the brick path to the T intersection with Hudson Road, turn right (east), and retrace the hike toward Sandy Hook Lighthouse, passing the National Park office. Retrace hike back to Fort Hancock parking lot.

6.9 Arrive at the Fort Hancock parking lot.

Hike Information

Local Information

Monmouth County tourism Web site: www.visitmonmouth.com. Monmouth County historic lighthouses Web site: www.visitmonmouth.com/lighthouses. Sandy Hook tourism Web site: www.sandy-hook.com

Local Events/Attractions

There are many natural and historical attractions at the recreation area, including Sandy Hook Lighthouse, Fort Hancock, exhibits, bird-watching, and others. Nearby in Highlands is the famous Twin Lights, a double stone lighthouse built in 1862 to provide a navigational beacon for the entrance to New York harbor. Now a State Historic Site, tours are available: Twin Lights Historic Site, Lighthouse Road, Highlands 07732; (732) 872-1814; www.twin-lights.org/home.htm

Lodging

Camping available at Cheesequake State Park; group camping only is available at Sandy Hook; contact the visitor center.

Hike Tours

Sandy Hook offers a variety of guided walks and tours at both natural and historic sites; contact the visitor center for details.

Organizations

A number of partner organizations assist the National Park Service in operating and developing the natural and historic resources at Sandy Hook; see www.nps.gov/gate/shu/shu_partners.htm for a complete list with contact information.

A MONUMENT TO ONE-TIME ENEMIES

One feature of the hike is a monument erected to the memory of 1st Lieutenant Hamilton Douglas Halyburton and twelve crewmen of the Royal Navy. On New Year's Eve 1783, the sailors launched a boat from their warship in pursuit of some deserters. They were almost immediately overtaken by a blizzard. Their boat foundered and the sailors died of drowning or exposure. They were buried here on Sandy Hook, but the site was lost to memory and only rediscovered when the Army was grading a railroad line in the early 1900s. Their bones were reinterred in Cypress Hill Cemetery in Brooklyn.

Of course, in December 1783 the British were still the *enemy* (even though the Treaty of Paris had just been signed). So how did the monument to enemy sailors get built? The Civilian Conservation Corps erected it in 1939 in honor of a visit by King George VI and the future queen Elizabeth of England to Canada and the United States—they passed here on their way from Red Bank to get their ship at Sandy Hook.

47 Finn's Point

Welcome to an unorthodox loop hike providing an interesting day. The route runs along the perimeter of Fort Mott State Park. Hugging the Delaware River, it crosses the top of the sea wall, meanders along the Interpretive Trail, and explores Finn's Point National Cemetery. There is a short road walk with little traffic, which continues along the parade grounds and Officers' Row. The hike concludes with a walking tour through the actual fort. Enjoy the grand view of Pea Patch Island, the state of Delaware, and traffic on the river from the parapet. The walk is made of lawns, paths, beach, and stairs; the only challenge you're likely to have is leaving.

Start: Fort Mott State Park parking lot off Fort Mott Road
Distance: 2.1-mile loop
Approximate hiking time: 2 hours
Difficulty: Easy
Trail surface: Lawns, paths, beaches, stairs, parapets, and a short roadwalk
Seasons: All
Other trail users: Multiuse except cemetery and fort
Canine compatibility: No dogs permitted in National Cemetery
Land status: State park and national cemetery
Nearest town: Pennsville
Fees and permits: None
Schedule: Fort hours vary by season; contact park office for details; national cemetery open 8:00 a.m. to dusk
Maps: *DeLorme: New Jersey Atlas & Gazetteer* p.60; USGS Delaware City, PA, quadrangle
Trail contacts: Fort Mott State Park, 454 Fort Mott Road, Pennsville 08070; (856) 935-3218; www.state.nj.us/dep/parksandforests/parks/fortmott.html. Finn's Point National Cemetery, Fort Mott Road, Salem 08079; (609) 877-5460; www.cem.va.gov/nchp/finnspoint.htm.
Other: This is a great hike for a picnic. Allow extra time to explore the fort and museum.
Special considerations: While in the National Cemetery, remember that special reverence is due this spot, and act accordingly.

Finding the trailhead: From the intersection of Route 49 and Route 45 in Salem, take Route 49 north for 2.7 miles. In Harrisonville turn left (northwest) onto Lighthouse Road (County Route 632) and drive 2.2 miles till you come to the Finn's Point Rear Range Light (left). Here there is a fork in the road. Bear left and in 0.2 mile, turn left (southwest) onto Fort Mott Road (County Route 630) and go 1.2 miles to Fort Mott State Park. Turn right (west) through the entrance, and the parking lot will be on the left.

The Hike

New Jersey was part of the Union during the Civil War, but today's walk brings us past a Confederate memorial. We begin at Fort Mott, the centerpiece of our hike. It was part of a three-fort defense system built in the 1800s to protect the Delaware Bay and Delaware River ports. The oldest was Fort Delaware, on Pea Patch Island in the river, built in 1848 (you can take a ferry there today). It was followed by Fort DuPont on the Delaware side of the river. Fort Mott was not built until after the Civil War, in 1872. Construction stopped on the unfinished fort in 1876 and did not resume until 1896, when the present structure was completed. The new fort was part of a broader American buildup of naval defenses and sea power, used to promote commerce and foreign policy. This aggressive posture led to, among other things, the Spanish–American War in 1898.

During the Civil War, Fort Delaware (conveniently located on an island) became a Union prison for captured Confederate soldiers. At its peak, some 12,500 prisoners were kept here, many captured at the Battle of Gettysburg but also some nonmilitary personnel. The fort-prison was makeshift, damp, and crowded, and while it was no Andersonville, its reputation among Southern soldiers was similar to that infamous Confederate prison for Union POWs. Some 3,000 Confederate prisoners died here (mostly from cholera), as did 135 Union guard soldiers. Early on, the soldiers' cemetery at Finn's Point, adjacent to Fort Mott, was used as a burying ground, and eventually all the Confederate dead from Fort Delaware were interred here. It became a National Cemetery in 1875 and is still used for military burials.

In 1910, an 85-foot-tall obelisk was erected as a memorial to the Confederate dead. Forts Mott, Delaware, and DuPont were rendered obsolete by construction of the more modern Fort Saulsbury in Delaware in 1917; all three forts passed into state ownership in the late 1940s, with Fort Mott being taken over by the state of New Jersey in 1947. The Finn's Point Rear Range Light, another local landmark, was built in 1877 as part

Fort Mott and a path along the Delaware River seawall.

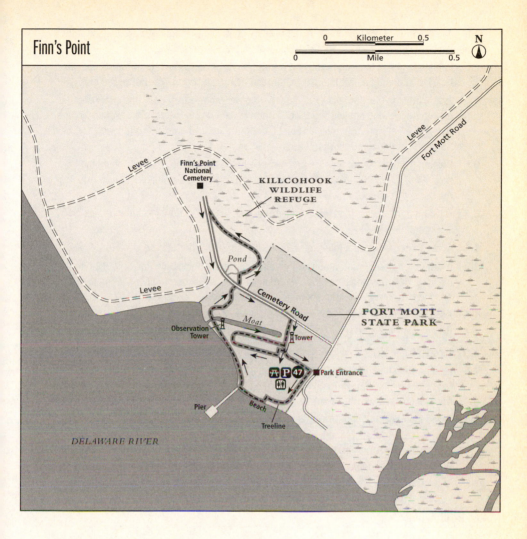

of a dual–light navigation system for the bay. The Front Range Light was demolished after channel dredging rendered it unnecessary, but the Rear Range Light survived. A unique lighthouse with an iron skeleton, the 115-foot structure was restored in 1983–84 and is now part of the Supawna Meadows National Wildlife Refuge.

The history and solemnity of this hike through a fort and a cemetery is enlivened by the beautiful views of the Delaware and the rich, beautiful habitat of the state park here. It's by no means just a hike for military history buffs.

Miles and Directions

0.0 From the south end of the parking lot, locate the gravel road on the edge of the tree line, passing the back of the restroom and the picnic grove. Begin to walk the perimeter of the open space.

0.1 At the corner of the tree line, turn right (west), continuing on the grass, edging the woods. Looking right gives you an expansive view of Fort Mott's parapet.

0.2 In the opening in the woods line and signage NO SWIMMING, turn left (southwest) onto the beach and immediately turn right (northwest) along the shore, heading for the pier.

0.3 Just before the pier, turn right (northeast) up a well-worn, sandy path and cross over the end of the pier and straight (northwest) onto the sea wall with its gravel (eventually paved) path, following signs to the Finn's Point Interpretive Trail. An awesome sight, with Fort Mott on your right and the Delaware River on your left.

0.5 Bearing right away from the river and just before the end of the sea wall, locate the Interpretive Trail, a gravel pathway. At Station 1 stop and pick up a trail guide, which explains the thirteen stations.

0.7 Heading north, zigzag (first left, then right) across paved Cemetery Road and back onto the Interpretive Trail.

1.1 At the T intersection, the Interpretive Trail ends. Turn right (north) onto Cemetery Road.

1.2 Arrive at the Finn's Point National Cemetery (part of the Pennsville Township Historical Trail). Walk the stonewalled perimeter or wander at will, eventually returning to the entrance. This may be one of the more solemn sections of our hikes.

1.5 From the entrance, retrace the route on Cemetery Road, heading south.

1.6 Pass (south) the north end of Interpretive Trail and continue on Cemetery Road.

1.8 Cross (southeast) the middle section of Interpretive Trail and continue on Cemetery Road.

2.0 After passing the maintenance yard and prior to the Post Headquarters (Building 9), turn right (southwest) through the opening in the fence and head down a paved road, passing the Welcome Center (museum), park office, and the restrooms.

2.1 At the fork, bear left onto the main entrance to the park and back to the parking lot (2.2 miles). (**Side trip:** Before arriving back at the lot, stop at Kiosk 1, picking up a map for the Walking Tour of Fort Mott. Take the tour, which adds 0.5 mile. It has amazing views from the fort's parapet, looking across the Delaware River. Besides, it is the only elevation gain of the day.)

Hike Information

Local Information
County of Salem, 94 Market Street, Salem 08079; (856) 935-7510; www.salemco.org

Local Events/Attractions
Supawna Meadows National Wildlife Refuge has wildlife observation trails in a tidal meadows environment: 197 Lighthouse Road, Pennsville 08070; (856) 935-1487; http://northeast.fws.gov/nj/spm.htm

Other Resources
The Three Forts Ferry Service (Delaware River and Bay Authority) provides ferry service to Fort Delaware; www.threeforts.com/index.html. It's worth the trip!

48 Liberty State Park

On this adventure the skyline isn't broken by towering oaks, sycamore, or white pines but by Lady Liberty, Columbus Monument, Liberation Monument, and Manhattan skyscrapers. The route takes advantage of walkways, the nature path, Interpretive Center, the Central Railroad of New Jersey Terminal, and especially the Liberty Walk. All these border salt marshes, coves, ponds, the Hudson River, and the Morris Canal Big Basin. This flat loop outing is bustling with bicycles, yachts, tugs, helicopters, and multinational sightseers. Come early to experience this Saroyan-esque scene. Side trips to Millennium Park, Ellis Island, and Statue of Liberty are doable along the route.

Start: Park Headquarters parking lot at Morris Pesin Drive
Distance: 5.1-mile loop
Approximate hiking time: 2.5 hours
Difficulty: Easy
Trail surface: Walkways, paths, and sidewalks
Seasons: All
Other trail users: Bicycles
Canine compatibility: Leashed dogs permitted
Land status: State park
Nearest town: Jersey City
Fees and permits: None

Schedule: Dawn to dusk
Maps: *DeLorme: New Jersey Atlas & Gazetteer* p.33, 81; USGS Jersey City, NJ, quadrangle; a map is also available at the park or online at www.getnj.com/lsp/lspmaps.shtml.
Trail contacts: Liberty State Park, Morris Pesin Drive, Jersey City 07305; (201) 915-3440; www.state.nj.us/dep/parksandforests/parks/liberty.html
Special considerations: The park may fill up on weekends or for special events/occasions.

Finding the trailhead: From the juncture of Interstates 95 and 78 in Newark, travel east on I-78 (also called New Jersey Turnpike Extension), crossing the Newark Bay Bridge. Take exit 14B (Jersey City/Liberty State Park). From the tollbooth bear left and then turn left onto Bay View Avenue, all the while following Liberty State Park signs. Travel 0.2 mile till you come to a rotary. Take the first exit from the circle onto Morris Pesin Drive, taking it 0.7 mile through the entrance to the park and following it to the third and final parking lot on your right (just past Freedom Way on the left). The park office, restrooms, and concession are at the southeast end of the parking lot.

The Hike

This hike takes us past the historic Morris Canal Basin, the world's best view of Manhattan, a spectacular historic train shed and railroad terminal, views of Ellis Island and the Statue of Liberty, and the site of an infamous island munitions depot. If you want to OD on history and landmarks, you're in the right place! Before this area was part of Jersey City, it was Communipaw Cove. The famous Morris Canal connected with the bay in the canal basin on the north side of the park here. Later, the Central Railroad of New Jersey (CRRNJ) bought acreage here in 1864 and built a rail terminal and depot. By the Civil War it was a hub of industry and transportation.

This Jersey waterfront became decidedly more high profile in 1886, with the dedication of the Statue of Liberty on nearby Bedloe's Island. First proposed in 1871, the Statue, a gift from France to the United States, rapidly became one of the great American icons. The current magnificent CRRNJ terminal and shed on the Jersey side was constructed in 1889. More activity came to the area in 1892, when immigration processing was transferred from Castle Clinton (The Battery) near the tip of Manhattan to a new immigration facility on nearby Ellis Island. The current landmark immigration building was built in 1900. From the time it opened in 1892 until it closed in 1954, some seventeen million immigrants entered the United States via Ellis Island. The immigration station greatly increased traffic through the CRRNJ terminal (most immigrants traveled not to New York, but to New Jersey and points beyond). Some eight million immigrants passed through the terminal over the decades. By 1915 the terminal was serving 300 trains and some 30,000 passengers each day. Industrial use of the area likewise grew apace.

▶ The park's Web site is loaded with lots of great information: www .libertystatepark.org.

In the 1880s the Lehigh Valley Railroad opened a dock, shipping, and storage facility on nearby Black Tom Island, linked to the mainland by a causeway. By 1915, it was used to store munitions being shipped to Europe, where World War I was raging. By July 1916, it is estimated some two million pounds of explosives were stored on the island. This was a tempting target for German saboteurs, who exploited the island's low security. In the early hours of July 30, 1916, several small fires started on

View the Statue of Liberty from Liberty Walk.

Black Tom Island. Some responsible personnel fought the fires, while others fled. At 2:08 a.m. the fires finally found explosives and the island went *kaboom*—to put it mildly. The explosion, it is calculated, registered something like 5.5 on the Richter scale and caused over $20 million in damage in the greater Jersey City/Manhattan area. Miraculously, only seven people died. It meant the end of munitions storage in the area, though other industry followed. The area between Black Tom Island and the rail terminal to the north was ultimately filled in; former Black Tom Island is now the area at the end of Morris Pesin Drive.

By the 1930s, both immigration, and rail transport here were in decline. Largely underused and abandoned, the area was nonetheless prized for its grand railroad terminal and close proximity to the Statue of Liberty and Ellis Island. In 1976 the property became Liberty State Park. As for the Black Tom Explosion, no saboteurs were ever conclusively identified, but a 1939 settlement over the matter with Germany was, rather obviously, interrupted by World War II. A subsequent 1953 settlement, combining Black Tom with other war-related damage, settled on $95 million in reimbursement. The last payment was made only in 1979, by which time the average person couldn't have told you what the Black Tom Explosion was. Tragically, it wasn't the last time foreign terrorists brought destruction and mayhem to this area: The World Trade Center was scarcely a mile across the Hudson.

The shadows of past tragedy can't dampen the generally ebullient atmosphere at Liberty State Park, however. It's often a busy and bustling park, the crowds a reminder of the days when the tired, the poor, the huddled masses yearning to breathe free passed through here. As brand-new Americans, they got the world's best welcome by the lady in the harbor, her torch held high as a beacon, guiding them to a better life.

Miles and Directions

0.0 Begin the hike by proceeding to the north end of the parking lot and out the entrance. Cross (northeast) Morris Pesin Drive and onto the paved walkway paralleling Freedom Way, a road that borders the undeveloped section of the park.

0.2 Turn right (southeast) onto the brick Nature Path.

0.3 Arrive at the Interpretive Center. Turn left (northwest) and within 40 feet turn right (northeast) before the Freedom Way and onto the paved walkway.

0.4 After passing a gravel road on the right (not shown on the park map), turn right (east) onto a paved walkway where you begin to have a spectacular wide-open view of Ellis Island, Statue of Liberty, and the Big Apple.

0.5 Ascend (east) up a grade to a brick-laid patio. Proceed directly across the circle to a T intersection; turn left (northeast) onto a paved walkway. General directions: Proceed straight (northeast) up the middle of the park on the paved path, ignoring the numerous intersections, which lead to either Freedom Way (left) or Liberty Walk (right).

0.7 Pass through a circular garden and continue straight (northeast) on the walkway.

1.0 Pass through a picnic area with restrooms, drinking water, telephones, and playground. Continue straight (north) on walkway.

Liberty State Park

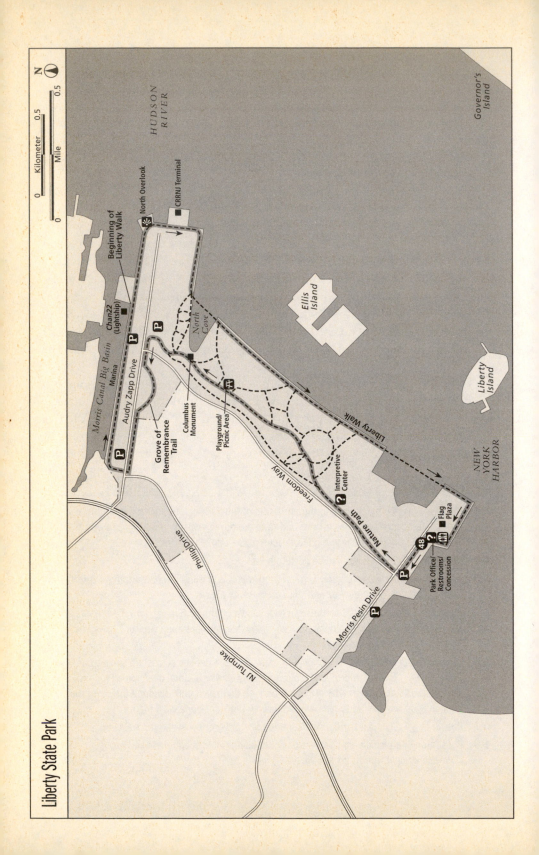

N

Kilometer
0   0.5

0   0.5
Mile

HUDSON RIVER

Governor's Island

North Overlook

CRRNJ Terminal

Beginning of Liberty Walk

Chan22 (Lightship)

Morris Canal Big Basin
Marina

Audry Zapp Drive

P

P

North Cove

Ellis Island

Grove of Remembrance Trail

Columbus Monument

Playground/Picnic Area

Liberty Walk

Liberty Island

Freedom Way

Interpretive Center

Nature Path

?

NEW YORK HARBOR

Phillip Drive

Flag Plaza

48

Park Office/Restrooms/Concession

P

Morris Pesin Drive

P

NJ Turnpike

1.1 Pass Columbus Monument. (**Side trip:** Turn right [southeast] to explore the monument and the North Cove.)

1.2 Just before the Freedom Way at the T intersection turn right (northeast) onto a walkway. (**FYI:** You are now passing the former sheds of the Central Railroad of New Jersey [CRRNJ].)

1.3 Just before Audrey Zapp Drive (cobblestone), turn left (west) crossing, Freedom Way, and onto a walkway, paralleling Audrey Zapp Drive. Immediately turn left (south) into the east entrance to Millennium Park/Grove of Remembrance loop and work your way west toward Phillip Drive.

1.8 Arrive at Phillip Drive where the Grove of Remembrance Trail ends. Turn right and cross (north) Audrey Zapp Drive through a lot and down a culvert to the Liberty Landing Marina walkway. Turn right (east) onto the path, putting the Morris Canal Big Basin on your left.

2.7 Pass *Chan/72*, a light ship, on your left, and the Liberty House, a restaurant, on your right. The Liberty Walk path, which runs along the bulkhead, also begins here.

2.8 Pass the North Overlook and the Liberty Walk turns right (south), placing the Hudson River to your left (east).

2.9 Pass the CRRNJ Terminal and continue south. (**Side trip:** Explore the interior of the terminal [an industrial cathedral], and visit the small museum. Restrooms are also available.) (**FYI:** You can access ferry service to the Statue of Liberty and Ellis Island from this spot for a fee and a security check.)

3.0 Turn right (northwest) and continue to edge the Hudson River.

3.1 Climb the stairs where the Liberty Walk veers left (west) onto a causeway between the Hudson River and the North Cove. General directions: Head southwest on the Liberty Way (bulkhead), ignoring the numerous paths coming in on the right.

4.8 Arrive at the end of Liberty Way. Turn right (northwest) onto a walkway, which continues to run the edge of the bulkhead.

4.9 Pass Liberation Monument on the right and shortly pass the Flag Plaza on the right.

5.0 Turn right (northeast) on the walkway, bordering the water and the picnic area. (**FYI:** This is the area of the Black Tom Disaster.)

5.1 Arrive back at the park office, restrooms, concession stand, and the parking lot.

Hike Information

Local Information

GET NJ, PO Box 3362, Jersey City 07303; www.libertystatepark.org (lots of great information on Liberty State Park and the area). Jersey City Online: www.jerseycityonline.com (information on nearby Jersey City).

Local Events/Attractions

No better time or place to visit the iconic Statue of Liberty, which along with nearby Ellis Island is a short ferry trip away. Both operated by the National Park Service. (212) 363-3200; www.nps.gov/stli/. In the park itself is the very popular and highly acclaimed Liberty Science Center, a hands-on museum and learning center for children and adults. 251 Phillip Street, Liberty State Park, Jersey City 07305; (201) 200-1000; www.lsc.org

Lodging

Lots of options in nearby Jersey City

Restaurants

Again, lots of options in nearby Jersey City

Hike Tours

The Friends of Liberty State Park, as well as park staff, run a variety of walking tours and programs; contact information below, or inquire at the park.

Organizations

The Friends of Liberty State Park have played an important role in advocating for the future of the park; call (201) 915-3403 or visit www.folsp.org/contact_us.htm.

49 Island Beach

Take a journey through the coastal dunes on a barrier island—Island Beach State Park. Ramble under thickets. Saunter along the Atlantic Ocean. Ask the fishermen what's the catch of the day: striped bass, bluefish, or seaweed? Stop at the Interpretive Center and pick-up "Twenty Common Shells" (a free handout) and have a scavenger hunt along the shore. This extensive out-and-back beach walk to Barnegat Inlet to view "Old Barney" (the lighthouse) is a good spot for lunch and to watch the boats navigate the channel.

Start: Interpretive Center/Forked River Coast Guard Station on Island Beach State Park main drive

Distance: 5.8-mile out-and-back

Approximate hiking time: 3 hours

Difficulty: Strenuous due to length of time of beach

Trail surface: Beach and dunes

Seasons: All

Other trail users: Anglers and sport fishing vehicles

Canine compatibility: Leashed dogs permitted

Land status: State park

Nearest town: Seaside Park

Fees and permits: Higher fee on weekends

from Memorial Day through Labor Day

Schedule: Dawn to dusk

Maps: *DeLorme: New Jersey Atlas & Gazetteer* p.58; USGS Barnegat Light, NJ, quadrangle; a map is also available at the park.

Trail contacts: Island Beach State Park, PO Box 37, Seaside Park 08752; (732) 793-0506; www.state.nj.us/dep/parksandforests/parks/island.html

Other: Be aware this park can fill up on nice summer weekends.

Special considerations: There is zero shade on this hike; be prepared. The jetties, while interesting, can be hazardous; use caution.

Finding the trailhead: From the Garden

State Parkway exit 82 in Toms River, travel Route 37 east for 6.8 miles, passing over the Tunney/Mathis Bridge onto Island Beach at Seaside Heights. Bear right (south) onto Central Avenue (Route 35), passing through Seaside Park and South Seaside Park. In 2.8 miles arrive at the entrance to Island Beach State Park. Continue traveling south on the park road for 7.1 miles. At the Interpretive Center/Forked River Coast Guard Station, turn left into the parking lot.

The Hike

Be sure to stop at the Nature Interpretive Center, located a mile past the entrance gate. Excellent displays and knowledgeable staff explain the ecosystem you are about to experience. While there, pick up their extensive handouts, enough to create a small book.

Our hike begins at the Forked River Coast Guard Station No. 112 Interpretive Center. Take a few minutes to tour the various displays relating to the island: boat building, beach buggies, fishing, clamming, hunting, oil spills, and Life-Saving Service.

The journey today winds through a good portion of the barrier island ecosystem. Waves, wind, and currents created this very large "sandbar," which remains above the tides. A shallow bay separates the barrier island from the mainland. Starting in the middle of the island, the path with its numerous interpretive kiosks immediately "tunnels" through a thicket. Emerge from under the black cherry, the cedars, and the holly into the secondary dune, carpeted by beach heather. Rise up onto the primary dunes, held in place by beachgrass, seaside goldenrod, and sea-rocket. Before you drop down from the dunes onto the beach, scan the horizon. The Jersey Coast has been nicknamed "The Graveyard of the Atlantic," and from this very location, there have been hundreds of shipwrecks and thousands of lost lives. The Barnegat Shoals, extending from the shore with its strong currents, undertows, and shifting sandbars, act like a flytrap for errant ships. It captures its prey and slowly destroys the ship by beam and mast, flinging the vessel's cargo, crew, and passengers into the sea.

▶ Island Beach was once known as Lord Stirling's Isle, owned by and named for William Alexander, Lord Stirling, of Basking Ridge (see The Great Swamp and Lord Stirling Park hikes). This guy owned land everywhere. King Charles I of England originally granted the island in 1635.

Gazing at the Atlantic, you just might imagine the *New Yorker,* a transatlantic packet, running aground minutes before midnight on December 19, 1856. Sailing for the Black Ball Line, notorious for their speed, might it have placed Captain Alexander McKennon under pressure to maintain the schedule? Did he mistake the Barnegat Light for a beacon aboard a New York–bound ship? Captain McKennon's actions stranded 280 terrified Irish and German immigrants along with his crew. The raging sea played tug-of-war with the ship. Waves crashed over her deck, coating it with sand. Adding to the horror, the hull sprang leaks, sloshing salt water around the lower passenger decks. One hundred fifty yards from the beach, gripped securely by the sand, the vessel swayed in 8 feet of frigid water. The launching of two small boats failed to bring about a rescue. At dawn a third attempt made by the captain landed a group of female passengers ashore. Due to the fury of the storm, the captain could not return immediately to his command.

THE LIFE-SAVING SERVICE

"You have to go out, but you don't have to come back," read the Life-Saving Service's motto. Their devotion and valor were unquestionable. Potentially, they dealt with the most terrifying forces on earth: the sea and the weather. They lived a dangerous and rigorous life, all for $40 a month. During ten months of the year (off June and July), they patrolled at night from sunset to sunrise and during adverse weather conditions. While on their four-hour watch, two surfmen (as they were called) walked the beach heading in opposite directions, carrying a lantern and a signaling device. They would meet the patrols from the other stations (1 to 5 miles apart) and exchange a check (proof they had walked their stretch) and return to the station. They also collected unique marine life found on the beach for the Smithsonian.

The surfman's life depended on his fellow surfmen, and how well they performed together as a crew, especially under the worst weather conditions. On scheduled days they practiced boat drills, a romantic idea till you imagine trying to launch a 15-foot skiff into the pounding surf from the beach, or for that matter, landing it. Would you dread or enjoy the cold Atlantic waters during the capsize drill? How about firing of the Lye gun at a target, or rigging the breeches buoy in the rough sea? On the following day you practiced Morse code in a four-man team. One member dictated the message while two more members, one waving the red flag (dash) and another waving the white flag (dot), sent the message, while the fourth received the reply. On Friday you trained in first aid, and Saturday you would grab a rag or a broom and clean. By Sunday, you'd have earned a day of rest, but not much, since the Forked River station was fairly active. Between 1883 and 1915, three volumes of Life-Saving Reports of Assistance Rendered were filled, an above-average number.

On January 5, 1877, surfman John Parker set out for night patrol from Forked River Life-Saving Station #114. The records read, "Died in the line of duty." What service was he rendering that took his life? Why was John Parker, the keeper of the station (1872–76) demoted to a surfman? Why does this site lack a monument for his heroic service? Just remembering, "You have to go out, but you don't have to come back" was a fact of life for these courageous men.

Those ashore packed into a wooden shack, while the passengers aboard the derelict experienced pillaging of their personal belongings by the crew. Aboard the Black Ball Line, the sailors notoriously fought and received brutal treatment; therefore, the packets bore the name "blood boats" and the crew, "packet rats." Consequently, by the time Captain McKennon returned, his crew mutinied, resulting in the captain's loss of an eye and the arrest of the errant crew. With the arrival of the Life-Saving Service (who had been on another rescue), a cable attached to the ship permitted the life-car to remove the remaining passengers from the ship. The castaways, no longer floating in the sea, found themselves hiking 17 miles on a desolate island before reaching shelter. A wrecking company salvaged the cargo of railroad iron, coal, hardware, and earthenware, but the sea claimed the *New Yorker*.

As you comb the Atlantic Ocean toward Barnegat Inlet, hopefully fair weather fills your sails and good companionship accompanies you.

Miles and Directions

0.0 From the east side of the parking lot walk between the Interpretive Center (left) and the former Coast Guard Station (right) on a paved sidewalk. There you will find a sign: JOHNNY ALLEN'S COVE SELF-GUIDED TRAIL. At the fence, pick up a trail guide and take the sandy trail, heading northeast.

Crossing the primary dune onto Atlantic Ocean beach.

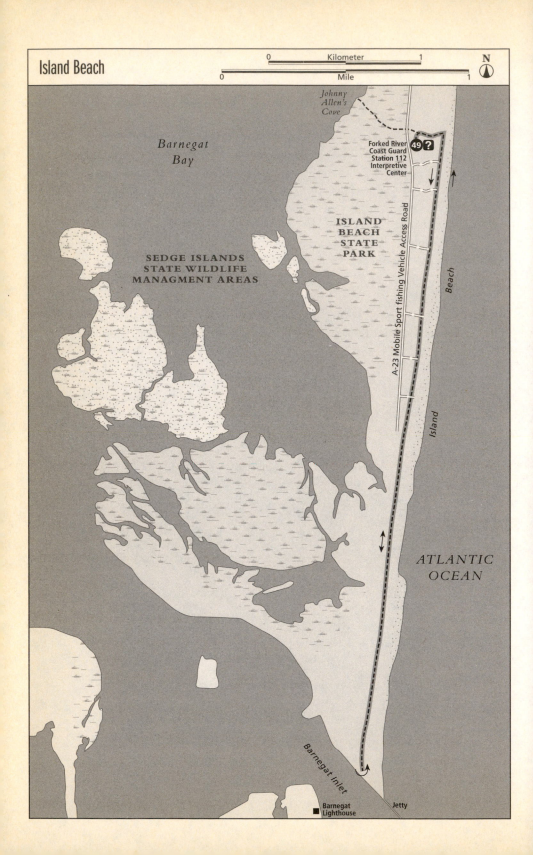

Island Beach

Kilometer

Mile

N

Johnny Allen's Cove

Barnegat Bay

Forked River Coast Guard Station 112 Interpretive Center

49 ?

SEDGE ISLANDS STATE WILDLIFE MANAGMENT AREAS

ISLAND BEACH STATE PARK

A-23 Mobile Sport fishing Vehicle Access Road

Beach

Island

ATLANTIC OCEAN

Barnegat Inlet

Jetty

Barnegat Lighthouse

0.1 At the T intersection turn right (southeast) and head for the Atlantic Ocean 0.2 mile (so noted by a sign). (**Side trip:** Consider taking the trail left to Barnegat Bay [0.3 mile] on the return leg.)

0.2 Cross through the dunes along a picket fence and onto the beach. The Atlantic Ocean is before you. You might want to tie surveyors' tape on the sign RIP CURRENTS CAN KILL, so on your return you can easily spot the path back to the Interpretive Center. Turn right (south) along the beach and the water.

0.3 Pass path (right/west) through the dunes.

0.4 Pass path (right/west) through the dunes. Sign reads A-18.

0.6 Pass path (right/west) through the dunes. Sign reads A-19.

0.9 Pass path (right/west) through the dunes. A-21 is unmarked.

1.1 Pass path (right/west) through the dunes. A-22 is unmarked.

1.3 Pass path (right/west) through the dunes. Sign reads A-23.

1.5 Pass A-23 Mobile Sportfishing Vehicle Access Road (right /west).

2.5 Pass path (right/west): Sign reads AUTHORIZED VEHICLES ONLY.

2.9 Arrive at Barnegat Inlet. Barnegat Lighthouse (State Park) and Long Beach Island is across the channel. The bulkhead and jetty are interesting areas to explore, but they can be bone-breaking slippery. At this point reverse the hike.

5.8 Arrive back at parking lot.

Hike Information

Local Information
Ocean County Web site: www.co.ocean.nj.us/. Ocean County Chamber of Commerce, 1200 Hooper Avenue, Toms River 08753; (732) 349-0220; www.oc-chamber.com. Seaside Heights Official Tourism Information Web site: www.seasideheightstourism.com

Local Events/Attractions
A walk up Barnegat Lighthouse is a must-do; from the inlet at Island Beach, however, Old Barney is so-close-yet-so-far, either a long but easy drive or a short but rough swim (only kidding! Don't try it!). Barnegat Lighthouse State Park, PO Box 167, Barnegat Light 08006; (609) 494-2016; www.state.nj.us/dep/parksandforests/parks/barnlig.html

Hike Tours
Canoe, kayak, and walking tours are available—contact the park.

Organizations
Friends of Island Beach State Park, PO Box 37, Seaside Park 08752; (732) 793-0506; www .friendsofislandbeach.com. Save Barnegat Bay, 906-B Grand Central Avenue, Lavallette 08735; www.savebarnegatbay.org

In Addition

Walt Whitman on Lifesaving

Walt Whitman honored the lifesaving station here with a poem that wonderfully evokes the experience of scanning the dark seas on a howling, snowy, stormy night here:

Patrolling Barnegat
Wild, wild the storm, and the sea high running,
Steady the roar of the gale, with incessant undertone muttering,
Shouts of demoniac laughter fitfully piercing and pealing,
Waves, air, midnight, their savagest trinity lashing,
Out in the shadows there milk-white combs careering,
On beachy slush and sand spirts of snow fierce slanting,
Where through the murk the easterly death-wind breasting,
Through cutting swirl and spray watchful and firm advancing,
(That in the distance! is that a wreck? is the red signal flaring?)
Slush and sand of the beach tireless till daylight wending,
Steadily, slowly, through hoarse roar never remitting,
Along the midnight edge by those milk-white combs careering,
A group of dim, weird forms, struggling, the night confronting,
That savage trinity warily watching.

—Walt Whitman

50 Cape May Point

Cape May Point State Park, the bird-watching mecca of the Northeast, provides a glorious hike on boardwalks, sandy paths, and the beach, passing through salt marshes and mixed forest; up and over dunes; and along freshwater ponds and the Atlantic Ocean. The Cape May Lighthouse is never out of sight. Once on the beach, the hike skirts a World War II bunker before it heads to an access point. Beware that there is little shade on this adventure. If you need elevation, you should take a side trip up the 157-foot-tall lighthouse for a spectacular view of the peninsula.

Start: Cape May State Park parking lot on Lighthouse Avenue

Distance: 2.6-mile loop

Approximate hiking time: 1.5 hours

Difficulty: Easy

Trail surface: Boardwalks, sandy paths, and the beach

Seasons: All

Other trail users: Hikers only

Canine compatibility: Dogs not permitted on beach April 15 through September 15; otherwise, leashed dogs permitted

Land status: State park

Nearest town: West Cape May

Fees and permits: None

Schedule: Dawn to dusk

Maps: *DeLorme: New Jersey Atlas & Gazetteer* p.73; USGS Cape May, NJ, quadrangle; a map is also available at the park.

Trail contacts: Cape May Point State Park, P.O. Box 107, Cape May Point 08212; (609) 884-2159; www.state.nj.us/dep/parksandforests/parks/capemay.html

Special considerations: There is zero shade on this hike; be prepared. The park may close due to capacity on busy weekends.

Finding the trailhead: From the south end of the Garden State Parkway, take Route 109 west for 0.7 mile. Bear right onto Sandman Boulevard (U.S. Highway 9). In 0.1 mile, bear right again, continuing on Sandman Boulevard, and travel west for 0.3 mile. Turn left (south) onto Seashore Road (County Route 626) and go 0.1 mile. Bear left (south) on Seashore Road (Route 162, CR 626) and cross the Intracoastal Waterway. In West Cape May (1.9 miles), Seashore Road becomes Broadway. Go 0.4 mile to the intersection with Sunset Boulevard (County Route 606). Turn right (west) onto Sunset Boulevard and drive 1.7 miles. Turn left (south) onto Lighthouse Avenue (County Route 629) and drive 0.7 mile to the Cape May Point State Park parking lot.

The Hike

A lighthouse keeper's life is stereotypically one of loneliness and isolation, but not so here at Cape May Lighthouse, a feature of this walk. Built in 1857–59, it's near the village of Cape May Point, an early shore resort, so from the beginning, Cape May Light was a popular attraction for shore visitors. Hundreds of people were annually climbing its 157-foot height even in the 1880s, and the keeper was as much a tour guide as a lens-polisher and oil-filler. This was the third lighthouse at this location. It was turned off from 1941 to 1945 as a wartime precaution.

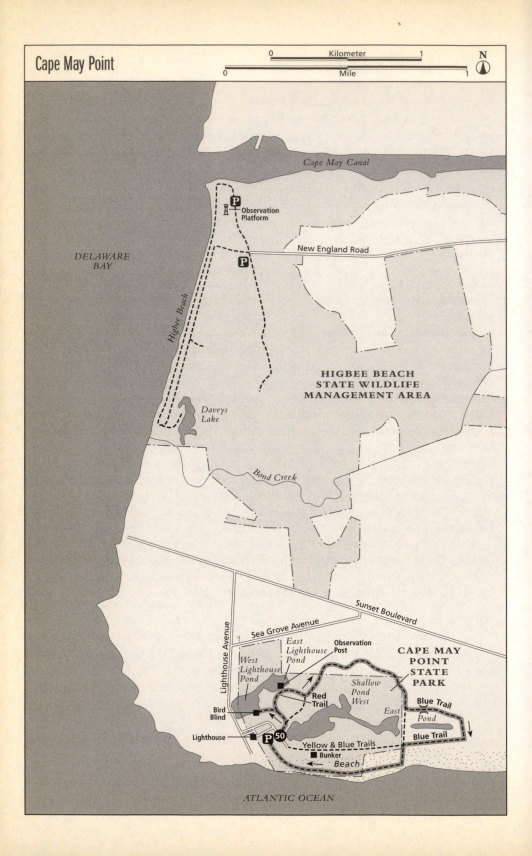

Cape May Point

0 — Kilometer — 1
0 — Mile — 1

N

DELAWARE
BAY

Cape May Canal

P Observation
Platform

P New England Road

Higbee Beach

HIGBEE BEACH
STATE WILDLIFE
MANAGEMENT AREA

*Daveys
Lake*

Bond Creek

Sunset Boulevard

Sea Grove Avenue

Lighthouse Avenue

*East
Lighthouse
Pond*

Observation
Post

CAPE MAY
POINT
STATE
PARK

*West
Lighthouse
Pond*

*Shallow
Pond West*

Blue **Trail**

Red
Trail

East

Pond

Bird
Blind

Blue **Trail**

Lighthouse

P 50

Yellow & Blue Trails

Bunker

Beach

ATLANTIC OCEAN

A major reminder of those dark war years sits in the shadow of Cape May Light-house: On the nearby beach are the ruins of a concrete artillery bunker built by the Army Corps of Engineers in early 1942. Originally some 900 feet from the shoreline, and covered in earth and sod, subsequent beach erosion has left it sitting on pilings over the surf. Two circular emplacements for 8-inch guns on either side of the bunker are now visible only at low tide. The 7-foot-thick walls of the bunker housed rooms for powder, shells, generators, and other necessaries. It was part of a defense system for Delaware Bay but never saw much action (although German U-boat U-*858* surrendered off the coast here in May 1945).

For decades the bunker was a popular feature of the beach. Erosion and decay have now rendered it an off-limits ruin, seemingly doomed to eventual collapse into the surf; some say ghosts of wartime solders can be seen manning it in the twilight. Cape May Lighthouse has a happier future. Still in use (automated), the Mid-Atlantic Center for the Arts leases it, gives tours, operates the adjacent museum, and has undertaken some $2 million in restoration on the scenic landmark.

Miles and Directions

0.0   Walk to the northeast end of the parking lot, where you will find trailhead signs and a bicycle rack. Proceed (northeast) onto the boardwalk, following the Red Trail (red blazes), which is co-aligned with the Yellow and Blue Trails.

0.1   Turn left (northwest) onto the south end of the Red Trail loop and continue on a boardwalk.

0.2   Side trip out and back: To a bird blind on Lighthouse Pond West, turn left following the boardwalk.

0.5   Side trip out and back: To a viewing platform over Lighthouse Pond East, turn left onto a footpath.

0.6   Arrive at the north end of the Red Trail loop and turn left (northeast) onto the Blue Trail, which is co-aligned with the Yellow Trail.

1.3   Turn left (southeast) at the blaze post, remaining on the Blue Trail and shortly crossing a bridge over standing water. The Yellow Trail continues straight.

1.5   At the T intersection with a blaze post, turn right (south) onto a sandy road, still following the Blue Trail.

1.6   Before the dune and between the pond, the Blue Trail turns right (west) onto a gravel road.

1.8   Between the two ponds there is a trail junction. In this open space, the Yellow Trail comes in on the right (north) and joins the Blue Trail, heading straight (west) back to the parking lot. This is an alternative; otherwise, turn left (southeast) and climb the ramp over the dune.

1.9   Turn right (west) before the Atlantic Ocean. The beach has become your trail.

2.3   After passing the World Was II bunker, head back (north) toward the lighthouse. Take the access before the People with Disabilities ramp. At the other end of the access, arrive at the southeast end of the parking lot, where you will find a faucet to wash the sand off your feet. (**Side trip:** Continue to explore the beach around the peninsula and climb the Cape May Lighthouse!)

2.6   Arrive at the parking lot.

Hike Information

Local Information

Cape May County Department of Tourism, 4 More Road, Crest Haven Complex, Cape May Court House 08210; (800) 227-2297; www.thejerseycape.net/. Cape May Tourism Web site: www .njsouthernshore.com/membership/member_pages/Cape_May_County_Tourism.html. And another Cape May Web site: www.beachcomber.com/Capemay/tourism.html

Local Events/Attractions

A walk through Cape May is a walk through Victorian architectural history and not to be missed. In Cape May you can visit the landmark Emlen Physick Estate, a landmark 1879 mansion rescued by the Mid-Atlantic Center for the Arts (which also operates the 1859 Cape May Lighthouse in the state park): Mid-Atlantic Center for the Arts, 1048 Washington Street, Cape May 08204; (800) 275-4278; www.capemaymac.org

Lodging

Lots of bed-and-breakfasts in Cape May, though usually a bit pricey; for economy accommodations, head just north to the glitz of Wildwood.

Restaurants

Many options in Cape May

Organizations

The New Jersey Audubon Society's Cape May Bird Observatory operates The Center for Research and Education, 600 Highway 47 North, Cape May Court House 08210; (609) 861-0700; as well as The Northwood Center, 701 East Lake Drive, Cape May Point 08212; www.njaudubon.org/ Centers/CMBO/. The former is for more serious avian research, while the latter has exhibits, books, and a gift shop.

Battery 223, built in 1942, protected the harbor with two 6-inch M1 guns. Since it was abandoned in 1962, the sea attempts to reclaim the beach.

Honorable Mentions

"Had we but world enough, and time," (as the poet says) it would have been marvelous to include every hike we love. But we don't, and our editor, while most forbearing, isn't coy. So with apologies and substantial guilt we list the following places that had to be left out. Some are great hikes that are problematic because they are closed during nesting periods. Others are under development or in various planning stages. Some trails are closed temporarily due to other problems. However, they're all wonderful, and we encourage you to visit them, too; they're well worth your time.

Allaire Village
Allamuchy SF/Village/Waterloo
Bass River SF
Brigantine NWR
Columbia Trail
Corson Inlet and Stone Harbor
EB Forsythe NWR
Farny Highlands
Garrett Mountain
Hacklebarney State Park
Highlands Trail
Holgate Beach
Jenny Jump SF
Kittatinny Valley State Park
Morris Canal
Ore Belt Trail
Patriots' Path
Pequannock Watershed
Ramapo Mountain State Forest
Ringwood and Long Pond (Hasenclever trail closed)
Six-Mile Run
Sourland Mountains
Sparta Mountain Wildlife Management Area and the Edison Ore
    Concentrating Works site
Turkey Mountain (Morris County)

New Jersey Backpacks

1. Short and Simple Outing: High Point to Culvers Gap

0.0 miles. Route 23: AT Parking

5.5 miles. Mashipacong Shelter

11.5 miles. Gren Anderson Shelter

14.5 miles. U.S. Highway 206: AT Parking Lot

2. Longer and Simple Tramp: High Point to Millbrook–Blairstown Road

0.0 miles. Route 23: AT Parking Lot

11.0 miles. Gren Anderson Shelter

18.0 miles. Brinks Shelter

29.0 miles. Millbrook–Blairstown Road

3. Gap Ramble: Delaware Water Gap to Culvers Gap

0.0 miles. Interstate 80: Dunnfield Creek Parking Lot

4.6 miles. Backpacker Site

12.7 miles. Catfish Fire Tower: make camp

24.7 miles. Brink Shelter

28.3 miles. US 206: AT Parking Lot

4. Kittatinny Ridge Trek: Delaware Water Gap to High Point

0.0 miles. Interstate 80: Dunnfield Creek Parking Lot

4.6 miles. Backpacker Site

13.0 miles. Hemlock Hollow: make camp

24.0 miles. Brink Shelter

34.3 miles. Gren Anderson Shelter

45.3 miles. Route 23: AT Parking Lot

5. Valley Vault: Vernon Valley to High Point

0.0 miles. Route 94: AT Parking Lot

7.0 miles. Pochuck Shelter

19.0 miles. High Point Shelter

21.0 miles. Route 23: AT Parking Lot

High Point to Cape May Point

		Date Hiked	Comments
1.	Steenykill Lk./HighPoint	_____	_____
2.	Lk.Rutherfurd/Appalachian Tr.	_____	_____
3.	Paulinskill Valley Trail	_____	_____
4.	Mt. Tammany/Sunfish Pond	_____	_____
5.	Culver's Gap/Stony Lake	_____	_____
6.	Wallkill River Valley	_____	_____
7.	Pahaquarry Copper Mines	_____	_____
8.	Millbrook Village/VanCampens Glen	_____	_____
9.	Buttermilk Falls/Rattlesnake Mt.	_____	_____
10.	Pochuck Valley/Wawayanda Mt.	_____	_____
11.	Pyramid Mt./Tripod Rock	_____	_____
12.	Bearfort Mt./ Surprise Lk.	_____	_____
13.	The Tourne	_____	_____
14.	Pequannock Highlands	_____	_____
15.	Saffin Pond/Headley Overlook	_____	_____
16.	Schooley's Mountain	_____	_____
17.	Terrace Pond	_____	_____
18.	Wyanokie High Point	_____	_____
19.	Black River	_____	_____
20.	Ken Lockwood Gorge	_____	_____
21.	Wawayanda Lake	_____	_____
22.	Great Falls of the Passaic	_____	_____
23.	Hudson Palisades	_____	_____
24.	Princeton Woods	_____	_____
25.	Jockey Hollow	_____	_____

	Date Hiked	Comments
26. Watchung Reservation	_____	_____
27. DRC–Millstone Valley	_____	_____
28. Great Swamp	_____	_____
29. DRV–Stockton to Bull's Island	_____	_____
30. DRV–Stockton to Lambertville	_____	_____
31. S. Mt. and the Rahway River	_____	_____
32. Hackensack Meadowlands	_____	_____
33. Lord Stirling Park	_____	_____
34. Belcoville and the S. River	_____	_____
35. Pakim Pond and Mt. Misery	_____	_____
36. Parvin Lake	_____	_____
37. Bear Swamp Hill–Pine Plains	_____	_____
38. Wells Mills	_____	_____
39. Apple Pie Hill	_____	_____
40. Batsto Lake	_____	_____
41. Lk. Nummy and E. Creek Pond	_____	_____
42. Cheesequake	_____	_____
43. Maurice River Estuary	_____	_____
44. Higbee Beach	_____	_____
45. Cattus Island	_____	_____
46. Sandy Hook	_____	_____
47. Finns Point	_____	_____
48. Liberty State Park	_____	_____
49. Island Beach	_____	_____
50. Cape May Point	_____	_____

Clubs & Trail Groups

New York–New Jersey Trail Conference
156 Ramapo Valley Road (U.S. Highway 202)
Mahwah 07430
(201) 512-9348
www.nynjtc.orgcontact.html

New Jersey Audubon Society
9 Hardscrabble Road
Bernardsville 07924
(908) 204-8998
www.njaudubon.org

Batona Hiking Club
1001 Second Avenue
Media, PA 19063
http://members.aol.com/Batona/

The Appalachian Mountain Club
5 Joy Street
Boston, MA 02108
(617) 523-0655
www.outdoors.org

Appalachian Trail Conservancy
799 Washington Street
PO Box 807
Harpers Ferry, WV 25425-0807
(304) 535-6331
www.appalachiantrail.org

Adirondack Mountain Club
814 Goggins Road
Lake George, NY 12845
(518) 668-4447
www.adk.org

Green Mountain Club
4711 Waterbury-Stowe Road
Waterbury Center, VT 05677
(802) 244-7037
www.greenmountainclub.org

Further Reading

Anderson, Elaine. *The Central Railroad of New Jersey's First 100 Years: A Historical Survey.* Easton, Penn.: Center for Canal History and Technology, 1984.

Beck, Henry Charlton. *Forgotten Towns of Southern New Jersey.* New Brunswick, N.J.: Rutgers University Press, 1994 (originally published 1936).

———. *The Roads of Home.* New Brunswick, N.J.: Rutgers University Press, 1956.

Bertland, Dennis N., Patricia M. Valence, and Russell J. Woodling. *The Minisink: A Chronicle of One of America's First and Last Frontiers.* For the Four-County Task Force on the Tocks Island Dam Project, 1975.

Cavanaugh, Cam. *Saving the Great Swamp.* Frenchtown, N.J.: Columbia Publishing Company, Inc., 1978.

Chavez, Steve R. Burns, and A. Berle Clemensen. *Pahaquarry Copper Mine: Delaware Water Gap* (Cultural Landscape Report, Vol.1). Denver, Colo.: US Dept. of the Interior and NPS, 1995.

Cohen, David Steven. *The Folklore and Folklife of New Jersey.* New Brunswick, N.J.: Rutgers University Press, 1983.

Collins, Beryl Robichaud, and Karl H. Anderson. *Plant Communities of New Jersey.* New Brunswick, N.J.: Rutgers University Press, 1994.

Cunningham, John T. *This Is New Jersey.* New Brunswick, N.J.: Rutgers University Press, 1985.

———. *Made in New Jersey.* New Brunswick, N.J.: Rutgers University Press, 1954.

Daniels, Jane, ed. *New Jersey Walk Book.* New York: The New York–New Jersey Trail Conference, 1998.

Dann, Kevin, and Gordon Miller. *30 Walks in New Jersey.* New Brunswick, N.J.: Rutgers University Press, 1982.

Della Penna, Craig P. *24 Great Rail-Trails of New Jersey.* Amherst, Mass.: New England Cartographics, 1999.

Eastman, John. *Forest and Thicket: Trees, Shrubs, and Wildflowers of Eastern North America.* Harrisburg, Penn.: Stackpole Books, 1992.

Field, Van R., and John J. Galluzzo. *Images of America: New Jersey Coast Guard Stations and Rumrunners.* Charleston, S.C.: Arcadia Publications, 2004.

Geology of the New York City Region (U.S. Geological Survey), http://3dparks.wr.usgs.gov/nyc/index.html.

Lawrence, Susannah and Barbara Gross. *The Audubon Society Field Guide to the Natural Places of the Mid-Atlantic States: Inland.* New York: The Hillton Press, Inc., 1984.

Lenik, Edward J. *Iron Mine Trails.* New York: The New York–New Jersey Trail Conference, 1996.

Lowenthal, Larry, and William T. Greenberg Jr. *The Lackawanna Railroad in Northwestern New Jersey.* Morristown, N.J.: The Tri-State Railway Historical Society, Inc., 1987.

———. *Chester's Iron Heyday.* Chester, N.J.: Chester Historical Society, 1980.

———. *Iron Mine Railroads of Northern New Jersey.* Dover, N.J.: The Tri-State Railway Historical Society, Inc., 1981.

Lurie, Maxine N., and Marc Mappen. *The Encyclopedia of New Jersey.* New Brunswick, N.J.: Rutgers University Press, 2004.

Mott, Schuylar L., editor-in-chief. *Among the Blue Hills . . . Bernardsville . . . a History.* Bernardsville, N.J.: Bernardsville History Book Committee, 1974.

New Jersey Geological Survey environmental education Web site, www.state.nj.us/dep/njgs/enviroed.

NJPinebarrens.com (Pine Barrens Web site), www.njpinebarrens.com.

Ransom, James M. *Vanishing Ironworks of the Ramapos.* New Brunswick, N.J.: Rutgers University Press, 1966.

Scherer, Glenn. *Nature Walks in New Jersey.* Boston: Appalachian Mountain Club, 1998.

Seibold, David and Charles Adams III. *Shipwrecks Near Barnegat Inlet.* West Reading, Penn.: Rieck's Printing, 1984.

Shanks, Robert. *U.S. Life-Saving Service: Heroes, Rescues and Architecture of the Early Coast Guard.* Petaluma, Calif.: Costano Books, 1996.

Wacker, Peter, and Paul G. E. Clemens. *Land Use in Early New Jersey.* Newark, N.J.: New Jersey Historical Society, 1995.

Wolfe, Peter E. *The Geology and Landscapes of New Jersey.* New York: Crane, Russak & Company, Inc., 1977.

WPA Guide to 1930s New Jersey, The. New York: The Viking Press, 1939. Reprint: New Brunswick, N.J.: Rutgers University Press, 1986.

Yoder, C. P. "Bill." *Delaware Canal Journal.* Bethlehem, Penn.: Canal Press, Inc., 1972.

Hike Index

Apple Pie Hill, 237

Batsto Lake, 242

Bear Swamp Hill and the Pine Plains, 226

Bearfort Mountain and Surprise Lake, 92

Belcoville and the South River, 210

Black River, 124

Buttermilk Falls and Rattlesnake
Mountain, 75

Cape May Point, 297

Cattus Island, 270

Cheesequake, 252

Coastal Plain and Pine Barrens, 208

Culvers Gap and Stony Lake, 53

Delaware and Raritan Canal—Millstone
Valley, 171

Delaware River Valley—Stockton to
Bull's Island, 182; Stockton to
Lambertville, 187

Finn's Point, 281

Great Falls of the Passaic, 142

Great Swamp, 176

Hackensack Meadowlands, 198

Higbee Beach, 265

Highlands Province, 80

Hudson Palisades, 148

Island Beach, 290

Jersey Piedmont, 140

Jersey Shore and Bays, 257

Jockey Hollow, 158

Ken Lockwood Gorge, 129

Kittatinny Ridge and Valley, 23

Lake Nummy and East Creek Pond, 248

Lake Rutherfurd and the Appalachian
Trail, 32

Liberty State Park, 285

Lord Stirling Park, 202

Maurice River Estuary, 260

Millbrook Village and Van Campens
Glen, 69

Mount Tammany and Sunfish Pond, 46

Pahaquarry Copper Mines, 62

Pakim Pond and Mount Misery, 216

Parvin Lake, 222

Paulinskill Valley Trail, 37

Pequannock Highlands, 100

Pochuck Valley to Wawayanda
Mountain, 82

Princeton Woods, 153

Pyramid Mountain and Tripod Rock, 87

Saffin Pond and Headley Overlook, 105

Sandy Hook, 274

Schooley's Mountain, 109

South Mountain and the Rahway
River, 193

Steenykill Lake and High Point, 25

Terrace Pond, 114

Tourne, 96

Wallkill River Valley, 58

Watchung Reservation, 165

Wawayanda Lake, 134

Wells Mills, 230

Wyanokie High Point, 118

About the Authors

Paul E. DeCoste is a native of New Jersey, brought up in a hiking family. As a nipper, he explored Mount Tammany, traversed the ice-covered Great Swamp, vacationed on Cape May Point, and tramped about Jockey Hollow on Sunday afternoons. As a member of the New York–New Jersey Trail Conference, he became part of the New Jersey volunteer management team for the Appalachian Trail, relocating it through the Great Valley and up the Wawayanda Mountain. As one of the creators, he taught *Take a Hike* and *Appalachian Trail as an Educational Resource,* encouraging folks to utilize the New Jersey park systems. A graduate of East Stroudsburg and Drew Universities, he taught for thirty years within the Garden State. Married with two children, he resides in Sussex County.

Ronald J. Dupont Jr. is a lifelong resident of northwestern New Jersey and a 1985 graduate of Columbia College, Columbia University. Over the last two decades, he has written three books and numerous articles on history in Sussex County and northern New Jersey. A Life Member of the New York–New Jersey Trail Conference, he is a longtime trail maintainer in High Point State Park. Among other trail-related activities, he prepared an historical and archaeological survey of the Appalachian Trail in New Jersey for the New Jersey Management Committee of the Appalachian Trail Conference. Married with two children, he lives in Highland Lakes, New Jersey.

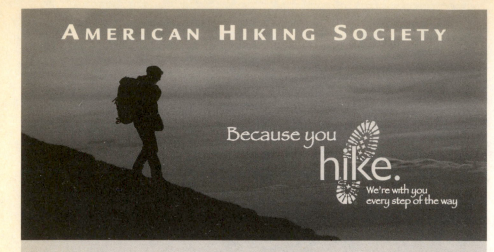
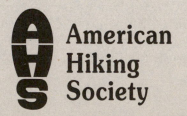